Women's Work

WOMEN'S WORK

Building Peace in War-Affected Communities
of Uganda and Sierra Leone

Jennifer Moore

PENN

UNIVERSITY OF PENNSYLVANIA PRESS

PHILADELPHIA

Published by
University of Pennsylvania Press
Philadelphia, Pennsylvania 19104–4112
www.pennpress.org

Printed in the United States of America on acid-free paper

10 9 8 7 6 5 4 3 2 1

A Cataloging-in-Publication record for this book is
available from the Library of Congress.

Hardcover ISBN 9781512827262
Paperback ISBN 9781512827279
Ebook ISBN 9781512827286

In grateful celebration of the life of my daughter
Tessa Irene Brandt Moore (1998–2024)

and in loving memory of my parents
Katherine Andres Moore (1935–2020) and
Jonathan Moore (1932–2017)

CONTENTS

PREFACE

My intention in conducting the research for this book was to probe my tripartite conception of postconflict transformation: a braid of peace with its three strands of reconciliation, retribution, and restoration, and an edifice of justice with its historical, corrective, and redistributive chambers. In order to develop a deeper appreciation of transformative justice, I wished to share in and learn from the perspectives of women who lived through the civil wars in their countries and are presently engaged in picking up the pieces of family and community life. This intention led me to conduct field research with rural women peacebuilders in Northern Uganda and Sierra Leone. Our interviews over a succession of summers are the mother lode of this book. I hope my work has some honest connection with their experiences and that my scholarly contributions will resonate with them—drawing on their intelligence, their sense of humor; reflecting in meaningful ways aspects of their daily lives; and also offering glimpses of their cultures, politics, psychology, and spirituality, expressed individually and collectively. The impulse to partake in and amplify these women's stories, their wisdom, their frustrations, and their triumphs percolates through this manuscript. At the same time, that impulse is reined in by my commitment to maintain professional integrity and personal humility, acknowledging the cultural distance between myself and the women peacebuilders themselves. Life has taught me that friendship is a powerful source of scholarly insight and social action. I am grateful for the friendships that have emerged from this work. I hope my scholarship will give back in some authentic way to those who have inspired it.

ABBREVIATIONS

AFRC	Armed Forces Revolutionary Council
APC	All People's Congress
CAT	Convention Against Torture and Other Cruel, Inhuman or Degrading Treatment or Punishment
CBO	community-based organization
CDF	Civil Defense Forces
CEDAW	Convention on Elimination of Discrimination Against Women
CERD	International Convention on the Elimination of All Forms of Racial Discrimination
DRC	Democratic Republic of the Congo
ECOMOG	Military Operations Group of the Economic Community of West African States
ECOWAS	Economic Community of West African States
FGC	female genital cutting
FGM	female genital mutilation
FIDA	Federación Internacional de Abogadas
FIDA-U	Uganda Association of Women Lawyers
GBV	gender-based violence
GWED-G	Gulu Women's Economic Development and Globalization Project
HDI	Human Development Index
HDR	United Nations Development Programme Human Development Report
HRAPF	Human Rights Awareness and Promotion Forum
HURIFO	Human Rights Focus
HURIPEC	Human Rights and Peace Centre of Makerere University Law School in Kampala
ICC	International Criminal Court
ICCPR	International Covenant on Civil and Political Rights
ICD	International Crimes Division of the Ugandan High Court

ICESCR	International Covenant on Economic, Social, and Cultural Rights (ICESCR)
ICJ	International Court of Justice
ICTJ	International Center for Transitional Justice
IDP	internally displaced person
IDPDC	Inclusive District Peace and Development Committee
IJM	International Justice Mission
JLOS	Justice, Law and Order Section
JRP	Justice and Reconciliation Project
LRA	Lord's Resistance Army
NaCSA	National Commission for Social Action
NGO	nongovernmental organization
NPFL	National Patriotic Front of Liberia
NRA	National Resistance Army
OCHA	United Nations Office for the Coordination of Humanitarian Affairs
PHU	peripheral health unit
PPP	People's Planning Process
RLP	Refugee Law Project of Makerere University School of Law
RUF	Revolutionary United Front
SLA	Sierra Leonean Army
SLPP	Sierra Leone People's Party
TRC	Sierra Leone Truth and Reconciliation Commission
UDHR	Universal Declaration of Human Rights
UNDP	United Nations Development Programme
UNICEF	United Nations International Children's Emergency Fund (now United Nations Children's Fund)
UPC	Ugandan People's Congress
UPDF	Uganda Peoples' Defence Forces (Ugandan Army)
USAID	United States Agency for International Development
VDC	Village Development Commission
VSA	village savings association (Sierra Leone)
VSLA	village savings and loan association (Uganda)
WAN	Women's Advocacy Network
WHO	World Health Organization

Figure 1. Walking from school in Northern Uganda. Photo by J. Moore, 2018.

Speaking Tree, by Joy Harjo

Some things on this earth are unspeakable:
Genealogy of the broken—
A shy wind threading leaves after a massacre,
Or the smell of coffee and no one there—

Some humans say trees are not sentient beings,
But they do not understand poetry—

Nor can they hear the singing of trees when they are fed by
Wind, or water music—
Or hear their cries of anguish when they are broken and
    bereft—

Now I am a woman longing to be a tree, planted in a moist,
    dark earth
Between sunrise and sunset—

I cannot walk through all realms—
I carry a yearning I cannot bear alone in the dark—

What shall I do with all this heartache?

The deepest-rooted dream of a tree is to walk
Even just a little ways, from the place next to the
    doorway—
To the edge of the river of life, and drink—

I have heard trees talking, long after the sun has gone down:

Imagine what would it be like to dance close together
In this land of water and knowledge . . .

To drink deep what is undrinkable.

Introduction

Rural Women's Perspectives on the Practice of Peace and the Meanings of Justice

When I woke up from a forty-year sleep, it was by a
song. I could hear the drums in the village. I felt the
sweat of ancestors in each palm. The singers were
singing the world into place, even as it continued to fall
apart. They were making songs to turn hatred into love.
—Joy Harjo

This book presents a reimagined theory of peacebuilding and transformative justice constructed through engagement with the experiences and insights of women farmers and microentrepreneurs who have lived through protracted civil conflicts in their native countries. It pieces together a practical and visionary approach to community life after violence from the core values, daily activities, and long-range goals shared among rural cooperative members in Northern Uganda and Sierra Leone. These commonalities manifest despite important differences in the preconflict and conflict histories and demographics of the two countries. The work draws on seven years of interviews with women activists across nine communities, four in the Acholi Region of Northern Uganda and five in the Moyamba and Koinadugu Districts of Sierra Leone. Their perspectives challenge the penal justice model that still dominates coordinated international responses to catastrophic armed conflict. These survivors of civil war demand a community-grounded peacebuilding model entailing advances in material well-being, the acknowledgment of state accountability

for community suffering, and the establishment of equitable and respectful gender relations.

Profiles in Peacebuilding Through Two Women's Stories: Boie Jalloh of Sierra Leone and Jane Orama of Northern Uganda

Boie of Dogoloya, Sierra Leone

Boie Jalloh[1] resides in a provincial community a day's journey by foot, mo-
torbike, and bus from her nation's capital of Freetown. She is a respected
mediator of disputes in her native Dogoloya, a section of the traditional
chiefdom of Folosaba Dembelia, within Falaba District, some twenty miles
south of the Guinean border in Sierra Leone's hilly Northern Province. Boie
is a recently widowed mother of five children and three more who died as
infants. A devout Muslim whose mother tongue is Fula, she also speaks her
national language of Krio and a bit of English. Boie was a preteen with no
formal education when the rebels of the Revolutionary United Front (RUF)
mounted an armed insurrection in 1991 against the military government of
President Momoh, reviled by some of his people for abuse of power and
corruption. When the populace did not rise up in support of their movement
as hoped, RUF forces increasingly resorted to looting and burning villages;
assaulting, raping, and killing civilians; and forcibly recruiting youth. Despite their relative isolation, Boie's community was not immune from the
violence of the so-called Rebel War. After attacks on Dogoloya by RUF
rebels, she was forced to flee to Guinea along with many of her relatives and
neighbors.

On the other side of the border, residents of Dogoloya encountered members of other communities also fleeing crossfire between the RUF and Sierra
Leonean Army (SLA) forces. These first refugees arriving in Guinea after the
Sierra Leonean conflict broke out in March 1991 were sheltered by farmers living along the border in the area of Guéckédou Prefecture in the forest region
of Guinea. Later in 1991, the United Nations High Commissioner for Refugees
established several settlements in and around Guéckédou. While they were
not confined to closed refugee camps, Sierra Leoneans like Boie and her family
were encouraged to congregate in such areas where they were eligible to re-

ceive humanitarian and medical assistance from the international community. For farmers like Boie and her family, accustomed to engaging in the "mixed cropping" of a wide variety of foodstuffs, life in the settlements was a sort of suspended animation under conditions of prolonged dependency with limited opportunities for collective subsistence and income generation. To Boie, "livelihood is making a farm, and feeding your family with rice and groundnuts and sometimes selling a part of the rice for clothing." Conditions of life in exile served to block her and her neighbors from their normal communal activities and their accustomed economic self-sufficiency.

Some Sierra Leoneans from the Northern Province resided as refugees in Guinea for the whole decade-long war. Others spent years in exile or fled to Guinea and returned when conditions changed, only to flee again when their communities suffered additional attacks from the RUF or other armed groups. After the Lomé Peace Accords were signed in 2002, Boie and most of her relatives and neighbors made their cautious return to Dogoloya. While relieved that *war don don* (the war has ended), the people of Dogoloya and other rural communities, so impacted by conflict, now faced additional hardships upon their return to a fragile peace. Community relations were frayed in the aftermath of violence in which Boie's neighbors had been both perpetrators and victims. Agricultural practices and cattle husbandry customary among the Fulbeh people were upended by years of armed conflict and displacement. Economic livelihoods became extremely precarious.

During the early years after the Lomé Accords, war crimes prosecutions were initiated in the Special Court for Sierra Leone and restorative justice hearings were held before the Sierra Leone Truth and Reconciliation Commission. Despite their importance, these national developments did not profoundly impact everyday life in Dogoloya, given the relative isolation of its inhabitants. For Boie and residents of rural communities like Dogoloya, certain aspects of the war persisted in the fear, tension, and breakdown in trust between community members.

When community organizers affiliated with a national NGO called Fambul Tok arrived in Dogoloya in 2007 to help instill a process of reconciliation at the local level, Boie willingly took part. She joined Dogoloya's newly constituted Peace Mothers group, first established as a talking circle to support women's trauma healing through the sharing of stories. Over time, the Dogoloya Peace Mothers took on a variety of new projects, including the organization of collective agricultural projects, the establishment of a village savings and loan association, the training of community mediators, the promotion of women's property rights, and the prevention of domestic violence. Boie and her fellow activists began to witness the palpable impact of improved social relations in jump-starting community life, in the form of increased cultivation, cattle breeding and informal trading.

Boie was particularly drawn to mediating disputes between community members. "I hope for a peaceful world," she explains, and "all that I do promotes a world in which we never quarrel." When she was a child, her mother and stepmother had a tense relationship and as a result their children were alienated from one another. "I was the one who helped bring them back together." She pleaded with the two women to love one another as mothers of siblings and members of one joint household. From then on, Boie was recognized as the family peacemaker. Three decades later, and after the death of her husband in 2018, "my half-brothers are now helping me to educate my children," thanks to her efforts to reconcile their mothers many years ago.

Despite her gifts in dispute resolution, Boie faced considerable obstacles in taking on such a public role. Before the war and according to cultural tradition, the women of Dogoloya were expected to remain silent in community gatherings. To organize effectively after the war, the Peace Mothers had to stretch customary gender roles. This required bold action on the part of individual women and a new open-mindedness on the part of male elders in the community. Supported by her husband and community mentors, Boie answered an inner call to lead. She committed herself to helping the women and men of Dogoloya resolve disputes before they festered or erupted into more serious violence. Several years ago, two neighbors were contesting the property line dividing their holdings. Boie encouraged the woman and man to sit down and talk it out with her and one another. "Today," Boie is proud to say, "the two are now cultivating the same piece of land."

Boie also mediates marital disputes, a painstaking process involving a succession of meetings with the couple and consultations with community elders. The resolution of family tensions proceeds in fits and starts. In some instances, Boie has helped the parties achieve what appeared to be a successful resolution, only to have their relationship devolve into further conflict. Her patience is tested as she renews her facilitation, again inviting each party to sit down with her one-on-one before bringing them together once more. She recalls one such difficult case, in which the third time was the charm. As for the couple's relationship today, Boie declares, "They are now good together."

Figure 2. Portrait of Boie and her grandchild, Dogoloya, Koinadugu District, Sierra Leone. Drawing by Taylor Noya, 2023.

Boie is proud of her reputation as a talented mediator of disputes. "My neighbors want me to lead," she explains. "When there's a problem, they say, 'call Boie. Boie is coming!'" In embracing interpersonal dispute resolution, she articulates a vision of peace and justice that prioritizes reconciliation over formal accountability or punishment. In this vein, Boie reflects on the meaning of *buti berende*, the "calm heart" of peace in her native Fula: "If I take from you, cheat you or cause you to suffer, we can never live together. I have a clean heart for everyone. If I'm in peace with others, I'll be happy."

Jane of Pader, Northern Uganda

Jane Orama[2] is a farmer and community elder from Dure, a rural parish less than two hours by road east of Gulu, the largest city in the Acholi Sub-region of Northern Uganda. Dure is part of Paibwore Chiefdom, located in the Latanya Sub-county of Pader District, one of the seven districts that make up Acholiland. Jane is Catholic, her first language Acholi. The widowed mother of nine grown children, she continues to advocate for vulnerable young people in her community. She supports herself and various orphans she has adopted through the cultivation of crops such as maize, *simsim* (sesame), cassava, potatoes, and groundnuts.

Jane was around thirty-three in 1986 when the rebels of the Lord's Resistance Army (LRA) launched a rebellion to end the repression of the Acholi people by the government of then-and-still-president Yowere Museveni. Not unlike the RUF in Sierra Leone, LRA commanders became frustrated when few of the local citizens greeted them as liberators. Their tactics increasingly entailed attacks on villages and the killing, rape, and assault of Acholi civilians. Like other small parishes throughout the Acholiland districts of Pader, Nwoya, Gulu, and Kitgum, Dure was a hot spot during the war, targeted by both LRA rebels and government troops of the Uganda People's Defense Forces (UPDF). Like others in her parish, Jane lost family members in this succession of attacks, many whose fates remain unknown.

During the ensuing twenty-two years and until the implementation of the Juba Peace Accords in 2008, Jane and many of her neighbors lived off and on in camps for internally displaced persons (IDPs) under a policy of forced relocation carried out by the UPDF as part of its counterinsurgency campaign against the LRA. These camps, meant to be refuges, were targets of attacks by rebel and government forces alike. As observed by Chris Dolan, the relocation centers were part of a system and strategy to impose conditions of social control, humiliation, calculated vulnerability, and material deprivation of the Acholi by the Ugandan state.[3] Jane and her neighbors from Dure and nearby communities are survivors of the ordinary traumas of prolonged camp life as well as the catastrophic violence of armed conflict.

Around 2007 the first of nearly forty IDP camps in Northern Uganda were closed as temporary inhabitants packed up their households and families. By 2009 IDPs from places like Dure were cautiously venturing back to their home communities. At the same time, international agencies stepped up their presence in the Acholi Sub-region, providing humanitarian support for returnees and gathering evidence of potential war crimes during the conflict. In particular, investigators of the International Criminal Court took testimony from survivors of war atrocities. While aware of the ongoing prosecution of LRA leaders in The Hague, inhabitants of Dure and rural communities throughout Acholiland had more immediate concerns. Their priorities were focused on the healing of wartime injuries, the prospect of reparations for those injuries, and questions of everyday subsistence. One organization that has provided psychosocial support to the returnees of Dure is the Refugee Law Project (RLP). Founded in 2009 to provide assistance and advocacy for war-affected people in Acholiland and other regions, RLP is a Ugandan NGO affiliated with the Human Rights and Peace Centre of the Makerere University School of Law in Kampala. RLP field staff based in nearby Gulu began outreach in Dure Parish in the early postwar period, initially focusing on psychosocial trauma healing activities for Jane and others struggling to reestablish their lives and livelihoods after losing so much during the war.

With RLP training and solidarity, Jane and other women of Dure founded a women's mutual assistance group, which they named Uketu wan Kwene (Where will you put us?), in tribute to their missing relatives. Uketu members came together to share traumatic experiences such as losing loved ones in attacks by both UPDF soldiers and LRA militants during two decades of war. Uketu and other parish-level women's collectives have also affiliated with the Women's Advocacy Network (WAN), a Gulu-based organization dedicated to women's equality and well-being, which seeks government reparations for war survivors in the Acholi Sub-region. Jane and other members of Uketu wan Kwene and WAN take part in numerous forms of collective action, similar to Boie and her fellow Sierra Leone Peace Mothers. In addition to trauma healing, they undertake cooperative farming activities, contribute to revolving credit funds, educate community members on women's inheritance rights, and promote their physical integrity and social well-being.

In her work with Uketu, Jane participates in collective efforts to secure government acknowledgment and reparations for the harms visited on their community during the war at the hands of government soldiers. Uketu members believe that their government is responsible for both its troops' direct role in attacks on communities and IDP camps as well as its failure to prevent the violence perpetrated by the LRA rebels, whose insurgency the government was unable to put down for over twenty years. They also engage in their own efforts to restore healthy social life in their community. In 2016 Jane and her fellow Uketu members created the Paibwore Chiefdom Cultural Centre, which they dedicated to their missing family members. The Centre was established as a museum and a place of sacred memory. Visitors enter a typical mudbrick and thatched-roof hut decorated with traditional Acholi animal skins, spears, and mixing gourds. From its whitewashed walls hang hand-painted scrolls listing the names of disappeared individuals along with the dates and locations of specific massacres against the people of Dure. These scrolls also identify the perpetrators of each attack, whether carried out by UPDF (Ugandan Army) or LRA forces.

While Jane values Uketu's role in founding the Cultural Centre, her focus is on the future. She values Uketu's community development activities and their contributions to mediating conflicts in the community, insisting that "when a dispute arises, the solution starts in the family." However, if the conflict persists and "the issues aren't well settled," she insists, "we can bring in others" with ultimate recourse in the courts. Dispute resolution is also essential, Jane points out, because it serves to facilitate collective farming and commercial activities. Her overriding concern is promoting women's economic livelihood in the face of changing gender dynamics in her community, in which women take on increasing responsibilities for family maintenance. "Reconciliation promotes unity so we can work together."

Of all the activities Uketu is involved in, Jane is "most proud of our village savings and loan association," particularly because women's access to revolving loans helps them pay school fees for their children. Jane believes that girls' education is essential to their future efforts to become self-sufficient. She would like to change the tradition in Dure that "if you have many children, boys are prioritized. . . . When funds are short, women are seen as a source of money through work." As a child, Jane was forced to leave school after her sixth year of primary. She is adamant that girls and young women should be educated and is proud that, with her support, one of her daughters was able to attend the Primary Teachers College in Gulu.

Jane also sees a downside to the resilience and economic vitality of the women of Dure. She is concerned that women have assumed an outsized share in livelihood activities since adapting to the physical displacement and cultural trauma of the war. "I see a negative strength," Jane cautions. "We women shouldn't have to take on such responsibility without support. . . . Due to the war, many things happened. Women have become men in their homes." At the same time, she also sees women's empowerment in positive terms: "Women have become stronger to push for their issues, to advocate. There is a high level of freedom of speech for women and men respect that."

As a widow, Jane is intimately aware of the heightened economic and social vulnerability of women in her community, given the Acholi tradition by which women "marry out" into the clan of their husband. Jane believes that widows should be able to choose to remain with their husband's family or return to their family of birth. Whether they remain or return, "they should be welcomed and treated with respect."[4]

In considering alternative visions of peacebuilding, Jane values improvements in material well-being over courtroom justice for past atrocities, prioritizing social and economic restitution to survivors over the punishment of offenders. Even when asking the government to acknowledge its role in wartime suffering, she takes a restorative approach. Jane believes that the state's payment of reparations to war-affected communities is the proper means of ensuring accountability. She envisions justice primarily in social, collective, and redistributive terms. At the end of the day, she is a pragmatist: "I would like to get involved in petty trading to add to my income from farming." Jane defines peacebuilding—*yupu kuc* in the Acholi language—in terms of economic sustainability. *Tic-cing* (livelihood), she declares, consists of all "the different things you do using your hands to change life for your family."

Figure 3. Portrait of Jane, Pader District, Northern Uganda. Drawing by Taylor Noya, 2023.

The Objectives of Women's Work: Embodying Social Transformation in the Daily Lives of Rural Women Peacebuilders

This book honors the experiences of non-elite women like Boie and Jane who lived through the recent civil wars in Northern Uganda and Sierra Leone and offers their practical wisdom as peacebuilders to others working in communities struggling to emerge from the violence of conflict and endemic poverty around the world. The term "non-elite" here refers to women who have modest incomes and limited access to electricity and running water, and who have completed on average less than eight years of formal education. These women survived armed attacks on their communities; assaults on themselves, their relatives and neighbors; the death of loved ones; the separation of their families; and the hunger, sickness, and trauma of displacement. Their practical insights on peace and justice emanate from the very wounds of these experiences and express their commitment to triumph over such adversity.

A study of women and social transformation after armed conflict must start with careful use of language. It is no small task for communities to emerge from the brutality of civil war and to establish enduring conditions of peace and well-being for all members. Rural peacebuilders' notions of justice are diverse and intricate. Transformative justice must be defined in terms that they find meaningful.

There is no shortage of technical definitions of "transitional justice," many centered on criminal trials, truth commissions, and symbolic reparations to redress past atrocities against civilians committed in time of armed conflict.[5] Yet for women like Boie and Jane living in the war-affected regions of Sierra Leone and Northern Uganda, transition from active combat to fragile peace is not enough. They seek enduring social change for their communities in the form of better access to credit, enhanced income opportunities, protection of their inheritance rights, and respect for the physical integrity of women and men. *Transformative justice*[6] or *social transformation* better captures their objectives. These rural women peacebuilders—transformative justice practitioners—strive to reform legal, political, and social service systems; create collaborative partnerships among men and women; and build vibrant economies in their communities from the ground floor up. Rather than electing reconciliation, retribution, *or* reparation in the aftermath of civil war, their goals are ambitious and interwoven. They work to affirm the historical record; they seek courtroom justice when feasible; and, most especially, they strive to improve the legal rights and socioeconomic welfare of women and men in their communities.

While the historical, courtroom, and social strands of justice are essential and intertwined, for women like Boie and Jane, the social dimension at the local level is particularly vital to their survival. Rural women peacebuilders' pronounced tendency to define peace and justice in communal and material terms is demonstrated in Boie's commitment to dispute mediation and Jane's efforts to enhance livelihood in their communities. Their focus on collective resilience and subsistence is shared with many other interviewees across the two countries, including those who were sexually assaulted by government troops, those captured and forced into marriages to rebel fighters, those whose families now include children who were born of rape in captivity, and those who continue to reckon with the loss of their missing loved ones.

Women peacebuilders throughout the world, including Jane Orama in Northern Ugandan and Boie Jalloh in Sierra Leone, have experienced and survived a multitude of traumas—physical and psychic, catastrophic and everyday, personal and systemic. Rape by combatants and forced marriage to rebels are not the central embodiment of women's suffering in war nor are they the principal causes of their postwar trauma, despite the widespread occurrence of these extreme violations of their human rights. The treatment of these tragic experiences in the literature about transitional justice and gender sometimes risks fetishizing such forms of wartime violence in unfortunate if unintentional ways. As noted by Aisling Swaine,[7] violence against women in wartime becomes aggravated because of the very prevalence of such violence against women during "peacetime." And as reported by the United Nations, "The home remains the most violent place for women."[8] By the same token, in both peace and wartime, women experience violence along a continuum, including sexual assault and rape, beatings and other nonsexual physical assaults, and other material forms of extreme suffering. In Uganda and Sierra Leone and many other societies around the world, violence against women before the war facilitates particularly catastrophic manifestations of violence during the war, which in turn feed the perpetuation of more normalized forms of violence in the postwar period.

In short, violence against women is a complex reality in war and peace. In both contexts, interrelated forms of violence occur against a backdrop of patriarchy, misogyny, and gender inequality. In war as in peace, domestic violence and marital rape are widespread, not to mention the material violence of not being able to provide food and medical care for your family or the crushing burden of not being able to educate yourself and your children. The ordinariness of violence against women in communities throughout the world demands greater recognition. It is this full spectrum of violence that women like Boie Jalloh and Jane Orama face in their communities in Sierra Leone and Northern Uganda today. As peacebuilders they confront these difficulties in order to create conditions of enhanced legal status and greater social well-being for themselves and their families in the future.

Related to the emphasis on sexual violence against women in the literature of transitional justice, is a prioritization of criminal prosecutions of war offenders. In Uganda and Sierra Leone, like other postconflict countries, the mainstream dialogue on transitional justice has focused on the pursuit of postconflict justice through criminal prosecutions of wartime perpetrators—for crimes such as rape and forced marriage—alongside the establishment of national truth commissions mandated to establish the historical record of the causes and conduct of the conflict. One of the central objectives of this book is to further expose the fundamental disconnect between an enduring preoccupation on the part of global transitional justice experts with war crimes prosecutions and national truth commissions, on the one hand, and the actual priorities of the people struggling, surviving, and thriving in war-affected communities, on the other. It is community peacebuilders like Boie and Jane who are creating most of the justice they experience in their daily lives. The juxtaposition of peace vs. justice—social reconciliation vs. criminal accountability—sets up a false and harmful binary. Women peacebuilders are very concerned with accountability, but they tend to define this concept in communal, moral, and material terms, rather than seeing justice solely as the work of formal or penal institutions. To the extent that women like Boie and Jane are concerned with "courtroom justice," it is the civil, reparative, and compensatory judicial mechanisms that most interest them, rather than individual criminal trials for perpetrators of militant violence.

Five objectives guide this inquiry into women and social transformation in Northern Uganda and Sierra Leone by defining essential terms, values, and intentions. These objectives help ensure that the analytic framework of postconflict justice is firmly grounded in the daily lives of women survivors of armed conflict.

Objective A: Exploring the resonance between the theory of "transformative justice" and the lives of women peacebuilders in Uganda and Sierra Leone

Rural women's ideas about the relationships and tradeoffs between the historical, courtroom, and social facets of justice will be explored throughout this book. In broad strokes, grassroots women like Boie and Jane present a vision of transformative justice that offers mercy, demands accountability, and seeks the common good, illustrated through myriad activities in communities across Northern Uganda and Sierra Leone. Their multifaceted conception of peace and justice emerges from individual conversations with women leaders in nine different communities across the two countries, which took place from 2016 to 2023.

This book spotlights non-elite rural women (women of modest income and limited schooling) who lived through the civil conflicts in Northern Uganda and Sierra Leone, focusing on the ways they envision transformative justice—and practice peacebuilding—in their home communities. It follows on my earlier monograph, *Humanitarian Law in Action Within Africa*,[9] which examines the formulation of national policies to promote transitional justice in Uganda, Sierra Leone, and Burundi during their postwar periods. Where *Humanitarian Law* took a top-down approach, comparing war crimes tribunals and/or truth commissions established at the international and national levels in each country, *Women's Work* looks at peacebuilding from the perspective of the women who are rebuilding their war-shattered communities by reunifying their families, restoring their local economies, and doing the work of justice on the ground.[10]

Objective B: Rethinking the partnership between academic and humanitarian "outsiders" and peacebuilders in Uganda and Sierra Leone

A careful balancing act is required to foster partnerships between local and international promoters of peace and justice. Human rights scholars, activists, technical experts, and civil servants often struggle to support community peacebuilders without dictating their agendas or purporting to guarantee their funding base. True solidarity requires more than shared rhetoric and mutual good will. An essential first step is for outsider scholars and advocates to learn from and cooperate with civil society organizations and individual community members like Boie and Jane as they practice social transformation in their own historical and cultural settings. Through an attitude of accompaniment and collaboration, we are more able to amplify the good that they are already doing and to follow their lead.[11]

Objective C: Defining women-centered peacebuilding

This book explores a vision of postconflict transformation implemented at the grassroots level and led by non-elite rural women committed to values of community empowerment, gender equality, and universal human rights. Without progress in all three endeavors, transformative justice for women and their communities is a hollow promise. But it is vital to understand what these concepts of community uplift, women's rights, and human rights mean to women who survived the wars in Northern Uganda and Sierra Leone. Their understandings of justice and their engagement in peacebuilding compose the heart of this book. In this spirit, Chapter 1 seeks to consider and distill the rhetoric and theory of feminism into relevant tools that are most meaningful to women living in communities emerging from violence, providing the conceptual foundation for a deeper exploration of their understandings of peace and justice in Chapters 3 and 4.

Objective D: Integrating human rights talk into the dynamics of transformative justice

This book starts with the supposition that the promotion of universal human rights is organically linked to women's empowerment and community uplift. Social empowerment and gender equality are part of the greater human rights continuum. However, this abstraction needs to be explored and refined in the context of the lives of war-affected women subsisting in rural communities.

Just as Chapter 1 provides a conceptual foundation for considering the relevance of feminist thought to grassroots women's peacebuilding, it also seeks to establish a parallel framework for examining the modern global human rights movement. A rural women-centric view of international human rights norms and instruments helps distill those principles most useful to rural women dedicated to economic well-being and conflict transformation in their communities.

Rural women peacebuilders in Northern Uganda and Sierra Leone, while not lawyers or academics, have nuanced ideas about justice and peace that resonate with the global human rights movement overall while challenging some of its tenets. Jane Orama speaks of the struggle for women's enjoyment of their rights to education and free expression. Boie Jalloh defines peacekeeping in terms of a fair and participatory process of dispute resolution. Both speak of women's property and inheritance rights. But the core of their worldview is relational and communal. Boie's and Jane's visions of human rights and their understandings of peace, along with those of their fellow community peacebuilders, are the lifeblood of this book. As those who understand the urgency for social change in their own societies, their experiences and insights redefine transformative justice in terms of collective resilience and daily subsistence.

Objective E: Offering a comparative analysis of women-centric peacebuilding in Northern Uganda and Sierra Leone

Sustained qualitative research within rural women's collectives in Sierra Leone and the Acholi Sub-region of Northern Uganda facilitates a rich comparative analysis of two contextualized national experiences with postconflict transition, identifying specific priorities set by various state and nonstate actors in the two countries. Civil society organizations in both countries, including Uganda's Women's Advocacy Network and Sierra Leone's Peace Mothers, have critiqued and cajoled governmental agencies to devote more resources and political will to the postconflict process. That work is ongoing as practitioners of transformative justice—from civil servants to community activists like Boie Jalloh and Jane Orama—continue to develop and reform programs and institutions to more fully confront past and ongoing experiences of violence in their particular country settings.

Uganda and Sierra Leone were selected as country sites for the field research underlying this book because they possess both fundamental similarities and important differences in their colonial and postcolonial experiences and institutions as well as in the nature of their civil wars and postconflict transitions. Their particular blends of ethnocultural and political factors contribute to a dynamic comparative framework from which to draw important lessons about durable peacebuilding in conflict-emergent countries throughout the world.

To begin, there are two important commonalities: both countries recently experienced more than a decade of armed conflict characterized by widespread attacks on civilian communities such as Dogoloya in Sierra Leone's Northern Province and Dure in Northern Uganda, and governments in both countries share a rhetorical and programmatic commitment to transitional justice in the long term. Resting on those commonalities are some interesting differences, starting with basic geography and colonial experience.

Uganda is located on Lake Victoria in Eastern-Central Africa, Sierra Leone along the Atlantic Coast of West Africa. In colonial heritage, while Uganda and Sierra Leone are both members of the British Commonwealth, their experiences under British authority were quite distinct. Uganda was a British protectorate subject to indirect rule through Great Britain's patronage of the Buganda Kingdom. Contrastingly, the Sierra Leone Protectorate was dominated by the Freetown Colony whose settlers included formerly enslaved Africans, some of whom earned their freedom from bondage in the American colonies and the opportunity to return to their ancestral homeland after supporting the British forces during the American Revolution. In Uganda, the prevailing economic inequality between Northern Uganda and the rest of the country is in part a legacy of the colonial era, reflected in much higher levels of poverty in Acholiland, including Jane's district of Pader, than in the nation overall. Similarly, in Sierra Leone, stark differences in the levels of development in the capital (the former Freetown Colony) and the upcountry provinces of the former protectorate also date back to colonial days—manifested in the lack of running water and electricity in much of Boie's community of Dogoloya today. In both countries, such regional inequalities were contributing causes of civil conflict and in both it is cause for concern that these inequities endure in the postwar era.

A few additional historical notes regarding the causes and conduct of the two civil wars suggest the rich contextual exploration of transformative justice to which these countries lend themselves. Uganda is emerging from a civil war characterized by the criminal militancy of the Lord's Resistance Army (LRA) in Northern Uganda and the Ugandan Army's counterinsurgency campaign against the LRA, central to which was the forced displacement and collective punishments of Ugandan civilians including Jane and her parish of Dure. Sierra Leone endured a civil conflict marked by competitive and collaborative brutality on the part of three major militant groups—the Revolutionary United Front (RUF), the Armed Forces Revolutionary Council, and the Civil Defense Forces—juxtaposed against the humanitarian law violations of the Sierra Leone Army. Collectively, these armed groups are responsible for the suffering of people in rural locales such as Boie's community of Dogoloya.

In Uganda the LRA War largely impacted the Northern Region of the country, particularly Acholiland where Jane resides, whereas Sierra Leone's Rebel War touched every district, including Falaba where Boie resides. Contrary to enduring stereotypical characterizations of armed conflict in Africa, neither Uganda's nor Sierra Leone's civil strife emanated from a predominant ethnic or religious fault line. In Northern Uganda Acholi were both perpe-trators of violence, particularly LRA militants, as well as survivors of wartime atrocities, including ethnic Acholi like Jane and other women peacebuilders across the districts of Nwoya, Gulu, Pader, and Kitgum.[12] In Sierra Leone, the Rebel War impacted people of Fulbeh communities like Boie and her neighbors in Dogoloya, but it also touched Mandingo, Limba, Koranko, Kono, Mende, Temne, and other ethnic communities throughout the country.

To an important extent, both wars were responses to corrupt governing institutions at the national level and outright disdain on the part of national leaders for entrenched poverty and underdevelopment concentrated in rural areas of both countries. In both Northern Uganda and Sierra Leone, there is a palpable longing on the part of rural people like Jane and Boie for their gov-ernments to take responsibility for their people's welfare, by committing national resources and budgetary expenditures to sustain strong systems of public education and health care, as well improved infrastructure in the form of roads, bridges, water and sanitation services, and functional electrical power grids.

Finally, the two countries undertook quite distinct approaches to postcon-flict transition at the national level. Where Uganda has so far focused on penal accountability for LRA atrocities, Sierra Leone combined limited criminal trials for a few representatives of each major armed faction with a national truth-telling process. Yet Jane and her fellow Uketu members believe that it is inappropriate for one LRA commander currently on trial in the International Criminal Court to bear the burden of criminal liability for Uganda's LRA War. As the late Daker Nighty of Uketu wan Kwene insisted, "Dominic On-gwen [one of the LRA leader Joseph Kony's top lieutenants], cannot take all accountability. The government must as well." As for Boie and her fellow Peace Mothers, they scarcely mention criminal trials at all, except in the context of peacetime assaults–namely, the prosecution of intimate partner violence after mediation has proved inadequate to resolve domestic conflict.

Despite the priorities and perspectives of community peacebuilders like Jane and Boie, international assessments of their countries' national transi-tional justice programs have remained remarkably focused on war crimes tri-bunals and national truth commissions. Uganda has pursued criminal prosecutions of leaders of the Lord's Resistance Army through international trials in the International Criminal Court (ICC) alongside national trials be-fore the International Crimes Division of the Ugandan High Court. The Ongwen ICC trial, conducted at the court's seat in The Hague, was live streamed in urban centers such as Gulu Town, although seldom could it be readily observed by Jane and others living in rural communities like Dure in Pader District.

In contrast, Sierra Leone pursued a two-pronged approach to transitional justice, starting with a limited number of trials in the Special Court for Sierra Leone of those "most responsible" for humanitarian law violations committed during the Rebel War, including rebels and soldiers alike. These trials ended in 2012 with the conviction of Charles Taylor, the former president of Liberia, for his role in arming the RUF. Overlapping with the first two years of the Special Court's mandate, national and district-level hearings were conducted before the Sierra Leone Truth and Reconciliation Commission, in which larger numbers of war offenders were able to seek amnesty in exchange for admitting and testifying in public hearings about their involvement in specific atrocities. While these symbolically and culturally significant hearings were held in provincial capitals, for the people in Boie's community of Dogoloya and other rural locales, there was little opportunity to experience such powerful reconciliatory events. It was for this reason that the NGO Fambul Tok launched a grassroots reconciliation movement back in 2007, now sustained by community activists such as Boie and her fellow Peace Mothers in Falaba, Koinadugu, Moyamba, and other upcountry districts throughout Sierra Leone.

For all the distinctions between the conflict and postconflict experiences in the two countries, the shared priorities of women dedicated to community justice work across the two settings are notable. In both Sierra Leone and Northern Uganda, women peacebuilders offer an approach to transformative justice that seeks concrete manifestations of accountability, reconciliation, and reparation at the national level while also focusing on local solutions, such as revolving credit funds, farming cooperatives, dispute mediation, the prevention of domestic violence, the protection of children, and the empowerment of women. Chapters 3 and 4 provide deep dives into the rich insights on peace and justice of women peacebuilders like Jane Orama and Boie Jalloh throughout Northern Uganda and Sierra Leone. In order to frame and shed fuller light on their contributions, the final section of this introductory chapter provides an overview of the evolution of transitional justice as a concept developed by activists and academics from the Global North, with an eye toward distilling and extracting those elements of transitional justice theory that are most relevant to rural women who are doing the work of peace and justice on the ground in violence-emergent communities.

Analytic Framework for Women's Work: Weaving a Braid of Reconciliative, Redistributive, and Retributive Justice

> By listening we will understand who
> we are in this holy realm of words.
> Do not parade, pleased with yourself.
> You must speak in the language of justice.
>
> —Joy Harjo[13]

Justice in Three Dimensions

Transformative justice is a modern phrase for an old phenomenon—a call for courtroom accountability, truth-telling, and social solidarity in the aftermath of the massive violations of human dignity occurring in a time of protracted armed conflict or despotic rule. Once the war or autocratic regime begins to wane, state and civil society actors alike seek an end to the violence, the prosecution of criminal perpetrators, the preservation of the historical record, and reparations for victims and survivors.[14] It is the non-penal dimensions of transitional justice, the historical and the social, that are most significant to women peacebuilders like Jane Orama of Dure in Northern Uganda and Boie Jalloh of Dogoloya in Sierra Leone.

This book engages in a combination of theory-testing and theory-building. It starts with a three-stranded concept of peacebuilding, adapted from the literature on transitional justice and my own scholarship, encompassing accountability or courtroom justice; reconciliation or historical justice; and material well-being or social justice. I explore and stretch this formulation through group conversations and more extensive interviews with women peacebuilders in the nine communities I visited over seven years of research. Their shared life experiences as well as their articulations of ideas of justice contribute to a more dynamic and nuanced vision of transformative justice after violence.

Some formal mechanisms for transitional justice seek to vindicate the principles of international humanitarian law, particularly through international prosecutions of war criminals for carrying out armed military attacks on civilians.[15] In contrast, the less formal grassroots reconciliatory activities prioritized by women like Jane and Boie, as well as the social welfare reforms they demand, find particular resonance in the principles of international human rights law, whether in the civil-political or socioeconomic realm. Reparations programs, a particular demand of women peacebuilders like Jane Orama in Northern Uganda, clearly fall within the doctrinal embrace of international human rights law. Such mechanisms are designed to acknowledge and repair the harms suffered by individuals and groups in society and to alleviate the causes of future violence through social welfare reforms that ensure greater enjoyment of economic and social human rights by all community members.

Over several decades, the evolving paradigm of *transitional justice* has highlighted a society's collective reckoning after a period of upheaval and massive human rights abuses. When the concept was analyzed in 2000 by the legal scholar Ruti Teitel, transitional justice was often associated with a liberal paradigm, implying movement from an autocratic to a more democratic political system.[16] More recently, the term has also been applied to post–civil war transitions, the focus of this book's comparative analysis.[17] But "postconflict transition" is a dry and euphemistic encapsulation of the messy, dynamic, and multilayered process of repair and revitalization that women's groups like Uketu wan Kwene in Northern Uganda and the Peace Mothers throughout Sierra Leone undergo after protracted and systemic violence. Members of communities torn apart by civil war like Jane and Boie cannot live by representative government and the rule of law alone. They seek an enduring experience of justice that is not subsumed in the prosecution of senior rebel combatants who ordered and perpetrated war crimes. Their understanding of justice also encompasses holding state actors accountable, restoring relationships between members of conflicted communities, in the case of Boie's mediation role, and redistributing resources through state reparations to survivors of wartime atrocities, as sought by Jane and the women of Uketu wan Kwene.

This book builds on a three-dimensional vision of *transformative* justice: justice that is restorative and redistributive as well as retributive and justice that enhances social well-being and communal reconciliation alongside demands for courtroom accountability.[18] That tripartite framework is articulated in this chapter and later adapted through conversations with women peacebuilders like Jane and Boie and their fellow community peacebuilders in Northern Uganda and Sierra Leone, portrayed in Chapters 3 and 4.

Like a braid with three strands, the restorative-retributive-redistributive conception of transformative justice intertwines three essential and interdependent components of peacebuilding into a greater whole. First, restorative justice encompasses the reconciling of war-affected communities through national programs, like Sierra Leone's Truth and Reconciliation Commission,[19] and local historical memory projects, like Jane Orama and Uketu's Cultural Centre in Northern Uganda. Second, retributive or "courtroom justice" has both penal and non-penal aspects: the trial and punishment of individuals for their role in perpetrating war crimes against civilians as well as civil damage claims seeking the payment of reparations. Non-penal accountability is most significant to rural mediators like Boie Jalloh in the Dogoloya community of Sierra Leone's Falaba District. Third and finally, redistributive justice takes a more structural approach, encompassing the dismantling of systems of inequality, particularly barriers to women's full enjoyment of their property, inheritance, and political rights. These challenges are front-and-center priorities for Jane and Boie and their community groups. Other redistributive measures entail increased public investment in rural health clinics and public schools and expanded civil society mobilization through collaborative agriculture, microenterprise, and community-based health promotion.[20]

Talking about transformative justice in these variegated and interdependent terms has two significant impacts. First, we recognize the complexity of social transformation for rural women and their communities; progress is often slow and uneven, reflecting the magnitude of the challenges they undertake. Second, we appreciate that like a wounded body which begins to heal from the moment of injury, war-affected communities are engaged in a constant process of renewal and reconstruction, led by grassroots women peacebuilders, which they realize in both incremental and dramatic ways. Together the redistributive, restorative, and retributive strands contribute to a three-dimensional vision of rural women-centric *transformative justice* that is gradual in pace, continuous in duration, and communitarian in nature.

The three-dimensional vision of transformative justice imagined by rural women peacebuilders in Northern Uganda and Sierra Leone is more ambitious than a mere penal accounting for specific crimes of war. Leaders like Jane Orama and Boie Jalloh further seek to restore and reconcile their still-fragile communities and to contribute to reinforcing the social and political fabric of their societies as a whole. As Chapters 3 and 4 illustrate, a communitarian vision of postconflict social change is particularly resonant with grassroots women peacebuilders throughout Northern Uganda and Sierra Leone. Jane and Boie's peace and justice work consists of concrete acts of individual, collective, and institutional healing. Their descriptions of peacebuilding activities in their communities articulate a *reparative* approach to postconflict recovery, encompassing truth-telling between individuals and their government, particularly for Jane and Uketu in Uganda; a restoration of community relationships, for Boie and the Peace Mothers in Sierra Leone; and the reformation of social, political, and judicial institutions, for women activists and peacebuilders throughout both countries. While penal justice is not their first priority, they nevertheless reject impunity for their governments and themselves. Jane and Boie seek an accountability defined in legal, moral, and material terms. Their insights suggest that the theory and practice of transformative justice must continue to evolve, as it has over the past century.

The Historical Antecedents of Transformative Justice

Over the past three decades, mechanisms to facilitate postrepression and postconflict transitions have been implemented in numerous countries throughout the world, including Argentina and Chile after the dictatorships of the 1970s and 1980s;[21] South Africa after the institutionalized violence and racism of apartheid throughout the latter half of the twentieth century;[22] and the former Yugoslavia,[23] Cambodia,[24] Rwanda,[25] Timor Leste,[26] Uganda, and Sierra Leone,[27] after the genocides and civil wars of the 1990s. In fact, these countries are celebrated for the modern institutions of transitional justice they have crafted or inspired: Chile and South Africa[28] for their pioneering Truth and Reconciliation Commissions; the former Yugoslavia and Rwanda for their International Criminal Tribunals, created by UN Security Council resolutions;[29] Uganda for its early self-referral to the International Criminal Court, relevant to Jane and Uketu in their attitudes toward the prosecution of LRA leader Dominic Ongwen; and Sierra Leone for its Special Court operating alongside its Truth and Reconciliation Commission, also of historical relevance to Sierra Leone's Fambul Tok Peace Mothers. These postviolence transition programs emphasize the retributive and restorative facets of justice, with some attention to redistributive justice, through modest reparations programs.[30]

But peace with justice long predates the 1970s. The period of American Reconstruction inaugurated a transitional justice program for the states of the former Confederacy after the American Civil War and the abolition of slavery, as did the establishment of the Nuremburg and Tokyo Tribunals and the institution of the Marshall Plan for European Recovery after World War II. American Reconstruction sought to punish the southern states for their acts of rebellion and prepare them for reentry into the Union; to enfranchise the former slaves; and to create a system of free labor. The Freedmen's Bureau Act of 1865 mandated the Bureau of Refugees, Freedmen, and Abandoned Lands to assist destitute war-affected southerners, Black and white.[31] While rural women peacebuilders may not speak of Europe's Marshall Plan or the period of American Reconstruction, there are important historical resonances between the Marshall Plan and the reparations programs demanded by Ugandan women of Uketu wan Kwene and other women's peacebuilding collectives. Similarly, there are commonalities between the mutual assistance societies formed among freedmen and freedwomen in the American South in the late nineteenth century and the Peace Mothers and Ugandan women's revolving credit associations and agricultural cooperatives today.

Historical precedents for postconflict transitions are also important for the light they shed on the role of nonstate actors and grassroots communities in transformative justice. In addition to the leading role of the US government in Reconstruction during the 1860s and 1870s, this period also illustrates civil society's essential contributions to the process of social transformation. After the American Civil War, freedmen and freedwomen founded community organizations as well as informal "neighbor to neighbor" networks to help African Americans search for and reunify with separated family members and to facilitate economic integration and sheer survival through collective subsistence efforts within their communities.[32] Benevolent organizations founded by and for Black Americans served and continue to serve as vital organs of social transformation throughout the United States, promoting self-help, community development, and civic engagement for their members as well as a more inclusive view of American democracy.[33] Despite historical differences, these post–Civil War African American mutual assistance networks bear important similarities to the Peace Mothers network in Sierra Leone and rural collectives like Uketu wan Kwene in Northern Uganda. Former slaves and war survivors alike have relied historically on economies of affection and collective survival strategies to a greater extent than they could on public or philanthropic support. While women's collectives in Sierra Leone and Northern Uganda continue to demand greater reparations from their governments for what was lost during the war, they survive to a large extent due to their own efforts in collective subsistence, microlending, and local advocacy. Their efforts are explored in greater depth in Chapters 3 and 4.

Historical "Transitions" in the Field of Transitional Justice

The International Center for Transitional Justice (ICTJ) talks about transitional justice as a process—encompassing criminal trials, truth commissions, reparations programs, and institutional reforms—which enables a society to emerge from periods of repression and widespread human rights abuses. Essential to the process are the structural and cultural changes necessary to prevent the recurrence of those violations in the future.[34] The reparations programs and social welfare reform components of the ICTJ's conception of transitional justice are most resonant with the work of Ugandan and Sierra Leonean women peacebuilders like Jane Orama and Boie Jalloh.

The modern conception of postrepression and postconflict justice was not cut out of whole cloth, but crafted from an earlier preoccupation with the abuses of twentieth-century authoritarian states. Early conversations about ending impunity for the crimes of totalitarian regimes led to subsequent demands for accountability for outrages against civilians committed during protracted civil wars. Only more recently has the concept of postconflict transition come to embrace a fuller spectrum of justice measures—from courtroom-retributive mechanisms to the historical-restorative and social-redistributive forms of peacebuilding, which are arguably of greatest relevance to rural women peacebuilders like Jane and Boie. Thus, the dynamic concept of *transformative justice* is the fruit of an evolution from what was essentially a program of international penal accountability to something much more ambitious and demanding—namely, a commitment to grassroots social transformation in communities like Dure Parish, Northern Uganda, and Dogoloya, Sierra Leone, as they continue to emerge from prolonged periods of entrenched violence and human rights abuses.[35]

In its historical evolution, the field of transitional justice has undergone several transitions of its own. The first involved a change in overall context—from a focus on postauthoritarian transitions to a concentration on post–civil war transitions in countries like Uganda and Sierra Leone. This contextual shift brought with it an increasing recognition that human rights abuses in wartime are committed by a wide spectrum of actors, state and non-state agents alike. For societies suffering under totalitarian abuses, like Chile under Pinochet or Argentina under its military junta, it may seem relatively uncontroversial to identify the chief bad actors as the all-powerful and repressive police state and its various agencies and armed security forces.

Contrastingly, in societies pounded by civil strife like Northern Uganda and Sierra Leone, blame is spread widely. On the one hand, we have the civilian and military leaders of the Ugandan government and the Uganda People's Defense Forces (UPDF) and the government and army of Sierra Leone (SLA). Clustered on the other are the soldiers, rebels, and mercenaries fighting for myriad armed factions, including UPDF and SLA forces as well as Revolutionary United Front (RUF) rebels in Sierra Leone and Lord's Resistance Army (LRA) insurgents in Uganda. "Internal conflicts" are seldom simple nor are they exclusively internal. In the conflicts in Sierra Leone and Uganda, outside actors included foreign military forces like the Sudanese People's Liberation Front, which compounded the conflict in Northern Uganda, and the ECOMOG peacekeeping forces of the Economic Community of West African States (ECOWAS), which both alleviated and participated in the conflict in Sierra Leone.[36]

Thus, an important "transition" in the early field of transitional justice was a concerted shift in focus from postauthoritarian to postconflict situations and from police states to fragile states.[37] It also entailed an attitude adjustment that acknowledged the shared agency in so-called civil conflicts spanning a wide continuum of internal and external actors.[38] Increased attention to the challenges of postconflict transition in countries emerging from civil wars is reflected in an emerging literature on transitional justice in Northern Uganda and Sierra Leone, including the work of Erin Baines, Sarah Nouwen, Chris Dolan, Mark Drumbl, Paul Bradfield, and others regarding Northern Uganda;[39] and the scholarship of Hawa Kamara, Jimmy Kandeh, William Schabas, Tom Perriello and Marieke Wierda, Joseph Opala, and others, regarding Sierra Leone.[40]

Moreover, as transitional justice theorists began to grapple with post–civil war transitions, the work of postconflict justice has increasingly come to encompass the reconciliation of former combatants with their communities of origin as well as institutional reforms—the building of new legal, social, and economic infrastructures, sometimes from the ground up. This focus on the social and communal realms is of particular relevance to Jane Orama and Boie Jalloh and their fellow women peacebuilders throughout Northern Uganda and Sierra Leone. The social reconstruction involved in postconflict transition requires particular attention to those members of society most vulnerable to exploitation and poverty, who demand more than penal accountability for some war criminals and amnesty for others. By the same token, deep-seated institutional and structural reforms in the postconflict period are powerful antidotes to resurgent militancy, repression, and armed conflict. To be successful in the long term, postconflict transition requires meaningful social transformation. Thus, another transition in postconflict theory is the shift from a narrower focus on courtroom justice to a wider spectrum encompassing the historical and social components of justice, and a changed focus from individual accountability to the repair of communities. Increased attention to the non-penal and informal dimensions of transitional justice is reflected in the scholarship of Aisling Swaine, Fionnuala Ní Aoláin, Dina Francesca Haynes, and Naomi Cahn,[41] as well as other writers who spotlight the social dimension of justice in Northern Uganda and Sierra Leone in particular.[42]

It is not an accident that blueprints for postconflict transformation in Africa—from South Africa to Libya[43]—typically involve the integration of criminal tribunals, truth commissions, and social service delivery systems. The courtroom-retributive, historical-restorative, and social-redistributive facets of justice interrelate in dynamic and creative ways, particularly at the grassroots level, as attested by individual women peacebuilders whose insights are explored in the text of the chapters that follow.

Yet another innovation in postconflict theory concerns new ways of conceptualizing the legitimacy of the state and the nature of state authority in societies emerging from protracted civil wars. This approach is particularly relevant to the attitudes of women peacebuilders like Jane Orama in Dure Parish, Northern Uganda, who seek shared accountability between the Ugandan government and the Lord's Resistance Army. Attention to the complicity of both state and nonstate actors in wartime offenses is reflected in the literature of William Schabas, among others.[44]

Criminal accountability, while it can be assigned to state and nonstate actors alike, still assigns penal responsibility to individual actors rather than the state overall. Individual actors are punished for committing war crimes and crimes against humanity as defined by domestic and international criminal law. Contrastingly, social and historical justice programs involve the collective responsibility of the society and its governing structures to protect the dignity and agency of all its members while providing for their basic needs. This approach is commensurate with the concept of state responsibility under international law.[45] For states to make progress in the domain of social and historical justice they must take seriously their obligations under human rights law, which requires the defense of civil and political rights as well as state support for the socioeconomic well-being of all people, in times of war and peace. State responsibility for social welfare through reparations is a particular priority of women peacebuilders like Jane Orama in Northern Uganda, who long for their government to fully recognize the Acholi as full citizens of the Republic of Uganda. For the theory of transformative justice to have meaning for peacebuilders like Boie and Jane it must grapple with the problem of state illegitimacy and irrelevancy in the everyday lives of war-affected people. Women peacebuilders demand a theory of justice embodied in the state's capacity and willingness to protect and provide for its people rather than its raw power to exert military and economic control over them.[46]

There is a powerful synergy at work within transformative justice initiatives in Northern Uganda and Sierra Leone today, modest in results and ambitious in demands. When grassroots women leaders like Jane Orama and Boie Jalloh engage in peace and justice work in their communities, to an important extent they are embodying and assuming the responsibilities of their governments under international and national law. In this sense they are getting out in front, pushing their communities and societies, and modeling good behavior for state and nonstate actors alike. Women peacebuilders show us how transformative justice is done in the lives of the people the state and the international community are meant to serve. In large part, the justice they seek is the justice they make, largely on their own.

Methodology for Women's Work: Qualitative and Narrative Interviews with Women Peacebuilders in Northern Uganda and Sierra Leone

Research Design

The research for this project is qualitative in nature, derived from group and individual interviews conducted with women active in peacebuilding in nine communities across Sierra Leone and Northern Uganda over a seven-year period from 2016 to 2023. The interviews were conducted using a Peacebuilders' Questionnaire, included as Appendix 1 in this volume. This research is derived from a longitudinal study of around thirty individual women. The questions posed gave rise to narrative responses that vary in length and detail depending on the individual interviewee.

In my research I utilized snowball or convenience sampling rather than blind sampling. By design, the technique built on my professional relationships with several national NGOs, prior relationships between my interpreters and the community groups with whom they worked, and my own interactions with the interpreters and interviewees over the course of seven years.

In essence, the methodology for this study is derived from a particular adaptation of convenience sampling—a "relational sampling" technique rooted in institutional, personal, and community relationships. I gained entry into the nine communities I visited on multiple occasions thanks to the links between my interpreters and their community networks. As analyzed in the scholarship of Sally Engle Merry, the role of cultural and social translators is fundamental in establishing creative connections between outsider academics and community insiders.[47] The trust and common cause between interpreters and community activists was the portal through which I walked. The growing rapport I built with my interpreters and our interviewees was the vehicle that transported me over that threshold many times.

With these prior and evolving relationships between interviewer, interviewees, and interpreters come constraints and biases as well as opportunities to take old ideas in new directions. The insights and experiences the women have shared were in part the product of their sense of what I wanted to hear, and in part a function of their willingness and desire to share, learn from, and engage in intellectual exchange with me and one another about ideas close to their hearts. Our interactions were both scripted and spontaneous. The exchanges were at times more brittle or reductive, at others more expansive or epiphanous. Our extended conversations most often occurred after repeated visits with individual women, some of whom I visited on as many as six different occasions over successive years. The seven-year relationships I have established with my principal interviewees have necessarily led to a degree of emotive bias, while also birthing opportunities for deeper relationships and creative explorations. These relationships and interchanges, and the learning gleaned from them, are the taproots of this book.

Implementation of Research Plan

From prior research and scholarship throughout the early 2000s, I became aware of a grassroots women's peace network active throughout Sierra Leone called the Fambul Tok Peace Mothers. During this same period, in consulting the scholarship of the Refugee Law Project, I became more knowledgeable about women's peace activism in Northern Uganda. In both countries, women's peace and development groups operate at the level of the parish or section, comprising a cluster of several villages in walking distance of one another within a particular district.[48] As my research plan evolved, I contemplated traveling to such communities to interview individual women as they pulled away from their daily livelihood activities to gather with fellow group members. With a few unexpected and often fortuitous wrinkles and twists, this was the way the work unfolded.

My research findings are drawn from interviews conducted over the seven-year period 2016–2023 with Jane Orama and Boie Jalloh and other non-elite women active in peacebuilding collectives in nine localities, four communities in Northern Uganda and five in Sierra Leone. I interacted in focus group discussions with a total of about sixty women across the two countries, thirty of whom I interviewed individually. The twenty women I interviewed in Northern Uganda included Jane Orama, two of her fellow members of Uketu wan Kwene, and members of three other community collectives–namely, Rwot Lakica, Alany pa Mony Lit, and Odoko Mit. The ten women I interviewed individually in Sierra Leone included Boie Jalloh and two of her fellow Peace Mothers from Dogoloya in Falaba District as well as one Peace Mother from Heremakono and two from Kaponpon, both communities in Koinadugu District, in the North of Sierra Leone. In the South of Sierra Leone, I interviewed two Peace Mothers from Palima and two more from Tawovehun, both communities in Moyamba District.

In order to identify specific women's community collectives in the two countries, starting in 2015, I began reaching out to key human rights agencies[49] in both countries. Meeting with staff, I explored their capacity to facilitate my introductions to local women's groups whose members might be willing to speak with me about their community activism. Through a combination of long-standing and newer contacts, I began to consult with individual staff members of nongovernmental organizations in both countries with track records of support for and partnership with women's community groups.[50] These NGOs share a philosophy and practice of collaborating with, but not controlling, grassroots activists. Their field staff are nationals who themselves lived through the armed conflicts in their countries, who have experience working with scholars and advocates researching postconflict recovery around the world, and who were willing to provide me with logistical and other forms of support throughout my research. Four of these field workers are profiled in Chapters 3 and 4.

In Northern Uganda, three agencies helped facilitate my research in four communities in Acholiland. My research in Gulu District was facilitated by the Women's Advocacy Network (WAN), originally a project of the Justice and Reconciliation Project (JRP), and based in Gulu Town, the largest urban center in Northern Uganda and the epicenter of violence and displacement during the LRA War. In my visits to rural communities in Nwoya and Pader Districts, I also benefited from the collaboration of the Refugee Law Project (RLP). With RLP's help, I met and interviewed Jane Orama and others in Dure Parish of Pader District, as well as members of Alany pa Mony Lit in Nwoya District. In Kitgum District, I collaborated with Human Rights Focus (HURIFO), a Ugandan nongovernmental agency. HURIFO staff facilitated my initial meetings and interactions with the women peacebuilders of Odoko Mit, located in the Mucwini Sub-county of Kitgum District. Both RLP and HURIFO have operated out of field offices in Gulu and Kitgum.

In Sierra Leone I consulted with Fambul Tok, the Freetown-based NGO that kindled the Peace Mothers movement, and whose team members introduced me to Boie Jalloh and her fellow Peace Mothers living in Falaba District as well as the individual Peace Mothers I interviewed in four other communities across the Koinadugu and Moyamba Districts. Fambul Tok staff, based in numerous field offices throughout the country, collaborate with local Peace Mothers groups in over two hundred communities throughout the Northern, Eastern, and Southern Provinces of Sierra Leone, all of which were sites of extreme violence during the Rebel War.

Around a dozen staff members and friends of WAN, RLP, and HURIFO supported my field work in all four communities in Northern Uganda, as did a dozen or so Fambul Tok staff members and affiliates in five rural parishes and chiefdoms across Sierra Leone. Particularly essential to my work was their expert assistance in translating my conversations and interviews with women, whether in the Acholi language, spoken by Jane Orama in Northern Uganda, or in the various languages spoken in different regions of Sierra Leone, including Mende, Mandingo, Limba, and Fula, the first language of Boie Jalloh.

The preliminary phase of the field research was structured around correspondence and consultations with the founders and staff of the Women's Advocacy Network, the Refugee Law Project, and HURIFO in Uganda, and the Fambul Tok Peace Mothers in Sierra Leone. These early conversations took place in the national and district capitals of the two countries. In 2016 I met with representatives of the various partner organizations in Kampala,

Gulu, and Kitgum, Uganda, and in Freetown, Moyamba, and Kabala, Sierra Leone. In both countries NGO staff described the grassroots networks with which their organizations collaborate. These senior staff members provided vital briefings and initial introductions to women engaged in peace and justice work in rural locales in both countries. The research studies I undertook would not have been initiated or completed were it not for the relationships of trust and confidence that these individuals and agencies have created and nurtured with local women throughout the postwar period and for the good will that they and members of the local women's groups were willing to extend to me. I was privileged by their willingness to share their time and insights in furtherance of my research.

The heart of my field research consists of a series of interviews with women peacebuilders spread out over a seven-year period. I started in 2016 with focus group discussions in each of nine communities—four across Gulu, Kitgum, and neighboring districts of Northern Uganda and five spread out between the Northern and Southern Provinces of Sierra Leone. These group interactions were followed by individual interviews with a select number of those who participated in the focus group discussions. The initial individual interviews occurred in 2016 and 2017. From 2017 to 2023 (interrupted by a two-year hiatus due to the COVID-19 pandemic), I organized successive yearly rounds of follow-up conversations with various individuals among my initial interviewees. In 2016 and 2017, subject to my ethical research protocol, I asked for and obtained oral consent from all my potential interviewees before proceeding with focus group or individual interviews. Each participant was also given the opportunity to be quoted by name or anonymously in the volume with her consent.[51]

The primary objective of all the interviews was to learn how the community activists like Jane and Boie define and describe their peace and justice work in Northern Uganda and Sierra Leone and to explore how peacebuilding emerges from their daily activities. The focus group interviews were structured around three initial questions posed to the women: What are your understandings of reconciliation? Of livelihood? Of accountability? The follow-up one-on-one interviews delved further into the perspectives of individual women with a series of twenty-four questions, including: What level of schooling did you complete? Have you or your family members visited a hospital or clinic in the past year? What collective activities among those your community group engages in are you most proud of? What protections against domestic violence exist in your community? Are women able to participate in politics and to purchase and inherit property on an equal footing with men? (The Peacebuilders' Questionnaire, which guided the individual interviews in Northern Uganda and Sierra Leone, is Appendix 1 in this volume.)

A further objective of the research was to seek and gather lessons and perspectives that grassroots women peacebuilders in Northern Uganda and Sierra Leone, like Jane Orama and Boie Jalloh, might offer to women and men working on postconflict social transformation at the local, national, and regional levels in various parts of the globe. Their insights and those of their fellow peacebuilders contributed to my reshaping and refining of the language and vision of transformative justice. They helped me winnow out rhetorical terminology and programmatic objectives that seemed remote or counterproductive, while leaving the essence—those concepts that resonate with and support women's experiences of collective action and social transformation in their communities. Their understandings of transformative justice offer important insights to institutions and practitioners working at the district, national, and international levels to better support grassroots peacebuilding in Uganda, Sierra Leone, and other parts of the world.

My interviews and interactions with grassroots activist women working in partnership with the Women's Advocacy Network and other agencies in Northern Uganda and the Fambul Tok Peace Mothers in Sierra Leone help identify the unfinished business of postwar recovery. Grassroots projects need to be paired with structural change, particularly if resurgent conflict is to be prevented. Women peacebuilders in Northern Uganda and Sierra Leone have refined an innovative and multifaceted practice of transformative justice that supports gender equity and promotes reconciliation, livelihood, and accountability in the near and longer term. Their visions of transformative justice have application in diverse communities and societies around the world seeking to survive and thrive in the aftermath of violent conflict. Chapters 3 and 4 discuss detailed insights drawn from dozens of interviews with grassroots peace workers in the two countries. Presenting, analyzing, and honoring these conversations with women peacebuilders in Northern Uganda and Sierra Leone form the heart of this book. Collectively, their stories illustrate that transformative justice is not only needed in the postrepression or postconflict phases of national development. Rural women peacebuilders understand that concepts of peace and justice are most ambitious and most meaningful when they are fashioned into practical tools for social transformation at the community and national level in societies continuously grappling with conditions of structural violence and social inequality.

Roadmap for *Women's Work*

Chapter 1: Feminist Critiques and Human Rights Implementation
of Transformative Justice

The first section of Chapter 1 examines transformative justice through a feminist lens, in order to consider what feminist thought offers to Ugandan and Sierra Leonean peacebuilders and to suggest what other feminists might learn from their grassroots insights. Feminist critiques of postconflict justice identify an essential weakness in the contemporary implementation of transitional justice programs—a stubborn fixation on retributive justice and criminal trials as the guarantor of accountability and the best response to the perpetration of violence against women. This insight resonates with the frustrations of women peacebuilders in both countries who are committed to the integration of reparative and redistributive measures of accountability and justice. Moreover, feminist academics and women peacebuilders agree that concern for women's physical and sexual victimization in wartime should not blind us to the contemporary realities of war-affected people in the two countries, including the structural violence of poverty.

In the second part of Chapter 1 we examine human rights treaties from the grassroots perspective, evaluating them in terms of their potential to support and magnify women peacebuilders' contributions to reconciliation, livelihood, and accountability in their communities. We examine in particular those human rights instruments designed to promote and[52] uphold gender equality, social welfare, and the reparation of injury—globally and in the African Region—probing for their relevance as practical tools for justice work on the ground.

Chapter 2: The Historical Roots of War and Peacebuilding
in Uganda and Sierra Leone

This chapter places peacebuilding in Northern Uganda and Sierra Leone in a historical framework by examining the colonial and postcolonial roots of the civil wars in the two countries. Uganda and Sierra Leone are interesting comparative cases because of the different ways in which their policy makers prioritized criminal trials, historical memory preservation, amnesty programs, and other transitional justice mechanisms once their civil conflicts finally wound down. These choices cannot be understood in a historical vacuum. Some of the ethnopolitical tensions and abuses of power that led to these civil wars have continued to express themselves in the formation of national policies in the postconflict periods. These same realities help explain certain prevailing critiques of those policies by members of civil society, including grassroots women peacebuilders in the two countries.

This historical approach will provide a basis for considering the variety of grassroots women's perspectives on peacebuilding in the two countries. Thus, Chapter 2 provides historical and institutional context for our examination of the work of the Sierra Leone Peace Mothers, in Chapter 3, and the work of the Ugandan Women's Advocacy Network and affiliated women's collectives, in Chapter 4.

Chapters 3 and 4: Conversations About Peacebuilding with Rural Women in Uganda and Sierra Leone

Chapters 3 and 4 are the bedrock of the book. They present detailed insights on the meanings of transformative justice drawn from community-based research conducted from 2016 to 2023 among grassroots women peacebuilders, including Boie Jalloh of Sierra Leone and Jane Orama of Northern Uganda. The field interviews provided opportunities for individual women in rural communities in the two countries to describe their peace and justice work, the values that motivate them, and the objectives they seek. Their understandings of such concepts as reconciliation, accountability, and livelihood help us refine and deepen our three-dimensional conception of transformative justice. A truer resonance between the theories of postconflict justice and the perspectives of women peacebuilders gives local and global advocates better tools for supporting positive and deep-rooted social change. Such organic social transformation will both serve and be animated by women and men in communities and societies emerging from armed conflict and other everyday forms of violence around the world.

Feminism, Human Rights, and Transformative Justice: From Patriarchy to Partnership, from Rights to Reparation

We have to send our children to school. In time,
attitudes about women's rights will change. It is
important for children to know that women and men
have the same rights.
> —Fatumatah, Peace Mother of Koinadugu District,
> Sierra Leone

This is the kitchen table university. Everything
you need to know is here. This corn we are serving
embodies lessons in geography, economics, culture,
and colonization. These utensils here tell a story of
materiality and socialization. Salt is about migrations.
Songs are born here to grow food and children. We sing
stories to acknowledge and grow love.
> —Joy Harjo

Women working within grassroots community development networks in Northern Uganda and Sierra Leone have strong views regarding gender equality, human integrity, and community well-being. This chapter draws from the considerable work of scholars and advocates in the fields of feminism and human rights to identify elements of those theoretical frameworks most relevant to the concrete endeavors of rural women peacebuilders in the two countries.

Feminism and human rights are terms that require thoughtful definitions, given their diverse interpretations and applications by academics and activists throughout the world. At the outset, I place these terms within one overarching normative framework, in which feminist thought and human rights thought share a fundamental commitment to gender equality and human integrity. As such, *feminism* here reflects a worldview that insists on the full equality of women, men, and all people in the face of centuries of patriarchy and misogyny in cultures and societies throughout the world.[1] By the same token, *humanism* is a mindset proclaiming the dignity of all people in all spheres of life, whether public or private, political or socioeconomic, individual or communal. Just as feminism is a movement and ideology intimately linked to respect for the full humanity of women and men, humanism is a movement and ideology rooted in a notion of dignity encompassing the full range of human experience and aspiration.

The main sources consulted in this chapter are academic writings and international legal instruments. I draw on the scholarship of contemporary feminist writers to distill important ideas relevant to grassroots peacebuilders. I then interpret specific instruments of international law to extract human rights concepts useful to women peacebuilders as advocacy tools. For our purposes, the doctrinal reach of human rights law extends broadly. Human rights treaties apply in times of peace and war. In this sense, human rights law overlaps with humanitarian law or "Geneva law," and encompasses the protection of vulnerable individuals in situations of armed conflict as well as postconflict. Moreover, this inclusive conception is not limited to the political realm in which freedom of expression and civil rights are prioritized. Human rights treaties also encompass the economic and social realms in which guarantees of food, shelter, health care, income, and education are recognized as necessary to rebuild societies after armed conflict and to prevent the resurgence of civil strife in the future.

In considering whether feminist thought and human rights law have anything to offer grassroots women's peacebuilding in Sierra Leone and Northern Uganda, it is not enough to answer in the affirmative. The deeper inquiry lies in evaluating the ways in which specific feminist concepts and human rights principles become meaningful and empowering to rural women contributing to social transformation in their two countries. Such understanding will allow for greater support for the work of women peacebuilders on the part of feminists and human rights advocates working in kindred domains. I will start by exploring the synergies between feminism and peacebuilding.

Feminist Principles as Tools for Social Transformation

What Feminist Scholars Have to Say About Women and Transformative Justice

There is a significant feminist academic literature around the impact of conflict and violence on women and the role of women in postconflict transition. The scholarly contributions that have inspired the theoretical framework of this monograph are myriad and can be clustered around five major analytic themes or propositions that scholars have brought to the study of women and transformative justice. *First,* gendered power relationships express themselves in the way that women experience violence before, during, and after armed conflict and help channel women's activism in the pursuit of transformative justice. *Second,* just as essentialized views of women contribute to women's subjugation in society and their victimization in wartime, women's roles in peacebuilding after armed conflict are often essentialized in both idealized and strategic ways. *Third,* physical and sexual violence against women during wartime is often studied at the expense of the socioeconomic and structural forms of violence that women experience after the war. It is the relationship between these types of violence that sheds the most light on the causes, conduct, and amelioration of armed conflict. *Fourth,* intersectional aspects of women's identity—namely gender, race, culture, and class—feed into the ways that women experience wartime violence and the ways that they mobilize in peacebuilding. *Fifth and finally,* women's empowerment has a complex relationship with masculine identities, which can fuel the phenomenon of backlash as well as prospects for partnership.

A paramount concern of this study of women and peacebuilding is the harnessing of theory in the service of social transformation. To this end, a brief elaboration of these five themes will help elucidate constructive insights that feminist scholarship offers to the work of transformative justice. I conclude this section with a rearticulation of these key feminist ideas in practical terms that have the most relevance to grassroots women peacebuilders in Northern Uganda and Sierra Leone.

EXPOSING GENDERED POWER DYNAMICS IN WOMEN'S DAILY LIVES

Feminist scholars often define gender in terms of the prevailing ideas about what it means to be male and female in a particular society. Gender roles, in the same vein, are defined in terms of the particular roles and duties typically assigned to men and women in given social contexts. Feminists classically analyze the power dynamics that create gender-specific expectations and the new dynamics that play out when individual women defy their prescribed gender roles, whether as a matter of principle, survival, or spontaneous self-expression. The feminist journalist Mona Eltahawy describes feminism as "a reckoning with power" and calls on feminists to "define power in a way that liberates us from patriarchy's hierarchies."[2]

Feminists unveil the subordination of women as a common denominator across cultures, ethnic groups, and social classes. Yet the feminist lens also reveals women's *insubordination* as pervasive as well. Power struggles and gender roles change over time. The dynamism of relations between men and women is all the more apparent in times of war, repression, and social change, as evidenced in the experiences and insights of Boie Jalloh and Jane Orama and their fellow women peacebuilders. Even as they are constrained by their gender in certain respects, they persevere in mobilizing their power as women—to survive, to resist, to participate, to build, and to effect change, individually and collectively.

CRITIQUING THE ESSENTIALIZATION OF WOMEN'S PEACEBUILDING ROLES

Feminist theory challenges essentialized or stereotypical conceptions of women and womanhood based on notions of male superiority and female inferiority—for example, women as delicate givers of life requiring male protection; female guardians of hearth and home depending on male leadership in the public square; and feminine power as emotive and relational alongside masculine power as strategic and competitive. Feminist scholars like Rita Manchanda also unveil the manipulation of idealized womanhood to justify the most violent forms of power politics—the idea that women are guardians of national purity[3] and that men must go to war to defend the female embodiment of the nation. In the name of combating patriarchy and

militarism, feminist scholars may run the risk of re-essentializing womanhood, as the subtitle of this book (*Women's Work*) and its central focus (*women
peacebuilders*) illustrate. Nevertheless, alongside the pitfalls of essentialization, Fionnuala Ní Aoláin identifies a "strategic essentialism" whereby women
claim their nurturing selves as a way of making their peacebuilding role more
effective or less threatening to men.[4] Essentialization is a versatile tool, as
complex and dynamic as the people it describes, with the capacity to disem-
power but at the same time to empower women.

RECOGNIZING WOMEN'S EXPERIENCES OF STRUCTURAL
AND WAR-RELATED VIOLENCE

United Nations Security Council Resolutions 1325 and 2467 are important
expressions of the commitment of the international community to gender
justice in the context of transitional justice. In 2000 the Security Council
affirmed in Resolution 1325 "the important role of women in the prevention
and resolution of conflicts" and "the need to implement fully international
humanitarian and human rights law that protects the rights of women and
girls during and after armed conflict."[5] Nearly twenty years later, the council
renewed its commitment to gender equality in the context of peacebuilding
in Resolution 2467.[6] In prioritizing women's participation in transitional justice endeavors, both resolutions highlight the tragedy of sexual violence
against women in conflict and postconflict situations.[7]

Despite these important diplomatic pronouncements, some feminist scholars take an extremely sober view of women's status in the postwar period, arguing that the reality for most women does not improve when armed hostilities
cease. Sheila Meintjes, Anu Pillay, and Meredith Turshen assert that "there is
no aftermath for women" given that they experience "so much misery, violence
and exploitation after the war."[8] They criticize an approach to postwar transition that focuses on women's political participation rights without challenging
"traditional gender restrictions," which endure past the war's formal conclusion. These scholars highlight "the real need women feel for social transformation rather than the reconstruction of the past."[9] Their work is related to the
scholarship of Aisling Swaine, who argues that the extraordinary forms and
levels of violence against women in times of war could not occur without the
tolerance for women's subordination in society during "normal" times.[10]

The enduring quality of women's marginalization and oppression is apparent in Northern Uganda and Sierra Leone, despite the winding down of
armed conflict in both countries. Over a decade since the Juba Peace Accords

were signed between the Lord's Resistance Army and the government of Uganda, Acholi women of Northern Uganda like Jane Orama continue to face high levels of poverty and illiteracy. Similarly, two decades after the Lomé Peace Accords were signed by representatives of the Revolutionary United Front and the government of Sierra Leone, rural agricultural women of Sierra Leone still face barriers in accessing education and health care, while their nation's maternal mortality rate remains one of the highest in the world.[11]

Transitional justice scholars recognize that the structural violence of poverty and inequality are powerful generators of armed conflict and may lead to its resurgence if economic suffering is not alleviated in the postconflict period. Paul Gready, director of the Centre for Applied Human Rights at the University of York, calls for "bottom-up approaches. If justice in transition is to be transformative, then it must address . . . the complex politics of transitional societies, including . . . histories of social exclusion and poverty, and the causes of conflict."[12] Feminist transitional justice scholars critique their field for giving lip service to structural violence without acknowledging the radical changes required to address entrenched poverty and without recognizing that it is women who bear the heaviest burden of such economic inequality. As Ní Aoláin pointedly states, "Placing the economic and social status of women squarely in the frame of analysis is critical to understand why transition often fails to deliver for women. Generally speaking, equality, economic redistribution, and social justice are off the table for the purposes of transition."[13]

According to these feminist perspectives, a focus on material conditions of life is vital to supporting the priorities of grassroots women peacebuilders like Jane Orama and Boie Jalloh in Northern Uganda and Sierra Leone, who tend to be less interested in war crimes prosecutions and more concerned with the status of women and their capacity to meet their basic needs and those of their families and communities.

ACKNOWLEDGING WOMEN'S INTERSECTIONAL COLLABORATION IN PEACEBUILDING

Intersectionality theory explores the power dynamics percolating through the multiple facets of human identity, including but not limited to ethnicity or race, socioeconomic class, and gender.[14] It gives us tools for addressing the phenomenon of overlapping spheres of oppression in the context of war and peace, highlighting the phenomenon of simultaneous "paradigms" or "abusive regimes,"[15] in which individuals experience multiple systems of subjugation and violence from a variety of standpoints or perspectives.[16] In this vein, for both Jane and Boie, their experiences before and during the armed conflicts in their countries as well as their approaches to peacebuilding and social transformation are colored by the various aspects of their identity, including their gender, their Catholic and Muslim faiths, their Acholi and Fulbeh heritages, and the vast development gaps they experience in their home regions compared to the wealth of elites in their respective countries.

As the transitional justice scholar Eilish Rooney points out, the tendency for the various components of our identity to be experienced as multiple vectors of subjugation and violence is particularly pronounced during and after armed conflict. Even as one basis for violence or inequality is ended or alleviated, other types of oppression and inequality may stubbornly persist, particularly for women. In time of transition, "women's lives are routinely invisible and fail to be improved."[17] At the same time, intersectional identities can also create common cause among women of different ethnic and linguistic groups. Rooney argues that "targeting deep-rooted inequalities reduces the divisiveness of identity politics and strengthens political stability,"[18] suggesting that intersectional mobilization and collective action by women can be powerful tools for social change.

CONSIDERING THE IMPACT OF WOMEN'S EMPOWERMENT ON MEN'S POWER AND IDENTITY

Another line of inquiry is the extent to which women are able to build common cause with men on issues of gender equality and community development in the postconflict period. Scholars suggest that this type of collaboration faces significant challenges. In the context of Northern Uganda, the gender scholar Chris Dolan attests that women's incremental gains are sometimes perceived as threats to the status of men, whether as heads of household, community and clan leaders, or property owners. Dolan points to the disruption of "gendered expectations" during and since the LRA War. Just as the inability to adequately nurture their children was painful to women, the inability to serve as breadwinner for the household was painful to men.[19] The reality that women's empowerment is sometimes equated to men's disempowerment complicates efforts for partnership between women and men in peacebuilding.[20] Yet scholars also attest to important ways in which some women and men in Northern Uganda are moving in tandem in the postwar period.

In Northern Uganda, among the multiple ways that men, women, and children suffered during the LRA War, sexual violence was common in military attacks on civilian communities as well as a means of humiliation and social control in the displaced persons camps. Rape was a tactic of both LRA and Ugandan Army (UPDF) forces. While sexual violence against women during the LRA War is well-documented, the systematic rape of men during the LRA War, particularly at the hands of the UPDF, is more slowly being acknowledged. Notably, Chris Dolan and others have documented the prevalence of sexual violence against men during the LRA War.[21] In certain communities in Acholiland, women's trauma healing groups have formed alongside men's trauma healing groups. Women's appreciation of the willingness of male survivors to speak out about male rape has strengthened their own commitment to collective healing. Moreover, men's exploration of "nonviolent masculinities" in such contexts may contribute to movement toward stronger partnerships between men and women within the home and the community overall.[22] The scholarship of Dolan and others suggests that the concept of "therapeutic activism" can be a basis for cross-gender collaboration among male and female peacebuilders who are able to acknowledge and somehow affirm their common experiences of surviving trauma.[23]

Toward a Contextualized Feminist Vision of Transformative Justice

Taking the five feminist themes presented above, we can transpose them into terms more rooted in the experiences of grassroots women peacebuilders in Uganda and Sierra Leone:

First, a community-engaged feminist worldview, dedicated to addressing gender power dynamics, rejecting misogyny, and dismantling patriarchy, is alive and well in Northern Uganda and Sierra Leone, although with certain caveats. Boie and Jane do not call themselves feminists. Nevertheless, they believe that women must work in partnership with men in the home and the society and they insist that women should have equal access to secondary education. They and their fellow peacebuilders agree fundamentally that a decent and healthy community cannot tolerate violence against women and children. They embrace women's empowerment in the service of community survival.

Second, "outsider feminists," working in partnership with women at the community level need to resist the tendency to idealize or essentialize women in Northern Uganda and Sierra Leone within an overly narrow conception of the female peacebuilder. Boie calls herself a "Peace Mother" and yet sought permission from her husband to participate in community dispute resolution. Jane functions as sole parent to a family of foster children yet rues the fact that women have "become men in their homes." Clearly, attitudes toward gender and gender roles are not static or monolithic for women peacebuilders and may not always align with the views of other feminist thinkers from around the globe.

Third, feminism, peacebuilding, and poverty alleviation are three legs of one stool among women peacebuilders in Northern Uganda and Sierra Leone. Boie, Jane, and their comadres agree, with rare exception, that women's access to health care, education, and income are the best insurance against violence in their families, community, and society. Moreover, grassroots women peacebuilders in Uganda and Sierra Leone are as concerned with alleviating structural violence and material suffering in the postwar era as they are with penalizing wartime instances of physical violence against women and men. For them, it is not enough to instill accountability for wartime offenses through criminal trials. Women peacebuilders also need access to food, income, credit, medical care, and education; they demand guarantees of property and inheritance rights; and they seek protection from domestic and community violence. Without economic and physical well-being for women, men, and children in war-emergent communities, the risk of renewed conflict is extremely high. Women peacebuilders in Uganda and Sierra Leone appreciate that macrolevel structural reforms of their social welfare, land tenure, and judicial systems are essential to break the cycles of violence and repression. In the meantime, they devote themselves to incremental, microlevel changes in their daily lives.

Fourth, coalition-building and "intersectionality" are dimensions of women's peace activism in the two countries. It is important to acknowledge the challenges and potential for collaborative engagement in peace and justice work across ethnic and faith communities in Uganda and Sierra Leone as in other parts of the world. Particularly in Sierra Leone, Peace Mothers groups include Muslims and Christians working together in the same communities and coalesce across Mende, Fula, and Limba-speaking regions, among others. Women's peace mobilization across cultural communities is not as apparent in Northern Uganda, partly due to the LRA War's singular impact on the Acholi people of Acholiland. Nevertheless, Northern Ugandan and Sierra Leoneans alike appreciate that interethnic solidarity is essential in both countries for social mobilization around goals such as state-funded reparations for long-term war injuries. Thus, the intersectional paradigm, while examining the complex causes of women's oppression, also reveals opportunities for women to collaborate across different identity groups. This potential is borne out in the collaboration of women peacebuilders across Northern Uganda and particularly in Sierra Leone.

Fifth, women's empowerment as community peacebuilders entails forging new partnerships with men and resisting the mentality that women's empowerment necessarily leads to the emasculation or displacement of men. The difficulty in doing so is reflected in Jane's comment about women "becoming men" in their homes across Acholiland. This phenomenon is not unique to Uganda, as peacebuilders in Sierra Leone also confront the impact on masculine identity when deep-seated patriarchal values are challenged. The Fambul Tok Peace Mothers in Sierra Leone have fashioned a concerted strategy to highlight the ways in which women's increased status also benefits their male partners and extended family members. The Peace Mothers utilize the slogan "woman power with man support" to affirm that as men get behind women's empowerment, women and men will be able to lift up the community, together.

The battle against gender inequality and gender-based violence continues in Northern Uganda and Sierra Leone in the postwar period. While acknowledging the persistent dynamics of gender oppression, the feminist concept of strategic collaboration is at work at the grassroots level among women peacebuilders in both Uganda and Sierra Leone as they forge new partnerships with men and with one another.

Now we turn to the synergies between human rights law and women's peacebuilding.

Human Rights Principles as Tools for Social Transformation

Prioritizing Human Rights Law over Criminal Law in Transformative Justice

Ugandan and Sierra Leonean women peacebuilders' central commitment to community healing and social well-being challenges the dominant global framework for transitional justice still preoccupied with determining individual criminal responsibility for war atrocities.[24] Theirs is primarily a restorative vision rather than a retributive vision. Defining wartime offenses as war crimes or crimes against humanity[25] creates an important benchmark for seeking reparations, civil remedies, and social reforms that will help alleviate the causes of conflict in the first place. Nevertheless, prosecutions do not take center stage. Human rights approaches are better designed to take on the structural and material changes that women peacebuilders seek. Penal justice is there, but it is a fallback.

Rather than concentrating on removing individual criminal actors from society, grassroots peacebuilders like Boie Jalloh of Dogoloya and Jane Orama of Pader hold themselves and their governments responsible for creating humane conditions of life for all people now and in the future. Their main focus is on state and community accountability rather than individual guilt. Their most urgent demand is for collective restitution rather than individual punishment. When women peacebuilders push their governments to implement changes under national law, they can utilize human rights principles to strengthen their call for social service reforms or reparations programs, for example. They may do so with explicit reference to international treaties or, indirectly, with reference to domestic legal mechanisms that dovetail with human rights concepts inscribed in treaty provisions.

Because so often discussions of international law and transitional justice begin with the analysis of penal mechanisms and the principles of international criminal law, it is important to push back and spotlight the specific and limited impact of these trials on individual war-affected people in the two countries and perhaps elsewhere. For many Peace Mothers in Sierra Leone, war crimes tribunals are remote, abstract entities that have played a largely historical role in peacebuilding. And for women peacebuilders in Uganda, ongoing war crimes trials are often regarded with skepticism if not outright derision. Instead, women peacebuilders in both countries are most committed to seeking improvements in the health care and educational systems and, particularly in Uganda, calling for reparations for wartime injuries. In both contexts, human rights principles are more useful than penal measures in pursuing vital structural reforms and reparative measures in the social and economic realms.

To better understand why women peacebuilders in Sierra Leone and Uganda prefer human rights and restorative mechanisms to the penal and retributive facets of transformative justice, it helps to consider their attitudes toward the conduct of the particular war crimes prosecutions that have occurred in their respective countries. In the case of Sierra Leone, it is perhaps more obvious why international criminal law is an abstract concept, given that the last proceedings in the Special Court for Sierra Leone concluded in 2015, after nine convictions, culminating in the sentencing of the former Liberian president Charles Taylor for directing and supporting war atrocities carried out by rebel forces of the Revolutionary United Front.

In Northern Uganda, contrastingly, war crimes prosecutions for rebel leaders of the Lord's Resistance Army are ongoing. The LRA lieutenant Dominic Ongwen's war crimes convictions were recently upheld in the International Criminal Court and arrest warrants are still outstanding for the LRA leader Joseph Kony and others.[26] At the same time, there have been no war crimes indictments of soldiers or officers on the government side. As further explored in Chapter 2, the prosecution of Ongwen for war crimes including the conscription of children was complicated by the fact that Ongwen himself was forcibly conscripted as a child many years before. Ongwen's case is also problematic for Ugandan women peacebuilders like Jane, due to the one-sided nature of ICC prosecutions overall and the Ugandan government's failure to hold the soldiers of the Uganda People's Defense Forces (the Ugandan Army) criminally accountable for their abuses as well.

In the opinion of Jane's fellow Uketu wan Kwene members (notably the late Daker Nighty), the LRA leader Ongwen should not bear all accountability for the LRA War. Members of women's collectives in Northern Uganda remain distressed that the Ugandan government denies its own responsibility for wartime suffering, through acts of omission and commission. As noted in interviews with survivors of the LRA War, the UPDF carried out their own attacks on civilians, and in addition they were largely powerless to protect the civilian population from attacks by the LRA.

Thus, the preference of women peacebuilders in Sierra Leone and Northern Uganda for reparations and structural reforms over criminal trials is not a rejection of accountability. Their commitment to social supports for a war-affected population bears witness to their insistence on equal justice and a restoration of the compact between themselves and their government. Human rights law is fundamentally about human dignity and the state's responsibility to guarantee the enjoyment of fundamental freedoms and social protections for all people, in times of peace and in wartime. The principles and mechanisms of human rights law are worthy of further exploration to determine their specific efficacies for women peacebuilders in the two countries.

The Essence of Human Rights Law: Dignity, Responsibility, and Complementarity
PROTECTING HUMAN DIGNITY

Human rights law is a body of international law[27] that affirms and promotes the physical integrity, political liberty, and social security of human beings, too often in the face of attacks on all three. As reflected in the 1948 Universal Declaration of Human Rights,[28] the human rights spectrum encompasses the principles of equality, humane treatment, civil and political agency, and economic and social well-being. Given the persistence of human rights violations around the world, the law of human rights too often comes up against the reality of human wrongs. Thus, advocates of human rights law must be stubbornly idealistic as well as defiant in the face of human suffering. Human rights practitioners continually seek to narrow the gap between the proclamation of human rights and their widespread enjoyment by human beings. But human rights law is not mere aspiration—it speaks the language of obligation and reparation.

STATE RESPONSIBILITY

The human rights treaties referenced below create binding obligations for both Uganda and Sierra Leone under international law. Those treaties signed and ratified by the two countries include the International Covenant on Civil and Political Rights (ICCPR), the International Covenant on Economic, Social, and Cultural Rights (ICESCR), the Convention on the Elimination of Discrimination Against Women (CEDAW), the African Charter on Human and Peoples' Rights (the Banjul Charter), and the Protocol to the African Charter on the Rights of Women in Africa (the Banjul Women's Protocol).[29] In each of these treaties, the state signatories are made the guarantors of the enjoyment of human rights by all people under their jurisdiction. The language of the International Covenant on Civil and Political Rights is illustrative in this regard: "Each State Party to the present Covenant undertakes *to respect and to ensure* to all individuals . . . the rights recognized in the present Covenant without distinction of any kind."[30] The same concept of state responsibility for the enjoyment of human rights is codified in other treaties to which both Uganda and Sierra Leone are parties.[31]

Thus, unlike international criminal law, which puts the onus for wrongful conduct on individuals, human rights law binds states, who are obligated to uphold the treaties they ratify and to remedy violations under the principle of state responsibility. Human rights law in this sense is a hybrid of contract and tort law at the global level whereby states create the compacts and states are liable for wrongful conduct. When states cause or fail to prevent human rights abuses against their people, in defiance of their treaty obligations, they are obligated to repair or provide restitution for those injuries. While most grassroots women peacebuilders in Northern Uganda and Sierra Leone lack professional training in treaty law, they often speak the language of human rights with regard to standards of right conduct and the fair resolution of disputes. They are invoking the principle of state responsibility when they demand reparations for the war-related and postwar deprivations they and their fellow community members have suffered.

COMPLEMENTARITY BETWEEN TREATIES, NATIONAL LAW, AND COMMUNITY ADVOCACY

Some international instruments create new mechanisms for the enforcement of human rights protections around the world. One example is the African Commission constituted by the African Charter on Human and Peoples' Rights,[32] which we will discuss further below. However, to a great extent, international treaties anticipate and rely on national measures to implement human rights in particular countries. This is the principle of complementarity. In fact, some treaties expressly require states to give effect to international treaty provisions under their national laws. The Convention on the Elimination of Discrimination Against Women illustrates this principle in providing that "states . . . shall take all appropriate measures, including legislation, to ensure the full development and advancement of women."[33]

There are important examples of complementarity in action in Sierra Leone and Uganda in the realm of women's rights. In 2007 Sierra Leone's Parliament passed so-called Gender Laws serving to criminalize domestic violence, to create a regular mechanism for the registration of customary marriages, and to recognize women's inheritance rights.[34] Since 1995 Uganda's Constitution has prohibited gender-based discrimination in the devolution of estates.[35] These national laws resonate with specific provisions of CEDAW and the African Women's Charter, explored in the text below, although they are not always fully honored in practice.

Beyond the global and national levels, there is an additional iteration of the complementarity principle that addresses the implementation of human rights protections at the community level. The idea of individuals as guarantors of human rights is expressed with particular clarity in the African Charter of Human and Peoples' Rights, which holds that "every individual shall have the duty to respect and consider his fellow beings without discrimination and to maintain relations aimed at promoting, safeguarding and reinforcing mutual respect and tolerance."[36]

Thus, human rights treaties provide a powerful framework for transformative justice work on the ground, particularly to the extent that human rights values resonate with national legislation and the objectives of women peacebuilders. Community leaders like Boie Jalloh and Jane Orama are committed to integrating respect for the dignity, integrity, equality, and well-being of all people within the daily life of their communities. They are particularly concerned with protecting women from physical harm and improving their access to education, health care, land, and credit. Their work dovetails most closely with provisions of human rights instruments that recognize and promote humane treatment, economic and social well-being, and gender equality.[37] These instruments include those discussed below, particularly the Universal Declaration of Human Rights, CEDAW, and the Banjul Women's Protocol.

Much of the time, grassroots women peacebuilders take it on themselves to do the work of human rights promotion—in their activism to improve material conditions of life, prevent domestic violence, challenge patriarchy when necessary, and facilitate peaceful dispute resolution in their communities. Nevertheless, they believe their governments should support them in realizing these goals, particularly when the state has played a role in causing or exacerbating violence and poverty. In this sense, the principles of state responsibility and complementarity work in tandem. The human rights framework promotes a restored relationship of trust between the individual and the government, something that Northern Ugandan peacebuilders demand in the form of reparations from their government for its conduct during the LRA War.

Despite the distance between international human rights treaties and enforcement mechanisms on the one hand and community-based conflict resolution and collaborative subsistence on the other, international human rights law inspires justice work on the global, regional, national, and local levels. This complementarity expresses itself even as international legal principles are utilized in different ways in the various arenas. In this chapter, I identify and explore those principles and provisions of international human rights law that are particularly relevant to women like Boie Jalloh and Jane Orama in their contributions to the various facets of transformative justice at the community level in Sierra Leone and Northern Uganda. They may employ these principles in their community work, through domestic advocacy, or in international forums. There is a symbiosis between all levels of human rights work, and indeed international human rights law is further strengthened and legitimized through its incorporation, application, and invocation at the state and local levels.

While grassroots women peacebuilders rarely make explicit reference to international treaties and institutions, they often employ universal human rights principles in their peace and justice work.[38] The principle of complementarity recognizes that women peacebuilders do not need to invoke formal human rights treaties and declarations directly to inspire or legitimize their human rights activism, to the extent that aspects of these instruments have been internalized within national law and cultural expectations. Moreover, human rights advocates who support human rights advocacy at the national and local levels are furthering the objectives of those very international treaties. Complementarity flows both ways as global norms and local actions mutually inspire and legitimize one another. To the extent that members of local women's collectives invoke human rights principles in their peace and justice work at the community level, their peacebuilding activities embody and strengthen the norms and principles that are codified in specific instruments.

In the ensuing passages I endeavor to link women peacebuilders' particular notions of rightful action with specific human rights instruments in order to strengthen a global human rights framework that better serves women's involvement in postconflict social transformation at the local level.

Distilling Human Rights Principles Vital to Women's Peacebuilding
GENDER EQUALITY, SOCIAL WELFARE, AND LEGAL REMEDIES

Women like Boie Jalloh and Jane Orama who are engaged in subsistence agriculture, dispute resolution, and the restoration of trust at the community level look at human rights in concrete terms. In particular, they ask to be respected as women and as people, for their property and inheritance rights to be protected, and for access to public education and health care on behalf of themselves and their families. Thus, our survey of the global legal framework for transitional justice focuses on those international human rights instruments that affirm respectful human interactions, sustainable livelihood, material well-being, and gender equity in ways that are relevant to women engaged in peacebuilding on behalf of themselves, their families, and their communities.

Below I explore three important concepts articulated in specific international and regional human rights instruments, highlighting their synergies
with women-centric peacebuilding at the local level. These human rights
principles include: *first*, respect for gender equality; *second*, recognition of
rights in the social and economic realms; and *third*, the provision of remedies for violations of rights. With respect to each, I will look at how specific
provisions of international instruments elaborate these ideas and then how
the various treaty provisions might apply in the lives and work of grassroots
women peacebuilders in Uganda and Sierra Leone.[39]

WOMEN'S RIGHTS ARE HUMAN RIGHTS: THE PRINCIPLE OF GENDER EQUALITY

The right to freedom from discrimination on the basis of gender (or sex) is
specifically enumerated in various treaties that the governments of both
Uganda and Sierra Leone have ratified. To begin with, the International Covenant on Civil and Political Rights prohibits discrimination against individuals "solely on the ground of race, colour, *sex*, language, religion or social
origin," even in times of national emergency.[40] In the Banjul Charter, another
treaty to which both countries are parties, there is similarly an unqualified
entitlement to enjoy enumerated rights "without distinction of any kind such
as race, ethnic group, colour, *sex*, language, religion, political or any other
opinion, national and social origin, fortune, birth or other status."[41] Addition-
ally, two international treaties are specifically dedicated to combating gender
discrimination—namely, the Convention on the Elimination of Discrimination Against Women (CEDAW)[42] and the Banjul Protocol on the Rights of
Women in Africa (Banjul Women's Protocol).[43] Both countries have ratified
CEDAW and the Banjul Women's Protocol. CEDAW defines discrimination
against women as "any distinction, exclusion or restriction made on the basis
of sex which has the effect or purpose of impairing or nullifying the recognition, enjoyment or exercise by women, irrespective of marital status, on a basis
of equality of men and women of human rights and fundamental freedoms in
the political, economic, social, cultural, civil or any other field."[44]

The Banjul Women's Protocol similarly defines discrimination against
women as "differential treatment based on sex and whose objectives or effects compromise or destroy the recognition, enjoyment or the exercise by
women, regardless of their marital status, of human rights and fundamental
freedoms in all spheres of life."[45] CEDAW and the Banjul Women's Protocol
go one step beyond the condemnation of gender discrimination to address

its root causes. Both treaties challenge states to take steps "to modify social and cultural patterns of conduct of men and women" in order to eliminate discriminatory or stereotypical attitudes in society, particularly regarding the purported inferiority of women.[46] In their advocacy for the inheritance and property ownership rights of women as well as women's right to be free from domestic violence, peacebuilders like Boie Jalloh and Jane Orama are invoking the spirit of the nondiscrimination and gender equity provisions of CEDAW, the Banjul Charter, and the Banjul Women's Protocol. Moreover, in their community advocacy work, they are making their own efforts to modify social and cultural patterns of conduct and to break down barriers to gender equality as contemplated in CEDAW and the Banjul Women's Protocol.

SOCIAL RIGHTS ARE HUMAN RIGHTS: THE PRINCIPLE OF SOCIAL WELL-BEING

The Universal Declaration and the Indivisibility of Human Rights

Since 1948 the Universal Declaration of Human Rights (UDHR)[47] has proclaimed the indivisibility of human rights, artificially divided in some international instruments. This indivisibility is particularly expressed in terms of the fundamental interdependence between rights in the economic-social realm and those in the civil-political realm.[48] The UDHR is an important legal and political tool for postconflict social transformation throughout the world due to its focus on human dignity and well-being in social, economic, and collective terms as well as in civil, political, and individual terms. The UDHR is regarded to have attained the status of customary law in the over six decades since its adoption by the United Nations General Assembly without dissenting vote.[49] As customary law, the Universal Declaration binds all states, even those like Uganda and Sierra Leone that achieved their independence after 1948. The UDHR remains the most influential instrument devoted to the protection of individual human rights because it is global in its geographical scope and expansive in its subject matter.

Because the UDHR contains numerous provisions in the economic and social realms—particularly upholding health, education, and property rights as well as gender equality—it is an important source of advocacy for women active in grassroots peace and justice work in Uganda and Sierra Leone. The legal stature of the UDHR has increased over time, notably when its principles were reaffirmed in the 1981 African Charter of Human and Peoples' Rights (the Banjul Charter),[50] a treaty ratified by both countries. It is also significant that the 1995 Constitution of Uganda and the 1991 Constitution of Sierra Leone incorporate many of the UDHR's substantive terms.[51] Those UDHR provisions relating to material conditions of life are also codified in the 1966 International Covenant for Economic, Social, and Cultural Rights,[52] a treaty ratified by both Uganda and Sierra Leone.

CEDAW and Rights for Women in the Social Realm

The Convention on the Elimination of Discrimination Against Women,[53] ratified by Uganda and Sierra Leone, also has specific references to women's social and economic rights. First, CEDAW devotes specific articles to the elimination of discrimination against women in the fields of education, employment, and health care and with regard to other forms of social support.[54] Another provision of CEDAW is particularly relevant to women in Northern Uganda and Sierra Leone who are involved in peace and justice work at the grassroots level. Article 14 recognizes "the particular problems faced by rural women and the *significant roles which rural women play in the economic survival of their families,* including their work in the non-monetized sectors of the economy." This article specifically references rural women's need for loans; their entitlement to participate in agricultural cooperatives, and formal and informal educational opportunities; and their right to access electricity, water, and sanitation facilities.[55]

When women peacebuilders like Jane Orama in Northern Uganda and Boie Jalloh in Sierra Leone advocate for better health care and educational, occupational, and financial opportunities for themselves and their families, they very seldom refer directly to CEDAW. However, when grassroots women peacebuilders utilize national laws and policies to further their social welfare rights, they are operating within the broader framework of CEDAW under the principle of complementarity described above. Moreover, they believe that their government has the responsibility to provide such services to them as a matter of right. Many women peacebuilders in Northern Uganda expressed the idea of a "covenant" that exists between the government and the people of Uganda, which has been breached by the state's failure to restore basic social services since the war. Community leaders have a profound desire to have this covenant restored and to once again experience that "the government is a part of us."[56] Only when the government acknowledges its role in the deprivations the people have suffered, and remedies their injuries, will unity be restored. In describing this covenant between the state and the people, Ugandan women peacebuilders are invoking the spirit of the third article of CEDAW, which requires that "States shall take in all fields, in particular the political, *social, economic and cultural fields*, including legislation, to ensure the full development and advancement of women."[57]

Banjul Women's Protocol: Health, Reproductive Freedom, and Marriage Rights

For grassroots women peacebuilders in Northern Uganda and Sierra Leone, it is somewhat artificial to address gender-based discrimination without circling back to women's extreme vulnerability in the economic and social realms. While both CEDAW and the Banjul Women's Protocol have provisions integrating antidiscrimination and social welfare, the Banjul Women's Protocol is particularly notable for the ways its provisions weave together gender equality and human security. The Banjul Women's Protocol is an important advocacy tool for women peacebuilders in Northern Uganda and Sierra Leone because it extends the scope of three important CEDAW provisions with respect to women's reproductive rights, marriage, and inheritance.

First, while CEDAW accords women and men equal rights "to decide freely and responsibly on the number and spacing of their children,"[58] the Banjul Women's Protocol acknowledges that women have "the right to decide *whether to have children*" as well as their number and spacing, and that women have "the right to choose *any method of contraception*."[59] Second, while CEDAW recognizes women's right to enter into marriage "only with their free and full consent," the Banjul Protocol provides that "the minimum age of marriage for women shall be 18 years."[60] Third, while CEDAW requires States Parties to accord women "a legal capacity identical to that of men,"[61] the Banjul Protocol enters more deeply into domains where women in fact seldom enjoy that equal legal capacity—namely, in inheritance, at the death of a spouse and upon remarriage. In special provisions devoted to "Widows' Rights," "Right to Inheritance," and "Special Protection of Elderly Women," the Banjul Protocol protects *women's rights to inherit equally* upon the death of a spouse or parent, *to retain the family home* when widowed or remarried, and *"to automatically become the guardian and custodian of her children*, after the death of her husband, unless this is contrary to the interests and the welfare of the children."[62] All these provisions of the Banjul Protocol are of special relevance to Boie

Jalloh and Jane Orama and their fellow community group members. Boie
and Jane are both widowed—Boie very recently and Jane some years back.
Hence the custody of their children and access to the family home are issues
of paramount concern for their welfare and that of their families.

Notably, the Banjul Women's Protocol addresses a very specific concern
related to women's physical integrity, which CEDAW does not address. Article 5, entitled "Elimination of Harmful Practices," requires states to *prohibit*
and sanction *"all forms of female genital mutilation,* scarification, medical-
ization and para-medicalization of female genital mutilation."[63] The provisions prohibiting and sanctioning female genital mutilation (FGM) are of
particular relevance in Sierra Leone, where the incidence of cutting is thought
to have returned to as high as 90 percent despite a temporary suspension of
the practice during the Ebola crisis of 2014 and 2015. Sierra Leone's Parliament has not explicitly criminalized FGM despite laws prohibiting acts that
are dangerous or harmful to women and girls.[64] Utilizing domestic law and
the Banjul Women's Protocol to push their government to take further steps
to eradicate FGM is a path open to women peacebuilders in Sierra Leone. At
the same time, the work they do to expand access to health care at the local
level serves a kindred purpose in modifying patterns of conduct and social
service provision that impact women's health and well-being.

There are several additional provisions of the Banjul Women's Protocol
not contemplated in CEDAW. Under article 10, women have *"the right to participate in the promotion and maintenance of peace,"* including programs of
community-based peace education and conflict resolution from the grassroots to the global level.[65] Article 11 obligates States Parties to *protect women*
"against all forms of violence, rape and other forms of sexual exploitation";
criminalize such acts as war crimes, genocide, and crimes against humanity; and "take all necessary measures to ensure that no child, especially girls
under 18 years of age, take a direct part in hostilities and that no child is recruited as a soldier."[66] Article 13 concerns women's economic and social welfare rights, including protections against sexual harassment at work; equal
pay for equal work; *protections for women in the informal sector,* including
social insurance; *protections against labor exploitation of female children*; and
the provision of pre- and postnatal maternity leave.[67] Finally, the Banjul Protocol includes provisions dedicated to "Food Security," "Adequate Housing,"
"Right to a Healthy and Sustainable Environment," and "Right to Sustainable Development."[68] All these provisions are relevant to women peacebuilders in Sierra Leone and Northern Uganda who are actively engaged in

peacebuilding (art. 10), working to prevent domestic violence (art. 11), and promoting women's access to health care (art. 13). To an important extent, the human rights they enjoy are the human rights they advocate for incrementally and devotionally in their daily work.

RIGHTS REQUIRE REMEDIES: THE AFRICAN COMMISSION AND THE UGANDAN PARLIAMENT

Individual victims of human rights violations—including grassroots women peacebuilders like Boie Jalloh and Jane Orama—may seek civil remedies against their state, based on its treaty-based obligations to protect the human dignity, political agency, and social welfare of persons subject to its power. State responsibilities under human rights treaties include acknowledging violations, paying reparations to the victims of human rights abuses or their next of kin, and reforming state law and policy to prevent future violations. To provide remedial mechanisms for individual victims of human rights abuses in the region of Africa, the framers of the Banjul Charter of Human and Peoples' Rights constituted the African Commission on Human and Peoples' Rights.[69] Boie, Jane, and their community groups have the capacity to bring claims against their governments before the African Commission.[70] As precedent, the African Commission has heard one important case relating to the civil war in Sierra Leone in which the government was found to have violated the Banjul Charter. This action was brought by a nongovernmental organization called the Forum of Conscience.[71]

The Forum of Conscience sued the government of Sierra Leone before the African Commission for its execution by firing squad on October 19, 1998, of twenty-four alleged participants in a coup attempt against the government of the former Sierra Leonean president Ahmed Kabbah in the waning years of the civil war. In 2000 the Commission on Human and Peoples' Rights agreed with the petitioners and held that Sierra Leone had violated the due process guarantees of the Banjul Charter in what was in essence an arbitrary and mass imposition of the death penalty. The commission found that the summary execution of the men violated their right to life as well as their right to appeal their criminal convictions, as guaranteed in articles 4 and 7(1)(a) of the charter, respectively.[72] The African Commission notes in its decision that after its investigation of the summary executions, Sierra Leone amended its military regulations to require appeals in cases involving criminal convictions by courts martial.[73] In 2021 Sierra Leone abolished the death penalty in all instances by unanimous vote of the Parliament.[74]

The outcome of the Forum of Conscience case illustrates both the power and limitations of human rights law. The commission ruled too late to save the coup plotters themselves. However, in a process stretching out over nearly a quarter-century, its decision contributed to the creation of new legislation in conformity with the human rights principles of the Banjul Charter. Thus, the case also illustrates the principle of complementarity and the ways that civil society organizations can employ international human rights mechanisms to change domestic law and to rectify injustice. Sierra Leone's rejection of the death penalty contributes to a global trend toward abolition, with tangible domestic legal implications for all Sierra Leoneans, including the Peace Mothers.[75]

The Prospect of Reparations Legislation in the Ugandan Parliament

In addition to bringing legal claims against their governments before international or regional bodies, women peacebuilders also have the capacity to bring claims before national institutions. In doing so, petitioners are appealing to concepts of state responsibility codified in international treaties like the Banjul Charter and their own national constitutions. By way of example, in 2014 the Women's Advocacy Network (WAN) took part in a coordinated advocacy campaign with women's community groups across Northern Uganda, including Jane's group, Uketu wan Kwene. In March of that year, WAN submitted a petition to the Uganda Women Parliamentarian's Association calling for reparations to survivors of wartime atrocities during the LRA War. On April 9, 2014, the Ugandan Parliament adopted a unanimous resolution calling on the government of Uganda to establish institutionalized reparations programs for Northern Uganda in the form of a gender-sensitive reparations fund, free and accessible health services for war-affected women and children, and a program of resettlement and reintegration for abducted women and children born in captivity.[76] To date, the government of Uganda has not implemented a large-scale structural reparations program as demanded by grassroots organizations advocating for war-affected women and men in Acholiland. However, as of 2023, there is renewed momentum in the Parliament to pass legislation establishing a specific reparations program for Northern Uganda.[77]

The failure of their government to acknowledge its responsibility for the long-term impact of war-related violence on the people of Northern Uganda is a major piece of unfinished business in the struggle for postconflict justice in Northern Uganda. Both national laws and international treaties affirm the state's responsibility to guarantee enjoyment of fundamental human rights. Closing this state accountability gap is at the heart of the transformative justice mission articulated by women peacebuilders throughout Acholiland.

Final Thoughts on Feminism, Human Rights Law, and Social Transformation

Typically, when Boie Jalloh, Jane Orama, and their fellow peacebuilders speak of women's rights or the "rightful" treatment of women, they do not identify themselves as feminists nor do they reference the international and regional treaties devoted to the human rights of women. Women peacebuilders in both countries advocating for women's property and inheritance rights are more apt to point to national legislation, such Sierra Leone's 2007 Gender Laws, one of which recognizes women's inheritance rights.[78] For their part, women in Northern Uganda may be more familiar with articles 21 and 33 of the 1995 Constitution of Uganda, which prohibit gender-based discrimination in the succession of estates, stubbornly patriarchal customary practices notwithstanding.

Nevertheless, when women peacebuilders in either country refer to their inheritance rights under the national laws of their country, they are at the same time invoking international principles. These state laws rest on the shoulders of international human rights obligations to women and all people that their governments have assumed under the Universal Declaration, the Banjul Charter, CEDAW, and the Banjul Women's Protocol, among other instruments.[79]

Two statements by women peacebuilders of Sierra Leone and Northern Uganda are particularly representative of their fluency in the language of feminism and human rights. Fatumatah of Kaponpon—a neighboring community to Boie's community of Dogoloya in Koinadugu District, Sierra Leone—described patrilocal Limba culture in normative terms: "When you're given to your husband [in marriage], you don't have rights. To me, that is not rightful." She further insisted, "We have to send our children to school [and] in time, attitudes about women's rights will change. . . . It is important for children to know that both men and women have the same rights." In resonant terms from the other side of the continent, peacebuilder Lucy from Nwoya District in Northern Uganda—which borders Jane's district of Pader—

Figure 4. Feminist street art, Freetown, Sierra Leone. Photo by J. Moore, 2023.

made an adamant reference to women's capacity to inherit property: "Equality is what accounts for this. The Constitution gives us this right."[80]

Even without utilizing the text of specific articles of the Banjul Women's Protocol, women peacebuilders like Boie Jalloh and Jane Orama are employing the rhetorical power of women's human rights in their transformative justice work. They are living examples of the principle of complementarity in action. On the ground in rural communities in Northern Uganda and Sierra Leone, women like Boie and Jane and their fellow peacebuilders are abundantly aware of women's subordination, legal vulnerability, and economic fragility in their daily experiences. Nevertheless, they are not afraid to challenge patriarchy and to confront misogyny. Their commitment to women's integrity, agency, and well-being is expressed in their contributions to dispute resolution, domestic violence prevention, and the promotion of women's property rights. Boie and her fellow Sierra Leone Peace Mothers speak explicitly about gender discrimination as a violation of their rights as women. Acholi women of Northern Uganda appeal directly to their government's responsibility to repair the breach of trust between the state and its people, through their demand for the payment of reparations to war survivors.

Building on this grassroots women-focused survey of feminist principles and human rights norms as tools of transformative justice, I now consider the historical frameworks for postconflict justice in both countries. Chapter 2 explores the causes, conduct, and consequences of the civil wars in Northern Uganda and Sierra Leone. Understanding the blueprints for postconflict transition established in their nations' capitals will enable us to appreciate more fully the priorities and activities of women peacebuilders active on the ground in nine rural communities across the two countries.

Historical Pathways: The Roots of Conflict and Peacebuilding in Uganda and Sierra Leone

For any spark to make a song it must be transformed
by pressure. There must be unspeakable need, muscle of
belief, and wild, unknowable elements. I am singing a
song that can only be born after losing a country.

—Joy Harjo

Historical Roots of War and Transition

This chapter places the conflict and postconflict periods of Northern Uganda and Sierra Leone in comparative historical context, recognizing that in both countries civil war was a product of specific colonial and postindependence dynamics in society. Analysis of these historical trends will help reveal the unfinished business of social transformation in the two countries, particularly regarding the status and well-being of women. This history will also provide a foundation for appreciating the perspectives and roles of women peacebuilders in sustaining social healing and collective livelihood at the community level in the two countries. In the first section, I will start with Uganda and the catalysts for the LRA War before examining the formal mechanisms for transitional justice that were established at the national level, including war crimes prosecutions in the International Criminal Court and the Ugandan High Court. The next section of the chapter is devoted to a similar historical

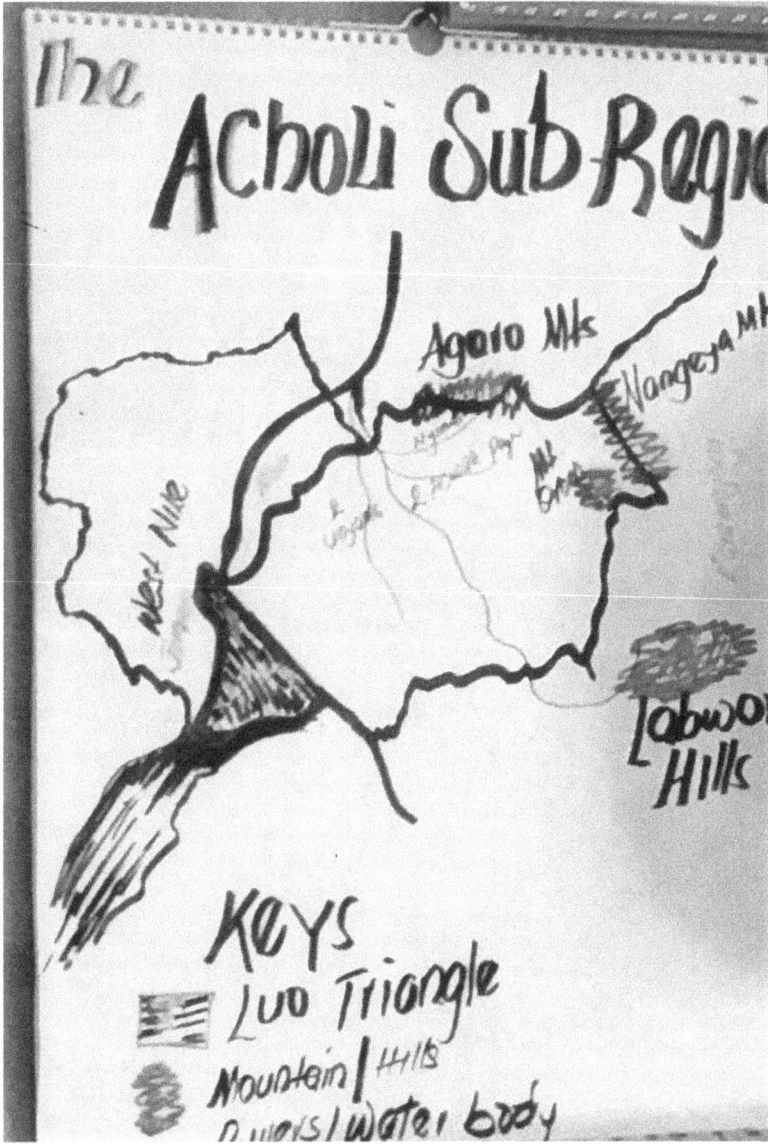

Figure 5. Hand-drawn map of Acholi Region of Northern Uganda. Photo by J. Moore, 2017.

Figure 6. Nile River rapids, crossing into Northern Uganda. Photo by J. Moore, 2023.

consideration of Sierra Leone's colonial and postcolonial experiences, its Rebel War, and the decision to pursue a two-pronged approach to transitional justice entailing the establishment of a Truth and Reconciliation Commission alongside a Special Court for Sierra Leone. Embedded throughout this chapter are comparative analyses of the similarities and distinctions between the two country's independence movements, their civil conflicts, and their national institutions of transitional justice, including their evolving policies regarding women's equality, integrity, and inheritance rights. Both sections end with critiques and responses to these national policies from grassroots women peacebuilders in either country.

Historical Foundations of War and Transition in Uganda
THE ROOTS OF THE LRA WAR

Exploration of Uganda's colonial and postcolonial history exposes certain prominent fault lines in the country's regional ethnopolitics and disparate social development manifested in the contemporary living conditions of Acholi people like Jane Orama and her neighbors in Pader District. Uganda's very name is derived from the Central Buganda Kingdom through which the British Crown exercised administrative rule over the territory under a protectorate established in 1894.[1] Indirect rule by the British facilitated a kind of informal regional caste system whereby northerners including the Acholi were more often recruited for military service while Ugandans from the Southern and Western Regions such as the Baganda and the Banyankole were more apt to be educated for colonial government service.[2] Regional social inequality dates from this period and endures to the present day. In 2023 the poverty rate in Northern Uganda was significantly higher than that of Uganda as a whole.[3] National dominance by leaders and parties associated with the relatively privileged Southern and Western Regions fueled the rise of military and political movements identified with the more economically marginalized northern tribes.[4] Where the protectorate era was emblematic of Baganda ascendency, political dominance in Uganda during the postindependence period has vacillated between heads of state affiliated with the North, such as Milton Obote and Tito Okello, and leaders with power bases in the Southern or Western Regions—namely, Idi Amin and Yoweri Museveni.[5]

A young Milton Obote became active in the Ugandan independence movement while an undergraduate at Makerere University in Kampala in the 1950s and later while in exile in Kenya. He returned to Uganda and became involved in politics, serving in the colonial Legislative Council in 1957.[6] Obote was a member of the Northern Lango community, a tribe with regional, linguistic, and political ties to the Acholi.[7] In 1960 Obote helped found the Ugandan People's Congress. He represented the UPC at the Ugandan Constitutional Congress organized by the British in the transition to independence. During this period, the UPC entered into an alliance of convenience with the Kabaka Yekka (King Only) monarchist party.

When Uganda won its independence from Great Britain in 1962, the Buganda Kabaka (king) Edward Muteesa II assumed the ceremonial post of president and Obote was appointed prime minister and head of state by the UPC, then the majority party. While Obote took power with the initial backing of the Baganda community, their support eroded over time, particularly when his national army recruited heavily in the Acholi Sub-region of Northern Uganda. Later, Obote abolished the traditional kingdoms of Uganda. This policy had a dramatic effect on the southern kingdoms, particularly Buganda, and reinforced the perception of a North-South ethnopolitical divide.[8] In 1967 Obote declared himself president and suspended constitutional checks on his executive power.[9] Obote had been in office for nearly a decade when in 1971 he was removed in a military coup led by his defense minister, General Idi Amin. Amin was a member of the Kakwa community of the West Nile region.[10]

During his repressive dictatorship, Amin's government stripped Ugandans of South Asian descent of their Ugandan citizenship, a policy rationalized in part by rhetorical appeals to an economic form of Black Nationalism.[11] At the same time, Amin's regime manipulated tribal differences and targeted perceived opponents. Amin's security forces were responsible for the death of as many as 300,000 Ugandans, many of whom were northerners singled out for their imputed loyalty to Obote.[12] Jane Orama's community and others in Pader and nearby districts were not immune from Amin's treatment of the Acholi as political enemies defined by their ethnicity and geography.

Opposition developed to Amin's regime throughout the 1970s, particularly fueled by Ugandan exiles in Tanzania, including one Yoweri Museveni who had studied economics and political science at the University of Dar es Salaam. Before graduating in 1970, Museveni led a delegation of student activists to anti-Portuguese rebel-held territory in colonial-era Mozambique, where they were exposed to guerrilla war tactics.[13] When the government of Tanzania decided to take military action against Amin, it did so in an alliance with Ugandan exiles led by Museveni, in what became the Uganda-Tanzania War. Amin was finally removed in 1979 by the Tanzanian Army mobilized alongside Museveni's Front for National Salvation.[14]

From mid-1979 to late 1980, Uganda was led by a series of short-lived governments under Yusuf Lule, Godfrey Binaisa, and Paul Muwanga.[15] Museveni served as defense minister briefly during the interim government that preceded general elections in 1980.[16] In democratic polling, Milton Obote of the UPC was reelected—returning to power in December 1980 after a nearly ten-year hiatus—at the start of what would be called the Obote II period.

Museveni contested the legitimacy of the 1980 elections and became increasingly disillusioned with Obote's rule.[17] One of Museveni's critiques was the perception that Obote favored the Acholi and members of other northern tribes in his government.[18] Museveni himself is a member of the Banyankole tribe, tracing his heritage to the traditional Ankole Kingdom of southwestern Uganda. Beginning in 1981, Museveni led the insurgent National Resistance Army (NRA) in a five-year Bush War against Uganda's armed forces under the command of Obote. General Tito Okello, an Acholi, deposed Obote in 1985 and one year later was deposed in turn by insurgent NRA troops as they stormed Kampala under Museveni's command. Three days later, on January 29, 1986, Museveni was sworn in as president of Uganda and leader of the new ruling party, the National Resistance Movement.[19] He has been head of state for nearly forty years.[20] From early in his first term, Museveni was perceived as hard on the Acholi in particular, targeting them in part for their support of his nemesis, Milton Obote.[21]

THE LRA WAR

Soon after the triumph of Museveni's National Resistance Movement in 1986, the insurgent Holy Spirit Movement rose up in Northern Uganda under the direction of Alice Auma Lakwena, an Acholi faith healer. Lakwena's followers were inspired by her charismatic spiritualism and her demands for regional development in the Northern Region, economic opportunity, and self-defense for the Acholi people. Many Acholi experienced painfully the "marginalization and oppression of northern Uganda under President Museveni."[22] Joseph Kony became the inheritor of Lakwena's mystical-militant leadership and her appeal to Acholi nationalism. He renamed their armed movement the Lord's Resistance Army (LRA). Kony mounted a twenty-year guerrilla war against Museveni's Uganda People's Defense Forces (UPDF) from 1987 to 2006 with cross-border support and safe havens provided by the government of Sudan.[23]

While Kony promised to redress the historical repression of the Acholi people, he gradually alienated much of the Acholi population in whose name he mobilized. Disaffection with the LRA by the local population was due in large part to rebel troops' practice of forced conscription and violent initiation ceremonies in which recruits, including children, were terrorized into committing atrocities against their own families and communities.[24] As described by Joseph Wasonga, the LRA "used extreme violence as a means of achieving psychological control over the abductees." When the Acholi communities of Gulu, Pader, and Kitgum resisted LRA tactics, Kony upped the ante, increasingly relying on "civilian victimization."[25] The LRA War led to the displacement of over two million Northern Ugandan civilians including Jane Orama, the death of tens of thousands of people, the forced conscription of thousands of children and adults, the forced marriage of hundreds of women, and the rape of countless women and men.[26]

DECONSTRUCTING THE LRA WAR IN NORTHERN UGANDA

The LRA is often depicted as a liberation movement of majority ethnic Acholi rebels that turned against its community of origin through forced recruitment of children and pillaging of Acholi villages. The catastrophic violence against civilians carried out by LRA militants remains emblematic of the civil war in Northern Uganda, evidenced by widespread accounts of child conscription by the LRA and sexual violence against women also perpetrated by rebels. In the Ugandan government's official narrative, Acholi civilians were preyed on by the LRA and protected by the Uganda People's Defense Forces. But this portrayal of the LRA conflict fails to take into account the historical ethnopolitical tensions between the northern tribes and the central government dating back to colonial times, which Jane Orama and her fellow denizens of Acholiland continue to experience today.[27] According to human rights monitors, academic researchers, independent journalists, and survivor accounts, Acholi civilians were systematically attacked throughout the conflict by the Uganda People's Defense Forces in the context of their government's counterinsurgency campaign against the LRA.

Nearly two million Acholi villagers were forcibly relocated by the Ugandan government and confined in concentration camp–like conditions on and off over the twenty-year conflict.[28] While living in so-called protected villages, civilians suffered periodic attacks by both UPDF soldiers and LRA rebels.[29]

In such encampments Acholi civilians were also subject to multiple deprivations, making camp life a "metaphorical prison"[30] and a collective experience
of "social torture,"[31] according to Chris Dolan. In addition to experiencing
widespread malnutrition and disease, limited opportunities to farm and
pursue livelihood activities, and inadequate public school and medical facilities, some researchers argue that more Acholi civilians died in the camps po-
liced by the UPDF than died in LRA attacks on their home villages.[32] In a
2008 interview, a Catholic priest in the Amuru District of Northern Uganda
identified two mass graves and testified about multiple cases of torture and
rape by UPDF forces. He described the displaced persons camps as "death
dens for eliminating the Acholi."[33] Included in the displaced population of
Northern Uganda were the majority of women peacebuilders like Jane Orama
who are active in the districts of Pader, Nwoya, Gulu, and Kitgum today.

THE 2000 AMNESTY ACT, THE 2006–2008 JUBA ACCORDS, AND THE CESSATION OF HOSTILITIES

In 2000 the Parliament of Uganda passed the Amnesty Act, which applied
broadly to immunize members of opposition forces, including the Lord's
Resistance Army, from criminal liability for "acts in furtherance of rebellion,"
based on their renunciation of continued involvement in militant action
against the Ugandan government.[34] The act was the expression of a wide consensus among legislators, community leaders, and war-affected people that
amnesty for militants was preferable to the continuation of a brutal conflict.[35]
Support for amnesty for LRA fighters reflected the extreme suffering of civilians in the LRA War and the awareness that many perpetrators of atrocities had themselves been forcibly inducted into the LRA cause as children.
By the time the Amnesty Act lapsed in 2015, 26,000 insurgents had received
amnesty certificates, including 13,000 LRA combatants.[36] Some of these "insurgents" had been forced wives of LRA combatants, including those who
later formed and joined the Women's Advocacy Network (WAN) in Gulu.
WAN members note somewhat ironically that after escaping from their LRA
captors after years of enslavement during which the state was powerless to
protect them, they were required to apologize to their government before they
were permitted to return to their families and communities.[37]

Despite the apparent broad reach of the Amnesty Act, the government of
Uganda in 2004 referred the situation on its territory to the International
Criminal Court, requesting the ICC prosecutor to investigate alleged inter-
national crimes by LRA leaders. Five indictments against LRA commanders

were issued against Joseph Kony and four of his top deputies. ICC prosecutions against the LRA are problematic to some Acholi war survivors, given the terms of the Amnesty Act and widespread popular support for a blanket amnesty program as well as the lack of ICC indictments of government troops for similar atrocities to those carried out by the LRA.

Between 2006 and 2008, the government of Uganda and the Lord's Resistance Army entered into six peace agreements, collectively known as the Juba Accords, encompassing separate treaties dealing with the establishment of a temporary ceasefire; commitment to a durable cessation of hostilities; provisions for accountability and reconciliation mechanisms; programs for the resettlement of internally displaced persons; rebel disarmament; and monitoring mechanisms.[38] The Cessation of Hostilities Agreement was signed in 2006 between the LRA and the government of Uganda, and the Accord on Disarmament, Demobilisation and Reintegration was signed in 2008. However, in the end Kony refused to sign a final peace agreement unless and until he was granted immunity in the ICC. The Ugandan government has consistently refused to ask the ICC to withdraw arrest warrants for any of the indicted LRA leaders.[39] Nevertheless, responding to the intervention of Acholi community leaders imploring on behalf of a war-weary population, Kony withdrew LRA troops from Ugandan territory into the Democratic Republic of the Congo.[40] Since 2006 there have been no significant military engagements between LRA and UPDF forces on Ugandan soil.[41]

Despite the lack of hostilities in Northern Uganda itself, in the postwar era, LRA insurgents have continued to attack civilians and move freely in the border region spanning southern Sudan, South Sudan, the Democratic Republic of the Congo, and the Central African Republic.[42] While a steady weakening of the LRA as a fighting force was cited as a basis for suspending US efforts to search for and capture Joseph Kony in June 2017, the United Nations reported a resurgence of LRA attacks in the DRC at that time, along with a spike in the forced recruitment of preteen boys and girls.[43] In March and May 2020, LRA troops reportedly carried out further lootings as well as abductions of civilians in the DRC. The violence increased food insecurity in the area and some Congolese nationals fled into South Sudan to seek refuge.[44]

PENAL JUSTICE FOR UGANDA: PROSECUTING THE LRA IN THE ICC AND UGANDAN COURTS

Since the Juba Peace Accords, and despite the Amnesty Act, the government of Uganda has stressed the retributive strand of transitional justice, exemplified in Uganda's "self-referral" to the International Criminal Court for investigation of the situation in Northern Uganda.[45] While the ICC Prosecutor's Office has maintained its prerogative to issue arrest warrants against both UPDF (Ugandan Army) soldiers and LRA militants, as of 2023 there have been no indictments against Ugandan soldiers or officers. Rather, the ICC has issued a total of five arrest warrants against Joseph Kony and four of his chief deputies. Of the five LRA indictees, Joseph Kony remains at large, three others are since deceased,[46] and only one has faced trial. In 2015 Dominic Ongwen surrendered and was taken into ICC custody[47] to face trial on multiple counts involving attacks on civilians.[48] In February 2021, he was convicted of sixty-one war crimes and crimes against humanity. Ongwen's conviction and twenty-five-year sentence were confirmed by the ICC Appeals Chamber on December 15, 2022.[49]

Ongwen's trial in the International Criminal Court was and remains controversial among Northern Ugandans like the members of Jane Orama's community group, Uketu wan Kwene. Jane and her fellow peacebuilders are well aware that he was forcibly recruited into the LRA at the age of fourteen while still attending primary school.[50] The ethical and legal questions raised in prosecuting offenders who were themselves victims of war crimes in the conflict between the LRA and the Uganda People's Defense Forces is a recurrent theme in community discussions about postconflict justice in Northern Uganda.[51] As expressed by the late Daker Nighty, Jane's fellow Uketu member, "Dominic Ongwen cannot take all accountability. The government must [as well]."[52]

The Ugandan Parliament also passed a statute in 2010 domesticating the Rome Statute of the ICC and creating an International Crimes Division (ICD) within the Ugandan High Court.[53] As of 2023, there have been no war crimes convictions in the ICD, although one person has been on trial for nearly fifteen years, "arguably one of the longest-accused persons on pre-trial detention in the history of International Justice," according to Avocats sans Frontières.[54] In 2009 the former LRA commander Thomas Kwoyelo was taken into custody. In 2011 he was charged before the ICD with twelve substantive counts of war crimes and crimes against humanity.[55] Also significant in Kwoyelo's case is the fact that he was recruited as a child.[56] Because Kwoyelo had submitted an application for amnesty under Uganda's Amnesty Act, his prosecution was suspended until 2015 when the Ugandan Supreme Court found that his case could proceed in the ICD. The Supreme Court's ruling was justified by Justice Katureebe's determination that "crimes committed willfully against civilians or communities would not ordinarily be covered by amnesty."[57] His trial was scheduled to resume in November 2018.

Kwoyelo's case was also impacted by the fact that in October 2012 he filed a petition in the African Commission on Human Rights alleging discrimination and deprivation of a fair and speedy trial in violation of the African Charter on Human and People's Rights.[58] Despite the commission's ruling in 2018 that Kwoyelo had indeed suffered discrimination and arbitrary detention in violation of the Banjul Charter,[59] his ICD trial resumed on schedule that year and has proceeded in fits and starts. In May 2023, the prosecution rested its case, with the defense case set to follow. The ICD hopes the case will conclude by 2025, given the characterization by one of its own judges that "this delay is a dark spot on our part as the judiciary in as far as justice is concerned."[60]

ASSESSING THE FORMS OF VIOLENCE AGAINST WOMEN DURING AND SINCE THE LRA WAR

Physical Violence Against Women During the LRA War

In addition to the conscription of young boys as child soldiers and men as adult combatants, the LRA also abducted girls and women into its ranks. Less often conscripted for direct combat activities such as military ambushes, looting, and abduction, typically adolescent girls and women were pressed into roles as porters and cooks, forced to become conjugal partners, or subjected to other conditions of exploitation and violence. Wasonga's research reveals a practice of young women being "assigned as brides to commanders in forced marriages, having to carry out grueling domestic tasks and endure long hours and continuous beatings." He emphasizes that sexual servitude was intrinsic to LRA forced marriages and so normalized that, "according to the LRA code of conduct, subjecting the girls to sexual activities against their will did not constitute rape." LRA commanders were known to permit rape by rebel troops as a form of reward or to inflict rape as a form of punishment on an abductee who had tried to escape.[61]

The Women's Advocacy Network, a women's collective based in Gulu Town, serves and is run by women who formerly were captives of the LRA. After escaping captivity and returning to their communities, WAN members became involved in trauma healing, livelihood endeavors, and community organizing activities. Evelyn Amony,[62] the chairwoman of WAN, was abducted by the LRA at the age of eleven from her grandmother's compound after she returned from school in 1994. Soon after her forced conscription, she was made to join the LRA leader Joseph Kony's household. In her memoir, Ms. Amony relates the day that Kony told her "I was to be his wife." She retorted, "How can I be your wife when up to this point you have called me your child?" When she tried to run, she was caught and caned by Kony's bodyguards. "I had to make the choice between life and death. If I wanted to live, I had to be his wife." Later that year, at the age of fourteen, she gave birth to Bakita, the first of her four daughters fathered by Kony.[63]

Structural Violence Against Women Since the LRA War

As important as it is to highlight the ways in which women and girls were brutalized during the LRA War, to Evelyn Amony, Jane Orama, and other women of Acholiland it is equally essential to address women's status and living conditions today. Fifteen years after the Juba Accords, Ugandan women are still experiencing ongoing threats to their bodily integrity and social well-being in the form of barriers to reproductive health care, limited educational opportunities, and sobering rates of domestic violence.

According to the United Nations Development Programme (UNDP), in 2018, over a decade after the LRA War ended, nearly 50 percent of Ugandan women aged 15 years or older had experienced intimate partner violence, as compared to a rate of slightly over 30 percent for developing countries as a whole and 29 percent for the United Kingdom.[64] More recent socioeconomic data from the United Nations has shed light on women's health and educational standards around the world. For Ugandan women, life expectancy at birth in 2021 was 64.9 years, as compared to 82.8 years for women in the United Kingdom.[65] The average years of schooling for Ugandan women over 25 years of age in 2021 was 4.9 years, as compared to 6.7 years for Ugandan men.[66] The maternal mortality rate for Ugandan women in 2021 was 375 deaths per 100,000 live births, as compared to 7 maternal deaths per 100,000 births in the UK.[67] Facing these statistical insights into the life of Ugandan women helps put into context their approach to postconflict peacebuilding in their country.

Efforts to Combat the Continuum of Physical and Structural Violence Against Women in Uganda

Unlike the postwar presidents of Sierra Leone, President Museveni has not made a public statement of apology to the women of Uganda for their suffering during the LRA War, nor has he made an official proclamation declaring the ongoing problem of sexual violence against women a national emergency. Nevertheless, there have been important advances as well as frustrations in the movement toward greater gender equality in Uganda. This dynamism relates to women's physical integrity rights as well as their inheritance and property rights.

Rhetoric Against Gender-Based Violence Yet Tolerance of Marital Rape

With respect to women's protections against physical violence, since as early as 2010, Ugandan NGOs and certain public figures have regularly endorsed a United Nations campaign called "Sixteen Days of Activism to End Violence Against Women and Girls," which since 1991 has been observed globally every year from November 25 to December 10.[68] In 2022 Uganda's launch of the 16 Days of Activism was sponsored by its Ministry of Gender, Labour and Social Development.[69] However, despite an increasingly powerful rhetoric defending women's physical integrity, legal protections are still inadequate. As a crucial example, rape in marriage is not acknowledged as an offense in Ugandan law. Neither the Ugandan Penal Code of 2007 nor the Domestic Violence Act of 2010 criminalize marital rape.[70]

Step Forward in Ensuring Women's Inheritance Rights

With respect to inheritance and property rights, 2022 proved a pivotal year for gender equality in Uganda, On April 10, 2022, President Museveni signed into law a bill that passed the Ugandan Parliament in 2021, amending the Ugandan Succession Act by eliminating or revising dozens of provisions that had discriminated against women in inheritance and property ownership. To start with, the amendments replace numerous references to "man," "his," "brother," "son," and so on, with "person," "his or her," "brother or sister," "son or daughter," and so forth.[71] More substantively, the new act establishes the penalty of a fine or up to seven years in prison for anyone who evicts or attempts to evict the surviving spouse from the family residence after the death of the other spouse.[72] The act also provides that where there is no will, the surviving spouse shall receive 20 percent of the value of the estate beyond the family residence.[73] These changes were long in coming. Fifteen years earlier the Ugandan Constitutional Court had called for such legislation, declaring numerous provisions of the prior Succession Act to be contrary to fundamental protections of gender equality in articles 21 and 33 of the 1995 Ugandan Constitution.[74]

Leap Back in Criminalization of the LGBTQ Community

In 2023 the Ugandan Parliament passed the Anti-Homosexuality Bill. The new act criminalizes gay sex and imposes the death penalty for so-called "aggravated homosexuality," defined to include homosexual sex with a person who has a disability or same sex acts by a "serial offender." Moreover, the act criminalizes the "promotion of homosexuality," a term likely to impede advocacy for LGBTQ rights.[75] Challenges to the constitutionality of the act are being brought by numerous NGOs and individuals, including the Ugandan Human Rights Awareness and Promotion Forum,[76] and faculty members of Makerere University School of Law.

The most direct negative impacts of the Anti-Homosexuality Act are on members of the LGBTQ community, particularly gay men who have consensual sex with other men. However, advocates who work in the field of combating gender violence are also concerned that the legislation will lessen protections for survivors of nonconsensual sex, both women and men, whether the sexual assault is against someone of the same or of a different gender. In fact, in some rural communities in Acholiland, the Acholi term for survivors of sexual violence is the same term used for gay men and is applied to both female and male survivors. In the climate of increased homophobia and the chilling of LGBTQ advocacy, concerns abound that survivors of rape and sexual assault in general will be associated with the LGBTQ community and, like them, wrongfully seen as unworthy of dignity and protection.[77] Another consequence of the Anti-Homosexuality Act is the fact that some international donors have pulled back funding for human rights and antipoverty related programs in Uganda, which will have a negative impact on all Ugandans, including women peacebuilders in Acholiland.

EQUAL AND REPARATIVE JUSTICE: WOMEN-CENTRIC PEACEBUILDING FOR UGANDA

To understand the attitude of Northern Ugandan women peacebuilders toward postwar justice in their country, it is essential to examine the history laid out above of the treatment of the Acholi by the various regimes and administrations that have ruled them. It is also crucial to consider the systematic attacks on the Acholi by their own government troops as well as the LRA during the Rebel War. Finally, it is necessary to grapple with the particular forms of violence that women experienced during the conflict and continue to experience in the postwar period. Only within this comprehensive historical, ethnopolitical, gendered, and socioeconomic framework can we understand why so many women in Acholiland might favor reparations over war crimes prosecutions.

One significant piece of unfinished business in Uganda's postwar transition for women peacebuilders remains a serious response to the accountability gap between government and rebel soldiers, illustrated by the enduring impunity for UPDF war crimes alongside a steady drumbeat of demands for LRA trials and convictions.[78] A second "justice gap" is the unmet demand

Figure 7. Mandate of the Special Court, Sierra Leone Peace Museum, Freetown. Photo by J. Moore, 2023.

Figure 8. Some of the many Sierra Leoneans who perished during the Rebel War, Sierra Leone Peace Museum, Freetown. Photo by J. Moore, 2023.

on the part of local people for the provision of broad-based reparations to survivors of atrocities. A third blind spot is the specific barriers women face in accessing health care and educational opportunities. From the perspective of Jane Orama's Uketu wan Kwene and other women's collectives, reparations should encompass financial support for resettlement, reintegration, and access to health care and other social services, including the treatment of war-related trauma. Despite a call for reparations by the Ugandan Parliament in 2014 and the Ugandan government's "National Transitional Justice Policy," which also contemplates reparations, the government of Uganda has yet to establish a reparations fund for survivors of the LRA War.[79] One women-led NGO that has spearheaded calls for broad-based reparations is the Women's Advocacy Network, based in Gulu Town. The experiences and perspectives of women peacebuilders throughout Acholiland are the focus of Chapter 3. I turn now to an examination of the historical roots of conflict and postconflict transition in Sierra Leone.

Historical Foundations of War and Transition in Sierra Leone
THE ROOTS OF THE "REBEL WAR"

As with Uganda, Sierra Leone's civil war arose out of a particular historical and social context. The preconditions for the armed conflict in Sierra Leone reach back to the founding of Freetown in the late eighteenth century, the designation of the Sierra Leone Protectorate in the late nineteenth century, and Sierra Leone's independence era beginning in 1961. Tensions and synergies between various ethnic and political groups have helped shape Sierra Leonean history and culture, including the particular dynamics that led to the Rebel War of the 1990s.[80]

Sierra Leone's modern history was inaugurated in 1792 when former slaves from the Americas founded the Freetown Colony along with "liberated Africans" who had escaped from their captors before being forced to embark on the Middle Passage.[81] The new arrivals to a literal "Freetown" came from different tribal and cultural backgrounds on both sides of the Atlantic, spoke a great variety of languages, and contributed to the diverse and cosmopolitan Krio (Creole) society that developed in the colony. The Krio dialect that evolved in Freetown was a blending of numerous sub-Saharan African languages along with English, French, and Arabic. Krio would later become the lingua franca and most widely spoken language of independent Sierra Leone.

While English is the official language of Sierra Leone today, Krio is the de facto national language.[82]

As the Freetown Colony developed into the nineteenth century, members of the Krio urban settler community engaged in economic exchange but less frequently intermarriage with members of local tribes from the inland or so-called upcountry territory of modern-day Sierra Leone. These ethnicities include the Mende, the Temne, the Limba, the Kono, the Mandingo, and the Fulbeh, Boie Jalloh's ethnic community.[83] Relations between the Krio people and the other tribal communities were not conducted on equal social or political terms.[84]

In 1896 the British designated the territory inland of Freetown as the Sierra Leone Protectorate, establishing a formal distinction between the Krio of the colony, who were British subjects, and the "protected persons" of the interior, who were not. Members of the various tribal communities living under the protectorate were not allowed to participate in colonial governing structures or have access to free movement and full employment rights in Freetown, in contrast to the greater political rights and economic privileges accorded the Krio subjects of the colony.[85] Such divisions did not end with independence from the British Crown in 1961. While it is true that Sierra Leoneans today are known for their multiethnic national identity, it is also apparent that pluralism and "politicized ethnicity" coexist in Sierra Leone's body politic. Powerful class and ethnic divisions endure, rooted in the colonial period and sometimes exacerbated by postindependence governments.[86]

In addition to the urban-and-Krio vs. upcountry-and-tribal distinction, there are also cultural differentiations between tribes that date back to the colonial era. For the two largest ethnic communities, the Mende and the Temne, these differences have often been endowed with political significance. The Temne, who represent around 35 percent of the population, have traditional roots in the North of Sierra Leone, where the Temne language predominates. The Mende, amounting to around 31 percent of the population, are based in the South, where the Mende language is most commonly spoken.[87] Historically, the two major political parties of Sierra Leone, both formed before independence, have been associated with either of these two most populous tribes. The Sierra Leone People's Party (SLPP), founded in 1951, has its power base in the South and is often seen as the traditional Mende party, although it has non-Mende members and constituents in the North. The All People's Congress (APC), founded in 1960, has its power base in the North and is typically depicted as the traditional Temne Party, although it also has a multiethnic membership that includes residents of the Southern and Eastern Provinces.

Beginning in the 1950s, Milton Margai, leader of the majority-Mende Sierra Leone People's Party, worked to unify politicians from the Mende, Temne, and Krio communities in the movement for Sierra Leone's independence. Sir Milton[88] served as Sierra Leone's first prime minister from 1961 to 1964, heading a government that included representatives of opposition parties and diverse tribal affiliations. According to Jimmy Kandeh, Milton Margai's leadership style was characterized by a "tolerance of the political heterogeneity of society." However, Kandeh also suggests that Margai's administration was a brief historical high-water mark for such an inclusive style of national politics in Sierra Leone.[89] Nevertheless, in their abiding affection for Sir Milton, the first leader of the sovereign Sierra Leone, Sierra Leoneans also express their regard for the ideal of a nontribal form of nationhood.[90]

During the administrations of successive heads of state, ethnopolitical tensions as well as official corruption and autocratic measures increased, reaching their zenith under Siaka Stevens of the Temne-dominated All People's Congress (APC). Stevens served as president from 1971 to 1985 and banned opposition parties in 1978. Stevens's time in office was evocatively termed the "plague of locusts" for his dictatorial policies and kleptocratic tendencies.[91] He was succeeded as head of state by Major General Joseph Momoh, against whose government the insurgent Revolutionary United Front mounted their rebellion in March 1991 at the start of Sierra Leone's Rebel War.[92]

Despite the predominant ethnic affiliations often attributed to the SLPP and its APC opposition, leaders of both dominant parties were guilty of manipulating tribal identity to enrich themselves and the business class of Sierra Leone.[93] It might be argued that the late nineteenth century fault line between the Krio bourgeoisie of the Freetown Colony and the tribal peoples of the interior had realigned by the 1980s into an even deeper chasm between a tiny economic elite with access to state resources on one side and, on the other, everyone else. The dispossessed included the great majority of Sierra Leonean people in rural areas struggling to meet their most basic material needs, including Boie Jalloh's Fulbeh community of Dogoloya in the northern district of Koinadugu.

In the words of the authors of the Final Report of Sierra Leone's Truth and Reconciliation Commission (TRC): "The central cause of the war was endemic greed, corruption and nepotism that deprived the nation of its dignity and reduced most people to a state of poverty. Successive political elites plundered the nation's assets, including its mineral riches, at the expense of the national good."[94] Speaking of the major political parties, the Final Report concludes that "neither the SLPP nor the APC made any genuine effort to attend to the debasement of the postindependence politics and economy of the country. On the contrary, history speaks of a systemic failure, whereby all the members of the political elite belong to the same failing system."[95] Certainly, Boie Jalloh's community of Dogoloya and rural people throughout Sierra Leone would agree that widespread poverty, endemic corruption at all levels of government, and the resultant misery of the population came together to fuel civil strife in the 1990s.

THE REBEL WAR

The "rebel" in "Rebel War" refers to the Revolutionary United Front (RUF). While the insurgency later morphed into a much more complex conflict, with numerous factions and subfactions, it began as an armed uprising by the RUF against the government of President Momoh in 1991. The roots of the RUF stretch back to the 1970s, during Siaka Stevens's first decade in office, when a Marxist-inspired student opposition movement flowered at Fourah Bay College, Sierra Leone's flagship liberal arts institution in Freetown.[96] Some of these students had been trained in military tactics in Libya in camps established by Muammar Gaddafi during the 1980s.[97] Another Sierra Leonean who received training in Libya was one Foday Sankoh, a former corporal in the Sierra Leone Army.

An important alliance was formed in Libya between Sankoh and Charles Taylor, the future leader of the National Patriotic Front of Liberia (NPFL), and later the president of Liberia (currently serving a fifty-year sentence for war crimes in The Hague).[98] When, under Taylor's command, NPFL forces invaded Liberia from Côte d'Ivoire in December 1989, Sierra Leoneans joined Liberian militants in launching Liberia's civil war. Later, in March 1991, when the Revolutionary United Front invaded Sierra Leone under the leadership of Sankoh, they did so from Liberian territory with arms supplied by Taylor's NPFL. The authors of the Final Report of Sierra Leone's Truth and Reconciliation Commission mince no words in assessing Sankoh's vision: "The original 'revolutionary' programme [of the RUF] never materialized in the form it was intended to take. It was supplanted by a deviant, militant agenda spearheaded by Foday Sankoh."[99] The TRC Final Report clarifies its meaning of this so-called "deviant agenda"—namely, one characterized by "the inclusion of civilian settlements within the scope of . . . RUF assaults."[100]

From 1991 to 2002, Sierra Leone's Rebel War engulfed all regions of the country across a complicated web of front lines defined by shifting and splintering alliances between the insurgents of the Revolutionary United Front (RUF), the soldier-rebels of the Armed Forces Revolutionary Council (AFRC), and the militia volunteers of the Civil Defense Forces (CDF). The RUF was intermittently armed and financed by Liberian and other transnational patrons, who were often compensated with access to Sierra Leone's diamond mines, intensifying the mercantile character of the conflict. The founding liberational appeal of the RUF waned as the movement degenerated into a militarized racketeering enterprise that principally sustained itself by preying on the civilian population of rural communities nationwide, including Boie Jalloh's parish of Dogoloya in Koinadugu District.[101] In a kaleidoscopic pattern across the country, RUF and rival commanders competed over territory and mineral resources, often taking, losing, and retaking small swaths of terrain in quick succession, each armed group attacking and brutalizing local villagers in turn.[102]

In a decade of conflict, close to 100,000 Sierra Leoneans were killed and two million people were forced to flee within the territory or into neighboring countries as refugees. These displaced people included the people of Boie's district of Koinadugu as well as Kono, Kailahun, Kenema, Bo, Pujehun, Bonthe, Moyamba, Tonkolili, Port Loko, Kambia, and Bombali. Led by the RUF in the sheer magnitude of war crimes committed, all parties to the conflict carried out atrocities against civilians, including targeted killings, child conscription, sexual slavery, rape, amputations, and torture in countless other forms.[103] Abducted children, boys and girls, swelled the ranks of all militant groups. They were forced to suffer and perpetrate brutal acts as young recruits and to mature into adulthood within a culture of violent militancy and banditry in which many were both victims and offenders.[104]

COMPARING SIERRA LEONE'S REBEL WAR TO UGANDA'S LRA WAR

Like Uganda's LRA War, Sierra Leone's Rebel War resulted in widespread civilian suffering in the form of targeted attacks and killings; sexual assault and other forms of torture; the forced recruitment of children; and catastrophic hunger, disease, and population displacement. Yet alongside these commonalities are three important differences between the two conflicts, concerning the number of armed groups, the geographic spread of the violence, and the multiethnic impact of the conflict.

Militant Groups

To begin with, rather than one main rebel insurgency challenging the national armed forces, as the Lord's Resistance Army contested the Uganda People's Defense Forces in Northern Uganda, Sierra Leone's Rebel War involved numerous factions and subfactions such that communities like Dogoloya were brutalized by various armed groups in turn. The RUF, the former army defectors who became the Armed Forces Revolutionary Council (AFRC), and the Civil Defense Forces (CDF) militia members were the three major armed groups. Other fighting forces included residual units of the Sierra Leone Army and regional peacekeeping battalions of the Military Operations Group of the Economic Community of West African States (ECOMOG). The haziness of Sierra Leone's civil war affiliations is evoked by the hybrid category of *sobels*—"soldiers by day, rebels by night"—and the division of the RUF and the AFRC into splinter groups. One of these rogue units, the West Side Boys, was responsible for killing six thousand civilians in seven days in an attack on Freetown in 1999 called "No Living Thing."[105]

Thus, the violence of Sierra Leone's Rebel War was notable for the blurring of distinctions between rebels and soldiers, militants and organized criminals, victims and offenders, and community protectors and those who came to prey on members of their communities. The resultant uncertainty about the authors of war atrocities impacted the nature of the trauma experienced by civilians in rural communities as well as the legacy of this trauma.[106] According to the authors of the Final Report of the Sierra Leone TRC, "there existed an astonishing factional fluidity among the different militias and armed groups. Overtly and covertly, gradually and suddenly, fighters switched sides or established new units on a scale unprecedented in any other conflict."[107]

The tendency for militant groups to morph, separate, and merge, in the end unified in their common commission of crimes against humanity, is illustrated in the formation and operation of the Civil Defense Forces themselves. Created as an expression of popular resistance to the outrages against civilians carried out by the RUF and other civil war factions, the CDF grew out of the traditional male hunting societies associated with particular regions of the country. The ranks of the CDF drew particularly from the Kamajors, a Mende tribal hunting society traditionally active in Moyamba and other districts in the Southern and Eastern Provinces of Sierra Leone. There is considerable pride, particularly in Mende communities, that the Kamajors and other CDF regiments were able to mobilize against RUF lawlessness and brutality. Nevertheless, Sierra Leonean war survivors also acknowledge that some CDF militias became notorious for criminal practices including violent initiation ceremonies.[108]

Geographic Range of Violence

Second, alongside the proliferation of factions in Sierra Leone's Rebel War, there was a proliferation of fronts as the conflict evolved. Unlike Uganda's LRA War, where violence was concentrated in the Northern Region of Acholiland, in Sierra Leone it is difficult to find a section, ward, or village throughout the country from Koinadugu in the North to Moyamba in the South that was not touched by the war. In the diamond-producing eastern district of Kono, formerly one of the most economically developed regions of the country, it is said that every village was burned or otherwise destroyed.[109] Throughout the country, some communities were attacked not once but twice or more as the RUF, AFRC, and CDF forces took and retook territory from one another with horrendous consequences for the civilian population. Included among the villages, sections, and parishes that suffered attacks during the Rebel War was Boie Jalloh's community of Dogoloya in Falaba District.

Multiethnic Impact of Conflict

Third, besides its pervasive impact geographically, the civil war violence in Sierra Leone cut across linguistic and religious communities—targeting all ethnic groups, including Mende from Moyamba and other districts; Temne from Bombali District in the North; and Mandingo, Limba and Fulbeh, like Boie Jalloh, from the districts of Falaba and Koinadugu in the Northeast. People of all communities suffered attacks, without regard for their Muslim or Christian faith.[110] The pan-ethnic nature of the Sierra Leonean conflict also contrasts with Northern Uganda's LRA War in which most of the violence occurred in the traditional Acholi homeland of Northern Uganda. Most of the civilian victims in the LRA War were of the Acholi and Langi ethnic communities while the perpetrators included the mainly Acholi rebels of the LRA as well as the more ethnically diverse members of the UPDF.

The remarkably diverse backgrounds of Sierra Leone's Rebel War survivors are reflected in extensive interviews with Sierra Leonean women peacebuilders, many of whom are part of a national network. The so-called "Fambul Tok Peace Mothers" live and organize in rural communities throughout the country. Both Christian and Muslim, they are of numerous ethnicities, including the Mende, Fulbeh, Mandingo, and Limba tribes. The Peace Mothers' insights on community-based peacebuilding are explored in depth in Chapter 4.

All three of these distinct aspects of Sierra Leone's Rebel War—multiple factions, multiple fronts, and multiple ethnicities of perpetrators and survivors—contribute to the postwar policies the nation embraced. In an important sense, a cultural awareness that both blame and suffering were widely shared created space for more comprehensive and innovative approaches to postconflict rebuilding in Sierra Leone. In contrast to Uganda's predominant emphasis on prosecuting the LRA in the International Criminal Court and domestically, Sierra Leone chose a hybrid approach. Sierra Leone's early postconflict policies paired a Truth and Reconciliation Commission with a Special Court mandated to prosecute high-ranking members of all major factions—the RUF, the AFRC, and the CDF alike.

SIERRA LEONE'S MIDDLE PATH TO TRANSITION: LOMÉ, THE TRC,
AND THE SPECIAL COURT

The Truth and Reconciliation Commission

When the Lomé Peace Accords between the Revolutionary United Front and the government of Sierra Leone were signed in 1999,[111] the short-term priorities of all factions and the civilian population were ending the hostilities, disarming the militant organizations, and granting amnesty to combatants for acts committed "in pursuit of their objectives."[112] The Lomé Accords also called for the creation of a Truth and Reconciliation Commission in order "to address impunity [and] . . . to facilitate genuine healing and reconciliation."[113] The TRC was mandated to establish a collective truth-telling and restorative justice process to help the people of Sierra Leone confront "the horrors of the past," based on the conviction that "knowledge and understanding are the most powerful deterrents against conflict and war."[114]

Sierra Leone's Truth and Reconciliation Commission conducted its work from 2002 to 2004.[115] During the first investigative stage, commission members conducted interviews with people willing to give statements about the human rights abuses they had suffered, witnessed, or perpetrated during the conflict. Based on their statements, individual victims and offenders were invited to participate in a series of hearings held between April and August 2003 in Freetown and in every district capital including Kabala, the headquarters town of what was then Boie's home district of Koinadugu.[116] In each district the commission held one week of hearings open to the public. An additional day of closed hearings was devoted to testimony from children, victims of sexual violence, and civilian or military officials with security concerns. The hearings were opportunities for war victims and survivors to testify about their experiences of war and suffering. Perpetrators were invited to listen, to explain their actions, and to atone for their offenses against individual civilians and the Sierra Leonean people.[117] The process culminated in 2004 with the issuance of the TRC Final Report, encompassing three multipart volumes, twenty-two chapters, and numerous appendices.

The TRC Final Report made a number of recommendations for law reform in Sierra Leone specifically crafted to cultivate a culture of nonviolence and respect for human rights throughout the country. In addition to calling for the abolition of the death penalty and the prohibition of corporal punishment in schools, the Final Report recommended laws recognizing women's equality and integrity and mandating the provision of reparations to war-affected individuals.[118] Women's equality and reparations remain of particular interest to the Peace Mothers of Boie's community of Dogoloya and rural communities across the country.

On June 19, 2007, the Parliament of Sierra Leone passed a package of bills, known collectively as the Gender Laws. These three statutes served, respectfully: (1) to criminalize domestic violence; (2) to create a regular mechanism for the registration of customary marriages; and (3) to recognize women's inheritance rights.[119] The latter piece of legislation, known as the Devolution of Estates Act, ensures that a women whose spouse died intestate is entitled to 35 percent of the estate of the deceased, with specific allocations to children and parents as well.[120] The meaning of "spouse" in the legislation includes a domestic partner or "cohabiting person" who has lived with the deceased in a marriage-like relationship for five years or more.[121] Also significant, the act gives the reviewing court equitable powers to ensure that appropriate distributions be made to a spouse or child in the case of a will that does not otherwise provide for them appropriately.[122]

The following year, 2008, in response to considerable testimony during the TRC hearings from war amputees and other survivors of violence, the government of Sierra Leone established a National Commission for Social Action (NaCSA). NaCSA issued payments valued at US$100 to eligible amputees, war wounded, and sexual violence survivors drawn from a registry of nearly thirty thousand victims.[123] As modest as these monetary reparations were, their symbolism spoke volumes in terms of acknowledging and seeking to alleviate the suffering of ordinary Sierra Leoneans.

Most recently, in 2021, the Parliament of Sierra Leone abolished the death penalty as punishment in all cases.[124] Sierra Leone was the twenty-third country in Africa to do so.[125]

The Special Court for Sierra Leone

Despite prioritizing disarmament and restorative justice, the Lomé Accords did not foreclose all criminal prosecutions of former combatants accused of committing attacks against civilians. The accords' amnesty provisions were ultimately interpreted to allow trials of high-level offenders for international crimes as the issue of penal accountability gradually came to the fore.[126] In 2002 the Special Court for Sierra Leone was created by treaty between the United Nations and the government of Sierra Leone to prosecute those offenders who bore "the greatest responsibility for violations of international humanitarian law and Sierra Leonean law" since 1996.[127] By that time the TRC had begun to fulfill its mandate, and thus the two institutions operated simultaneously from 2002 to 2004, when the TRC issued its Final Report.[128] The Special Court went on to indict thirteen individuals representing the three major armed factions, of whom nine were convicted. In addition to eight Sierra Leoneans from the RUF, the AFRC, and the CDF,[129] Charles Taylor was sentenced in 2012 to fifty years of imprisonment for supplying arms and training to the Revolutionary United Front.[130] Foday Sankoh was also indicted by the Special Court in 2003. He died in a hospital later that year. Thus, his indictment was withdrawn before trial.[131]

In both Sierra Leone and Uganda, war crimes prosecutions had to contend with strong popular support for widespread amnesty for combatants. These amnesty programs were based on legislation, in the case of Uganda, and treaty provisions, in the case of Sierra Leone. Ultimately, the Lomé Accords' amnesty provisions were deemed compatible with prosecutions pursuant to the Statute of the Special Court for Sierra Leone.[132] As in Uganda, amnesty was determined to be limited to lawful objectives of insurgents— namely, acts of violence against combatants or military targets and exclusive of direct attacks on civilians and their communities in violation of international law.[133] But unlike Uganda, the scope of prosecutions in Sierra Leone was explicitly limited by degree of culpability. Only those "who bear the greatest responsibility" for war atrocities were subject to trial in the Special Court.[134] Also in contrast to Uganda, among the nine individuals convicted of war crimes and crimes against humanity in the Special Court were leaders of all three major militant groups.

Thus, unlike Uganda, where LRA leaders have been the sole targets of ICC and domestic war crimes prosecutions, the mixed affiliations of the accused promoted a greater sense of equal justice in the Special Court for Sierra Leone. At the same time, the requirement of "greatest responsibility" created a sense of restraint and moderation in the implementation of criminal justice in the case of Sierra Leone.

DECONSTRUCTING SIERRA LEONE'S "MIDDLE PATH" TO TRANSITIONAL JUSTICE

It is tempting to romanticize Sierra Leone's hybrid approach to reckoning with the prolonged suffering of its Rebel War period. According to some scholars and others involved in implementing national transitional justice policies, Sierra Leoneans refused the "either/or" binary choice between retributive or restorative justice, choosing instead to embrace the "both/and" marriage of accountability and forgiveness.[135] In fact, the intertwined values of acknowledgment and mercy are reflective of the moral framework of many of the Peace Mothers whose perspectives are shared in Chapter 4 of this volume.

Nevertheless, it is crucial not to allow idealized notions of justice to cloud our vision of the actual results delivered by the institutions of the TRC and the Special Court. As exposed in the scholarship of Rosalind Shaw, some Sierra Leoneans conflated the mandates of the TRC and the Special Court. Others were concerned that the two institutions shared information, such that testimony before the TRC might be provided to officers of the Special Court, despite a prior offer of amnesty to a particular witness. This concern was only reinforced when it was reported that the Special Court indeed hired former TRC staff once the commission's work was concluded in 2004.[136]

Most significantly, Shaw's field research reflects the awareness of ordinary Sierra Leoneans that neither the TRC nor the Special Court were able to alleviate the deep-rooted rural poverty and official abuse of power that gave rise to the Rebel War and which endure long after its conclusion. In particular, Shaw interviewed former combatants who explained that they were made to "humble themselves" in the presence of local elders and cultural leaders before being permitted to return to their communities of birth. In so doing, they were subjecting themselves to the very "pre-conflict structures of inequality and marginalization" that had helped inspire the Rebel War.[137]

To meaningfully contend with "structural poverty" in Sierra Leone today, it is important to put this term in a comparative and quantitative light. To do so, I consulted data on relative levels of human development around the world. The United Nations Development Programme uses a so-called Human Development Index, or HDI, to compare the 191 countries of the globe for which there is sufficient data. The HDI ranks the level of human security in a particular country based on a composite of life expectancy, average years of schooling, and gross domestic income per capita.[138] In 1990 near the start of the Rebel War, Sierra Leone fell within the lowest 5 percent of countries globally in terms of socioeconomic development. Twenty years after the end of hostilities, Sierra Leone is still part of that 5 percent sector of countries many of whose people live in extreme poverty. As of 2021, Sierra Leone was still ranked 181 out of 191 countries, one rung below Afghanistan and two rungs higher than Yemen. For comparative purposes, Uganda's HDI rank is 166 and that of the United Kingdom is 18.[139]

The fact that twenty years after the end of the conflict, some war survivors are still waiting for compensation is a source of deep frustration for ordinary Sierra Leoneans today who struggle to subsist despite the rising cost of living. Sky-high inflationary trends for fuel and food by late 2023 are rooted in both external and internal forces, including the impact of the Ukraine conflict on the price of basic commodities and the fallout from reports of election improprieties during Sierra Leone's 2023 presidential elections,[140] which have resulted in decreased levels of funding for development projects by foreign governments and NGOs. Thus, even as they are committed to blending accountability and mercy in their local organizing activities, women peacebuilders throughout Sierra Leone struggle to provide for their families. They understand intimately what Shaw terms "the quiet violence of socioeconomic marginalization."[141] This structural and everyday violence has continued largely unabated since the war ended in 2002, as I will explore further below and in Chapter 4.

ASSESSING THE FORMS OF VIOLENCE AGAINST WOMEN DURING AND SINCE THE REBEL WAR

Above we emphasized three distinctions between Uganda's LRA War and the Rebel War—namely, the greater number of armed groups who fought, regions that were attacked, and ethnicities who suffered in Sierra Leone's conflict. Nonetheless, what is highly similar in broad strokes between the two civil wars is the direct targeting of civilians and the disproportionate impact of those attacks on women.

In the Sierra Leonean conflict, countless men, women, and children were killed and assaulted by members of various armed factions and subjected to extreme conditions of social distress caused by lack of food, sanitation, and basic medical care. This was true in Boie's community of Dogoloya and nationwide. The country was unified in its shared experience of both the catastrophic and commonplace sufferings of war. Against this brutal backdrop of daily atrocities against civilians, the Rebel War was characterized by particular patterns of gender-related violence.

Physical Violence Against Women During the Rebel War

The gendered nature of wartime violence in Sierra Leone was reflected in both magnitude and form. With respect to sexual violence, women were not the sole victims,[142] but they were undeniably the primary ones.[143] During the Rebel War the physical violence against woman took various characteristic forms. The pervasive use of rape against women of all ages, like the amputation of hands, feet, and limbs of men and women, was a signature form of violence utilized by militants of the Revolutionary United Front. While statistics are incomplete and difficult to verify, it is said that 50 percent of all women who encountered RUF forces in their communities were raped by one or more RUF fighters over the course of the war.[144] The practice by rebels and other combatants of forcing male family members to sexually assault their female relatives was also prevalent and resulted in some displaced families scattering into male and female bands, to avoid being subjected to forced incestuous violence when they encountered armed militants.[145] Finally, pregnant women reportedly had their babies cut from their wombs in seemingly random acts of gratuitous violence. While only a few cases of the disembowelment of pregnant women were reported to the Sierra Leone TRC after the Rebel War, it is believed that the practice may have been underreported due to the trauma of witnessing such an event.[146] As with other patterns of war-related physical violence, even isolated anecdotes of such cruelty toward women served to engrain more deeply the climate of abject fear that members of all the warring parties propagated throughout the layers of Sierra Leonean society.

In assessing the gender-related wartime violence perpetrated against Sierra Leonean women, there is no intention to treat as exceptional the brutality that women experienced in the Rebel War, as compared to the LRA War or other civil conflicts. In her own comparative work of conflict-related violence against women in Liberia, Northern Ireland, and Sri Lanka, Aisling Swaine cautions against ranking countries in a sweepstakes of wartime brutality.[147] That same caution applies here.

Structural Violence Against Women Since the Rebel War

The Rebel War and the LRA War share another similarity. Alongside the sharp focus on physical, and particularly sexual, violence against women during both conflicts, there is a parallel tendency to downplay or ignore the other forms of violence that Sierra Leonean and Ugandan women have suffered and survived beyond the sexual brutalization of their bodies by soldiers and rebels in wartime. As Aisling Swaine also argues, violence against women is pervasive worldwide and does not start or end with armed conflict.[148] This is as true in Sierra Leone as in Uganda. The extreme social marginalization of Sierra Leonean women—particularly rural women—has been documented since the availability of gender-differentiated human development data. Over the twenty years since the conclusion of the Rebel War, Sierra Leonean women's life expectancy and access to secondary education remain extremely low, and their level of maternal mortality is close to the highest in the world. According to the United Nations Development Programme (UNDP), in 2018, over a decade after the LRA War ended, nearly 45 percent of Sierra Leonean women aged fifteen years or older had experienced intimate partner violence, as compared to rates of around 50 percent for Uganda, slightly over 30 percent for developing countries as a whole, and 29 percent for the United Kingdom.[149]

More recent data from the United Nations help place Sierra Leone within the context of women's socioeconomic well-being globally. For Sierra Leonean women, life expectancy at birth in 2021 was 61.4 years, as compared to 64.9 years for Ugandan women, and 82.8 years for women in the United Kingdom.[150] In 2021 the average years of schooling for women over 25 in Sierra Leone was 3.5 years as compared to 5.8 years for Sierra Leonean men; whereas, in Uganda, women on average completed 4.9 years, Ugandan men 6.7.[151] The maternal mortality rate for Sierra Leonean women in 2021 is difficult to contemplate, estimated to be 1120 deaths of expectant mothers per 100,000 live births as compared to 375 maternal deaths per 100,000 births for Uganda and 7 such deaths for women in the UK.[152] Only Chad and Sudan have higher rates of maternal mortality than Sierra Leone.[153]

Efforts to Combat the Continuum of Physical and Structural Violence
Against Sierra Leonean Women
Rhetoric Against Gender-Based Violence

On March 27, 2010, the country's then-president, Ernest Bai Koroma, made a public apology to the women of Sierra Leone for the outrages they had suffered during the conflict. His statement is notable for linking physical violence during the war to long-standing denials to women of their social and economic human rights: "For decades women have had to battle it out with the constraints of culture to get justice and education; for decades women have been denied access to their just inheritance; and for a whole decade during the war we fell short in our obligation to adequately protect women from the brutalities of armed conflict."[154] Almost a decade later, on February 7, 2019, President Julius Maada Bio announced a national emergency in response to increased reporting of cases of rape and sexual violence against women and girls.[155] Like the former president Ernest Bai Koroma's apology, this national proclamation is symbolic yet powerful as it pushes back against a culture of women's subordination that tolerates everyday violence against women and girls.

Changing Attitudes and Policies Regarding Female Genital Cutting

Alongside the frank national conversation confronting gender-based violence, and the passage of legislation criminalizing marital rape and protecting women's inheritance rights, Sierra Leoneans continue to engage in a widespread cultural practice of female genital cutting (FGC). In Sierra Leone, FGC is carried out in the context of coming-of-age ceremonies for girls typically between the ages of 10 and 14. FGC entails removal of part of the girl's clitoris by a female traditional birth attendant. As further discussed in Chapter 4, UNICEF statistics indicate that, as of 2018, over 90 percent of Sierra Leonean women had been subjected to the ritual cutting, despite the fact that over 30 percent of women believed that the practice should be abolished. In recent years, changing attitudes toward FGC have had an impact on cultural practices. As of 2022, around 40 percent of girls between 15 and 19 had not been cut, either because they had refused or due to their not being subjected to the ritual.[156]

While FGC is not criminalized under Sierra Leonean law, the Child Right Act of 2007 does prohibit "any cultural practice which dehumanises or is injurious to the physical and mental welfare of a child."[157] Moreover, a bill debated in the Parliament in 2023 would require Sierra Leone's National

Commission for Children to undertake training and public education programs to eliminate "female genital mutilation, sexual abuse and economic exploitation of children."[158]

These enduring statistical indicators of gender inequality—alongside increasing public recognition of women's subordination in Sierra Leonean society—help put into context women's approaches to postconflict peacebuilding in their country.

TRANSFORMATIVE JUSTICE AT THE LOCAL LEVEL IN SIERRA LEONE

There are three important differences between grassroots peacebuilding in Sierra Leone and Uganda that reflect the distinctions in the nature of their civil wars and their different national approaches to transitional justice. Sierra Leone's Rebel War had more factions, more fronts, and more ethnic groups involved on all sides of the conflict than Uganda. Moreover, one faction was not demonized in the Sierra Leone TRC or the Special Court, unlike Uganda's focus of blame on the LRA. The composite impact of all these factors in the Sierra Leone case has facilitated a more positive feedback loop between the central authorities and the local communities in the postwar period. The various wartime and transitional justice dynamics have created ongoing peacebuilding opportunities in three areas. These include (1) the recognition of the suffering of the Sierra Leonean people; (2) the mobilization of political will; and (3) the creation of space for rural communities to take the lead on the ground and across the country.

Government Acknowledgment

First, the government of Sierra Leone has addressed the plight of war-affected people to a greater extent than the government of Uganda has. This state expression of empathy has been facilitated by the fact that Sierra Leone has had two democratically elected administrations since the end of the Rebel War—those of Ernest Bai Koroma of the APC, and Julius Maada Bio, the current president, of the SLPP. Former president Koroma in particular expressed his concern for the welfare of his people in public proclamation and through overseeing the disbursement of modest reparations payments to war-injured individuals under the NaCSA program described above. Contrastingly, President Museveni of Uganda, in power during and since the LRA War, has been unwilling to take responsibility for the suffering of his people caused by his armed forces during the conflict. There appears to be less anger and resentment toward the central government on the part of rural Sierra

Leoneans than that expressed by Northern Ugandans concerning official attitudes toward postwar healing.

Political Will

Second, Sierra Leone has had a legitimate national reconciliation program under the auspices of the TRC. Uganda has a policy on paper with little to no implementation. Symbolic as the work of the Sierra Leone TRC may have been, it created a historical record and a blueprint for change. As limited as the government's implementation of reparations programs has been, it has taken steps. This creates a stronger foundation on which to build and innovate reconciliation programs at the local level in Sierra Leone.

National Mobilization

Third, Sierra Leone's Rebel War impacted the entire country, and therefore there is a basis for a peacebuilding movement which is multiethnic, interregional, and grassroots in nature. Given the limited impact of Sierra Leone's Special Court and its Truth and Reconciliation Commission on the lives of the vast majority of war-affected women and men, the real work of peacebuilding began when the mandates of those national institutions ended. As acknowledged in the TRC Final Report, the cause of reconciliation would require the ongoing work of rural community members across the country for many years.[159]

SIERRA LEONE'S FAMBUL TOK PEACE MOTHERS

In 2007 a group of Sierra Leonean human rights activists launched the NGO Fambul Tok in collaboration with supporters in the international community. Fambul Tok, which means "family talk" in Krio, is a community revitalization organization committed to peaceful dispute resolution, restorative justice, and collaborative development activities throughout Sierra Leone. Its founders envisioned an ambitious, organic, and long-term process of national reconciliation, facilitated through regular consultations with Sierra Leoneans in rural settings about how best to effect concrete and meaningful changes in their daily lives. In its initial phase, Fambul Tok outreach staff partnered with local communities to facilitate mediation and dialogue between individual victims and offenders, often culminating in an atonement ceremony around a bonfire.[160] These cleansing rituals went beyond mere public expressions of responsibility and forgiveness. They were linked to the reestablishment of cooperative agricultural projects in communities where such collective enterprises had been largely abandoned during the course of the Rebel War. Fambul Tok has documented increased productivity and more bountiful harvests in communities that have undergone reconciliation and atonement programs.[161] Thus, in addition to restoring community ties, Fambul Tok has sought to promote peacebuilding in material terms, integrating the socioeconomic and interpersonal aspects of reconciliation.

Despite the powerful symbolism of neighbor-to-neighbor atonement and forgiveness, community-based organizations like Fambul Tok have had to work harder to ensure the equal partnership of women and men in social healing at the local level. Public cleansing rituals often assert a kind of social control or pressure in which some women feel compelled to forgive their offenders even when silence is their preferred form of speech and witness.[162] At the same time, the lasting value of such rituals can be questioned, particularly when public expressions of remorse by a male offender toward a female survivor seldom alleviate the pronounced power imbalance between men and women in the community.

Partially in response to such critiques, in 2009 Fambul Tok launched the Peace Mothers, a program established to focus on the particular experiences, needs, and leadership skills of women in communities like Dogoloya and across the country. Like the women's collectives in Northern Uganda, the Peace Mothers groups initially served as talking circles within which women could confide in other women friends in private about the trauma they had experienced, "to know that they're not alone, that time will help, to allow them to speak, to be encouraged, to be unburdened."[163] Over time, the activities of the groups expanded in scope, first to collaborative agricultural projects and microfinance activities, and later to mediation and advocacy work. It is a point of pride among Peace Mothers that their network has led to an increase in women's participation within Fambul Tok overall.[164]

Activism and organizing within the Peace Mothers and Fambul Tok evidence the importance of civil society as a voice for community resilience and economic development throughout Sierra Leone. In particular for women, who participate in formal governing structures to a much lesser extent than men,[165] involvement in women's collectives expands their historically limited opportunities for leadership in the public realm.[166]

The role of Peace Mothers in mobilizing community-based public health responses to the 2014–15 Ebola emergency and in preventing violence in recent elections has become a model for a village level "People's Planning Process" in Sierra Leone's health, education, and economic development sectors.[167] The

Ebola crisis in particular, like the Rebel War itself, devastated social networks and subsistence economies in Sierra Leone. The Peace Mothers' response to the Ebola emergency—building trust and educating community members about hand-washing and safe burial practices—is an apt metaphor for peacebuilding itself, a process that is pragmatic, community-based, women-centric, education-focused, and fundamentally collaborative.

Peace Mothers such as Boie Jalloh bear witness to the immense task of reestablishing social networks and rebuilding the economy after military, economic, and social devastation. Their work illustrates the power of women-centered community revitalization in Sierra Leone and other postconflict societies throughout the world. Insights on grassroots peacebuilding drawn from interviews with members of five local Peace Mothers groups in the southern district of Moyamba and the northern district of Koinadugu are the focus of Chapter 4.

In both Sierra Leone and Northern Uganda, the distance between national capitals and rural communities is great, and the struggle for material subsistence is intense. Thus, it is understandable that women peacebuilders in both countries tend to view peace and justice in gritty, down-to-earth terms. Their experiences and wisdom regarding the work of social transformation are the subject of the remaining two chapters of this book. I start in Chapter 3 with a presentation and discussion of the perspectives and contributions of rural women peacebuilders from the Acholi Sub-region of Northern Uganda.

Peace in the Home, Peace in the Nation: Conceptions of Justice Within Women's Collectives in Northern Uganda

And when my sister
Is grinding simsim
Mixed with groundnuts
And I am grinding
Millet mixed with sorghum
You hear the song of the stones
You hear the song of the grains
And the seeds
And above all these
The beautiful duet
By Lawino and her sister.
  —Okot p'Bitek, *Song of Lawino*

Women are like teachers everywhere.
They don't go with a lot of
aggression.
They take things systematically.
They have a lot of mercy.
  —Lucy, Peacebuilder of
    Nwoya District

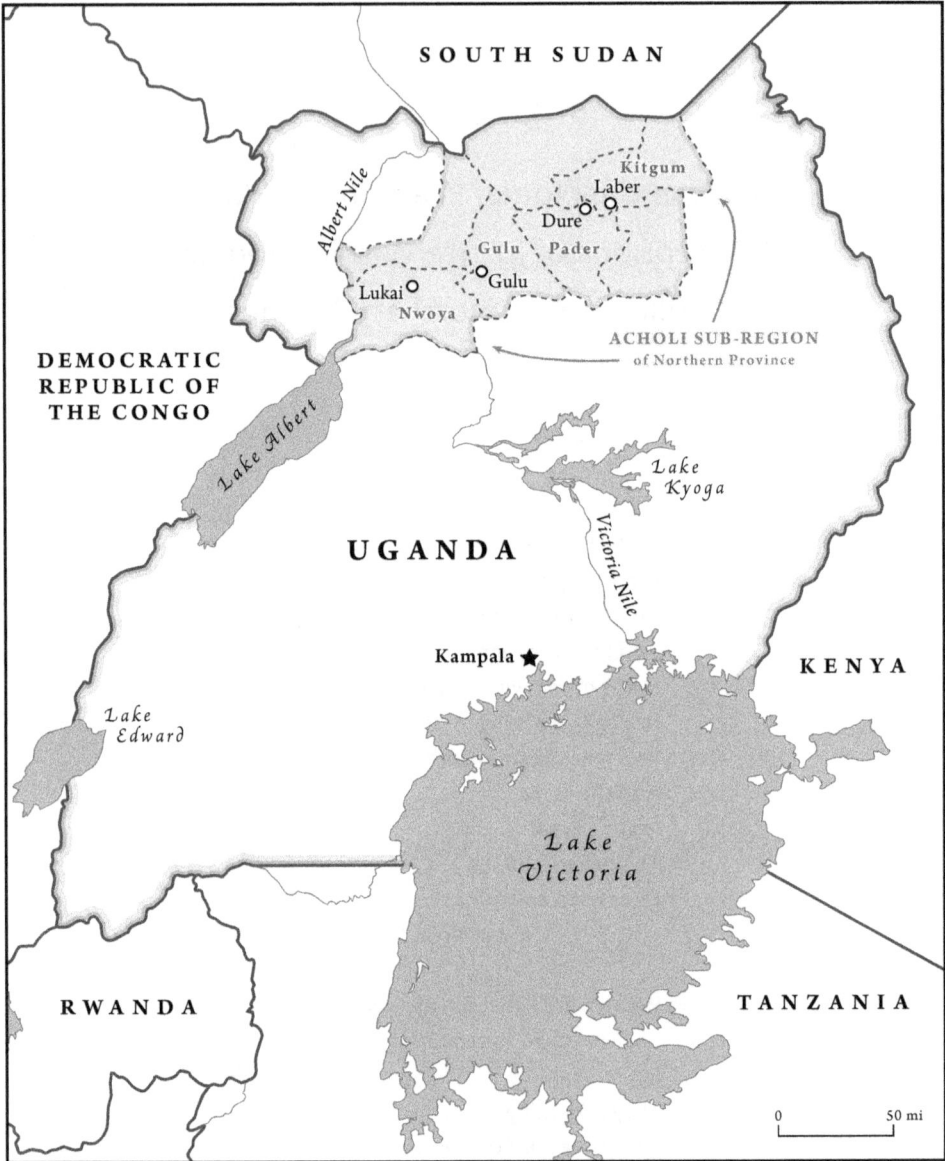

Map 1. Map of Uganda by Erin Greb.

Place, Partnerships, and Methodology

The Cultural Milieu of Acholiland

Lawino is the narrator of the Ugandan poet Okot p'Bitek's *Song of Lawino*.[1] Her description of grinding grain with her beloved sister is evocative of the cultural milieu of Northern Uganda in which Lucy Okello and Jane Orama[2] and their fellow women peacebuilders find themselves—the demands of agricultural subsistence; the physical labor, both hard and devotional; the sisterly collaboration, companionship, and celebration. P'Bitek's epic poem threads the rhythms of daily Acholi life through the narrator's running commentary on religion, politics, gender roles, and social well-being. Lawino shares her ethnic heritage and maternal language with the twenty women peacebuilders I interviewed in Northern Uganda over a seven-year period from 2016 to 2023. Her thoughts on liberation, self-actualization, and speaking truth to power in mid-twentieth-century Acholiland establish a fitting backdrop for interviews with contemporary women peacebuilders like Jane and Lucy, who devote their daily lives to the work of subsistence, community healing, and collective empowerment.

Lawino's ballad is both a song of lamentation and a forceful declaration of personal agency in response to her husband's thoughtless embrace of Western ways. At one point she calls Ocol "a dog of the white man" and encourages him to return to his roots and to appreciate "the wealth in his house."[3] While Ocol is the self-described modernist, it is Lawino who questions why things should be a certain way, particularly for women. Her words resonate with the challenges of women's empowerment in Acholiland today:

> I am not a shy woman
> I am not afraid of anybody
> And I am not easily browbeaten.
> I know that the person who asks
> Has done no wrong.
> I will not be frightened
> By those who say
> Asking questions is mortal sin.[4]

ETHNICITY, GENDER, AND WOMEN'S IDENTITY IN POSTWAR NORTHERN UGANDA

Acholi identity is an important factor in understanding the context and consequences of Uganda's LRA War for rural women who survived the conflict and have been engaged in the work of community building ever since.[5] Acholiland, the traditional homeland of the Acholi people, is one of four subregions of Northern Uganda, alongside Lango, Karamoja, and West Nile. As described more fully in Chapter 2, the Lord's Resistance Army was founded by an Acholi faith healer, Joseph Kony, who mobilized and forcibly recruited among the Acholi and the Langi, appealing to the historical oppression and neglect of northerners during both the colonial and postindependence eras. In response to LRA militancy, the Uganda People's Defense Forces mounted a counterinsurgency campaign involving the massive forced displacement of wide sectors of the civilian population of Acholiland, including Jane Orama, Lucy Okello, and the other members of the women's collectives who took part in my interviews. The army's civilian relocation policy was widely perceived by Acholi people as punishment for their imputed support for the LRA and their assumed historical support for the president's political adversaries, including the former president Milton Obote, whose second term in office ended abruptly in two coups in 1986, the first short-lived and the second leading to Museveni's nearly forty years as head of state.[6] Since the 2007 Juba Accords, Acholi community leaders have sought reparations from the Ugandan government for the wartime atrocities suffered by members of their ethnolinguistic community. Such calls for restorative justice have remained largely unanswered.

As an Acholi woman, Lawino would likely have joined her husband's family when she married Ocol, as was the expectation for Jane Orama and Lucy Okello. By cultural practice, Acholi women "marry out," with profound implications for their material circumstances and inheritance rights. As Jane's fellow group member Mary expressed it, "Traditionally, a boy brings a continuation of the clan and a girl brings a continuation of another clan."[7] Thus, when Jane Orama became widowed, she looked to her late husband's family to ensure her economic subsistence. Acholi women today confront the legacy of this cultural system, compounded by the aftermath of the LRA War and the government's forced relocation policy. The displacement of wide sectors of the population disrupted traditional land tenure systems and compromised clan-based social support mechanisms. Although Uganda's amended Succession Act of 2022 recognizes the equal claims of daughters and sons to inherit from their fathers and the rights of widows to inherit property left by their deceased husbands, the reality on the ground in communities can be quite different, given generations of cultural practice prioritizing the rights of male children in inheritance.

Today many Acholi women like Jane Orama and Lucy Okello cope with the uncertain terrain between progressive national norms promoting gender equality that are not yet fully implemented and traditional kinship networks sustaining collective subsistence that are no longer fully functional.[8] The challenge of harmonizing traditional practices with contemporary legal rights is one that Jane and Lucy and their fellow women peacebuilders face on a daily basis as they engage in community and familial life. In our field interviews, Northern Ugandan women shared their varied experiences navigating these turbulent social crosscurrents.

The Structure of the Portal Organizations
WOMEN'S ADVOCACY NETWORK, REFUGEE LAW PROJECT, AND HUMAN RIGHTS FOCUS

In Northern Uganda, numerous community-based and nongovernmental organizations (CBOs and NGOs) work with grassroots women's collectives devoted to peacebuilding and community healing in the postwar period. In seeking partner agencies for my study of the grassroots women's peace movement in Uganda, I was assisted by colleagues from the Human Rights and Peace Centre (HURIPEC) of Makerere University School of Law in Kampala. In 2016 Zahara Nampewo, then HURIPEC's executive director,[9] and a succession of her community partners eventually led me to Jane Orama, Lucy Okello, and eighteen other women active in community development in their rural locales across Acholiland. The selection of three particular organizations as entry points for my research in Northern Uganda was inspired by a characteristic dynamism between each NGO or CBO and its affiliated community groups, in which organizational energy flows in two directions—up from the collectives to the agency and down from the agency to the local women's and mixed groups.

My three portal organizations were the Women's Advocacy Network of the Gulu-based Justice and Reconciliation Project (WAN),[10] the Refugee Law Project of Makerere University School of Law (RLP), and Human Rights Focus (HURIFO), all three active in various sub-counties of the Northern Ugandan districts of Gulu, Nwoya, Pader, and Kitgum.[11] Each nonprofit agency interacts with a network of women's or mixed-gender collectives active at the village level in one or more districts.[12] In some cases, as in Kitgum with Human Rights Focus, the groups were formed spontaneously as village savings and loan societies and later affiliated with a nonprofit or community-based organization. Elsewhere, particularly in Gulu, Nwoya, and Pader with the Women's Advocacy Network and the Refugee Law Project, most of the women's groups were inspired or launched by NGOs and subsequently achieved considerable autonomy through the formation of leadership teams and the establishment of self-financing structures linked to microcredit programs. Jane Orama and Lucy Okello are members of two of the women's collectives affiliated with the Refugee Law Project.

HURIFO, unique among the three portal agencies in this regard, has a track record of working with mixed community groups composed of male and female members, with women typically making up the majority. The groups were founded initially as social solidarity organizations and revolving credit funds. These so-called village savings and loan associations (VSLAs) subsequently affiliated with HURIFO after taking part in the agency's trainings on dispute resolution and inheritance law. The Women's Advocacy Network, a community-based organization, serves as an umbrella for local groups whose members are exclusively women, many of whom spent years as abductees and captives of the Lord's Resistance Army (LRA). The Refugee Law Project, an NGO operating under the administrative rubric of Makerere University School of Law, has in recent years provided training and nominal material support for women's groups such as Alany pa Mony Lit in Nwoya District and Uketu wan Kwene in Pader District.[13] Lucy Okello is a member of Alany and Jane Orama is a member of Uketu.[14] Community groups working with RLP are composed of individuals like Lucy and Jane who survived wartime abuses at the hands of both the LRA and the Uganda People's Defense Forces (UPDF) during Northern Uganda's twenty-year civil conflict.

The Vision of the Portal Organizations and Their Affiliated Women's Groups

WAN, RLP, and HURIFO share three foundational attributes. First, these organizations are committed to women's leadership, whether in women's collectives or within mixed groups of men and women. Second, each NGO or CBO is connected to a network of community groups, each of which is tightly knit into the fabric of its local parish and chiefdom. Third, they share a mission to provide support to their affiliated women's or mixed groups largely in the form of solidarity and training, with minimal financial contributions. The nonprofits thus facilitate the self-sufficiency and dynamism of their individual women's groups and mixed collectives. The partnership between each agency and its affiliated groups honors the integrity of each local entity and helps guard against a relationship of dependency.[15]

Nevertheless, at times group autonomy may verge on economic marginalization. Alany pa Mony Lit member Esther bore witness to the increased isolation experienced by Alany given an extended hiatus in contact with the Refugee Law Project. She quipped in a 2023 interview, "If you will take another five years to return, then please leave me one small goat!"[16]

While Jane, Esther, Lucy, and their fellow groups' members value their relationships with the staff of their partner agencies and sometimes yearn for more material support, their group solidarity is palpable, as is their pride in the self-generating character of their activities. Underlying the livelihood and advocacy projects of each community group is the principle on which it was founded: the women came together to share their stories of suffering, resilience, and hope. The social and psychic solidarity that the members provide one another remains integral to group identity and provides the grounding for their microcredit, collective agriculture, and women's empowerment projects. Their peacebuilding activities are continuously sustained by the friendship and cooperation between group members.[17]

WOMEN'S PEACE MOBILIZATION IN THE RESTORATIVE JUSTICE ARENA IN NORTHERN UGANDA

The Ugandan government's national policy for postwar transition has highlighted the individual penal accountability strand of transitional justice. This predominantly retributive approach is manifested in the war crimes trials of former insurgents of the Lord's Resistance Army in the International Criminal Court in The Hague and the International Crimes Division of the Ugandan High Court in Kampala. In the restorative arena, Uganda has not yet established a national Truth and Reconciliation Commission, despite a succession of political and legislative efforts to create one.[18] Moreover, the government has failed to provide significant compensation to war survivors or to trace missing relatives still unaccounted for, some fifteen years after the end of LRA hostilities in Northern Uganda.[19] The government's drive to prosecute rebel offenders is seriously out of sync with the overriding concerns of

Jane, Lucy, and their fellow peacebuilders. Seeking reconciliation at the grass-roots level, they are frustrated with their government's merely token overtures in the name of social welfare enhancement. They subscribe to a nuanced definition of accountability that combines truth-telling, apology, and the payment of material compensation. Even those supportive of judicial trials for suspected war criminals see a significant gap between the government's emphasis on rebel accountability and the realities of life in war-affected communities of Northern Uganda, where women peacebuilders and many of their neighbors were abused by government soldiers and rebels alike.

Many war survivors in Northern Uganda seek an apology from their government for its failure to protect the population from LRA attacks and forced conscription. It is also vital to Ugandan women peacebuilders that the government acknowledge its direct complicity in the wartime abuses carried out by its own UPDF forces. Interviewees recounted various offenses perpetrated by both the UPDF and the LRA: sexual violence against women and men, disappearances, targeted killings, forced displacement, destruction of property, and other attacks on civilian communities, all occurring over two decades of civil war from 1986 to the Juba Accords in 2007.

Women's collectives working in concert with WAN, RLP, and HURIFO seek state compensation for war victims and their communities, without being naive about the prospects for broad-based reparations in the near term. In the meantime, women peacebuilders like Jane Orama maintain memorials to their loved ones killed in wartime massacres. Group members such as Lucy Okello participate in village savings and loan societies, microenterprises, and agricultural cooperatives. Those who have benefited from NGO trainings in turn train other members of their communities in dispute resolution and violence prevention.[20] Women's collectives engage in grassroots activism in its most vibrant and unvarnished form.

Language and Methodology
LINGUISTIC NOTES: TALKING ABOUT RECONCILIATION, LIVELIHOOD, AND ACCOUNTABILITY IN THE ACHOLI LANGUAGE

In speaking with Jane, Lucy, and their fellow group members, certain Acholi phrases flow through the descriptions of their daily work—*yupu kuc* (peacebuilding), *mato oput* (an Acholi reconciliatory rite), *tic-cing* (the "work of one's hands" or livelihood), *adwogi metic* (payment due for one's labor or a fair accounting for one's conduct), and *kwayo kica* (the heartfelt plea for forgiveness). Their vocabulary of peacebuilding includes phrases and concepts that do not neatly separate out into punitive, historical, or material notions of postconflict justice. Typically, these various notions of peace and justice diverge and converge, weaving themselves into a vibrant fabric of community reconciliation, subsistence, and development.

While individual interviewees like Jane and Lucy might wax philosophical at times regarding the restorative, retributive, and redistributive strands of peace, their comments are also grounded in the heavy doses of the realism and sheer grit required to get through their days. Many women in Acholiland spoke of their personal resilience in terms of *oteka*, a kind of strength associated with the ability to sustain constant devotion to subsistence activities, despite great difficulties.[21] Such resilience is closely linked to the notion of perseverance. When asked to describe the concept of perseverance, my RLP interpreter and research partner Fred Ngomokwe used the Acholi phrase *bedo ki tek cwin mi timo tic ikare matek*, translated as "building a mechanism to finish a task within a very difficult situation." He alluded to the proverbial cook who needs to be able to withstand the heat and smoke from the cooking pot if she is to remain in the kitchen. Winifred Arima Abalo, another interpreter and colleague, retranslated Fred's phrase to signify "having strength in time of hardship."[22] Interwoven with Fred and Winnie's understandings of resilience and perseverance is the capacity for endurance—the ability to bear a difficult experience or memory and to move forward with it. Fred illustrated this capacity for endurance with the Acholi phrase *dano ma kanyo lok* (literally, "you absorb something") and pointed to the mother who bears the secret of her household, even if it is very painful. Such Acholi notions of resilience, perseverance, and inner strength pervaded the conversations and interviews with members of the four community groups in Northern Uganda.[23]

DEVELOPING A FIELD METHODOLOGY FOR NORTHERN UGANDA

Over a seven-year period, I engaged in conversations with Acholi women active in peacebuilding collectives in four different war-affected communities, inviting them to talk about the various concepts, metaphors, and values that guide their daily work in the service of conflict resolution and daily subsistence. Through a series of focused interviews, I developed deeper relationships with nearly twenty of these individuals, including Jane Orama and Lucy Okello.

The conversations within the WAN, RLP, and HURIFO community networks in Northern Uganda gave each participant several opportunities to

articulate her own understandings of the various dimensions of peacebuilding. The first phase of the research encompassed focus groups, one in each of
four community settings, followed by extensive interviews with select individuals from each group. In 2016 a total of thirty women took part in the focus groups, of whom twenty agreed to take part in individual interviews. I
returned three times to their communities for follow-up interviews, in 2017
and 2018 and again in 2023.

The focus groups were structured around three questions concerning the
meaning of the terms "reconciliation," "livelihood," and "accountability," answered in turn by each participant. Each woman shared her understanding
of *mato oput* (reconciliation), *tic-cing* (livelihood), and *adwogi metic* or *kwayo
kica* (two interlinked dimensions of accountability).

Following the focus groups, each individual interviewee orally answered
a series of twenty-four questions from the "Peacebuilders' Questionnaire,"[24]
spanning seven main topic areas: (1) the interviewee's life circumstances and
experiences; (2) her community involvement and her assessment of the value
of such activities; (3) her articulation of the interrelationships between reconciliation, livelihood, and accountability; (4) her perceptions of the current
state of women's protection and empowerment; (5) her attitudes and experiences with regard to access to health care, education, and employment opportunities; (6) her perspective on women's property ownership, inheritance
rights, and access to the political process; and (7) her estimation of women's
status and roles in her community.

The second phase of the research took place over successive years, involving two rounds of follow-up conversations with those individuals I had interviewed in 2016, including Jane Orama and Lucy Okello. In 2017 I sat down
once again with the women in their local settings. We touched on a variety
of essential themes, including their understandings of the essence of peace,
their personal wellsprings of courage, and their most vital engagements in
community subsistence. I asked Lucy, Jane, and the others one additional
question: "If your work in the community were a tree, composed of roots,
branches, and fruit, what would each part of the tree represent?"[25] Many but
not all described reconciliation as the roots of the tree of peace, accountability as its branches, and livelihood as its fruit.[26] Again, in 2018, I returned to
each of their communities to verify the accuracy of the women's impressions
as I had recorded them in the previous years, and to confirm their willingness to be quoted in the text of the manuscript.[27]

The final phase of the research took place in 2023, after a hiatus due to the COVID-19 pandemic. I returned to the four communities to assess how the women's collaborative activities might have been impacted by emergent local and global developments such as worsening drought, the war in Ukraine, and the passage of the 2023 Anti-Homosexuality Act by the Ugandan Parliament as well as ongoing inflationary trends.

The Wisdom of Women Peacebuilders in Acholiland

In the first section below, I draw from my interactions with *Rwot Lakica*, a women's collective affiliated with the Women's Advocacy Network, originally a project of the Justice and Reconciliation Project,[28] then based in Gulu Town.[29] The second section conveys the substance of conversations with members of *Alany pa Mony Lit* and *Uketu wan Kwene*, two women's groups based in Nwoya and Pader Districts with historical support from the Gulu field office of Makerere University's Refugee Law Project. The third and final section is devoted to contributions from the women of *Odoko Mit*, a mixed group based in the Lagoro Sub-county of Kitgum District. Odoko, while self-sustaining, has benefited over the years from trainings provided by Winnie Arima, formerly of the Ugandan NGO Human Rights Focus.

Rwot Lakica and the Women's Advocacy Network in Gulu
CULTURAL NOTES REGARDING RWOT LAKICA AND GULU TOWN

Rwot Lakica (God Is Merciful) is one of a number of local women's groups situated in Gulu District, Northern Uganda, that are affiliated with the Women's Advocacy Network (WAN). The women of Rwot Lakica came together spontaneously in 2006 based on their common experiences as former abductees of the Lord's Resistance Army, who were forced into marriage-like relationships with rebel soldiers and commanders and later escaped from the LRA or were liberated by the end of the LRA War. In 2012 they formally launched themselves as a women's group affiliated with the Gulu-based Justice and Reconciliation Project and later the Women's Advocacy Network.[30] Like the members of other community-based women's groups clustered under the umbrella of WAN, many of the women of Rwot Lakica had given birth to a child or children while in LRA captivity. Rwot Lakica members take part in a variety of group activities related to education, advocacy, and economic development. Among their accomplishments they emphasize the value of group counseling and sharing stories with other members as vital to their own emotional health and the well-being of their families.

The members of Rwot Lakica are ethnic Acholi or Langi, part of the greater Luo tribal community historically based in the southern part of Sudan (now South Sudan), Northern Uganda, and Western Kenya. Group members are acculturated to the urban setting of Gulu Town. Their levels of education range from a few years of primary school to successful completion of a bachelor's degree. Near the end of the conflict, beginning around 2006, several were trained in tailoring at St. Monica's, a local school run by a Catholic order under the leadership of Sister Rosemary Nyirumbe.[31] Several others are employed by or volunteer for the Women's Advocacy Network. While most earn modest salaries or make their living selling handicrafts and other goods in the informal economy, they struggle to support their families.

IDENTIFYING AN INTERPRETER FOR CONVERSATIONS WITH SURVIVORS OF LRA CAPTIVITY

In preparation for my interviews with members of the Women's Advocacy Network, I sought an interpreter, bilingual in English and Acholi, who was also well versed in the culture of Acholiland and the impact of the LRA War. I was fortunate to meet with Victoria Nyanjura in July 2016, shortly after I arrived in Gulu on the bus from Kampala for the first time. A native Langi speaker who communicates fluently in Acholi as well as English, she was both a member of Rwot Lakica and a staff member of the Women's Advocacy Network. Victoria was eager to introduce me to members of Rwot Lakica and other WAN-affiliated women's groups, and willing to serve as my interpreter for the focus group and individual interviews. She identified six group members available to meet with me the very afternoon of the day we first met.

Victoria Nyanjura plays a special role in the struggle for women's full participation in community life and peacebuilding in Northern Uganda due to her experiences and insights as a survivor-advocate. She provides encouragement and guidance to former LRA captives, having benefited from such support herself when she returned from captivity some fifteen years ago. Her perspective is particularly relevant because she experienced firsthand the stigma often directed at former rebel captives even as they are struggling with the long-term impacts of trauma.

When she was in her mid-teens Victoria was captured by rebels in 1996 in an infamous LRA raid on St. Mary's College, a private secondary school for girls located some forty-five miles south of Gulu Town in the town of Aboke.[32] One of her fellow Rwot Lakica members, Grace, was abducted from St. Mary's at the same time. During their LRA captivity, she and Grace were at one point part of the same household. As Victoria put it, "We ate from the same pot." Life behind rebel lines was a fluid network of temporary encampments and households that were formed and disassembled as the conflict progressed. Victoria described life in captivity as extremely frightening. Individual women would sometimes try to escape. In addition to specific punishments imposed by rebel soldiers on the attempted escapees, all the captive women in that encampment would be beaten "to make them fear." At a certain point, Victoria explained, she became aware that this was her life for now, that somehow she had to abide it and "to obey, because I had no . . . other option."[33] While in captivity Victoria gave birth to a son in 2000 and a daughter in 2002. In 2004, at the age of twenty-one, she fled with her children during crossfire between the LRA rebels and government soldiers of the UPDF.

After her escape, Victoria took part in a reintegration program implemented by World Vision. She then moved to Kampala to continue her studies, successfully completing her Advanced Level secondary school exams in preparation for earning a bachelor's degree in Development Studies from Kyambogo University in Kampala. Given the prohibitive cost and competing family responsibilities, few former LRA captives are able to finish secondary school, although some pursue vocational training and go on to engage in skilled craftwork, farming, or petty trading.[34] Victoria's academic accomplishments have deepened her capacity to reflect on her own life experiences in the broader context of postconflict transition for the people of Northern Uganda. Those insights feed her commitment to healing trauma and empowering women in communities emerging from violence.

After completing her university studies, Victoria was hired by the Justice and Reconciliation Project to help organize and support women's groups in the Gulu area under the auspices of the Women's Advocacy Network. From 2016 to 2018, she served as after-care specialist for the Washington, DC–based International Justice Mission (IJM), providing social support and legal advocacy for war-affected women, including widows whose land had been grabbed by family members. In August 2018, Victoria began work on a master's program in international peace studies at the University of Notre Dame.

Figure 9. Victoria Nyanjura Gulu, Northern Uganda. Photo by J. Moore, 2016.

Upon completion of her degree, she founded the CBO Women United for Women, which is active in the eastern part of Northern Uganda. Victoria played an important role in facilitating the research for this chapter. Her insights into self-advocacy and empowerment on the part of war survivors illuminate this study of grassroots peacebuilding.

TALKING WITH MEMBERS OF THE WOMEN'S ADVOCACY NETWORK
Initial Impressions of Rwot Lakica Members' Lives in Captivity

We conducted our focus group and individual interviews[35] in 2016 on the terrace of the Pearl Afrique Hotel in central Gulu Town, which members of the Women's Advocacy Network reached by *boda* (motorcycle taxi). I chose not to start with pointed inquiries about the women's abductions or other personal experiences with the LRA. Some in-depth discussions of life in captivity happened outside of the formal interviews, in the context of background and follow-up conversations with Victoria and several other Rwot Lakica members. Other individuals broached questions of abduction, forced marriage, and sexual violence spontaneously during their interviews, typically in the context of questions relating to childbirth and health care, their attitudes toward the government, and issues of accountability.

One typical opportunity for an interviewee to share about her life with the LRA came in response to a question about where she gave birth to her children—at home or elsewhere; and under what circumstances—alone, with a local midwife, or in a clinic or hospital. Several of the women explained that one or more of their children had been born "in the bush"—a reference to captivity behind rebel lines, whereas others were born at home or at a health center, normally before or after the LRA conflict.

Often the interviewees did choose to share certain aspects of the circumstances of their abduction, captivity, and escape. Typically, they were captured by the LRA at school or en route; they endured captivity on average from eight to ten years; and most took advantage of crossfire between the rebels and UPDF (Ugandan Army) soldiers, to run away into an area of denser vegetation and eventually to reach safety. At that point, they made their way to a town or UPDF reception and reintegration center where they were granted amnesty. Reflecting on the reality of her involuntary servitude at the hands of the LRA, Grace saw considerable irony in the fact that although her government had failed to protect her from rebel abduction and enslavement, after escaping from a decade of captivity it was she who had to seek an official state pardon for being associated with the LRA.[36]

Focus Group Discussion with Rwot Lakica and WAN Members, 2016

As became customary with my community dialogues among members of women's collectives in Northern Uganda and Sierra Leone, the women of Rwot Lakica and other WAN members sat in a circle for the focus group, in this case around a table on the terrace of the Hotel Pearl Afrique. Participants included Alice, Agnes, Santa, Stella, Evelyn, and Grace,[37] four of whom also took part in individual interviews after lunch. In a pattern followed during all four focus groups among women's collectives in Northern Uganda, this one started with the theme of *reconciliation*. I invited each participant to share her understanding of the concept—"Grace [for example], what does reconciliation [*mato oput*] mean to you?," proceeding in that manner around the circle.

Three responses stood out among WAN members: reconciliation entails forgiveness and healing; it is brought about by the mediating role of broadminded community leaders; and, fundamentally, reconciliation requires honesty by the government regarding offenses committed by army (UPDF) soldiers, not merely the acknowledgment of atrocities committed by LRA rebels. Stella, then in her late twenties and the mother of two children, spoke of reconciliation in the postwar context as a mechanism for conflict resolution within the community: the parties who 'fail to understand' one another must first agree to designate someone with 'vast knowledge' to 'bridge the gap' between their positions.[38] Another spoke of reconciliation in the context of the government's failure to protect civilians during the LRA War: 'Since all of us were abducted,' she argued, 'the government should acknowledge its part in our plight.' This honesty, she noted, would give women like herself the confidence to speak candidly about their experiences.

Moving on to the theme of *livelihood* (*tic-cing*),[39] five insights emerged: livelihood is self-sufficiency; it promotes healing; it is collective; it is empowering; and livelihood requires the acquisition of skills, such as the cultivation of new crops and the utilization of new farming methods. Agnes, then thirty-nine with five children, emphasized a symbiosis between individual sustenance and community unity: 'If you are making a living, it is easy to reconcile.' Several Rwot Lakica members spoke of the restorative nature of livelihood activities—involvement in productive activities has helped them bear the emotional burdens of their wartime experiences.

The discussion concluded with *accountability* (*kwayo kica* or *adwogi metic*). Four themes dominated: the importance of truth-telling; the government's ultimate responsibility for wartime offenses; the requirement of compensation; and the recognition that accountability facilitates both reconciliation and livelihood. Accountability is a layered and nuanced concept in Acholi. Many participants across all four community groups in Northern Uganda stressed two components of accountability: *kwayo kica*, the request for forgiveness for acknowledged wrongdoing; and *adwogi metic*, signifying what the perpetrator deserves, or has earned, based on their actions or labor.[40] While there were differences in the way these two notions were defined, most women agreed that both the acknowledgment of wrongdoing and a willingness to make amends are vital components of accountability. Agnes focused on the interconnections between accountability and reconciliation. She specified that first the community and then the individual offender must acknowledge the wrong that has occurred, followed by those individuals most impacted by the wrongdoing. After the wrongdoer acknowledges the offense, they ask for forgiveness (*kwayo kica*) and then appropriate compensation or accounting is made (*adwogi metic*).

Individual Interviews with Rwot Lakica Members in 2016

After our focus group discussion, Grace, Stella, Santa, and Agnes volunteered to take part in individual interviews in the afternoon. These conversations followed our standard Peacebuilders' Questionnaire.[41]

Life Circumstances and Experiences

The Rwot Lakica and WAN members who took part in the individual interviews in 2016 ranged from twenty-eight to forty years of age. Grace speaks Langi, Acholi, and fluent English. The other three are Acholi speakers with limited facility in English. One is Anglican and the other three are Catholic. Stella was ten years old at the time of her abduction by the LRA, and the others were in their teenage years. They were abducted on a bus, at home, or at school. Three were still in primary school (between P-2 and P-7) at the time of their abduction, while Grace was abducted from St. Mary's College (secondary school) in Aboke. After returning from captivity, Grace completed her secondary studies in Kampala, going on to receive her bachelor's degree in development studies from Gulu University. The others completed their studies during their primary years.

Each woman spoke of her children. They have two, three, four, and five surviving children, respectively. Three of the four delivered one or two children in captivity and then gave birth to one or more after they returned from the bush. Agnes was abducted after she had given birth to two sons, from whom she was separated throughout her captivity, and one daughter, who was abducted with her and remained with Agnes in captivity. After escaping and returning to her community, she and her daughter were reunited with her two sons and her parents, who had cared for her boys while she was in captivity. Agnes has since given birth to another girl and another boy. Grace had a son and daughter in captivity. Her son was killed when she attempted to run from the rebels with him and his sister. Grace and her daughter survived their escape. She has since married and given birth to another son.

Three of the women spoke of the response of their families and new partners when they returned from the bush. Grace explained that her parents had formed an association of the parents of abducted children after her abduction. This organization helped facilitate Grace's return with her daughter, and her reconciliation with her family. Now married, Grace and her husband are raising her daughter and their younger son. Stella explained that the father of her second child 'accepts but does not support' her older son who was born in captivity. Santa described a situation in which she initially returned to live with her parents but moved out because of her father's mistreatment of her daughter. She and her daughter now live with her partner, the father of her three younger children. Santa explains she is 'mother and father' to her eldest daughter, who is now pursuing her advanced secondary school studies.

Community Involvement

One question on the survey asks the participants what aspect of their community work brings them the most pride or enthusiasm. This tended to be a bright spot during the individual interviews among the members of Rwot Lakica, a pattern which played out over the other community groups based in the districts of Nwoya, Pader, and Kitgum as well, and similarly for the members of the five Peace Mothers groups in Sierra Leone. Of the four Rwot Lakica women interviewed, three pointed to "peer support and storytelling" as what they value most among their group activities. There was a clear sense that the mutual support they provide one another is a source of solidarity, resilience, and joy. Grace, the only university graduate of the four, had recently found employment with the Gulu-based Justice and Reconciliation Project, working in the area of returnee reintegration. Because she was personally acquainted with the phenomenon of stigmatization, she felt that she was able to be more effective in her work with returnees from the LRA conflict.[42]

All four WAN-affiliated women have goals and aspirations for further professional growth. Stella expressed the desire to continue her studies and Agnes aspired to start a business. Grace hoped to find more stable employment since she had been managing on a series of short-term contracts with the Women's Advocacy Network. Santa wished to acquire land for a women's settlement and to attain further educational opportunities for her children.[43]

One part of the questionnaire asks the interviewee to explain how disputes are resolved in her community. All four Women's Advocacy Network members described a process whereby local cultural leaders or relatives are called in to mediate. Grace described mediation as a "win-win" for both sides. Stella emphasized the need for the parties to "humble themselves" before reconciliation can be achieved.

Interrelationships Between Reconciliation, Livelihood, and Accountability

An important link between the focus group and the individual conversations is a question concerning the relative significance of reconciliation, livelihood, and accountability. Each of the four interviewees of Rwot Lakica answered

this question with distinction and clarity, some slightly favoring one component or another, others emphasizing the symbiotic relationship between
the various facets of peacebuilding. Agnes stressed that 'livelihood takes priority' but noted that accountability is also important because through the
'acknowledgment of mistakes [we] resist repetition.' Santa insisted on the importance of reconciliation, which 'requires the two parties to ask one another for permission to live in harmony.' For her part, Stella suggested that
there is something of a chicken-and-egg relationship between livelihood and
reconciliation. At one point she stressed the primacy of livelihood: 'Reconciliation is fine, but if I cannot eat, there is a problem. If you're dead, what's
to reconcile?' Later, she turned the coin on its head, arguing: 'Without
acceptance' of former captives and combatants by the community, there can
be 'no training, no livelihood.'

Finally, Grace shared her views on the various strands woven into the
peacebuilding process. The most formally educated of the four, she explored
certain nuances of the language around peace and justice. While Grace recognized forgiveness as vital to peacebuilding, she also stressed the crucial role of
livelihood in allowing community members to live a dignified life in material
terms. Interestingly, she posed economic well-being as a counterweight to formal notions of penal accountability. She questioned the value of having someone jailed for war atrocities or other crimes and the futility of "living with a
grudge," insisting that "Women can do without accountability, but not without livelihood." There could be "no peace," "with a perpetrator who made you
poor." Nevertheless, Grace also acknowledged the interconnections between
all three components of justice and healing, stating that reconciliation, livelihood, and accountability were "equal and interrelated, like brothers."[44]

Attitudes Toward Women's Empowerment

Several questions addressed the interviewees' sense of their own empowerment over time, their perception of protections against violence in their
community, and their perspectives on the government of Uganda. Agnes
described herself as being weak and unable to talk when she returned from
captivity, in contrast to the strength she now feels. Santa also remembers being unable to speak when first liberated from captivity. Prayer, she explained,
and the opportunity to tell her story in the reception center and since have
enabled her to have a positive attitude and to accept herself for the beloved
human being she is. As for Stella, she emphasizes that she is now able to talk
about her past experiences and to provide for her children. Grace is convinced

that she is stronger as a result of her time in captivity and her struggle upon her return: "I have more skills due to my suffering."

In cases of domestic violence, Agnes explained that the local council gathers the family of the abuser and the family of the victim to sort things out. Santa, in her interview, also pointed to the local council as an important resource in conflict resolution. Stella described a process through which the victim might first report an incident of violence to her neighbors and then to the police. However, she was somewhat qualified in her faith in law enforcement, stressing that police officers captive to their own avarice might be incapable of taking necessary action without the payment of a cash incentive. Grace asserted that "these days we have the law and local leaders to call on." Nevertheless, she emphasized that respect for women must be internalized within families and communities, not merely imposed by outside forces, in order for the incidence of gender-based violence to be lessened. When the police are called to respond to a report of domestic abuse, Grace insisted that the offender must have some degree of self-awareness and integrity for the intervention to be successful. If he is willing to change, Grace insisted, "he may learn his lesson."

Some WAN members were skeptical of the government's commitment to addressing the needs of war-affected Northern Ugandan women, suggesting that corruption and nepotism might distract public officials from postwar rehabilitation. One member referred to a unanimous resolution of the Ugandan Parliament in 2014, endorsing the WAN's petition calling on the government to establish a reparations fund for war survivors, on which the government has taken no action as of 2023.[45] She lamented the fact that while there had been compensation for the victims of the July 2010 al Shabab terrorist bombings in Kampala, no such payments were made to the women abducted by the LRA over twenty years of civil war.[46] An adequate response, she argued, would require the government to admit responsibility for wartime atrocities. She also recognized that such an outcome might require pressure from outsiders, including the United Nations.

Access to Education, Health Care, and Employment

All four Rwot Lakica interviewees identified the payment of school fees as a barrier to education for their children. Agnes praised her children's intelligence only to lament that, due to lack of funds, they all remained at home, helping her in cultivating crops. She specified that primary school fees are 360,000 Ugandan shillings per year (approximately US$120), whereas annual secondary school costs amount to 900,000 shillings (around US$300). Santa explained that she was able to pay the school fees of all her children at present but that doing so becomes more difficult as rates go up at the secondary level. Others identified early pregnancy as an additional barrier to girls' successful pursuit of their secondary studies.

For medical needs, all four WAN members have access to free health clinics in their communities and most of them have delivered several of their children in a clinic or hospital. However, three stressed that public health services in their area are very basic, and that specialized care in hospitals, including surgery, is far beyond the financial means of most people.

The interviewees painted a relatively bleak employment picture overall, particularly for women without advanced schooling. Santa drew a distinction between more accessible occupations such as farming and informal selling, on the one hand, and salaried employment opportunities with a business or agency, which are few and far between, on the other. Stella also stressed that women in Northern Uganda commonly hire themselves out to do casual labor, whether washing clothes or babysitting other people's children. Grace pointed out that unemployment levels are high, and that educated people may end up in jobs such as hawking goods, for which they are overqualified.

Property Ownership, Inheritance, and Women's Access to the Political Process

Questions regarding property ownership, inheritance rights, and women's political agency highlighted gaps between legislation and formal rules, on the one hand, and community practice or incomplete implementation of formal rules, on the other. In terms of property ownership, all four Rwot Lakica members clearly articulated that women of sufficient means could and sometimes did purchase property, either in their own name or in the name of one of their children. While Grace stated that some "families know the law," others do not. She and her fellow WAN members emphasized the daunting practical impediments to women's effective enjoyment of their land and property rights.

Interviewees suggested an even more marked divide between women's de jure and de facto rights with respect to inheritance. Despite constitutionally mandated equal inheritance rights for daughters and sons, Agnes described the community practice whereby the property goes to a male child upon the death of the father. In the case of the death of the husband, she explained, the wife's prospects were dependent on the relatives of her deceased spouse—she might inherit all his property, a portion, or none at all. Santa said something very similar, pointing to the Acholi tradition by which a woman "marries out" of her community of birth and hence cannot inherit from the father. As for inheriting her husband's estate, this depends on his family's inclinations. Stella had a slightly different take on inheritance rights. In most cases the widow should be able to inherit from the husband's estate, she explained, although if he had more than one wife, she might inherit less. As for property descending from the father, she agreed with her fellow group member that a brother was more likely to inherit than a sister. Grace put it bluntly: women's right to inherit property exists only "in theory."

With respect to holding public office, all four WAN members indicated that women sometimes vie for public office, particularly at the local level. However, several acknowledged that the number of women serving in elected positions in Northern Uganda remains low.

Estimation of Women's Roles in the Community Overall

Finally, I asked all Rwot Lakica interviewees to indicate ways in which *"women are helping to make decisions about how to move your community forward."* Agnes painted a full tableau—'Women are struggling hard to participate in advocacy, development, trying to keep their kids in school, getting them to the hospital, and sharing information with [visitors] like you.' Santa was characteristically concise—'Women's groups help improve the lives of their members.' Stella stressed that 'women are working hard. The Women's Advocacy Network is a shining example of women's leadership.' Grace acknowledged that "some women are empowered," depending on their level of education, values, and attitude but cautioned that "men are still there with their strong views."

WAN INITIATIVES IN 2023

During the last phase of my field interviews, members of the Women's Advocacy Network expressed cautious optimism around reparations policy at the national level. In 2023 legislative momentum to resurrect the moribund Reparations Bill in Parliament resulted in consultations between legislators, WAN, and other NGO representatives. WAN members in particular insisted on specific language mandating assistance to survivors in tracing their relatives still missing since the end of the war. To the Women's Advocacy Network, meaningful reparations policy entails truth-telling on all sides, including the government's accounting for its failure to protect civilians during the war.[47]

Figure 10. Mandate of the Women's Advocacy Network, Gulu, Northern Uganda, J. Moore, 2023.

WEAVING TOGETHER THE INSIGHTS OF WOMEN'S ADVOCACY GROUP MEMBERS

The four main themes that emerged from the focus group and individual interviews with members of the Gulu-based Women's Advocacy Network entail their gratitude for the moral support of their peers in trauma healing; their demand for more affordable and adequate education and health care; their commitment to advocacy to promote women's property and inheritance rights; and, critically, their insistence on government accountability for its role in the LRA War. These themes continued to play out in the interviews with women in the districts of Nwoya, Pader, and Kitgum.

Alany pa Mony Lit and Uketu wan Kwene in Nwoya and Pader

The women of Alany pa Mony Lit (Alany) and Uketu wan Kwene (Uketu) live in rural parishes in the Nwoya and Pader Districts of the Acholi Sub-region of Northern Uganda. As illustrated in the map of Uganda printed opposite the first page of this chapter, Nwoya is west of Gulu, and Pader is located east of Gulu and south of Kitgum.[48] Alany and Uketu are two among a network of grassroots women's community groups with historical linkages to the Refugee Law Project. Both groups have collaborated with RLP's field office located in Gulu Municipality, the headquarters town for Gulu District and the second-largest city in Uganda after Kampala. Support from RLP has ebbed and flowed over the years, given the evolving political dynamics in Uganda. Such developments include the passage by the Ugandan Parliament of the Anti-Homosexuality Act in 2023 and the foreseeable negative impact of such policies on external foundation support.[49] Nevertheless, Alany and Uketu retain their connections to RLP and appreciate occasional visits to their communities on the part of current and past RLP staff. Like the community groups affiliated with the Women's Advocacy Group and HURIFO, Alany pa Mony Lit and Uketu wan Kwene are largely autonomous, existing by virtue of their own microsavings programs and collective subsistence activities.

The Refugee Law Project was founded in 1999 as the action-oriented research arm of Makerere University Law School's Human Rights and Peace Centre (HURIPEC). RLP has its main office in Kampala, Uganda. RLP staff conduct research, publish human rights reports, and offer outreach and training for self-sustaining community groups. They advocate for and assist urban refugees and those living in encamped settlements in various parts of the country; and they prioritize the needs of internally displaced and returnee populations affected by the two-decade-plus civil war in Northern Uganda as well as refugees from neighboring countries like South Sudan. An important focus of RLP's work in Northern Uganda is the physical and psychosocial rehabilitation of war survivors and refugees. In this sense RLP is both a research-based advocacy organization and a direct service provider. While RLP is not a community-based organization per se, it is closely linked to CBOs and individuals who reside in the rural parishes and sub-counties of Northern Uganda. RLP's tightly imbedded relationship to communities and war survivors in the North is facilitated by the fact that its staff in the Gulu and Kitgum field offices are native Acholi speakers who themselves lived through the LRA War.[50] Since the conflict began winding down in 2006, RLP has engaged in a variety of reintegration and human rights empowerment activities, including collaborating with women's and men's community groups engaged in reconciliation, group healing, collective agriculture, microcredit, and violence prevention initiatives.

IDENTIFYING A RESEARCH FACILITATOR EXPERIENCED IN TRAUMA HEALING

On my first visit to Kampala in 2010, I had the opportunity to meet with several members of the staff of Makerere University Law School's Human Rights and Peace Centre who were involved in the work of the Refugee Law Project. These colleagues provided a comprehensive overview of the priorities and philosophy of the organization. Nevertheless, on arriving in Gulu in July 2016 to conduct the first phase of my field research, I still had a limited understanding of the work of RLP on the ground. I was grateful to get an appointment with Fred Ngomokwe, then coordinator of RLP's Gulu field office.

I explained to Mr. Ngomokwe that I wished to interview women war survivors working in grassroots community groups and asked him if he might facilitate my introduction to women willing to share their experiences during and since the war. He suggested two groups: the women of Alany pa Mony Lit, survivors of sexual violence living in Nwoya District; and the women of Uketu wan Kwene in Pader District, relatives of "lost ones"—individuals who had disappeared during the war and remained unaccounted for.[51] Within two days Mr. Ngomokwe and I set out by back roads in a locally hired car to the home parishes of the Alany and Uketu women's groups. There Fred served as facilitator, interpreter, and technical consultant for focus group and individual interviews with members of the respective women's groups. The insights derived from these interviews formed the conceptual foundation for the two subsequent research trips I organized to Nwoya and Pader in June 2017 and July 2018 as well as another trip during the final phase of the research in 2023.

In addition to providing expert interpretation and linguistic insights, Fred educated me on the nature and legacy of the LRA War, in particular its impact on the Acholi people of Northern Uganda. He endeavored to impress on me the historical and contemporary marginalization of the Acholi, the virtual containment of the Rebel War in Northern Uganda, and the apparent disdain of the national government for the plight of the Acholi during the conflict and since. Fred pointed to President Yoweri Museveni's tendency to blame the LRA War on the Acholi themselves: "Acholis," the president famously said during the conflict, "are like grasshoppers [trapped] in a bottle biting themselves to death." Mr. Ngomokwe further elaborated that,

Figure 11. Fred Ngomokwe and members of the Women's Advocacy Network, Gulu, Northern Uganda. Photo by J. Moore 2023.

for Museveni, the LRA War "started in Northern Uganda, was affecting Northern Uganda, and was killing Northern Uganda." The president, he explained, viewed the conflict as a "family issue"—a problem for Northern Ugandans but not for Ugandans as a whole.[52]

Like Victoria Nyanjura and Winifred Arima Abalo, who also served as cultural and linguistic interpreters for the Ugandan community visits, Fred Ngomokwe was raised in Northern Uganda where he and his family experienced and survived the LRA war. Mr. Ngomokwe's mother tongue is Acholi. He grew up in Gulu District and completed his secondary education at St. Joseph's College Layibi in Gulu Municipality. He graduated in 2009 from Kampala International University where he earned a bachelor's degree in social work and social administration, which prepared him for a career in peacebuilding and conflict management. Fred became the RLP field office coordinator in Gulu in 2013.

Mr. Ngomokwe is particularly known within RLP, Ugandan, and broader transitional justice circles for his experience working with male survivors of sexual assault. He has worked extensively with two community groups based in Lukai Parish in Nwoya District, one composed of male and the other of female survivors of sexual violence. Both groups were created to provide mutual support for their members and to reduce stigma in the community.[53] When asked how he came to this work, Fred explained that he and his friends and family were painfully aware of the high incidence of sexual violence against women during the LRA War. Years later in 2009, upon completion of his university degree, the Juba Peace Accords implementation process was underway. Fred was hired to work with an International Criminal Court–sponsored project in which he conducted interviews with Acholi-speaking survivors of the LRA War. One day during his field work, a local man confided in him, "I hear you speaking of 'survivors'—where would you put me?" Fred responded, "Tell me your story." He was profoundly impacted by the man's experience of sexual assault and his willingness to speak of his trauma.

In subsequent testimonial sessions, men continued to share their painful and buried memories. Fred developed an ability to listen and foster trust. "My approach starts with a story," he explains, "to lead you to understand you are not the only one who has suffered. I believe so much in stories." These interactions became pivotal in the direction of Fred's future work counseling and advocating for male victims of rape and solidifying his broader commitment to postconflict social healing for men, women, and their communities. Since 2013 he has worked with numerous men's and women's community groups under the auspices of Makerere University's Refugee Law Project. While such groups are gender-specific, they often operate side by side. In fact, in Lukai Parish it was the men who helped inspire the women to form their own group and call it Alany pa Mony Lit (Mistreatment of Women Is Painful). As neighbors, relatives, and fellow survivors, the women were moved by the men's willingness to share their painful experiences in the respectful company of those who carry similar burdens.

Refugee Law Project's Work with Women Survivors of Violence

Overall, RLP researchers and field staff such as Fred Ngomokwe recognize that men and women alike require trusting and safe environments to address the consequences of their past trauma. At the same time, RLP staff acknowledge the fraught nature of male and female relationships in a society still emerging from a prolonged conflict saturated by multiple layers of violence. Women remain particular targets of brutality and bear disproportionate burdens of exploitation and entrenched poverty. Yet, in emerging from the period of armed conflict, many women have successfully under-taken new roles in the home and community, whether to triumph over such abuses or as a matter of sheer survival. Clearly, "gender empowerment" in Acholiland remains a mixed bag of aspiration, realization, and frustration, as men and women continue to grapple with the legacy of the past as well as current social realities, including resurgent homophobia manifested in the 2023 Anti-Homosexuality Act.[54] The challenges of shifting gender relations are particularly pronounced in the face of increased rates of unemployment among men; persistently high rates of illiteracy, early marriage, and mater-nal mortality among women; and widespread unhealed trauma in the pop-ulation at large.[55] In the dynamic social climate in Northern Uganda today, there is a fragile and growing commitment to strengthened partnerships between men and women in the home and in society at large.[56] RLP staff and community group members, male and female alike, foster collaborative projects and consultations with women and men at the community level. The shape and impact of such community efforts are revealed in conversa-tions with the women of Alany pa Mony Lit and Uketu wan Kwene, ana-lyzed in the sections below.

TALKING WITH MEMBERS OF ALANY PA MONY LIT

Lucy Okello and the other women of Alany pa Mony Lit reside in the vicin-ity of Lukai Parish in Alero, a sub-county of Nwoya District bordering Gulu District to the west. The group comprises women who are survivors of rape and sexual violence perpetrated against them during the LRA conflict. The women of Alany pa Mony Lit participate in a broad spectrum of community empowerment activities. Like other peacebuilding groups in Northern Uganda, Alany operates as both a community savings and loan association and a framework for mutual support and collective action for its members.

Alany pa mony lit is an Acholi phase meaning "Mistreatment of women is painful." As a discussion with Fred Ngomokwe revealed, in Acholi usage the term *alany* connotes humiliation of various kinds. *Alany pa mony lit* is a euphemism for the sexual violation of women, a common occurrence often attributed to the LRA throughout the conflict. However, in the case of Lukai Parish, given the history of widespread attacks on civilians by UPDF and LRA rebels alike, it is also a thinly veiled reference to the rape of women by the army. Many of the women of Alany were assaulted by UPDF soldiers.

In contrast to the women of Rwot Lakica who are acculturated to the urban setting of Gulu Town, Lucy Okello and the other women of Alany pa

Mony Lit reside in a rural environment and spend much of their time cultivating crops, tending orchards, and keeping livestock. All six members of Alany who took part in the interviews are ethnic Acholi and Catholic. Most of the women gave birth to their children at home, whether alone or with a traditional birth attendant. All are native Acholi speakers, although one also speaks some English and another some Swahili. One group member did not attend school and the others attended between two and six years at the primary level.

Alany members are proud of their farming activities and other cooperative endeavors. They point to a moment in 2014 when the community of Lukai came together to rebuild after much of their settlement was destroyed in a wildfire. The community is known for its agricultural productivity, particularly the cultivation of groundnuts and a variety of trees, such as pine, eucalyptus, banana, and yellow acacia. Alany pa Mony Lit members also value the mutual assistance they provide and receive from their fellow group members, both emotionally and materially. They point to their progress in fighting the stigma linked to sexual assault and their ability to open up to one another as peers with mutual compassion.

As was the case in conversations with the other women's groups, the focus of the discussion was not on the interviewees' traumatic experiences. I asked no pointed questions about sexual violence at the hands of government soldiers. As in other locations, some women were moved to share their personal experiences in response to specific questions concerning childbirth or their pursuit of treatment for enduring injuries resulting from an assault. They also alluded to past experiences in expressing their appreciation for the power of friendship among Alany members.

Focus Group with Alany pa Mony Lit, 2016

The women of Alany pa Mony Lit first assembled in a group to share their impressions on the interlocking themes of reconciliation, livelihood, and accountability.[57] We conducted our focus group conversation sitting on a large tarpaulin on the ground under the full sun, sharing groundnuts, which the women had harvested and boiled in the shell. In Lukai Village the circle included eight women—six group members, me, and one law intern; and two men—another intern and our interpreter, Fred Ngomokwe. Fred made initial introductions and shared with group members the context of my book project on women peacebuilders in postconflict communities in Northern Uganda and Sierra Leone. In the same pattern followed with the other community groups in Gulu, Pader, and Kitgum, we started with the theme of *reconciliation*.

Three perceptions of reconciliation stand out among those shared by members of Alany pa Mony Lit. First, reconciliation is often described with reference to the Acholi practice of *mato oput*—the ritual sharing of the "bitter herb," traditionally conducted to reconcile two families after an interclan killing. Second, reconciliation is typically understood as a collective process embraced by the community in order to restore unity. Third, Alany members share a common concern that reconciliation with the government has not yet been achieved in Northern Uganda. Public officials have not acknowledged the wrongdoing of state actors during the war nor have they compensated many of those war survivors who suffered specific injuries—whether material, physical, or psychological. These three impressions—the importance of ceremony, the role of the collective, and the missing element of state accountability—overlap to some extent with the understandings shared among the members of Rwot Lakica and the Women's Advocacy Network, who emphasized forgiveness, elder-led mediation, and government honesty. Alany group members also emphasized the qualities of unity and healing as paramount ingredients in the process of reconciliation.

Of the six women of Alany pa Mony Lit who joined in the 2016 focus group discussion, one was in her forties and the others in their fifties. Group members Filda and Esther, both fifty-three, stressed that *mato oput* traditionally takes place at the clan level. They described the typical context in which an act of violence was perpetrated by an individual of one clan against a member of another. In such situations members of the offender's clan would sit down to pool their resources prior to the ceremony. In this way they were able to pay a particular form and level of compensation to the victim's family at the conclusion of the rite and on behalf of the offender's clan. Esther stressed the essential communal character of *mato oput*: because it is the clan that assumes responsibility for wrongdoing by its member, clan leaders must agree to the amount and nature of any compensation.[58] Understandably, it is something of a stretch for Northern Ugandans to adapt traditional cleansing ceremonies designed for interclan killings to the postwar context, especially if there is a lack of community ties between perpetrators and survivors and given the passage of time since the acts of violence occurred. Group members hope that *mato oput* and other cleansing rites will become a more common means of reconciling perpetrators and survivors of atrocities associated with the LRA War.

One Alany member addressed a particular challenge for war-affected people in Acholiland—namely, the need for reconciliation between the government of Uganda and survivors of atrocities perpetrated not by insurgents but by agents of the state. Having acknowledged that reconciliation is vital to community unity, she stressed that the process is best initiated by the individual soldier or other state actor who is ready to acknowledge wrongdoing. Where such individual accountability is not realistic, she suggested that the government as a unified body might accept responsibility for the collective offenses committed by its troops during the LRA War or since. The problem, she cautioned, is that the notion of government accountability remains largely in the theoretical realm. The government has not yet made a clear acknowledgment of state wrongdoing during the Rebel War, and many victims remain uncompensated. This puts community groups in a vulnerable position when they ask the government to account for sexual assault and other atrocities carried out by its soldiers. Until such time that the government acknowledges its complicity, she cautioned, 'the people live in fear.'

The Alany focus group then moved on to a discussion of *livelihood* or *tic-cing*. Three common threads emerged representing group members' understandings of livelihood—sustainability, collectivity, and investing for their children's futures. For her part, the Alany vice-chairwoman Aida emphasized four manifestations of *tic-cing*: the fruit of one's creative energy; the generation of cash to purchase other goods; collective efforts, particularly in the domain of agriculture; and productive activities that require specialized training. The finance chairwoman Alice talked about livelihood in terms of "situational productivity," which for her involved alternating seasons of tree cultivation with periods of brewing alcohol. In detailing the chain of production and distribution, she highlighted the importance of human energy itself as an investment resource. To illustrate, she described the process of fermenting cassava and teasingly identified George, one of the two RLP summer interns, as a potential customer.

Lucy Okello[59] spoke of livelihood as an investment for her children's future needs as well as their immediate sustenance. By way of example, she pointed to her cultivation of banana trees and her hopes to cultivate pine, eucalyptus, and fruit trees in the future. Concluding their roundtable discussion of *tic-cing*, the Alany chairwoman Evelyn[60] suggested that successful livelihood activities satisfy a combination of short- and long-term goals—livelihood entails the family's daily consumption of a portion of their harvested crops as well as the sale of any surplus to generate cash. Such funds can be utilized in life-sustaining ways, including replacing livestock lost during the war or paying for school fees for children in the coming months. She highlighted the value of Alany members' collective activities, both their cooperative agricultural projects and other microfinance activities organized through their village savings and loan association.

Finally, Alany pa Mony Lit members turned to the concept of *accountability*. The term *adwogi metic* roughly translates as "wages due," signifying either cash for labor or "just deserts" in the sense of consequences for one's actions. Our focus group discussion of *adwogi metic* expressed the strong resonance that Alany members perceive between livelihood and accountability—the former being material (the fruit of one's labor), and the latter ethical (the fruit of one's character). Our exchange of views on *adwogi metic* was nuanced and slippery, in part because accountability in Acholi connotes both financial accounting and a sort of moral bookkeeping. Group members sketched out a variety of illustrations of accountability: their efforts to establish the historical record, petitioning the government for compensation, their drive to "even out the score," their need for courage in seeking compensation, and their yearning for a renewed sense of unity between the people and the government.

The vice-chairwoman Aida defined accountability as the appropriate consequences of a past event, whether positive or negative. She also talked about accountability as a potential means of restoring the broken covenant between community members and their leaders, even if the government has yet to answer this call. Aida identified three components of accountability—establishing the record, acknowledgment, and apology. She also emphasized that self-advocacy by community members is now happening for the first time. For example, when the Women's Advocacy Network petitioned the Ugandan Parliament in 2014, individual women peacebuilders from their area supported the call for reparations for the people of Northern Uganda. Several Alany members emphasized the courage that women must summon to speak to outside agencies about their suffering and the burdens they carried during the war.[61]

Filda pointed to the importance of documenting the animals and resources they had lost during the war in any claim for compensation. She observed that while values of acceptance and forgiveness are all well and good, the return of lost items is also essential as is the material compensation of war-disabled people like herself, who deserve support in providing for their biological children and the orphaned children they have taken under their wing. The Alany chairwoman Evelyn completed the circle, speaking of *adwogi metic* as the link between the government's authentic plea for forgiveness and the survivors' fervent hope for reparations. She clarified that although losses can seldom be fully compensated, the Ugandan president will be able to restore some vital measure of social unity once he has sincerely apologized for the injuries the people suffered during the war.

Individual Interviews with Alany pa Mony Lit, 2016

Each Alany pa Mony Lit member who participated in the morning focus group volunteered to take part in the individual interviews scheduled after lunch, following the Peacebuilders' Questionnaire[62] used for all nine Ugandan and Sierra Leonean women's community groups. I interviewed Aida, Alice, Lucy, Filda, and Evelyn, all of whom gave me permission to quote them by name.[63] As with the focus group conversations, Fred Ngomokwe provided Acholi interpretation for the one-on-one interviews.[64] We conducted most of our individual interviews on a bench inside a cool, thatched-roof circular hut serving as a meeting place for the community.

Life Circumstances and Experiences

The members of Alany pa Mony Lit who participated in the focus group and individual interviews in 2016 ranged in age from forty-four to fifty-six years of age. Four speak only Acholi, one Acholi with some facility in English, and one Acholi with a bit of Swahili. All six are Catholic. All six were sexually assaulted by UPDF soldiers. One Alany member is HIV positive and has no children. The others have between two and six kids. All of them gave birth to their children at home. Filda, for example, gave birth to her six children alone, with quick labors, and even cut their umbilical cords herself, as she matter-of-factly explained. She lost four of her six children, likely due to malaria she thought. Filda explained that she did not go to school because, after her mother died, she was raised by an aunt who lacked sufficient funds for her school fees. The others attended primary school for between three and seven years. As for the Alany vice-chairwoman Aida, she left school in P-7 without sitting for her exams. Daughters, she explained, are not the priority when the family has limited funds for school fees.

Community Involvement

A popular question on the survey asks each woman which aspect of her community work brings her the most pride and joy. The common themes among

Alany members were their agricultural productivity, their efforts to alleviate the shame of sexual assault, and the mutual support between group members. The vice-chairwoman Aida first pointed to her farm work: 'I am proud
of what I produce out of my sweat.' She then emphasized her role in fighting
stigma in her community, acknowledging the peer-counseling training Alany members have received from staff of the Refugee Law Project. The Alany
finance chairwoman Alice also highlighted their community activism: 'I'm
proud of our coming out as a team of victims who have been raped at some
time in this community.' She also expressed pride in her community's increased agricultural productivity, which went from nominal cultivation,
while they were in the relocation camps, to prodigious agricultural yields over
the past seven years. Their harvests include rice, groundnuts, sweet potatoes,
cassava, and tik trees, a local species of hardwood.

A subsequent survey question concerns the members' priorities for future
group activities. The vice-chairwoman Aida stressed the need for Alany
members to work collectively on multiple fronts: 'People have come all the
way [home] from the [IDP] camps, so we need to impact knowledge in the
community. Agriculture is the backbone so additional training in new methods is needed. Advocacy, which has enabled us to speak out, requires . . .
more networking.' The finance chairwoman Alice hopes their bee project will
grow. She also recollected the disaster in 2014 in which her two houses burned
to the ground: 'When I lost everything due to the wildfire, the group members came together to help us with food and supplies. This showed us how
unified our group was. This unity is continuing. The group supports those
who have lost loved ones.'

Alany members had pointed comments on the subject of dispute resolution within the family and community, an activity in which women are playing more central roles since the LRA War. The finance chairwoman Alice
stressed a local preference for "ironing things out" within the family but also
indicated that community leaders and the LC 1 (village council members) can
be called on for assistance if required. In addition to her leadership in Alany,
Alice is also the finance chairwoman of another community-based organization that mediates land disputes. Conflicts over boundaries are high-stakes
contests that without mediation might otherwise end in violence.

Interrelationships Between Reconciliation, Livelihood, and Accountability

As with the four interviewees from Rwot Lakica, the members of Alany pa
Mony Lit answered the question relating to the interrelated facets of peace-

building with thoughtfulness and nuance. To an even greater extent than Rwot Lakica members, who sometimes prioritized livelihood, the members of Alany tended to see the interdependence of the three components of community transformation. For the Alany chairwoman Evelyn, 'they are interrelated—if they're used concurrently, they can yield one fruit: unity and acceptance.'[65] Lucy Okello, the youngest group member, promoted a particular succession for the three facets of peacebuilding: 'reconciliation . . . first, then accountability, and then livelihood.'

Attitudes Toward Women's Empowerment

Various common themes emerged in the responses of the members of Alany pa Mony Lit to three questions concerning their perspectives on government accountability, the changing nature of women's status since the war, and available avenues of redress for violence against women in the family and community. With regard to the government of Uganda, some interviewees suggested that, left to its own devices, the state is self-interested and actively discriminatory against the people of the North. At the same time, they expressed confidence that the state is capable of responding to pressure and is slowly doing so, thanks to the collective action of women's networks and with the support of advocacy groups like the Refugee Law Project.

Some Alany members took a skeptical view of the president's motivations, suggesting that although Museveni purported to 'speak for everyone,' his policies were short on implementation, and what little action taken was thanks to pressure from nongovernmental agencies. One member stated: 'In Northern Uganda, it's as if we don't have a president. Our leaders come on our side when they need our votes. Our president is more of a dictator, and yet the people form the country.' Another member charged the government with 'open discrimination, massive killing, raping of men, raping of women.' Alongside some skepticism that the president would accept responsibility for the atrocities that occurred, group members expressed their gratitude that 'at least we have the capacity to speak the truth without fear because there is someone behind us—Refugee Law Project.'

In terms of women's status, all the Alany interviewees feel that they are stronger today in their families and communities, playing key roles in agriculture, business, and family decision-making. Once again, this evolution did not happen spontaneously and requires ongoing organization and activism to maintain. One member, while skeptical of the state's commitment to women's empowerment in the North, also saw certain benefits for going it alone: 'Women have become stronger than ever, but even so, the government doesn't care about us, and this pushes us toward further advocacy.' Filda gave a moving rendition of women's changing roles: 'During the war we were like young ones.' After the Peace Accords, 'the way we were resettled was as painful as the way we were taken to the camps.' As for now, 'I get emotionally rehabilitated in the group, which gives me strength in life. There is always vulnerability, and the impact on my children is difficult to see, and yet I have the capacity to help my children.' In a kindred spirit, Lucy Okello emphasized that a woman may now take on land ownership and may even be in a position to manage the land of her deceased father: 'Equality is what accounts for this. The Constitution gives us this right.'[66]

As for protection against gender violence, Alany members describe a process whereby the aggrieved individual goes to family and village leaders, followed by appeals to various tiers of higher authority as necessary. The finance chairwoman Alice addressed the initial level of conflict resolution between those directly affected: 'Respect has to be given. If something occurs, we sit down to iron it out.' Filda gave the example of an abusive husband who was withholding the children's school fees but eventually paid them once a local advocacy group wrote him a letter on his wife's behalf explaining his obligations. Lucy Okello pointed to the positive impact of dispute mediation by community elders, 'who will recommend dialogue rather than blows.' Their chairwoman Evelyn injected a note of caution regarding the impact of dispute resolution on wartime abuses: 'The violence and humiliation that a woman receives from her family is easier to resolve than violations by the army.'

Access to Education, Health Care, and Employment

Like the women of the Women's Advocacy Network, the members of Alany are reminded on a daily basis of their limited opportunities as women in the arenas of education, health care, and employment. The vice-chairwoman Aida described her difficulties financing the education of her hearing-impaired child, for whom the fees to attend an institution for pupils with special needs amounted to 80,000 Ugandan shillings (around US$25) per term.[67] She noted that similar barriers exist for health care, with its 'big gap in the provision of services. The hospital writes a prescription, but it has to be paid for.' Finally, Aida lamented the lack of public service employment opportunities at the village level. For this reason, income-generating opportunities for women are largely limited to agricultural day labor and piecework such as laundry and tailoring. For her part, Filda pointed to recent efforts to improve educational outcomes for young women, including a new local ordinance that imposes fines on parents who do not send their children to school. She stressed that most parents indeed have the funds to pay the relatively modest school fees that are assessed, particularly in the primary years. 'The issue is will.' She pointed to a case where the local authorities seized a family's goat and sold it to pay for their child's school fees.

Lucy addressed both open doors and barriers that women face in all the social service sectors. In terms of education, there are schools, but family support must be forthcoming. In health care, antiretroviral medications for HIV-positive individuals are available, but to obtain them one must be ready to walk to the hospital in Gulu Town. There are opportunities for employment in the formal sector, such as a position at the farm registry in the district of Pader, but only for those who have obtained a certain level of secondary or postsecondary education. Lucy Okello ended on an upbeat note. For women who left school in the primary years there are special classes provided with their needs in mind. Lucy spoke of several women she knows who are working hard to improve their lives through adult education.

Property Ownership, Inheritance, and Women's Access to the Political Process

The members of Alany pa Mony Lit painted a nuanced picture of women's property, inheritance, and political rights. For the vice-chairwoman Aida, the purchase of land by women is 'very possible,' including in her case, where she was raped and subsequently abandoned by her husband yet has the option of buying in her own name. For married couples, however, the husband may block the wife's attempt to purchase land in her own right. As for inheritance, Aida acknowledged that the realities of polygamy may pose challenges for women, especially if they are young or have no children. In terms of political office, she pointed to the recent election of several women as members of Parliament, stressing that women's activism 'starts in the home,' but does not end there.

Lucy Okello took somewhat of a good-news-bad-news approach to gender and the law in contemporary Northern Uganda. She stated frankly that while a single woman might purchase land freely, for a married woman 'domestic violence might result' if she were to seek to buy land without her husband's permission. Inheritance rights seem a bit hazy. It is 'very normal for women to inherit when the husband dies since his wealth was amassed partly through her efforts,' according to Lucy. But when women are the children of the deceased, she sketches a different picture altogether: "When the father dies, first the brothers inherit, then the sisters."

In contrast, the Alany chairwoman Evelyn outlined a strategy for how women could best exercise their legal right to purchase property: 'Women need to control their own finances. When women have a brain to think and act and use their own money' they can do so. 'If you wait for the man, he may block' you. She stressed that 'women have equal inheritance rights. To realize [these rights, they must] start collaborating with their brothers from an early age, to become peers.' This idea of the need for partnership between women and men is an important theme, expressed by women peacebuilders across Northern Uganda and Sierra Leone and discussed throughout our text.

Estimation of Women's Roles in the Community Overall

The members of Alany pa Mony Lit described a variety of contributions women were making to help develop their community. 'Charity begins from home,' said the vice-chairwoman Aida. 'The way you take leadership in your house should be exemplary so even your children become a point of reference of how simple it is to become a leader in the community. [As] women become opinion leaders that also shows that you are leading a positive life in the community that can transform the community.' 'Women are very fast in decision-making,' stated the finance chairwoman Alice. 'They will never surrender or retreat.' For her part, Filda stressed that 'women's decisions are moving the community forward. Both men and women have been empowered in decision-making regarding land, domestic issues, and domestic violence. We've seen women reporting cases to the police and legal services, [and] women bring husbands before clan leaders to expose them for overdrinking.' For Lucy Okello, quoted in the epigraph to this chapter, 'Women are like teachers everywhere. They don't go with a lot of aggression. They take things systematically. They have a lot of mercy.'

New Challenges and Opportunities for Alany pa Mony Lit in 2023

The passing of the chairwoman Evelyn on July 17, 2023, marked a great loss for Alany pa Mony Lit in terms of friendship and leadership. Nevertheless, their collective commitment remains strong. During the final round of interviews that year, participants spoke of challenges facing the group. One member noted that their bank loan applications were typically denied due to age discrimination and the stigma they faced for their open identification as survivors of sexual assault. When asked about the prospects for govern-

Figure 12. Members of Alany pa Mony Lit, Nwoya District, Northern Uganda. Photo by J. Moore, 2017.

ment support or reparations, she laughed and insisted that 'waiting for the government is like chasing after a dead chicken.' In the face of the impediments they face, Alany members stress the healing power in the group. The finance chairwoman Alice spoke of the importance of the emotional support they give and receive. The vice-chairwoman Aida put it simply: 'Without this group, I would not be here.'

Weaving Together the Insights of Alany pa Mony Lit Members

Four powerful impressions emanated from the focus group and individual interviews with members of Alany pa Mony Lit over the seven-year research period: group members' pride in their expertise and initiative in agriculture; their strength in fighting the stigma of sexual assault; their commitment to women's empowerment in the economic and political domains despite great odds; and their relentless advocacy for reparations and acknowledgment from the government for its role in the LRA War while resisting any tendency to engage in magical thinking in this regard. Many of these themes will continue to resonate as we turn to conversations with women's community collectives in Pader and Kitgum.

TALKING WITH MEMBERS OF UKETU WAN KWENE

The women of Uketu wan Kwene (Where will you put us?) reside in Dure Parish, within the traditional Paibwore Chiefdom, located in Latanya Subcounty of Pader District.[68] Like the women of Alany pa Mony Lit, they have collaborated with the Refugee Law Project, benefiting from training and outreach activities. Whereas the women of Alany came together as survivors of sexual assault by Ugandan soldiers, the women of Uketu all lost family members in massacres during the LRA War. The fates of their loved ones remain unknown and unacknowledged by the government of Uganda. Like the women of Alany, many women of Uketu engage in farming—including cultivating tomatoes, beans, maize, *simsim* (sesame), cassava, potatoes, and groundnuts and raising chickens. Agricultural yields in Pader over the 2016–2023 period have been less than in Nwoya District due to the dryer terrain and reduced rainfall. A drought in 2016–17 hit the area particularly hard, and severely parched conditions were again apparent during the last phase of research in 2023.

The women of Uketu wan Kwene dedicated a cultural center in 2016 as a living memorial to their loved ones killed or disappeared during the civil war.[69] Between 1990 and 2003, 413 families in Paibwore Chiefdom were victims of a series of attacks, massacres, and abductions carried out by both Ugandan Army and LRA forces. The community lost family members, homes, and livelihoods. Because the cultural center is located within the compound of Rwot (Chief) Dermoi—at that time the leader of the Paibwore Chiefdom—certain ceremonial duties were carried out by the late Daker Nighty, wife of the Rwot, who died of heart disease in 2018.[70] Prior to her death, and while the Rwot was absent, Daker Nighty would welcome and orient visitors to the center. She also acted as an informal ombudsperson for women's issues within the chiefdom. In her personal capacity, Nighty chose to become a member of Uketu wan Kwene, for which she served as finance secretary up until her death in 2018.[71]

On July 16, 2016, the day of our initial focus group and individual interviews, the Rwot and Daker invited me and the two Refugee Law Project interns to take part in a tour of the cultural center. It is housed in a traditional mud-brick and thatched-roof hut of the sort commonly used as homes and community spaces throughout the region. On display were household necessities, including pots for water and cooking and animal skin mats for sleeping as well as important tools and symbols of Acholi culture, such as shields, spears, sisal baskets, and mingling sticks (mixing spoons). The cultural center was created to serve as a place of remembrance and historical record. Hanging from the walls of the hut were banners with hand-painted chronological notations indicating the dates and places of specific attacks and listing the individual names of those who were killed or disappeared. The place had the air of a house of worship—calm, somber, dark, and cool. It had been dedicated by community members earlier that year in a traditional ceremony for calling back their lost ones. Around the outside circular wall of the beehive-shaped building are soft-hued paintings of Acholi words and symbols, including a grieving parent kneeling in profile, the symbol of Uketu wan Kwene; a chain with the words *wek jong* (let my people go); and a dove and hand of friendship (see Figure 14).

The women of Uketu are proud of their cultural center, created to serve as a living memorial to their lost relatives as well as an educational and historical resource for their community and war-affected Northern Ugandans overall. Part of Uketu's community outreach work involves educating neighbors and other visitors about the history and ongoing challenges of their region. A tribute to their departed loved ones, the center also represents the community's demands for acknowledgment of its wartime suffering at the hands of the Ugandan government, which failed its people through acts of omission and commission. Uketu members are grateful for the training, advocacy, and moral support of the Refugee Law Project. The warmth and familiarity between community members and RLP staff was palpable as we sat down for our initial conversations.

Focus Group Discussion with Uketu wan Kwene, 2016

The five women who took part in the Uketu wan Kwene focus group were between twenty-four and sixty-five years of age, including the youngest and oldest women among the twenty that I interviewed in Northern Uganda over a seven-year period. Within the Rwot and Daker's compound, amid bright ornamental shrubs and flowering trees that provided shade from the hot sun, we were invited to sit on sturdy, brightly colored plastic chairs next to a small table with flowers. Like the Rwot Lakica and Alany pa Mony Lit focus groups, in which participants acknowledged but did not dwell on experiences of abduction and sexual assault, the Uketu focus group discussion did not start with the massacres or losses the women suffered during the war. Instead, individuals commented on these events when moved to do so or when pertinent to specific questions. As with the other focus groups, we started with the theme of *reconciliation*.

Six facets of *mato oput* emerge from the insights shared by the women of Uketu wan Kwene: reconciliation is a form of sharing, mediated and supported, that promotes unity, nonrepetition, and healing. There is a powerful sense among all the Uketu participants that reconciliation ensures community vitality and survival. Juxtaposed against this positive depiction of *mato oput* is the utter failure of the government of Uganda to make an official gesture of reconciliation to the people of Northern Uganda, a reality that some find deeply troubling.

Like the women of Alany pa Mony Lit, the women of Uketu wan Kwene spoke about the traditional ceremony of *mato oput*. Several participants suggested new potential uses for *mato oput*, notably instances of violence in the home, civil war atrocities, and abuses specifically requiring government accountability. Daker Nighty, fifty-two, insisted that '*mato oput* can come even in a situation when death has not occurred, [as] in a situation of domestic violence, where people are brought together to have a thorough look [and provide] counseling and guidance. Traditionally, we have a custom where we gather the sand and put our hands into it, vowing nonrepetition and unity.' Another member expressed considerable urgency regarding the application of *mato oput* to wartime offenses by the government: 'If you look thoroughly into the war in Uganda, it has left wounds. We can't heal the wound ourselves; we need external support.' Another stressed that reconciliation, particularly with the government, requires the acknowledgment of wrongdoing. Later she clarified: 'There is a need for acceptance on the side of the government that an incident of that kind—war, or conflict—has happened. That [acknowledgment] should be coupled with asking for forgiveness. . . . Without acknowledgment and forgiveness, there can be no *mato oput*.'[72]

The women of Uketu wan Kwene then moved on to address *livelihood* (*tic-cing*). They echoed some of the themes of Alany members, including the need for skills and training, and their drive to support their families. Jane Orama started with the literal meaning of *tic-cing* (the "fruit of one's hands") in her daily life: 'To me, livelihood is the different things you do using your hands to change your life for your family. I'm also a farmer since I lost my husband. I always [seek] subsistence to help raise the orphans I'm taking care of and send them to school.' Mary, at thirty-six, is the secretary of Uketu wan Kwene and a schoolteacher who is fluent in English. She had her own perspective on livelihood. Mary included among the diverse forms of *tic-cing* increased opportunities for those with advanced schooling: 'Livelihood to me is all about putting together the different skills and knowledge I have into action that shall yield a product; I cultivate maize, *simsim*, cassava, potatoes and ground nuts, but not enough for my family. [I have] a lot of interest but not much knowledge. I also work with the government, which helps to raise funds. I'm a primary school teacher.'

Finally, the women of Uketu wan Kwene turned to the topic of *accountability*. Like the members of Alany pa Mony Lit, they emphasized the need to account for wrongful conduct, using the term *adwogi metic* (wages due). Two important themes emerged: first, *adwogi metic* is the natural consequence of one's actions, the metaphorical "reaping of what one sows." Second, members identified the problem of "negative accountability," as in situations where blameworthy conduct goes unacknowledged and uncompensated. Daker Nighty addressed this second theme of "nonaccountability," putting the onus squarely on the government: 'We have a lot of missing persons; we know those whom we have buried, [but] the others we do not know if they are dead or alive. To me accountability is the positive result of an effort that has been put. [But there is] also a negative part. For instance, if my sister was abducted and there is no news [of her fate], I'm asking for accountability. Dominic Ongwen[73] can't take all accountability. The government must [as well].' Another Uketu member seconded Nighty's objection to state impunity: 'Accountability can't come if one-sided. If only the LRA but not the government gives accountability, [there's] no accountability. We've been left in this community with much disability, widows and orphans, which reopens old wounds.'

Individual Interviews with Uketu wan Kwene, 2016

We conducted the interviews with individual members of Uketu wan Kwene after the focus group discussion. These interviews were guided by the Peacebuilders' Questionnaire (found in Appendix 1 of this volume). My comparative analysis focuses on interviews with those three members of Uketu that Fred and I interviewed on multiple occasions—in 2016, 2017, 2018, and 2023.[74] Jane Orama, the late Daker Nighty, and Mary each gave me permission to quote them by name. Jane Orama is profiled in our Introduction. Daker

Nighty died of heart disease in the summer of 2018, a month after our last interview in July of that year.

Life Circumstances and Experiences

In 2016 Jane, Daker Nighty, and Mary were 65, 51, and 36 years of age, respectively. During our interviews, Jane spoke Acholi with no proficiency in English; Daker Nighty spoke some English; and Mary was proficient in English, code-switching between Acholi and English with ease. Jane and Mary are Catholic, and Daker Nighty, Protestant.

The women of Uketu wan Kwene of Paibwore Chiefdom are less geographically isolated than the members of Alany pa Mony Lit, owing to the fact that the home of the Rwot and Daker is situated along the asphalt road between Gulu and Kitgum. For most Uketu members, this means easier access to health care facilities, as reflected in their childbirth experiences. Jane gave birth to nine children, of whom the first six were born in a health center and the other three at home with the help of a traditional birth attendant. Daker Nighty gave birth to eight, one of whom died, and all were born in Kitgum Hospital. Mary delivered three children, all in Kitgum Hospital. In terms of schooling, Uketu members have generally completed a bit more formal education than members of the other women's groups, who on average left school after three or four years of primary instruction. Jane continued up to her sixth year of primary school (P-6), while Nighty completed P-7. Mary continued to the secondary school level, excelling in her lower secondary examinations and qualifying for employment as a primary school teacher.

Like the members of Rwot Lakica and Alany pa Mony Lit, the women of Uketu wan Kwene have experienced considerable loss in their lives. Alongside the pride and enthusiasm they express for their vital engagement in their community, Uketu members face significant challenges on a daily basis. In addition to war-related suffering, they face ongoing struggles with subsistence and access to adequate health care. The stark reality that 413 families in this area lost loved ones to war-related atrocities over a thirteen-year period during the LRA War is coupled with their everyday struggles to satisfy the basic needs of their families.

Community Involvement

When asked what aspect of her community work gives her the most satisfaction, Jane Orama identified their village savings and loan association (VSLA). For Daker Nighty and Mary, it was the cultural center they dedicated in February 2016. In speaking of their cultural center, Nighty explained that 'the history of the place represents the missing persons and our loved ones lost in the war.' As for their priorities in the future, each mentioned specific initiatives she felt should be undertaken or expanded. Jane would like to get involved in petty trading as a way to supplement her household income. Nighty spoke favorably of Uketu members' plans to one day register as a community-based organization for purposes of applying for grants and loans. Mary 'would like to see that our cultural center grows into one that will be referred to by many clans.'

Uketu members are committed mediators and express a strong preference for dispute resolution at the community level. Jane explained that when a dispute arises, 'the solution starts in the family. Members sit and strategize about the way forward. If the family fails to resolve the situation, then we bring others in, agencies [and] government structures, if the issues aren't well settled.' For her part, Daker Nighty stressed that ordinarily matters of domestic violence are resolved by the family members themselves and seldom need to be brought to the level of the chiefdom.

Interrelationships Between Reconciliation, Livelihood, and Accountability

Throughout the field research in Northern Uganda, individual group members' perspectives on the relationship between the various components of *yupu kuc* (peacebuilding) never failed to inspire interesting conversations and comparative analysis. In the case of Uketu wan Kwene—in contrast to Alany members—Nighty and Mary tended to prioritize livelihood. Jane, on the other hand, saw the three components as interdependent, with reconciliation the first among equals: 'Traditionally, they move together; the three should stand as one. [However,] if parents are divided, the future will not be there. . . . Reconciliation promotes unity so you can work together.' While Jane suggested that reconciliation promotes livelihood, Nighty put livelihood first. She emphasized that reconciliation does not happen instantaneously, requiring energy and hard work over time: 'Reconciliation comes after a very serious process. . . . Livelihood is at the top, then accountability, then reconciliation. Reconciliation is the culmination and requires the others to be established first.'[75]

Attitudes Toward Women's Empowerment

The members of Uketu wan Kwene were not shy about sharing their attitudes toward the national government, women's changing roles, and protections against gender-based violence in their community. They expressed considerable reservations about the central government's concern for war-affected people in the North, even suspecting that funds designated for Northern Uganda might be being diverted to other regions of the country. One put it simply: 'For us, living far away from Kampala, were it not for NGOs, we would not know anything about the government.'

Regarding the impact of the war on gender roles, Jane Orama was characteristically direct: 'Life has really changed. Before, women had less responsibility. Due to the war, many things happened. Women have become men in their homes.' On further reflection, she identified downsides as well as advances for women: 'I see a negative strength. We women shouldn't have to take on such responsibility without support. [Yet] women have become stronger to push for their issues, to advocate. There is a high level of freedom of speech for women and men respect that.' For her part, Mary stressed that despite the rhetoric of women's empowerment, the war and postwar periods exacerbated gender inequities to some extent: 'In the camps, women were active to provide for the children while men were waiting for relief. Things are changing. There's a shift toward women. Survival of the fittest and male privilege have been moved from the camps home. Now men just drink. Men do nothing. Men are more privileged, on the take. This doesn't make women stronger. They should be supported by men. Women have a very strong heart for their kids.'

Uketu members finally spoke out on gender-based violence. Jane insisted that women have the same rights as men to seek recourse against mistreatment in the home. Nighty struck a more cautionary tone regarding women's ability to access meaningful protections: 'There are situations [in] which men reject decisions of the women's group or chief's wife [and] where women are forced to go to the police. But the police are corrupt, and women have to pay cash to the police for transport to arrest the man. At times the women lack funds and the men go free.' For her part, Mary expressed confidence in the rule of law: 'If violence [in the home] leads to injury, that goes straight to the police.'

Access to Education, Health Care, and Employment

Jane, Nighty, and Mary echoed their fellow women peacebuilders in Gulu, Nwoya, and Kitgum in starkly illustrating the powerful barriers to women's enjoyment of their social and economic rights. With regard to education, Jane stated that 'women have the same ability and opportunity, but if you have many children, boys tend to be prioritized. . . . When funds are short, women are seen as a source of money through work . . . [and] the problem of [early] pregnancy is still there.' You will find girls 'even thirteen and pregnant.' As for salaried work, Jane was blunt that there is 'nothing here in terms of employment, unless a woman is hired in someone's garden.' Mary saw some movement in the domain of education: 'Girl child education depends on the financial strength of the family and that's why most stop at primary. If [the family is] educated, then they do push for girl child education.'

Property Ownership, Inheritance, and Women's Access to the Political Process

Like the women of Alany pa Mony Lit, Uketu wan Kwene members emphasized the gendered aspects of land tenure as well as traditional inheritance practices among the Acholi. Daker Nighty's take on property and inheritance rights distinguished between married and single women and between the rights of widows and daughters. She explained that cultural practice in Acholi 'determines women's ownership. Land is collective. If you marry, you have the right to own in that area. If you have funds, you can purchase land, but it's best to put [it] in your brother's name or consult with your husband.' As for inheritance, she explained, 'it's easy for a married woman to inherit from the husband, but harder for a girl to inherit from the father.' In explaining why daughters generally inherit 'a small share,' Nighty again referenced the Acholi tradition of "marrying out," clarifying that 'when girls marry, they go to the husband's place.' Mary stressed the particular vulnerability of women living in common law unions without a marriage certificate. 'Traditionally, a married woman can inherit what belongs to her husband. [As for] a cohabiting woman, she gets nothing.'

In their realism about persistent gender inequality, the members of Uketu wan Kwene see a silver lining—or breakable glass ceiling—in women's access to elected office. Jane, Nighty, and Mary agree that if women have the desire, skills, and charisma, they can succeed in the democratic process. As Daker Nighty stated, 'It is our dream that we will have a woman president.'[76] In explaining women's innate capacities for public service, she credits women's special abilities in caring for the hearth and home.

Estimation of Women's Roles in the Community Overall

Finally, Jane, Nighty, and Mary were asked to take the long view regarding women's contributions to community development. Their answers conveyed an inveterate spirit of optimism, mixed with a healthy dose of realism. Jane

Orama commented, 'These days, we see women giving advice about how to live in the community. These good-hearted women become exemplary . . . showing the young ones how to learn from the elders.' For her part, Mary warned that women have become victims of their own success. 'Women are struggling to move the community forward but aren't being supported,' she insisted. 'When women form a VSLA [self-funded community bank] and register at the sub-county level, the community thinks they no longer need help.' Mary's insights suggest that women's empowerment comes at a certain price. Even as the contributions of activist women are praised and valued by their relatives and neighbors, they are expected to assume ever-increasing responsibilities for the material upkeep of their families and the economic vitality of their communities.

New Challenges and Opportunities for Uketu wan Kwene in 2023

Like Alany pa Mony Lit in 2023, Uketu wan Kwene has experienced a change in leadership, in this case due to the passing of their former chairwoman Daker Nighty in 2018. Even five years after her death, conversations with Uketu members indicated they were still struggling with this loss, complicated by uncertainty regarding the continuity of Rwot Dermoi's position since the death of his wife. It is not clear whether he will continue as chief or if this role will be delegated to another community leader.

Despite the power vacuum at the chiefdom level, when our research team returned in July 2023 it was clear from conversations with Uketu members that the group remained active, particularly compared with other women's collectives in neighboring Kitgum District, who were facing extremely severe drought conditions. Uketu members continued to engage in microlending, collective farming, traditional dancing, and elder-mediated dispute resolution at the community level. Moreover, their new chairwoman, Christine, noted that the group had recently received a "Parish Development Model" grant from the local governing council, a modest infusion of funds to supplement their VSLA earnings and agricultural income.[77]

On a more critical note, Mary reflected on the enduring Acholi understanding that "a boy brings a continuation of the clan and the girl brings a continuation of another clan." So long as the cultural practice of women "marrying out" is maintained, she suggested, inheritance rights would remain problematic for women in Paibwore Chiefdom.[78] Finally, several group members returned to the fundamental value of peer support among group

Figure 13. The late Daker Nighty and friends of Uketu wan Kwene, Pader District, Northern Uganda. Photo by J. Moore, 2018.

members, 'in times of trouble and joy.' As Uketu member Evelyn noted with a wry smile, 'We are struggling together.'[79]

Integrating the Perspectives of Uketu wan Kwene Members

Four major insights emerge from the focus group and individual interviews with members of Uketu wan Kwene over the period from 2016 to 2023: reconciliation is impossible without accountability, especially on the part of the government; preserving the memory of loved ones lost in the war unifies the community; the traditional Acholi practice of women "marrying out" makes them economically vulnerable in marriage and widowhood; and women's empowerment will be a "negative strength" unless they can share responsibilities and privileges with men. These perspectives from the women of Pader, alongside those of women peacebuilders in Gulu and Nwoya, provide a foundation for interpreting conversations with the women from Odoko Mit, a community collective based in the Kitgum District of Acholiland.[80]

Figure 14. Uketu wan Kwene Memory Center honoring lives lost in the LRA War, Pader District, Northern Uganda. Photo by J. Moore, 2017.

Perspectives of Odoko Mit in Kitgum
CONTEXTUAL NOTES ON KITGUM

Odoko Mit (Life is becoming good) is one of a network of community organizations collaborating with the Ugandan NGO Human Rights Focus (HURIFO). Odoko is located in Kitgum District, which neighbors Pader to the north. Like the RLP-affiliated groups Alany pa Mony Lit and Uketu wan Kwene, the members of Odoko are villagers involved in agriculture and some petty commerce. In contrast to RLP, all the community groups linked to HU-RIFO are composed of both women and men who spontaneously organized themselves into village savings and loan associations (VSLAs) and subsequently affiliated with HURIFO. Odoko Mit members benefit from HU-RIFO trainings and consultations but receive no direct cash outlays. As my

HURIFO interpreter and research facilitator Winifred Abalo puts it, "We are fighting dependency syndrome."[81] While the individual interviews were conducted exclusively with women, men participated alongside women during the initial Odoko focus group discussion.

IDENTIFYING A RESEARCH FACILITATOR WITH EXPERIENCE
ORGANIZING IN KITGUM DISTRICT

My bridge to Odoko Mit in Kitgum was Winifred Arima Abalo. In 2016 Winnie was the HURIFO field officer responsible for outreach, human rights monitoring, and training for around fifteen community groups located in the Kitgum and Lamwo Districts of Northern Uganda. Like Victoria Nyanjura and Fred Ngomokwe, Winnie Abalo has become a colleague and trusted source of information over the years we have worked together. In speaking about her own professional development, she reflected on certain life experiences that drew her into human rights advocacy.

Ms. Abalo was raised in Kitgum during the LRA War. By the time she reached secondary school, her parents could no longer afford her school fees. Winnie was fortunate to have a close relative who offered to sponsor her education. She studied for her senior secondary school examinations at home in the evenings amid the sound of LRA and Ugandan Army (UPDF) gunfire in the area. Based on her exam scores she earned a competitive full tuition scholarship to Makerere University in Kampala, where she studied philosophy and history. During university holidays, Ms. Abalo regularly returned to Kitgum to stay with her family in an IDP camp where they had been relocated by the UPDF as part of the government's counterinsurgency policy against the LRA. With other young women of her community, Winnie often ventured from the camp at night to fetch water and firewood for her family. They were occasionally shot at by patrolling UPDF soldiers who likely mistook them for rebels.

In 2011 Ms. Abalo received her bachelor's degree from Makerere University. Two years later she was hired by Human Rights Focus to serve as their human rights monitor for Kitgum. Positions in Northern Uganda's NGO sector are precious and precarious, given the stiff competition for limited grants from philanthropic foundations. Throughout the period of our collaboration from 2016 to 2023, compensated or not, Ms. Abalo continued to perform her community outreach work with the community groups she has worked with in Kitgum District.

TALKING WITH MEMBERS OF ODOKO MIT

Odoko Mit started as a community savings and loan association. This is in contrast to Rwot Lakica, Alany pa Mony Lit, and Uketu wan Kwene, which were founded initially as collective healing circles centered around their members' shared traumatic experiences, including forced marriage, sexual violence, or the disappearance of family members. Nevertheless, individual members of Odoko are also united by common experiences of violence, displacement, and deprivation during the LRA War. Moreover, the essential components of their peacebuilding work are remarkably similar to the activities of members of the other collectives. Mutual support, conflict mediation, women's empowerment, and community development are the core ingredients of their collective action, just as they are for the other interviewees. Bichentina, the Odoko Mit chairwoman, could have spoken for any of the Northern Ugandan collectives when she stated: 'Because of the work we are doing as a group, women's rights and children's rights are being respected.'[82]

The women and men of Odoko Mit reside in Laber Parish of Lagoro Sub-county in Kitgum District, Northern Uganda. As with other community groups affiliated with Human Rights Focus, the women of Odoko Mit formed their group spontaneously before affiliating with Human Rights Focus.[83] Odoko Mit members are farmers of maize, *simsim*, sorghum, millet, beans, and cotton. They are native Acholi speakers with little or no proficiency in English. Most of the women did not have the opportunity to go to school or ended their studies after a few years at the primary level. They mention with special pride their local VSLA (village savings and loan association) and mediation activities. For their part, the men reflect on their traditional contributions to community well-being, including fashioning handles for hoes and felling timbers for table-making.

Reflections on Our Initial Encounter with Odoko Mit in Laber Parish, 2016

Our initial July 2016 visit with Odoko Mit members in Mucwini Sub-county had a number of unique dimensions. It was not unusual that the chairwoman, Bichentina, gathered six women to sit on the ground in a clearing while offering Winnie and me a seat on a nearby bench. Similar scenarios unfurled in the other settings in Northern Uganda. What was special about the Odoko Mit focus group was that the original invitees were later joined by other group members, both women and men, and possibly a few nonmembers who were strolling by. As the discussion progressed, new arrivals continued to squeeze in. By the time we were halfway through our discussion, as many as twenty people were companionably jumbled together in two intermingled rows. Because our process involves three questions to be answered in a series of round-robin exchanges, only women and men who had arrived by the start of the first round were expected to participate in the various stages of the discussion. This minor chaos somehow orchestrated itself naturally, as the original nine members answered the questions while latecomers listened, made occasional sotto voce comments to a neighbor, laughed appreciatively, and generally enjoyed themselves.[84]

The men of Odoko Mit clearly valued their opportunity to participate, even in a secondary role. Throughout the focus group discussion, the men naturally joined in the conversation, given the easy rapport between the group members.

Focus Group Discussion with Odoko Mit, 2016

Nine Odoko Mit members participated in the July 2016 focus group discussion, six women and three men, with Winnie Abalo serving as our interpreter. Bichentina, 58, serves as the Odoko chairwoman. Of the others—Pasca was 47 years old in 2016; Concy, 29; Nighty, 32; Florence, 30; Ellen, 50; Vantorino, 54; Alfred, 34; and Godfrey, 25. As with the other focus groups, we started with the theme of *reconciliation*. Each participant was invited to share in turn their understanding of *mato oput*. For Odoko Mit members, the traditional cleansing ritual involves three crucial elements—an apology for wrongdoing, the payment of compensation, and the sharing of food, typically a goat or sheep. Compensation is paid to the clan rather than directly to the aggrieved person or family.

Members described the ceremony from their own experiences or imaginations. Florence shared a vivid childhood memory: 'I witnessed *mato oput* involving a sheep and a goat. One clan killed the sheep and gave half of it to the other; the other clan killed the goat and gave half of it to the other; then they greeted one another, and the participants danced until morning with drumming and a lot of joy.' Ellen added a poignant suggestion: 'If my child were killed, I would insist on compensation, so the lost one would know' the value of her life. 'The money could be used for dowry for my son's wife, and their child could be named for the lost one.' Godfrey, the youngest focus group participant, offered his concise final word: '*Mato oput* is forgiveness. Problems arise and members mediate—that is how I see *mato oput*.'

Of all the Odoko women's insights into reconciliation and *mato oput*, Concy's reflection stands out. While she herself had not witnessed a *mato oput* ceremony, she was confident that 'if someone killed my child, the clan leaders would take it up in a clan meeting and advise me not to [take] revenge. There would be extensive discussion. The wrongdoer would ask for forgiveness. As the bereaved parent I would forgive, but I would ask for compensation,' in the form of a symbolic cash payment to the clan. Concy drew a clear distinction between *mato oput* as a ceremonial process and *timo kica* (the granting of forgiveness) as the desired outcome. Without the asking and granting of forgiveness, she insisted, *mato oput* is an empty ritual. Its power lies in its capacity to restore social cohesion and community vitality. While Odoko Mit members believe it would be possible to adapt the ceremony to the atrocities that occurred during the LRA War, this would require the government's willingness to participate, which is not yet forthcoming. Concy's words echo those of an Uketu member in Paibwore Chiefdom: 'Without acknowledgment and forgiveness, there can be no *mato oput*.'[85]

The nine Odoko Mit focus group participants proceeded to an exchange of views about *tic-cing* or *livelihood*. For most Odoko members, *tic-cing* involves farming. The four Northern Ugandan community groups had diverse takes on *tic-cing*. While Rwot Lakica participants emphasized the role of livelihood in the promotion of healing, Alany and Uketu members stressed the collective dimension of *tic-cing*. For their part, Odoko Mit members envisioned *tic-cing* as a mechanism for meeting material needs in the future, speaking of livelihood in terms of investment. When agricultural surplus is sold, the cash can go to essential household needs, such as the payment of school fees or the purchase of medications.

Finally, the participants of Odoko Mit turned their attention to *accountability*. Where Rwot Lakica and Alany pa Mony Lit members stressed the lack of government accountability for wartime suffering, Uketu members focused on accountability overall as the consequences flowing from conduct, especially wrongdoing. For their part, the members of Odoko Mit talked about accountability as encompassing both *adwogi metic* (wages due, or consequences for wrongdoing) and *kwayo kica* (seeking forgiveness). Alfred started the round-robin on accountability, emphasizing the quality of mercy: 'I'd like to talk about asking for forgiveness [*kwayo kica*]. If Godfrey and I have a disagreement over land, I will go to the elders to ask for help in asking Godfrey for forgiveness for fighting him. *Kwayo kica* is applicable to land-wrangling.' Bichentina and Pasca, on the other hand, fell soundly within the accountability-as-wages-for-honest-labor camp. Bichentina insisted 'If I do hard work, I can earn what I need for the household. Nothing is better than getting the worth of what you've done [adwogi metic].' Pasca agreed that 'if I cultivate for this year, [the harvest] may bring income that I give to my son to pay the dowry to bring his wife into the home. That woman will bring more energy [into the household] and her contribution will be traced back to my labors.'

Individual Interviews with Odoko Mit, 2016

At the conclusion of the Odoko Mit focus group we conducted individual interviews with three participants—Bichentina, Concy, and Pasca. Each woman gave her permission for me to quote her by name.

Life Circumstances and Experiences

Bichentina, Pasca, and Concy are between 30 and 60 years of age. Like the other women of Odoko Mit, they reside in Lagoro Sub-county, a remote region of Kitgum District. To reach Lagoro in 2016 required a two-hour journey from Kitgum Town over dirt roads.[86] All three Odoko members are native Acholi speakers, with no facility in English, and all three are Catholic. Bichentina, 59 years old in 2016, did not attend school; Pasca, 49 years old, completed two years of primary school; and Concy, 30 years old, left school in P-4. In contrast to the women of the other community groups in Acholiland, some of whose children were born in a health center, members of Odoko Mit who were pregnant during the LRA War generally gave birth at home.

Like the women of Rwot Lakica, Alany, and Uketu, the women of Odoko Mit draw from a broad range of life experiences, from bountiful joy to deep trauma. Concy was expecting her sixth child at the time she participated in the 2016 focus group. She gave birth to a daughter in September that year.[87] Pasca has lost five of her children, four of them to malaria, flu, polio, and measles. At the time of our conversations in July 2016, Pasca's adult son had recently committed suicide. Amid her sorrow she expressed profound gratitude to her fellow group members for lending their support in her time of grief and for helping her to perform the traditional ritual of cutting down the tree from which her son hung himself.

Community Involvement

Asked about those aspects of their community work that give them the most joy and satisfaction, Bichentina and Pasca pointed to Odoko's VSLA and Concy mentioned the group's mediation activities. Bichentina was very

precise in her descriptions of the requirements of VSLA membership, starting with a weekly deposit on 'savings day' of a minimum of 1,000 Ugandan
shillings, maximum 5,000 (approximately US$1.25).[88] The fee for late contribu-
tions is 200 shillings. As for loans, a borrower of 50,000 shillings (close to
US$15) has one month to pay it off at 20 percent interest. Two months is allotted
to repay a loan of 100,000 shillings. In addition to extending credit, the VSLA
provides emergency grants to members who face special difficulties. Pasca received such a gift after her son's death, in the form of 200,000 shillings (around
US$60) to buy the goat for his funeral rite.[89] In assessing her contributions to
dispute resolution, Concy noted proudly, 'I've been trained and have participated in many mediations. The families continue well.'[90]

Regarding conflicts at the family and community level, all three women
emphasized the value of mediation. Bichentina was matter-of-fact: 'Dispute
resolution is always done through mediation. The group assesses fines for intentional wrongdoers. Mediations are quite successful, thanks to trainings
from Human Rights Focus. Problems do not recur.' Concy focused on the
mediation of family disputes involving child truancy or parental failure to
pay school fees: 'We talk with parents of children who aren't in school. Ha-
bitual offenders are referred to the local police Child and Family Protection
Unit.' Pasca stressed that mediations are an important way to resolve conflicts informally. 'They put the parties together to talk and resolve' their issues, without recourse to the courts.

Interrelationships Between Reconciliation, Livelihood, and Accountability

As with the other community collectives, Odoko members were thoughtful
in describing the connections between *mato oput, tic-cing, adwogi metic,* and
kwayo kica. In the case of Odoko Mit, all three interviewees emphasized the
interdependence between the main components of *yupu kuc* (peacebuilding).
As Bichentina stated: 'All three go together. When you [accomplish] *mato
oput* (cleansing), you can work hard for *tic-cing* (livelihood). And if you don't
work hard, you can't [earn] *adwogi metic* (wages for your labor).'

Attitudes Toward Women's Empowerment

Like their counterparts in the other community groups, the women of Odoko
Mit had strong opinions on the national government, the changing status of
women, and the viability of protections against gender-based violence. There
was a split among the Odoko interviewees regarding whether President
Museveni cares about the women of Northern Uganda. One member was

unequivocal: 'I am not seeing anything good from this government. Only from NGOs are good things coming. We struggle on our own. We have been trained in life skills, livelihood, and *yupu kuc* (peacebuilding).' Another had a different take: 'To me, Museveni cares.' With respect to the status of women, Bichentina, Pasca, and Concy agree that women's circumstances have improved since the war, largely due to their own efforts. In particular, Concy declared: 'Women are stronger since the war. Almost all work in the home is being done by women. Most men drink. Women farm and pay school fees and are stronger than they were before and still strong up to now.'

In terms of efforts to combat violence against women, all three pointed to specific remedial actions. Bichentina explained that 'if a woman is beaten . . . the group mediates, sitting husband and wife down together. They inform the man that they can report [him] to the police. The mediations are mostly successful.' Concy acknowledged the capacity of the LC 1 (village council) to take action in cases of domestic violence if the problem cannot be resolved through informal mediation.

Access to Education, Health Care, and Employment

Members of Odoko Mit were more upbeat about opportunities for women in the education, health, and employment sectors than interviewees in other communities. Pasca painted a rosy picture in all three areas. She noted that 'most girls are in school.' She pointed to the Lagoro Health Center and the existence of private clinics. As for employment, she attested to the fact that young women were being hired for government jobs. Their chairwoman Bichentina was somewhat more qualified, first noting a positive trend in attitudes toward education. These days, 'they are preaching girl child education to the parents. There are secondary schools in Kitgum and Lagoro.' On the health care side, she lamented the lack of sufficient rural health clinics in their district. Finally, Bichentina urged realistic expectations for women in the employment sector: 'For the ones who went to school, there are opportunities, but for others, it's farming.'

Property Ownership, Inheritance, and Women's Access to the Political Process

Bichentina, Pasca, and Concy share a sense of progress regarding women's property and inheritance rights and their participation in the political realm. By the same token, all three are deeply aware of the implementation gap between law and practice at the ground level. They clearly appreciate the role of community education in instilling support for gender equality. As Bichen-tina noted, 'I can buy property because I'm married, but I could not without telling my husband.' Nevertheless, she was confident he would support such a move on her part, 'for the children's future.' As for inheritance rights, she pointed to the positive contribution of Odoko Mit in 'sensitizing the popula-tion that boys and girls inherit land equally.' Pasca painted a more nuanced picture regarding inheritance rights. 'It is possible for a woman to inherit her late husband's property along with their children,' she acknowledged. How-ever, 'girls and boys get shares of the property, but boys get more. I feel that boys and girls should inherit equal shares. Some people accept this idea, some do not.'

Regarding women's role in electoral politics, all three Odoko interview-ees distinguished between women competing for legislative seats set aside for women,[91] on the one hand, and their running against men for open seats in the various legislative councils, a much rarer occurrence, on the other. Concy noted that in Kitgum, 'women contest only for women's positions. Women will contest with men soon.'

Estimation of Women's Roles in the Community Overall

As with the other community groups in Northern Uganda, the Odoko Mit interviews concluded with a final question regarding the decisive ways in which women are helping to move their community forward. While Bichen-tina, Concy, and Pasca all believe women are playing a vital role in commu-nity development, they stress the need for greater support if women are to realize their considerable potential. Concy pointed to the many things 'women are doing to bring development to the community, by working hard to support their children in school and to provide food' for their families. Pasca insisted that 'given women's central role, they need to be supported economically.'

New Challenges and Opportunities for Odoko Mit in 2023

Drought conditions in 2023 were having a visible impact on farming for Odoko Mit in Mucwini Sub-county. Moreover, when we returned for the fi-nal research phase in July of that year, interviewees spoke of the recent deaths of two of their members. Their collective farming activities were in-frequent compared to past years, but impressively their savings and loan ac-tivities continued at a healthy level. Odoko Mit members highlighted their

Figure 15. Winifred Abalo and members of Odoko Mit, Kitgum District, Northern Uganda. Photo by J. Moore, 2023.

child advocacy work and efforts to combat gender-based violence (GBV). Florence spoke with pride about a parent in their community who had nearly abandoned a child and was now ensuring the child's school attendance, down to purchasing the necessary uniform, thanks to her efforts. For her part, the Odoko chairwoman Bichentina declared 'I'm most proud of stopping GBV' and also pointed to her successful intervention to stop the neglect of an orphan in foster care.

Encapsulating the Wisdom of Odoko Mit Members

Five major perspectives were expressed during the focus group and individual interviews with members of Odoko Mit: forgiveness and compensation are essential to the ritual and reality of reconciliation; land disputes are a significant source of conflict; women want to share livelihood duties with men; gender equality in the domain of property and inheritance is still a work in progress; and, most vitally, Odoko members' concerted efforts in conflict

resolution and child advocacy make a difference in improving the lives of
women and children in their community.

Common Threads in the Fabric of Peacebuilding in Acholiland

This chapter has presented a close reading of interviews on the subject of
peacebuilding with women who belong to grassroots collectives based in
the Gulu, Nwoya, Pader, and Kitgum Districts of Northern Uganda and
who partner with the Women's Advocacy Network, the Refugee Law Project, and Human Rights Focus. The interviews were designed to give each
individual the opportunity to define notions of peace and justice in her own
terms. The discussions touched on multifaceted and interlocking themes:
the symbiosis between reconciliation, accountability, and livelihood; the
meaning of women's empowerment; the nature of resilience; and the heart
of collective survival itself. Distilling the women's insights into a coherent
analytic whole is no simple task. The process cannot and should not be reductive. It starts and ends with the women's stories and the sense that they
make of their own lives.

Reflecting on their personal narratives and insights, each woman's steeli-
ness of character is undeniable, her resilience often incandescent. Our conversations were inspiring and at times difficult to get through. It is moving and
painful to listen to a woman talk about escaping captivity with her children
through crossfire between the LRA and the UPDF; to bear another's description of laying to rest her firstborn son who hung himself from a tree, and then
ritually cutting down that tree with other members of her community to prevent recurrence of his tragic fate; to hear a woman describe her desire to be one
with her government if only it would acknowledge its part in the wartime suffering of her community; to share a woman's plan for selling her extra produce
to finance her daughters' school fees and her dream of enrolling in adult education classes herself one day; to be reassured by a mother of six that I, too, could
have cut the umbilical cords of my own two children had I faced that necessity.
As expressed by Filda of Alany pa Mony Lit, 'We bring forth the strength that
we need.' Their stories, dreams, and testimonies resound with courage and
heart. At times the listener can but hope to channel some of the women's tena-
cious hope and sheer grit; their capacity to forgive self and others, and to endure; their imperative to survive and somehow to thrive; their acceptance of
what is, paired with their demands for much more.

Drawing from the essence of their stories, six basic peacebuilding insights emerge from conversations with women active in community collectives in the Gulu, Nwoya, Pader, and Kitgum Districts of Northern Uganda.

First, *reconciliation is not a sentimental notion, but the very basis of collective survival.* Violence serves to shut down community life and livelihood. Reconciliation is the restart button. In communities where drought imperils the food supply, medical clinics are distant, and school fees are high, discord is an unaffordable luxury.

Second, *reconciliation can only happen if the offender is willing to make amends.* Reconciliation requires the acknowledgment of wrongful conduct by the offender and his or her request for forgiveness (*kwayo kica*). As Daker Nighty of Uketu wan Kwene and Concy of Odoko Mit expressed in almost identical words, 'There is no reconciliation [*mato oput*] without accountability [*adwogi metic*].' The ultimate expression of accountability is the willingness to repair the harm. The granting of forgiveness (*timo kica*) rests on the faith that compensation will be paid, in symbolic and material terms. *Adwogi metic* literally means accounting for one's labor, and it applies equally to wages for honest work and the 'wages of sin'—in the sense of consequences for wrongful conduct. In either case, compensation is due. For the women of Alany pa Mony Lit in particular, *adwogi metic* is the way for the Ugandan president to reconcile with the Acholi people. Only when the government seeks forgiveness from the people and is willing to pay compensation for wartime atrocities will accountability be realized in Northern Uganda.

Third, because of the lack of reparations, *there remains a 'negative accountability'—quite literally a debt—between the government and the Acholi people.* Many women spoke of the government's failure to take ownership of its role in the wartime suffering of Northern Ugandans. As Nighty of Uketu wan Kwene put it, 'Dominic Ongwen [convicted LRA leader] can't take all accountability. The government must' also. A member of the Women's Advocacy Network stressed similar concerns on the part of former captives of the LRA: 'Since all of us were abducted, the government should acknowledge its part in our plight,' insisting that accountability 'requires the involvement of those at the top.' The women of Northern Uganda voice their demands while acknowledging the risks. They are proud of their involvement in calls for the government to pay reparations to war-affected people, including those who are former LRA abductees and those who are survivors of sexual violence committed by government soldiers. As one peacebuilder insisted,

'Women have become stronger than ever' and the government's inaction 'pushes us toward further advocacy.'

Fourth, *there is a yawning chasm between law and practice concerning women's property and inheritance rights.* Women in Northern Uganda are impacted in myriad ways by the gap between the letter of Uganda's Law of Succession and the enduring power of patriarchal traditions. Despite constitutional provisions recognizing gender equity in the devolution of estates, Mary of Uketu wan Kwene states that in too many cases women do not take ownership of the husband's property when he dies. Women peacebuilders advocate for de jure equality while they navigate their de facto inequality.

Fifth, *women peacebuilders yearn for equal partnership with men.* Women of all four collectives in Northern Uganda are proud of their leadership role in community dispute resolution, microfinance, collective agriculture, domestic violence prevention, and the fuller implementation of women's inheritance and property rights. At the same time, they are concerned that as they take on more of the burdens of community subsistence and development, they may not fully enjoy their fruits. Mary of Uketu wan Kwene spoke of 'male privilege' migrating from the IDP camps to the villages, commenting on their alcohol consumption and observing that 'men are on the take.' Nighty of Uketu alluded to men's displacement from their traditional roles, cautioning that 'women suffer more because men behave as if they are insane.' Jane of Uketu put it this way: 'Women have become men in their homes. I see a negative strength. We women shouldn't have to take on such responsibility without support.' As noted by the late chairwoman Evelyn of Alany pa Mony Lit, women instead need men to work *with* them. Their vision of partnership starts in childhood, when sisters should 'start collaborating with their brothers from an early age, to become peers.'

Sixth and finally, *restored relationships are the very fiber of peacebuilding.* Community integrity is the heart of collective survival, peaceful coexistence (*bedo kacel*), and peace (*kuc*) itself. Mary of Uketu wan Kwene spoke of unity (*ribbe*) and collective well-being (*be bedo*) as the building blocks of peace. Her comember Jane Orama identified dialogue (*lok*), unity (*ribbe*), *mato oput* (the reconciliatory rite), and joyful togetherness (*yom cwing*) as the elements of her metaphoric tree of peace. Connection to others is the font of an individual's strength and resilience (*diyo cwing*). The late Daker Nighty of Uketu wan Kwene insisted that she was able to persevere thanks to her dedication to the young ones' future, her commitment to unity, and her drive to prevent the recurrence of violence in her community. As Grace of Rwot Lakica summed it up, reconciliation is "mending broken relationships."

THE WAY FORWARD

Grassroots women peacebuilders in Northern Uganda are optimistic pragmatists. Each conversation reveals the interviewee's appreciation of her own contributions to social transformation, even as she acknowledges the immensity of the tasks she and her sister community leaders undertake. This balance between idealism and realism is expressed in countless specific ways. Women peacebuilders yearn for restored relationships with their wartime offenders through traditional rites like *mato oput*. But in the meantime, they experience reconciliation on a daily basis in their work as trained mediators who successfully resolve disputes between community members. Women community leaders seek accountability from their government in the form of compensation for war-related injuries. Meanwhile, they strengthen their community's commitment to values of gender equality and individual integrity by advocating for women's inheritance and property rights guaranteed by law and by taking specific action against instances of domestic violence that occur locally. Rural women aspire to a social service system in Uganda that guarantees welfare for all, but for now they enhance livelihood and increase family and community wealth by participating in community banking, pooling resources, making loans, and engaging in collaborative agriculture. Women peacebuilders in Northern Uganda do not wait for transformative justice to arrive from an external source. Every day in their communities, collectively and incrementally, they are making their own peace and justice on the ground.

Women in Power with Men's Support: Social Transformation Among the Peace Mothers of Sierra Leone

We must learn to give,
To work together,
To eat together from the same bowl,
To play and to laugh,
To share the kola nut.

      —Lamrana, Peace Mother
      of Dogoloya

Go up-country, so they said,
To see the real Africa.
For whomsoever you may be,
That is where you come from.
Go for bush, inside the bush,
You will find your hidden heart.
Your mute ancestral spirit.
And so I went, dancing on my way.

      —Abioseh Nicol, "The Meaning
      of Africa"

Lamrana Bah[1] is a Fambul Tok Peace Mother from Dogoloya, a village in Koinadugu, one of the rural districts of Sierra Leone's Northern Province. She is Fulbeh, like all the Peace Mothers of Dogoloya, including

Map 2. Map of Sierra Leone by Erin Greb.

Figure 16. Peace Mothers of Dogoloya, Koinadugu District, Sierra Leone. Photo by J. Moore, 2017.

Boie Jalloh, profiled in the Introduction. Lamrana describes her grassroots activism in communal terms. To her, peacebuilding embodies collective labor as well as shared celebration in which neighbors "eat together from the same bowl." To join Lamrana and Boie, we must indeed "go up-country," as the poet and diplomat Abioseh (Davidson) Nicol wrote of his rural Sierra Leone some sixty years ago. Today as then, getting to places like Dogoloya requires a journey up winding and rutted roads cut through dense vegetation, off the few main highways that link Freetown to its provincial capitals. Nicol's romanticized depiction of dancing along his journey through "the bush" somehow rang true as I arrived in Dogoloya for the first time in 2016. I was drawn by Lamrana and the other Peace Mothers into a ceremonial dance of hospitality amid gentle chants of "jabba hey, jabba hey"—"welcome" in Fula.

Partnerships, Vision, and Methodology

The Structure of Fambul Tok and the Peace Mothers

A variety of perspectives from participants in the grassroots women's peace movement in Sierra Leone are examined in this chapter through the qualitative analysis of conversations with members of local groups affiliated with the Fambul Tok Peace Mothers in Sierra Leone's Moyamba and Koinadugu Districts. Fambul Tok was an ideal entity to facilitate research among women peacebuilders because of the organization's dedication since 2007 to grassroots restorative justice in war-affected communities throughout the country. Fambul Tok maintains collaborative partnerships in all three of Sierra Leone's up-country provinces, encouraging community reconciliation initiatives in the Bombali and Koinadugu Districts of Northern Province; the Kono and Kailahun Districts of Eastern Province; and the Moyamba and Pujehun Districts of Southern Province. Moreover, its staff work with public officials, cultural leaders, and citizens at all tiers of Sierra Leonean society from the national authorities down through the district, chiefdom, and section leaders, penetrating all the way to the village level.[2]

The Fambul Tok Peace Mothers program was founded in 2009 in an attempt to prioritize women's voices and stories, incubate women's leadership, and capitalize on women-centered initiatives for trust-building and community development.[3] As of 2019, there were 271 Peace Mothers groups in rural communities throughout Sierra Leone.[4] Given its broad geographical and cultural reach, the Fambul Tok Peace Mothers network provides a solid framework within which to conduct qualitative research with rural women peacebuilders in Sierra Leone.

Peace Mothers groups sustain themselves through their microfinance and collective agricultural activities, additional characteristics shared with their sister organizations in Northern Uganda. Peace Mothers groups are commonly known for their village savings associations (VSAs), similar to the Northern Ugandan VSLAs, into which members deposit small amounts of cash regularly and from which they take out small loans on a rotational basis with modest interest accruing after a defined term. Like those in Uganda affiliated with the Women's Advocacy Network, Refugee Law Project, and Human Rights Focus, the Peace Mothers groups do not receive regular grants or other significant forms of ongoing material assistance from their parent organization. The main inputs and support they receive from Fambul Tok take the form of outreach, training, consultation, and solidarity, which ebb and flow with Fambul Tok's funding levels. The Peace Mothers survive and thrive due to the work of their own hands and the psychosocial support they provide each other and their extended families.

From 2016 to 2023, Fambul Tok staff helped me organize focus groups and individual interviews with a culturally diverse cross-section of Sierra Leonean women active in their local Peace Mothers groups. Some interviewees, like Boie and Lamrana, are ethnic Fulbeh and Muslim; others are Mandingo, Limba, and Mende of both Muslim and Christian faith traditions. In our interviews, participants shared details about their efforts to transform their communities after conflict, often touching on the interlocking themes of reconciliation, accountability, livelihood, women's equality, and women's partnership with men.

The Vision of the Peace Mothers

Unifying the interviewees as research subjects is membership in their local Peace Mothers' group and their dedication to common activities such as community banking, collective farming, domestic violence prevention, and dispute resolution. They define justice principally in terms of restored relationships at the community level; enhanced health care, education, and income-generation opportunities; and community "sensibilization" (consciousness raising) to ensure fuller implementation of laws mandating gender equality in inheritance, property ownership, and the political sphere.[5]

Essential to the Peace Mothers' notion of women's empowerment is the idea that when women are stronger, their families and communities are stronger. By the same token, members believe that when a woman's spouse actively supports her, together as a couple they can further contribute to the uplift of their community. These core principles are reflected in one of the Peace Mothers' slogans, often chanted at community meetings by women and men alike: "woman power—man support."[6]

At first blush, the statement seems to illustrate what some feminist scholars refer to as "strategic essentialism,"[7] signifying here an appeal on the part of women to traditional gender roles in order to make their activism more palatable to men and other women. But as the insights of the Peace Mothers shared below will show, there is much more to the Peace Mothers' name and their work than a mere adaptation of the trappings of women's subservience in the service of women's empowerment. In an environment where material survival is a daily struggle, women's need for the support of men is incontrovertible, as is men's reliance on women. Separate struggles are not viable.

The Peace Mothers are aware that full implementation of women's formal rights is a work in progress. Widows and women living in polygamous households whose marriages are not registered remain extremely prone to economic destitution. Because domestic violence is underreported and seldom prosecuted, local mediation and educational outreach are essential alternatives to law enforcement. Without ready access to courts of law and judicial orders of protection, rural women facing violence in the home increasingly participate in collective advocacy and call on trained community mediators for lifesaving interventions. This is the work of the Peace Mothers. They are essential guarantors of women's equality in their communities.

The Peace Mothers' vision is rooted in their dedication as community members to work together for their collective subsistence. Group members understand that women's empowerment can only happen within the context of enhanced social welfare for all. That said, the Peace Mothers do not speak with one voice. Members share a variety of perspectives regarding women's power and influence in the home, community, and society. Their views are both diverse and dynamic, interacting with the realities they face and the perspectives of their relatives and fellow community members. Moreover, women's roles as helpmates and leaders—as keepers of the flame and breakers of glass ceilings—are not mutually exclusive. Individual Peace Mothers thoughtfully formulate their peacemaking and mothering roles in ways that ideally serve both their community's survival and their own vitality and integrity. At the very least, the rallying cry "woman power—man support" merges two conceptions of gender roles. The first is the more familiar and traditional notion that women need men to support them. The other is a more demanding and transformative idea—that as women empower themselves, so too they challenge and strengthen their domestic partnerships and their communities to the benefit of women, men, and children alike.

Cultural and Linguistic Interpretation and Methodology
IDENTIFYING A RESEARCH FACILITATOR AND CULTURAL AMBASSADOR

Lilian Morsay was an early leader of the Peace Mothers program within Fambul Tok. I first came to know of her in 2015 from watching an online video about the Fambul Tok Peace Mothers. In the short film, she speaks frankly about the slow and inexorable work of restorative justice: "Reconciliation is not an event. It is a process. It won't happen spontaneously. It goes on as long, as long, as long as you live."[8] Lilian's words evoke the depth of commitment that peacemaking demands—the energy, devotion, patience, stubbornness, and creativity.[9]

Lilian facilitated several of my Sierra Leone research visits over the 2016–2023 research period and helped me formulate my research methodology. She first introduced me to community members and leaders, providing linguistic translation and cultural interpretation whenever necessary.[10] An experienced Fambul Tok team member who has worked among Peace Mothers communities throughout the country, Lilian is dedicated to women's peace activism at the local level, having started organizing in her native Kono District of Eastern Sierra Leone. As Peace Mothers coordinator for Kono, she conducted regular outreach, training, and coordination activities for all the local Peace Mothers groups in her district. She later took on the role of national Peace Mothers coordinator for Fambul Tok, serving as a resource for Fambul Tok field staff throughout the country and nurturing bonds of friendship with Peace Mothers in the various districts.

Like my translators and research facilitators in Northern Uganda, Lilian lived through the civil war in her country. During the Rebel War, she and her family fled Kono and sought refuge in neighboring Guinea. At one point during their flight she, her sisters, and their mother separated from her father and brothers. This situation was not uncommon, particularly given the rebels' practice of attacking civilian communities and forcing local men and boys to commit rape and other forms of assault on their own family members. Her family was reunited after the war. Lilian has a bachelor's degree and advanced certification in education from the Milton Margai College of Education and Technology in Freetown and a diploma in community development studies from Northern Polytechnic in the city of Makeni, the capital of Bombali District. In addition to Kono, she is fluent in English; Krio, Sierra Leone's national language; Koranko, widely spoken in Koinadugu District; and Mandingo, most commonly spoken in pockets of Northern and Eastern Sierra Leone and elsewhere in West Africa. After her father died, Lilian cared for her mother until her death in 2022. As a single mother, she raises her five children in her household in Kono.[11]

Figure 17. Lilian Morsay, Palima, Moyamba District, Sierra Leone.
Photo by J. Moore, 2019.

DEVELOPING THE FIELD METHODOLOGY

Given its ethnic diversity, Sierra Leonean society is culturally integrated to a remarkable extent, reflected in the way local communities are organized and in the interactions of their members. Sierra Leone's characteristic pluralism is evidenced in the multilingualism and religious fluidity of the Peace Mothers collectives. They express their inveterate interfaith sensibility in the common village practice of welcoming visitors with paired benedictions from the Muslim and Christian traditions. To ensure that my research drew from the country's rich cultural spectrum and represented the transregional and collaborative nature of women's peace activism in Sierra Leone, I hoped to spread the interviews across several ethnogeographic regions. Lilian recommended that we organize meetings with women of four maternal language groups, from both primary faith communities, and in at least two different provinces of the country. Thus, we decided to conduct the research for this chapter in two districts: the southern district of Moyamba, whose inhabitants are majority Mende, one of the two largest tribes in Sierra Leone; and the Northern districts of Koinadugu and Falaba, today the most ethnically diverse region of the country. We identified the communities of Palima and Tawovehun, two Mende-speaking communities in Moyamba to the south; as well as Dogoloya, Heremakono, and Kaponpon, three communities in Falaba and Koinadugu to the north, where the most common mother tongues are Fula, Mandingo, and Limba, respectively.

Our team visited all five communities in March 2016 for the first phase of the research. We then returned to the same communities on five occasions on a nearly yearly basis from 2017 to 2023 for individual and follow-up interviews.[12] Each time we embarked on a community visit, Lilian and I started with a fairly open logistical plan that took shape as we traveled, given the availability of transport and language interpretation and in deference to the vagaries of weather and agricultural work cycles. The research commenced in March 2016 with five focus group discussions, each composed of five to ten members of the local Peace Mothers group in that community. As with the Ugandan focus groups conducted in July 2016, the Peace Mothers' focus group discussions were structured around questions related to three basic components of peacebuilding—reconciliation, livelihood, and accountability. As in Northern Uganda, these common elements became points of departure for turn-taking around the talking circle as each woman took the opportunity to share her understanding of each concept. The insights I derived from these preliminary group interactions created the foundation for us to return to the same communities to conduct individual interviews and follow-up sessions in the ensuing years.

In each Sierra Leonean community we visited in July 2017 I interviewed between one and three of the women who had participated in the focus group the year before, using the same set of questions I used in my research with women peacebuilders in Northern Uganda.[13] The Peacebuilders' Questionnaire was designed to encourage each interviewee to talk about her life; highlight the peacebuilding activities that bring her the most pride and satisfaction; share her perspectives on women's status and access to social services; offer her assessment of women's rights to own and inherit property as codified and expressed in legislation, cultural norms, and local community practice; voice her satisfactions, frustrations, challenges, and goals; and identify the words, metaphors, and values that embody her vision of the peacebuilding process.

A total of thirty Peace Mothers joined in the five focus group discussions in March 2016. Ten of these focus group participants, one or more from each of the five communities, took part in individual interviews in July 2017 as well as in one or more follow-up interviews in May 2018, May 2019, July 2022, and October 2023. The focus groups in 2016 and the individual interviews in 2017 yielded the most substantive insights from individual Peace Mothers. The follow-up interviews in 2018 were focused on verifying and elaborating information and quotations that I had gleaned from earlier sessions. The meetings in 2019 were opportunities for me to give token gifts to individual interviewees in the form of photo albums with pictures and text memorializing our interactions together in their communities. In 2022 and 2023, I returned to their communities once COVID travel restrictions were lifted. My chief objective for the most recent visits was to renew contact with the Peace Mothers, find out whether their groups were still thriving, and inquire about current economic conditions. While all the groups are still active, their chief concerns since the COVID-19 pandemic and Russia's 2022 invasion of Ukraine are high inflation and the decreased availability of extra cash to invest in microlending and collective enterprises. According to Boie, a cup of rice that would have cost around 2,000 leones (approximately ten cents in US currency) in 2021 cost 4,000 leones (around 20 cents) in 2022 and 5,000 leones (around 25 cents) in 2023.[14] Given that the average Sierra Leonean lives on US$3 per day,[15] these inflationary trends make it very difficult to procure supplemental food, purchase medicines, and pay for children's school fees, particularly in the time periods between agricultural harvests.

The stories and perspectives the Peace Mothers shared over the 2016–23 period provide the foundation for my analysis of the women-centered grassroots peacebuilding movement in Sierra Leone. These women's stories invite the listener and reader into a deeper appreciation of rural non-elite women's contributions to postconflict social transformation in a variety of cultural contexts throughout their country. While the intricacies of their lives cannot be fully conveyed on the written page, with their enthusiastic consent I share certain details. In this way their insights into the meanings of peace and justice are illuminated in the light of their past and present experiences.

The analysis below of conversations with Sierra Leone Peace Mothers is organized around the five communities: starting with focus group and individual interviews among the women of Palima in Moyamba District, Southern Province; continuing to the community of Tawovehun, also in Moyamba; and then on to the three Northern Province communities of Falaba and Koinadugu Districts—Dogoloya, Heremakono, and Kaponpon. For each of the five communities I synopsize and integrate the contributions of the women belonging to the local Peace Mothers group, selecting particular details in order to illustrate and personalize the main themes that emerge. Based on contributions from the individual Peace Mothers interviewed, my explorative analysis is progressively comparative: first pairing the insights of women in the same community (such as Palima); then contrasting communities in one district (for example, Moyamba); later comparing insights between women of different districts (that is, Moyamba and Koinadugu); and, finally, integrating the contributions of women across Sierra Leone and Northern Uganda. We begin in Moyamba District of Southern Province.

Talking with the Peace Mothers in Five Rural Communities in Sierra Leone

Southern Province: The Two Moyamba Field Visits

ASSEMBLING OUR FAMBUL TOK RESEARCH TEAM FOR THE MOYAMBA COMMUNITY VISITS

Shortly after arriving in Freetown in March 2016, I met with Lilian Morsay and the Fambul Tok director John Caulker to map out a plan for my research. With their direction, we assembled a traveling research team composed of Lilian and me; Mustapha Rogers, our driver; and Aminata Sheriff, then serving as consultant for the Fambul Tok Peace Mothers program. We decided on an itinerary that included two community visits in Moyamba, followed by three community visits in Koinadugu. That very afternoon our team set out from Freetown toward Moyamba Town, a three-hour journey over sections of road alternately paved, graded, and deeply rutted.

We arrived at our destination in the afternoon and met with Theresa Kamara, the Fambul Tok field officer for Moyamba responsible for outreach and training with the various Peace Mothers groups in her district. Theresa got a sense of our research plan and agreed to accompany us on the field visits to Palima and Tawovehun. There she would facilitate introductions to local community members and provide Mende interpretation. Theresa's role was essential in helping me establish a foundation of trust and good will with the Peace Mothers of Moyamba, given her close connections to these communities. Building on Lilian and Theresa's bonds of affinity and solidarity with the local residents, I was better able to establish my own rapport with each woman I interviewed.

Demography, Culture, and Gender Politics in Moyamba District

Moyamba is the largest district of Sierra Leone's low-lying Southern Province, touching the Atlantic on its western coastline. Its inhabitants are mainly Mende speakers of both Muslim and Christian faith traditions, who are often related through interfaith marriages. Its major economic activities are the mining of bauxite, rice cultivation, fishing, and palm oil extraction. There is an engrained tradition of men's and women's cultural societies in Moyamba District, and women commonly participate in the collective life of their communities. The historical precedent of women's political leadership among the Mende dates back to the time of Madam Yoko, a powerful paramount chief during the latter half of the nineteenth century.[16] Madam Yoko founded a network of women's Bondo societies (the "Bondo")[17] throughout Moyamba charged with conserving cultural practices and initiating girls into womanhood. Ritual dance ceremonies from the Bondo tradition are a vital aspect of women's daily life, as I witnessed from the moment we arrived in Palima and Tawovehun. Since the time of Madam Yoko, Mende women have continued to assume political leadership positions, serving as paramount chiefs in a significant minority of Mende chiefdoms.[18]

The Bondo, like women's cultural societies in other parts of provincial Sierra Leone, is associated with the cultural practice of female genital cutting (FGC), a component of the traditional coming-of-age ceremony for young women. In Sierra Leone, FGC typically involves excision of part of the clitoris.[19] Young women are expected to submit to the cutting based on the Bondo teaching that it will lessen a young woman's sexual desire, thereby preserving her fidelity to her future husband.[20] The ritual cutting is traditionally performed by *soweis* ("experts" in Mende), respected female community elders trained as midwives to assist women during childbirth. FGC may be performed on a young woman without her consent.[21] The practice causes considerable pain and ongoing risks of infection and death throughout the healing process and later in the woman's life, particularly after intercourse and childbirth.[22]

Despite international and local campaigns for eradication and criminalization, FGC remains widespread throughout the rural areas of Sierra Leone, including communities in which the Peace Mothers are active. As of 2018, over 90 percent of Sierra Leonean women and girls had been subjected to the ritual genital cutting.[23] At the same time, nearly one-third of women nationwide were opposed to the practice being continued.[24] More recently, opposition has grown into action, and increasing numbers of young women are refusing to undergo FGC. In 2022 90 percent of women over 30 years of age had been cut, whereas only 61 percent of teens between 15 and 19 had submitted to the procedure.[25]

Increasing numbers of Sierra Leonean women believe that the practice of FGC—an affront to women's self-determination and a threat to their health—should end. They also insist that eradication must be endorsed at the community level and not be imposed nationally or internationally.[26] Upholding patriarchal traditions while also promoting women's community activism, the Bondo endures as a framework for cultural expression and an incubator for civic participation by rural women in Sierra Leone, particularly among the Mende of Moyamba District. Its practices, including FGC, continue to evolve, animated by both internal and external forces.

A Word on the Language of Peace in Mende

Almost all the women of Palima and Tawovehun speak Mende as their mother tongue. Most speak Krio, their national language, as well. In both communities during our initial visit in 2016, I was fortunate to have the interpretation skills of Theresa and Aminata, both native Mende speakers.[27] Lilian would provide supplemental interpretation in Krio when I wished to ask a follow-up question or to elaborate on a particular point. When asked to define peace in terms of its most important attributes, the interviewees often spoke in terms of unity, friendship, and development. Unity—or togetherness—is *ngoyela*;

friendship—or love—is *ndomeh*; development is *ndeguloma*; and peace itself is
ndeleh. The interrelationships between these words and concepts, particularly
ndeleh and *ndeguloma*—peace and development played out in the focus groups
and individual conversations with Peace Mothers in Palima and Tawovehun.

TALKING WITH THE PEACE MOTHERS OF PALIMA, MOYAMBA DISTRICT

Cultural Introduction to Palima, 2016

After arriving in Moyamba Town and spending the night in local guesthouses, we drove to the community of Palima the following morning. Palima
is both the name of a section composed of thirteen villages and the headquarters town of that section. Part of the Bagruwa Chiefdom, most of Palima's residents are engaged in agriculture and processing garri, a milled
form of cassava that can be stored long-term and used to make bread and
porridge. The people of Palima include Christians and Muslims, the latter
constituting a slight majority.[28]

Upon our arrival in their community we were greeted by a friendly
throng of women who sang, clapped, and swayed, drawing us into their
dance of welcome. The dancers were accompanied by male drummers and a
few "Bondo devils"—mysterious, playful, comic female personages wearing
elaborate carved wooden masks and dressed in costumes of thatch and bur-
lap. Men and children of the community were a relaxed, quizzical, often de-
lighted presence on the sidelines. The hour-long celebration was interspersed
with laughter, much teasing, and spontaneous dancing lessons. As Lilian put
it, "The women are jubilating." We joined in their celebration, dancing to the
point of exhaustion.

Palima Focus Group Discussions, 2016

After the jubilation time came the first focus group discussion. As was typical of all nine community dialogues across the women's collectives of Northern Uganda and Sierra Leone, our research team invited a small group of
women from the community to gather for a group conversation, deferring
to the local Peace Mothers leadership to designate a representative group of
women of different ages and roles. We welcomed Jenebah, Ademah, Theresa,
Fatumatah, and Hannah to join us in a small hut serving as a storage and
meeting room. Of these five, Hannah and Theresa were the two Palima Peace
Mothers who went on to participate in individual interviews with me in 2017
and subsequent years.

In the same pattern followed across the women's collectives in Uganda and Sierra Leone, we started with the theme of *reconciliation*. Hannah, then forty-eight and mother of eleven, is the Peace Mothers chairwoman for Palima. She defined reconciliation as 'forgiving and coming together,' and clarified that forgiveness requires remorse on the part of the wrongdoer. Fatumatah, fifty-seven and mother of twelve, elaborated on the distinction between forgiving and forgetting: 'If one is alone, one can forgive,' but 'with others, one can forget.' Her words suggest that only in community with others can one begin to let go of the pain of the past.

All five Peace Mothers of Palima seem to take for granted the notion that reconciliation stems from forgiveness, extended to wrongdoers to ensure the survival of the community. But nested within this conviction is another core belief: just as reconciliation requires forgiveness by those who suffered wrongdoing, forgiveness requires acknowledgment of misconduct on the part of the wrongdoer. There is a widespread understanding among Peace Mothers that reconciliation and accountability, meaning forgiveness and acknowledgment, are mutually dependent. Moreover, relationships are the heart of peacebuilding in all its various manifestations: community restoration, offender-victim conciliation, and collective livelihood. Individual survival depends on the vitality of family and community. The offender comes clean to the victim but also to her clan, thus reconciliation is both personal and communal. This theme of collectivity continues to emerge in subsequent interviews with Peace Mothers throughout Sierra Leone.

Exploration of the theme of *livelihood* followed. Fatumatah emphasized the need to link subsistence and cash-generating activities through her characterization of two crops commonly grown in Palima: 'If you farm rice and you don't cultivate cassava, your children suffer.' As I learned from this assembly of Peace Mothers, rice is typically grown as a food crop for family consumption, whereas cassava is often processed into garri and then stored and sold to generate cash for essential purchases. Both are needed for the family to flourish.

The five Palima Peace Mothers who participated in the 2016 focus group were interested in expanding their cash-generating activities to further supplement their subsistence agricultural work. They value hard currency as a tool to "solve their children's problems"—an ever-needed resource to finance education and medical needs. Cultivation of food crops sometimes went unmentioned as a form of livelihood, taken for granted as the center of women's daily life and the bedrock of community survival. Nevertheless, it was crystal clear from the group as a whole that livelihood is both surviving and thriving—a means of getting through the week and the season as well as a strategy for enhancing the well-being of their families now and in the future.

Finally, the group turned to a discussion of *accountability*. In contrast to their predominant description of livelihood in terms of capital investment, the woman of Palima tended to define accountability spiritually in terms of remorse, forgiveness, and love. All these notions are vitally linked back to the concept of reconciliation itself. For Ademah, the community *sowei* or midwife, 'accountability is love for one another, based on the faith we have in our religions.'[29] Both Ademah and Theresa see acceptance of responsibility as the prerequisite for the forgiveness that allows community cohesion to be restored. As Theresa expressed it, 'After taking responsibility, we will come together as one.' Finally, for the Peace Mothers chairwoman Hannah, accountability has two essential and interdependent components: the wrongdoer takes responsibility so that the offended person can forgive. 'Accountability is a relationship, an agreement between two people, a bond. When the bond breaks, there must be forgiveness.'

The Peace Mothers of Palima have a nuanced view of accountability, starting with their recognition of the vital link between acknowledgment of wrongdoing and forgiveness. It makes sense that the offender seeking redemption should apologize to the victim. But on a deeper level, they believe that the victim is also accountable. Her refusal to redeem the offender would threaten the collective survival of her community. As reconciliation requires accountability, the inverse is also true: accountability to the collective requires reconciliation between individuals. Thus, the victim's willingness to forgive her offender expresses her sense of obligation to the community. The symbiotic relationship between reconciliation and accountability described by the Peace Mothers in Palima reinforces a broader cultural imperative at work throughout rural Sierra Leone: individuals define themselves in relationship with others in recognition of the material and spiritual sustenance that the collective offers to its members. Additional perspectives on their identities as women and community members also emerged during the individual interviews with Palima Peace Mothers conducted the following year.

Reassembling Our Team and Returning to Moyamba for Individual Interviews in 2017

Sixteen months later in July 2017, I returned to Sierra Leone to conduct individual interviews with a representative group of those Peace Mothers who had taken part in the 2016 focus groups. I felt privileged to return to Moyamba, hoping to deepen my connections to the women I had met the year before. As in the previous year, we decided to initiate the field visits in Moyamba District, starting with Palima.[30] Due to heavy rains that month, what was a three-hour journey from Freetown in 2016 stretched into a six-hour excursion in 2017, including a prolonged roadside delay awaiting the ultimately successful repair of a washed-out bridge. Our journey went quickly with talk of family, culture, and politics on both sides of the Atlantic.[31]

We arrived in Moyamba Town by nightfall and in bright sunshine the following morning we drove another two hours over winding, rutted roads to our first community. As we stepped down from our vehicle upon arriving in Palima, we were again surrounded by a circle of singing, clapping, dancing women. Perhaps mindful of the impending rain and wanting to take advantage of clear skies to cultivate in their fields, the women abbreviated their welcome dance that year. Within fifteen minutes we were assembled on wooden benches for the community gathering outside the home of one of the Peace Mothers. Lilian expressed our appreciation for the local hospitality and reminded community members of my research project and interest in learning about the work of the Peace Mothers. When she informed our hosts that my father had passed away a few months before, the women spontaneously offered a Muslim blessing in hopes that he might rest in peace.

We then invited the Peace Mothers Hannah and Theresa to participate in individual interviews, as participants in the focus group discussion that had taken place the previous year. Hannah is the Peace Mothers chairwoman for Palima, and Theresa is the section chairwoman for Palima. While both are community leaders, Hannah's role is as head of their local civil society network whereas Theresa serves within the local leadership structure. Typically, the section chairwoman is appointed by the section chief, particularly if he is a man, to advocate for the interests of women in their cluster of villages.

To conduct the interviews, we went inside the sitting room of Hannah's home and gathered on benches arranged around a long wooden table. Given competing duties that day for the Mende-speaking Fambul Tok staff based in Moyamba, we elected to conduct the interviews in the national language. Lilian Morsay interpreted between Krio and English. I used the Peacebuilder's Questionnaire[32] formulated for the research in Sierra Leone and Northern Uganda and described in the methodology section above.

Linking Impressions of Palima, 2017 and Subsequent Years (2018–2023)

We interviewed Hannah and Theresa individually and separately in a private room in Hannah's house. They have much in common as Peace Mothers and leaders in their community. Both are women in their late forties who ended their formal education after the fourth year of primary school, both are mothers of four or five surviving children, both are Mende speakers and practicing Muslims, and both play leadership roles within the Fambul Tok Peace Mothers and in Palima as a whole. Hannah and Theresa farm for their livelihood and point to their participation in the collective agricultural activities of the Peace Mothers as an important way in which they survive individually and give back to their community collectively. They see reconciliation and accountability in concrete and everyday terms, inextricable in the same way that true forgiveness by the one who was offended requires the honest expression of remorse by the perpetrator.

As for attitudes about the government, Hannah explained, 'We are not getting anything.' In her own private interview, Theresa echoed Hannah in declaring: 'They are not doing anything.' Both defined the material and economic self-reliance of the women in their community as both a necessity and a triumph. As Hannah put it, 'For women, if you don't work, you don't eat.' 'Agricultural work is it,' insisted Theresa. Both lament the forces that compel young women to leave school before finishing, particularly early pregnancy and limited family means. Both acknowledge that public health services are severely lacking at the local level. Both see farming as their only choice and their greatest accomplishment. Theresa emphasized the importance of cassava as both a means of subsistence and a source of funds for education, medications, and other essentials. She ended our interview with an invitation she might extend to her daughter: 'Come, my child, and join our group. We will go to the farm, cultivate cassava, process it, make garri [cassava flour] and fufu [fermented cassava] to sell. We will use the money to feed and clothe you and pay your school fees.'

Turning to the themes of women's status and protection, the two women emphasized strengthened accountability mechanisms in their community and a heightened level of awareness that domestic abuse is a crime. Both spoke of a continuum of approaches to violence intervention, from mediation to more formal mechanisms of accountability. Hannah believes that one way to resolve marital disputes is to calm the parties down, 'lowering the temperature' of the 'annoyed wife' and encouraging husband and wife to 'come together.' Theresa was adamant that 'if a man beats a woman,' in her capacity as the Palima section chairwoman, 'I will take that man to the chief.'[33]

On land ownership and inheritance, the views of Hannah and Theresa suggest a very slow evolution with regard to women's property rights in Moyamba District or at least in Palima. Hannah stated plainly that a woman cannot buy land without her husband's permission, nor has she any hope of judicial protection 'without a strong man behind her.' Theresa said a woman has the right to purchase property so long as her husband is living. Nevertheless, Theresa conceded that women's property rights are vulnerable if legally challenged. Hannah and Theresa had somewhat differing views on women's inheritance rights. Hannah said that a widow who had lived on her husband's land would inherit all his property. Theresa, on the other hand, could state from experience that a widow might not inherit anything, save the right to inhabit and cultivate the land, which devolved to her husband's blood relations. It is worthy of note here that under the Devolution of Estates Act, as discussed in Chapter 2, widows are entitled to inherit 35 percent of the deceased spouse's property. Clearly, there remains a gap between law and practice in Palima.

Importantly, for both Hannah and Theresa, reconciliation and accountability are two sides of the coin of unity (*ngoyela*) so essential for survival and collective livelihood in their community. As they see it, the fullest expression of that unity is participation in community projects dedicated to collective development (*ndeguloma*). Thus, sustainable livelihood is the product of reconciliation—as development (*ndeguloma*) is the fruit of unity (*ngoyela*). As Hannah concluded, 'The first and foremost thing is that the women of Palima . . . are working together. Even now, we are on it. We have no fear to enter any house in the village because we are all one.' After interviewing Hannah and Theresa, it was time for our team to move on to Tawovehun.[34]

TALKING WITH PEACE MOTHERS OF TAWOVEHUN, MOYAMBA DISTRICT

Like the other four interview sites throughout Sierra Leone, I visited the community of Tawovehun in March 2016 and July 2017 with a local team led by Lilian Morsay. I returned in subsequent years (2018, 2019, 2022, and 2023) to verify certain facts and quotations and to maintain contact and solidarity with group members. Translation from English to Mende and Krio was provided by Fambul Tok staff, including colleagues based in the Fambul Tok field office in Moyamba Town, during all the field visits.

Figure 18. Theresa, Peace Mother of Palima, Moyamba District, Sierra Leone.
Photo by J. Moore, 2018.

Cultural and Demographic Notes on Tawovehun

Tawovehun is part of the chiefdom of Kowa, in the northern part of Moyamba. Like Palima, Tawovehun includes Christian and Muslim families, although for Tawovehun it is Christians who are in the slight majority, in
contrast to the roughly 70/30 Muslim-Christian demographics of Palima and
Sierra Leone as a whole. Tawovehun is the name of a section whose headquarters is in the village of Batema, where we conducted our interviews. As is
true for Moyamba overall, the majority of Tawovehun residents speak Mende
as their maternal language. Most residents are farmers engaged in the cultivation of rice, beans, cassava, groundnuts, and yams. Some villagers also
catch fish for consumption or sale. Batema is in walking distance of the municipality of Njala in the neighboring chiefdom of Kori. Njala is a university
town where Tawovehun residents can also seek medical treatment. Although
there is no attending physician in Njala, it has a mobile health clinic with a
traditional birth attendant in residence and is staffed by rotating community
health workers who visit once or twice per month.

Welcoming Ceremony in Tawovehun, 2016

In March 2016, our research team returned to Moyamba Town after our first focus group discussion in Palima, spending a second night in local guesthouses. We drove the following morning to Tawovehun, a journey of some two hours. As in Palima, the custom in Tawovehun is for women of the community to greet visitors in a ceremony of song, dance, and drumming. The celebration in Tawovehun that first year was extraordinarily exuberant. Among the dancers were several masked Bondo devils. The jubilation lasted for nearly two hours until Lilian Morsay and others suggested it might be time for us all to sit down and begin the focus group discussion.

While the conversation was meant to include five women, gradually five became six, seven and more, as one woman invited a sister, another her neighbor, and so forth. Finally, ten local women were squeezed together companionably on two benches in a shady area near one participant's family home. My analysis of the Tawovehun group interview focuses on the contributions of Nannah and Mami J.,[35] who would go on to take part in individual interviews in subsequent years.

Tawovehun Focus Group Discussions, 2016

As in all the field sites in Sierra Leone and Uganda, we started with the theme of *reconciliation*. Not unlike Palima, most of the Tawovehun Peace Mothers described reconciliation in terms closely allied with forgiveness. The focus group members stressed the importance of ending the cycle of wrongdoing. They noted that reconciliation is essential to the relationship between two individuals but also to the very survival of their community. Nannah, around forty years old in 2016, is the mother of nine children. Of the six who remain,[36] four are boys and two are girls. For Nannah, '*ngoyela* [unity] is healing. If you refuse to heal or forgive, the wrong will continue. In community, wrongs will happen, [but] life must continue.' Mami J., forty-five, explained that of the twelve children she gave birth to, only one survived. She put reconciliation in very personal terms: 'I gave birth to one child, a son who has done wrong and has been forgiven. I know I must also forgive.'

Our discussion of *livelihood* followed. Paralleling the Peace Mothers of Palima, the women of Tawovehun emphasized the need to earn some amount of cash income, largely from the sale of surplus crops, which enables the family to pay for school fees as well as medications and other essential household items. As Nannah put it, 'School is compulsory. To keep a child in school and to buy clothes, farming is necessary. Sustenance farming entails producing rice, beans and yams—rice for eating and the others for sale in the market.' Mami J. engages in farming to be able to provide for her son and is grateful that 'my husband helps as well.'

We ended with a round-robin on *accountability*. In contrast to the women of Palima, who defined accountability in spiritual terms linked to reconciliation, the Peace Mothers of Tawovehun tended to talk about accountability in financial and material terms. For Nannah, accountability requires 'honest money transactions, and returning loans.' For Mami J., accountability is being 'trustworthy. If someone gives you something for safekeeping, you will keep it safe.'

Reassembling Our Team and Returning to Tawovehun for Individual Interviews in 2017

In July 2017, I returned to Moyamba District with our research team including Lilian Morsay and our driver Mustapha Rogers. After interviewing Hannah and Theresa in Palima, we drove a couple of hours in the direction of Tawovehun. As it got late, we decided to stop for the night in Mano, a town on the banks of the wide, deep, and gently flowing Mano River. In the morning, we drove up the short but steep and rocky road from Mano to Tawovehun.

We arrived in Tawovehun before the sun was very high in the sky and joined in the ceremonial dance of welcome before being led to a nearby clearing next to a family home. There we were joined by our Mende interpreter Bashiru Yankuba, another local Fambul Tok staff member, who had gotten transport from Moyamba Town to help with the interviews. About a dozen townspeople gathered in, leaning against a tree or sitting on the front steps of the house. The community members were familiar and welcoming, appreciating that our research team had returned for a second visit after a year of absence. The group included about a dozen women, two with babies in their arms; a couple of men; and several children. Again, we received benedictions in the Muslim and Christian traditions and, as in Palima, Lilian shared that I was in mourning over the passing of my father. The townspeople offered a loving prayer in his memory.[37]

After the welcome, Nannah and Mami J. agreed to take part in individual interviews, having been among the ten women who had participated in the focus group the year before. The others were gracious about our desire to focus on just a few interviewees in order to spend sufficient time with each. They also appreciated our awareness that they had important family and farm duties to attend to, and they expressed their confidence that Nannah and Mami J. would well represent their Peace Mothers group as a whole.

Ushered into a cozy sitting room in the cement-block dwelling, we sat on velour-upholstered chairs and prepared for interviews using the standard Peacebuilders Questionnaire referenced above. Nannah and Mami J. gave their interviews separately and in private, starting with Nannah. Bashiru translated into Mende and Lilian into Krio when she wished to help the interviewee to elaborate on a given question.

Linking Impressions of Tawovehun, 2017 and Subsequent Years (2018–2023)

Nannah and Mami J. of Tawovehun have certain unique perspectives, starting with their individual life experiences. Still in their early to mid-forties, Nannah has lost three of her nine children while Mami J. has lost all but one of the dozen or so babies she delivered. Both women recognize the barriers to women's equal enjoyment of property and inheritance rights. At the same time, they also acknowledge Sierra Leone's progress in implementing the new Gender Laws, particularly regarding the devolution of estates, even as that progress is spotty and incomplete. Against the backdrop of a recent consciousness-raising campaign regarding women's inheritance rights, Nannah described a new tendency for community members to insist that the husband's relatives 'responsibilize,' meaning that they do right by his widow.

Both women talked about the relationship between the facets of peacebuilding. For Nannah it is livelihood, especially through women's agricultural cooperatives, that makes reconciliation and peace possible. For Mami J., education for her young granddaughter Hawa is the gateway to Hawa's meaningful understanding of *ndeleh* (peace). During our follow-up conversation in May 2018, she expanded on her own understanding of *ndeleh*: 'Presently, as I am sitting here, I am at peace because now there are two other women to help me with the farming.' As an elder, she can now concentrate on the household and caring for the children.[38] Already a grandmother at forty-six, Mami J. can ease back a bit on her physical labor, thanks to the strong arms and solidarity of her fellow Peace Mothers.

An important link between the 2016 focus groups and the individual conversations, conducted in 2017 and subsequently, is the question concerning the relative significance of *reconciliation, livelihood, and accountability*. The women of Palima tend to see reconciliation and accountability together as constituting *ngoyela* or unity, which they believe comes to fruition in the form of livelihood, expressed as *ndeguloma* or development. Nannah had a somewhat different conception. For her, the roots of community transformation are togetherness and unity (*ngoyela*). That unity then branches into development (*ndeguloma*), which in turn flowers in the form of reconciliation (*degoleh*). Rather than defining reconciliation as synonymous with *ngoyela* or unity, Nannah sees *degoleh* or reconciliation as built on a foundation of unity and development.[39] Thus, where for Hannah and Theresa of Palima reconciliation bears the fruit of livelihood, for Nannah unity in the pursuit of livelihood bears the fruit of reconciliation. Mixing some metaphors, these kindred conceptions of the tree of peace are two sides of the same coin or continuous loops in a spiral of sustainable community life.

Comparing and Contrasting Impressions of Peacebuilding from Tawovehun and Palima, 2017

Hannah and Theresa of Palima have quite a bit in common with Nannah and Mami J. of Tawovehun. All four Peace Mothers are Mende speakers who make their living through farming. Only Mami J. completed her first year of secondary school, the others having ended their studies after a few years of primary school. Where Hannah and Theresa are Muslim and Nannah and Mami J. are Christian, they all live in interfaith communities and are fluent in the practices and prayers of one another's faith traditions. They each value the mutual assistance activities of the Peace Mothers, making specific mention of the vitality of their agricultural cooperatives. They do not romanticize their situation as women; their self-sufficiency is a necessity, which they achieve through shared livelihood activities. These women are proud of their success in resolving community disputes that might otherwise bring collective life to a standstill. They share the painful experience of losing children due to illness. All of them identify education as key to women's development and each lament the lack of sufficient opportunities and resources for girls and women to further their education. All four of them see the national government as quite distant from their daily lives.

Northern Province: The Three Koinadugu Field Visits
DEMOGRAPHIC NOTES ON KOINADUGU

Koinadugu is the largest district of Northern Province and Sierra Leone overall and borders on the Republic of Guinea to the north.[40] Its district capital of Kabala is only about thirty miles south of that border. Aside from gold

Figure 19. Nannah, Peace Mother of Tawovehun, Moyamba District, Sierra Leone.
Photo by J. Moore, 2022.

mining and alluvial and terrace mining of diamonds,[41] its major economic
activities are cattle herding and the cultivation of rice, beans, and various veg-
etables. In contrast to the low-lying or coastal terrain of Moyamba District,
Koinadugu's capital city of Kabala is located at 1,500 feet above sea level. The
nearby peak of Loma Mansa (Mount Bintumani) is located at an elevation of
nearly 6,400 feet.[42] Where the majority of Moyamba's residents speak Mende
as their mother tongue, in Koinadugu numerous maternal languages are spoken, including Fula, Koranko, Limba, Mandingo, and Yalunka. Koinadugu
is the most ethnically diverse district of Sierra Leone, known for its inter-
tribal and interfaith marriages. In addition to the devotional practices typical of their individual faith traditions, Muslims commonly attend church
services and likewise Christians sometimes pray in mosques.[43]

Dogoloya, Heremakono, and Kaponpon are the three field research sites
in Koinadugu District. Each community is within fifteen miles of Kabala, the
district capital: to the southwest Heremakono; to the west Kaponpon; and to

the north Dogoloya, only about twenty miles south of Sierra Leone's northern border with Guinea. Despite the short distances, vehicles may travel less
than ten miles per hour over unpaved roads. Our research team selected the
three sites to provide a representative linguistic and cultural mix: Dogoloya
is a majority Muslim and Fula-speaking settlement, Heremakono is primarily composed of native Mandingo speakers who are Muslims, and Kaponpon is home to a majority of Limba who are both Muslim and Christian. The
Fambul Tok team members based in the Koinadugu District Office in Kabala collectively speak the full spectrum of regional languages as well as Krio
and English.

Assembling Our Research Team for Koinadugu

Lilian Morsay accompanied me to Koinadugu in 2016, 2017, 2019, and 2023,
serving as cultural interlocutor and translator (for Krio and Mandingo) during
the field visits. She introduced and reintroduced me to community leaders
and individual Peace Mothers in successive visits to the three communities,
providing continuity and helping establish and reestablish trust on each occasion. Interpretation and cultural insights for the focus group and individual
interviews were also provided by Fambul Tok colleagues Issa Kamara (fluent
in Fula and Mandingo), Zainab Kamara (fluent in Limba), and Emmanuel
Mansaray (fluent in Mandingo). Komba Moiwa of the Fambul Tok Freetown
office also provided Krio translation and vital logistical support in 2018,
2022, and 2023.[44]

Dogoloya, the home of Boie Jalloh and Lamrana Bah, was our first site
visit in 2016.

TALKING WITH THE PEACE MOTHERS OF DOGOLOYA, KOINADUGU DISTRICT

A Word on the Language of Peace in Fula

Dogoloya, located in the Folosaba Dembelia Chiefdom just north of Kabala,
is home to the Fulbeh people, whose native language is Fula. Among the
Mende of Moyamba Province, peace is *ndeleh*, unity is *ngoyela*, and development is *ndeguloma*. Among the Fulbeh of Dogoloya and nearby areas of
Koinadugu District, peace is *buti berende* (calm heart), unity is *yokere-enda*,
and cooperation or working together is *fotande*. Another important Fula concept is *mijade*, which means contemplation, meditation, or deep thought,
particularly about something painful or difficult.[45]

Cultural and Historical Notes on Dogoloya

Land is fertile and relatively abundant in Dogoloya. Many Fulbeh families here raise cattle, goats, and sheep, in addition to tending gardens.[46] The vast majority of Fulbeh people who reside in Northern Sierra Leone are practitioners of the Muslim faith. Non-Fulbeh Sierra Leoneans sometimes observe that patriarchy and male authority are more pronounced in Fulbeh settlements than elsewhere in Northern Sierra Leone.[47] Nevertheless, gender relations are changing among the Fulbeh as in other ethnocultural communities, particularly since the end of the Rebel War. This dynamism is evidenced by the strengthening of women's cooperative networks, including the Peace Mothers, and growing awareness and respect for the Gender Laws, including the Devolution of Estates Act.

While their precise history and provenance are debated, the Fulbeh are generally considered relative newcomers to Sierra Leone compared to other ethnic groups. Many geographers and anthropologists identify the seventeenth century as a key period for Fulbeh migration across much of West Africa.[48] Although traditionally nomadic, throughout West Africa today only roughly a third of the Fulbeh maintain an itinerant lifestyle, the majority living in settled communities.[49] Fulbeh communities in Northern Sierra Leone have thrived for generations in relative isolation and self-sufficiency through cattle husbandry and the cultivation of vegetable gardens. However, during the Rebel War the isolation of Fulbeh settlements became unsustainable. These communities were attacked by rival factions like those in all regions of Sierra Leone. War-related violence all too often involved neighbors forced by militants to commit violence against their own neighbors. It is an understatement that the aftermath of such brutality caused internal divisions in communities like Dogoloya. Thus, when Fambul Tok outreach workers arrived in 2008, a few years after the end of the Rebel War, the people of Dogoloya expressed a profound desire for local reconciliation. Even today, they celebrate the role of Fambul Tok and the Peace Mothers during the postwar period in restoring social ties and encouraging women's participation in all aspects of community life.

Two concrete examples of the impact of Fambul Tok's postwar reconciliation process in Dogoloya are notable. First, after Fambul Tok's community outreach efforts to promote peaceful national elections, village leaders proudly attest that there was no violence associated with local polling in Dogoloya in 2012 nor in subsequent elections, including the presidential contest in July 2023.[50] Second, these Fambul Tok networks were tapped during the Ebola epidemic of 2014 and 2015 to support the organization of public health initiatives at the local level. The Peace Mothers spearheaded a public education campaign throughout Sierra Leone to promote handwashing, the hygienic treatment of bodies, and the safe and dignified burial of those who succumbed to the disease. Crediting these efforts, Dogoloya had no deaths from Ebola during the epidemic. This outcome is in contrast to other communities throughout Sierra Leone reflected in the large number of cases and the nearly 30 percent national death rate for individuals infected with the Ebola virus in 2014 and 2015.[51]

Making Our Way to Dogoloya

In March 2016, our research team set out by road from Moyamba to Koinadugu District, a journey of some five hours over mostly paved roads. We spent the night in guesthouses in Kabala, the headquarters town of Koinadugu District, and drove to Dogoloya the following morning, a distance of less than ten miles over paved secondary roads.[52] Upon reaching the community, we were received by Peace Mothers and local leaders in a one-room building with a raised floor and a thatched roof, its walls constructed of interwoven boughs of wood. Rather than meeting our vehicle in a dancing multitude, as is customary in Moyamba District, the Peace Mothers of Dogoloya waited until we had stepped up into their meeting room to draw us into their dance of welcome. They wore floor-length light cotton robes, their printed headscarves loosely framing their faces. In turn several women warmly extended their upraised hands to us and we shared a little waltzing step, twirling around the room in the dappled sunlight.

After greetings from the various village leaders, Lilian asked the women to designate five representatives to take part in the focus group interview. We took our places on benches in a shaded area outside, joined by Mr. Jalloh, a local elder. "Dr. J," fluent in English, offered to assist our interpreter Issa Kamara with Fula translation for the focus group discussion. Issa described Mr. Jalloh as a "change agent" for his community. Upon his first conversations with Fambul Tok field workers in 2008, Dr. J had embraced the concept of women's community activism and encouraged other men of Dogoloya to do the same.[53]

Dogoloya Focus Group Discussions, 2016

As in the other villages throughout Sierra Leone and Northern Uganda, we started with the theme of *reconciliation*. Not unlike the women of Moyamba District, the Peace Mothers of Dogoloya chiefly defined the concept in terms of forgiveness, tolerance, and ending malice. Lamrana, Ayeba, and Boie were the three participants in the focus group who also participated in individual interviews over the following years. Boie Jalloh is also profiled in the Introduction. Her ideas about reconciliation and those of Ayeba and Lamrana are the focus of the qualitative analysis below.

Lamrana, then fifty years old and mother of six, is a traditional birth attendant. She emphasized that 'we must learn to give, to be able to work together, to eat together from the same bowl, to play and laugh, to share the kola nut.'[54] Ayeba, then forty years old and mother of five, contrasted the period just after the war, when there was quite a bit of malice between people, to the present moment, in which 'there are no grudges.' She spoke of the importance of a handshake, which symbolizes that 'what the other did was wrong but that she is forgiven.'[55] Boie, then thirty-seven years old and mother of four, stressed the importance of tolerance and used the metaphor of a shared river between two villages, to which neither has a superior claim: 'We should realize that the water belongs to us all.' As commonly understood in Moyamba as well, the women of Dogoloya recognize the practical and spiritual links between reconciliation and collective survival.

Next, we turned to *livelihood*. Not unlike the women of Moyamba, the Dogoloya focus group participants emphasized farming as the essence of their material subsistence. At the same time, they related livelihood to reconciliation, again reinforcing the vital link between reconciliation and survival. Lamrana plainly stated, 'Livelihood is peace, to start with; when there is peace, livelihood is assured.' Ayeba was somewhat more concrete, explaining that for her, 'livelihood is making a farm, and feeding your family with rice and groundnuts, and sometimes selling a part of the rice for clothing.' Boie combined the material with the philosophical: 'Livelihood is mixed cropping, cassava, rice, and groundnuts. Since there's peace, husband and wife can agree to work together.'[56]

Finally, we turned to *accountability*. The women of Moyamba defined the term variously, whether as honesty in business transactions, or taking responsibility and showing remorse for wrongdoing. Contrastingly, the Peace Mothers of Dogoloya concentrated on the internal aspects of accountability as a manifestation of moral character and integrity, rather than an accountability imposed from the outside as a mark of punishment or control. Accountability from within requires the courage to admit wrongdoing. Lamrana defined accountability in terms of discretion and not returning evil for evil:

'If you meet someone gossiping about you, and you tell your children and they quarrel with the gossiper, it's your fault. Instead, keep quiet.' Ayeba stressed the importance of acknowledgment: a wife should be able to apologize to her husband if she wrongs him, 'and men also should be able to apologize.' Boie agreed, positing a village misunderstanding and declaring that 'if a person admitted to being the source of the error that would end the problem.' At the end of the day, the women of Moyamba and Dogoloya tend to view accountability in terms of remorse by the wrongdoer as well as mercy on the part of the victim. They link accountability between individuals to the health of the collective.

Reassembling Our Team to Conduct Individual Interviews in Dogoloya in 2017

In July 2017, I returned to Dogoloya with our Fambul Tok team, including Lilian Morsay, Mustapha Rogers our driver, and Issa Kamara as our Fula interpreter. Due to the rainy season many Peace Mothers were busy in their fields, so this time it was an intimate group of women who gathered for the second time, chanting their song of welcome (*jabba hey*) and waltzing gently with Lilian and me, with warm recognition in their eyes. One by one, the three interviewees sat with our team on benches under a tree. Mr. Jalloh, proud gender relations "change agent" for the community, soon walked by and reintroduced himself. At one point, he seemed to want to participate in the conversations, until it was suggested that he might be making the women self-conscious, then he graciously took his leave. Later, we took a break and women of the community offered us a typical meal of cow's milk yogurt and a fluffy polenta made of ground corn, which we could season with sugar or salt.

As in all ten interview sites in Uganda and Sierra Leone, I used the standard Peacebuilders' Questionnaire[57] for the individual interviews.

Linking Impressions and Insights from Dogoloya, 2017 and Subsequent Years (2018–2023)

Like the women of Palima and Tawovehun, the Peace Mothers of Dogoloya are engaged in agriculture with the important addition of cattle husbandry so vital to Fulbeh identity and livelihood. In contrast to the women of Moyamba who are Mende speakers from both Christian and Muslim traditions, Boie, Ayeba, and Lamrana are all Fula speakers and practicing Muslims. Like in Moyamba, the Peace Mothers of Dogoloya are proud of their farming cooperatives and their revolving credit funds or VSAs. Their community has access to one health clinic, with trained nurses but no doctors; and their children can attend the local junior secondary school, although the closest senior high school is around ten miles away in the district capital of Kabala. The birth rate in Dogoloya seems to be around six or seven children per mother. Child mortality is a sad fact of life, as it is in Moyamba. Unlike the women of Palima and Tawovehun, who received some primary education, Lamrana, Ayeba, and Boie did not have the opportunity to attend public school, although they benefited from some religious instruction.

All three women of Dogoloya emphasized the value of their contributions to peacebuilding in their community of Dogoloya. Lamrana spoke poetically about the linkages between women's various contributions to community transformation. If women's peacebuilding efforts were a tree in the center of Dogoloya, she analogized, the roots would be unity (*yokere enda*), branching into cooperative work (*fotande*), and bearing the fruit of *buti berende*, the calm heart of peace itself.[58] For her part, Ayeba expressed her view that women's overall status now is 'comparatively much better than during the war. Now we women, we're doing more, like running the home. Before, men were shouldering everything, but now we women are doing a bigger part.' Boie also noted women's mediating and supportive roles: 'We promote peace and if there is any [collective] activity in the community, we as Peace Mothers come together to help in whatever little way we can.' At the same time, Boie emphasized that women in turn receive support back from their community. Recently when she faced a personal crisis, 'thirty-five men and women came to help me,' with no thought of compensation, 'simply because I've been promoting peace in the community.'

Lamrana, Ayeba, and Boie were interviewed separately, yet their responses conveyed a strong sense of common cause and shared values. Daily life in Dogoloya is challenging on a material level—resources are slim, farming is demanding, social services are few—yet essential material needs are being met at the community level. It's a given that life is a struggle, yet women are energized by their collective work, both materially and spiritually. The women of Dogoloya are good at survival. They know that and so do the men of their community. Their gentle and humble demeanor is grounded not in self-effacement but in self-respect.

After the individual interviews in Dogoloya, our research team moved on to Heremakono, also located in Koinadugu District.

Figure 20. Peace Mothers of Dogoloya, Koinadugu District, Sierra Leone. Photo by J. Moore, 2022.

TALKING WITH THE PEACE MOTHERS OF HEREMAKONO, KOINADUGU DISTRICT

A Word on the Language of Peace in Mandingo

Heremakono is part of the Wara Wara Yagala Chiefdom, home to a majority of Mandingo speakers. In Mende, it may be remembered, peace is *ndeleh*, unity is *ngoyela*, and development is *ndeguloma*; whereas in Fula, peace is *buti berende* (calm heart), unity is *yokere-enda*, and cooperation is *fotande*. In Mandingo, peace is *jusu-suma* (cool heart), unity is *kan-kelail* (one world), and collective work is *jama-bara*.[59] There is a compelling symmetry between the calm heart of *buti berende* in Fula and the cool heart of *jusu-suma* in Mandingo.[60]

Cultural and Historical Notes on Heremakono

Located about ten miles southwest of Kabala, Heremakono is the name of a cluster of four villages in Wara Wara Yagala Chiefdom, named for a prominent and beautiful mountain in the area. Heremakono's majority Mandingo residents are mainly Muslims who typically speak Krio in addition to Mandingo. Whereas the ancestors of the Fulbeh[61] people of Dogoloya are said to have arrived in Sierra Leone as pastoral nomads centuries ago, many Mandingo in the area of Heremakono are the descendants of missionaries who migrated to the Northern Province of Sierra Leone from Guinea in the late nineteenth century to establish Koranic schools.[62] Over the ensuing generations, Mandingo families have integrated with Sierra Leone's other major ethnic groups and settled around the country. Their population remains concentrated in various areas throughout Northern Province. In Koinadugu and elsewhere, most Mandingo make their living in commerce and agriculture.[63]

Assembling Our Team and Making Our Way to Heremakono, 2016

In March 2016, after visiting Dogoloya, our research team spent another night in Kabala. We learned early the next morning that a woman from Heremakono had recently passed away. Anticipating the postponement of our focus group discussion, we nevertheless proceeded to the community, a journey of less than thirty minutes along the main paved road heading southwest toward Freetown. Some local leaders invited us to sit with the gathered townspeople for a remembrance ceremony in the center of the village, where men and women of the community were seated in side-by-side clusters. Issa Kamara and Emmanuel Mansaray, another Fambul Tok staff member based in Kabala Town, provided Mandingo-to-English translation as we interacted with some local residents.[64] We joined in expressing our *woma-toro* (condolences) to the family and friends of the departed. Directly translated, *woma-toro* means "We are part of your loss."[65]

After the visiting time, community members encouraged us to proceed with our conversation with the Peace Mothers, foregoing the customary dance of welcome out of respect for the bereaved family. Peace Mothers Mariam, Hawa, Kaday, Fanta, and Mbalia came forward to meet with our team. We joined with them on benches in a shaded area near the village center, with Issa and Emmanuel serving as interpreters for the group interview.

Heremakono Focus Group Discussions, 2016

We started as always with the theme of *reconciliation*. Like the Fulbeh women of nearby Dogoloya, the Peace Mothers of majority-Mandingo Heremakono linked the concepts of reconciliation and accountability. In their understanding, the over-arching elements of reconciliation include mediation, often led by elders, and an apology by the offender that is typically followed by the victim's offer of pardon. For the Peace Mothers of Heremakono, reconciliation is more than a symbolic ritual. It is a painstaking and interactive process that requires the participation of numerous actors. It is ultimately dependent on the willingness of the wrongdoer to acknowledge their wrongdoing. He or she must be willing to make amends before forgiveness can flow.

Kaday, fifty and mother of six, shared her perspective as an elder who often leads mediations. As she noted, while present in such procedures from the start, Kaday tends to hang back at first to give the parties a chance to reach their own resolution, only stepping in to prevent an escalation of tensions. What is essential is that she accompanies the participants through the process to its final resolution. Fanta, fifty and mother of four, declared that 'for us, reconciliation is unity.' She elaborated on several details, specifying that the offender speaks first in the mediation process, then the victim. She insisted that where an apology is freely given by one party, pardon will tend to be forthcoming from the other. For her part, Mbalia,[66] forty-five and mother of five, described what ensues in the event that the parties become violent. In such rare instances, fines are levied on both. Only when the disputing parties have calmed down, she concluded, can the reconciliation process begin again in earnest.

Next, we turned to *livelihood*. Like the women of Moyamba and Dogoloya, the five Heremakono focus group members point to farming as a major subsistence activity. What distinguished Heremakono from other communities was the fact that its Peace Mothers place farming and revolving credit on an equal footing in terms of ensuring the material well-being of themselves and their families. They spoke at length about their village savings association (VSA), through which they manage a self-financed informal banking system. Kaday described the Peace Mothers' VSA as a well-maintained engine of cash generation requiring the regular collection of dues and orderly turn-taking by members in need of small loans.

Fellow group members Fanta and Mbalia elaborated on the lending process, detailing their individual 2,000-leone weekly contributions (around 10 cents in US currency), followed by the group's set-aside of a portion of that cash to buy rice for resale by group members, and the preservation of the remainder to support periodic loans. Fanta explained that the typical loan of 100,000 leones (around US$5) must be paid back after one or two months, with the possibility that the group will levy a fine or charge additional interest for late payment. Mbalia pointed out that while on her own she is able to cultivate small plots of groundnuts and okra, it is only in collaborating with the Peace Mothers that she is able to cultivate rice and cassava as well. Mbalia added one final detail concerning the social support component of their VSA. In addition to their weekly 2,000-leone deposit to the revolving credit fund, group members also regularly donate 500 leones to a separate fund to support outright grants to individual Peace Mothers facing special hardships.[67]

Finally, we turned to *accountability*. In contrast to the women of Moyamba, who often focused on good stewardship of entrusted funds alongside remorse for wrongdoing, the Peace Mothers of Heremakono spoke almost exclusively in terms of moral accountability for offending others. Mariam, thirty-five and mother of two, talked about the absolute necessity of owning up to one's bad conduct. If the wrongdoer 'takes responsibility for it and makes the first move, the other person will love that, and will forgive.' She concluded that 'accountability promotes reconciliation.' Hawa, forty-eight and mother of four, agreed that accountability requires that 'you take ownership of wrongdoing and ask for mercy. The other person is happy and apt to consent to work alongside you.' Finally, Mbalia put accountability and dispute resolution into a personal and historical perspective. 'Terrible things were done to me during the war by community members. We were like enemies.' She credited the role of their ceremonial bonfire in promoting reconciliation. 'Fambul Tok brought us together with the idea of community healing. In the interest of peace, we were encouraged to come clean with our offenses. Forgiveness became more forthcoming, and [we] were less apt to go to the police to resolve disputes.'[68]

Reassembling Our Team and Returning to Heremakono in 2017

Our team returned to Heremakono in July 2017, in the heart of the rainy season. Lilian Morsay facilitated the visit and also provided Mandingo translation. While rains complicated interview conditions throughout Sierra Leone that year, in Heremakono our timing was particularly difficult. Upon our arrival from Kabala we met with Mbalia, Peace Mothers chairwoman, who helped us identify one other woman who was also available for one-on-one conversation. However, after interviewing Mbalia that afternoon, her colleague was no longer available. Having waited for us as long as she could, she had returned to her plot to tend her crops. When we returned to interview her the following day, she was busy again, this time standing before a huge pot of steaming palm oil, which she was preparing to bottle. We were grateful for our conversation with Mbalia, the only individual interview we were able to conduct in Heremakono that year.

In my interview with Mbalia, I used the standard Peacebuilders' Questionnaire.[69]

Individual Interviews with Mbalia in Heremakono, 2017, 2018, and 2019

Although she did not attend school past Form 3, Mbalia has held numerous leadership positions in her community. In addition to being the Peace Mothers chairwoman for Heremakono, she also served for some time as the assistant section chief of Heremakono. Notably, this position was created for her by the Heremakono section chief himself, in recognition of her track record of community activism and so that she might serve as a role model for other women. Mbalia's other leadership positions include the Heremakono section chairwoman[70] and vice-chairperson of the Inclusive District Peace and Development Committee (IDPDC) of Koinadugu.[71]

Mbalia is aware that women's leadership at the local level in Sierra Leone is still largely limited to "affirmative action" positions set aside especially for women.[72] In fact, her roles as Peace Mothers chairwoman, section chairwoman, and assistant section chief are all nominally "women's positions." Contrastingly, her position as vice-chairperson of the IDPDC stretches that mold, subtly evidencing the slow but inexorable trend toward women's more equal participation in public life. Given that these district-level development committees are part of a nationwide trend to integrate local populations more fully into the nuts-and-bolts process of community development, the involvement of women in such local power-sharing exercises will help ensure that these structures are not merely cosmetic but are transformative over time.

Despite the limited historical and contemporary cases of women serving as paramount chiefs in districts such as Moyamba, at the national level women remain marginalized in the cultural and customary leadership structures of Sierra Leone. Mbalia fully recognized that for women to engage in political and civil life on an equal footing with men, they will need to attain greater power within these traditional and customary leadership structures. This will require their being *elected* by their fellow clan members as section or paramount chief, and not merely *selected* by the chief to serve as his female deputy. In a sign of slow and meaningful progress in this regard, Mbalia noted with pride that as of 2017 a woman was serving as town chief of the nearby community of Yagala, the headquarters town of the Wara Wara Yagala Chiefdom.[73] Nevertheless, Mbalia remained cautiously optimistic. The cresting wave of women assuming official positions of power in her country is yet to come. Despite her own political activism, she noted that local attitudes still discourage women from stepping forward. Moreover, given the high level of illiteracy among women, the fact that town and section chiefs must be able to read and write remains a barrier for many. As Mbalia attested, the expansion of women's political power will require their enhanced access to education, health care, and credit.

Mbalia's perspective on women's property and inheritance rights also bears witness to the slow progress toward gender equality. Regarding women's purchase of land, she explained that 'in the old days, the husband's consent was needed, but no longer.' As for inheritance upon the death of the husband and householder, she stressed the importance of recent changes in national legislation,[74] as well as public education campaigns conducted at the community level. 'Before now, when the husband died, the relatives would take his property. Now, given the law and sensitization, property is left with the wife and kids.'

Mbalia finally spoke of peacebuilding in metaphoric terms. She visualized the reestablishment of community unity—*kan-kelail*—as the root of all peacemaking. The trunk and branches of her tree of peace grow out from that unity as community members rededicate themselves to collective work—*jama-bara*. *Kan-kelail* and *jama-bara* then bear fruit, Mbalia explained, in the sustained peaceful coexistence of *buti berende*, the cool heart of peace.

Generalized Insights from Heremakono, 2017

Mbalia's conception of a continuum between unity, cooperation, and durable peace is consonant with the insights expressed during the Heremakono focus group the year before. She and other Peace Mothers of her community visualize reconciliation and accountability as inextricably enmeshed. There can be no reconciliation or forgiveness on the part of the offended until they are inspired by the offender's apology and their willingness to be held accountable. Only when apology is followed by forgiveness—as accountability leads to reconciliation—are conditions ripe for the reestablishment of unity. In turn, that unity empowers livelihood by facilitating collective work. It is precisely because they have leveled with and forgiven one another that community members in Heremakono are able to commit to the burden-sharing intrinsic to the success of their revolving work crews and microloan initiatives. Solidarity is not an abstract or sentimental concept in Heremakono. Unity may arise from the ashes of violence and alienation, but such trans-

Figure 21. The late Mbalia Koroma, Peace Mother of Heremakono, Koinadugu District, Sierra Leone. Photo by J. Moore, 2018.

formation only occurs when community members acknowledge their need to survive together.

Linking Impressions of Heremakono, Dogoloya, and Moyamba, 2017–2023

Just as Mbalia's insights were representative of her Heremakono Peace Mothers group, there were strong resonances between conceptions of peacemaking in Heremakono and those expressed by the women of Dogoloya. In Dogoloya, the Peace Mothers' metaphoric tree of peace is rooted in unity or *yokere enda* and its branches emerge from *fotande*, or collective work. In Heremakono, the tree of peace is also rooted in unity or *kan-kelail* and its branches likewise emerge from *jama-bara*, or cooperative work. In both communities, the calm, cool heart of peace—*buti berende* in Fula and *jusu-suma* in Mandingo—is the fruit of women's daily devotional acts of honest accounting, willing redemption, and shared labor. While the language of peace in the Fulbeh and Mandingo communities of Koinadugu differs somewhat from the Mende terms used by

Peace Mothers in Moyamba, the common link is unity: *ngoyela* in Mende, *yokere-enda* in Fula, and *kan-kelail* in Mandingo. Unity through reconciliation is deemed intrinsic to peace in all three cultural contexts.

An important distinction between the life experiences of the Fulbeh women interviewed in Dogoloya, the Mende women of Moyamba, and the Mandingo women of Heremakono concerns their level of education. Neither Ayeba, Lamrana Bah, nor Boie Jalloh of Dogoloya had the opportunity to go to public school; whereas Hannah and Theresa from Palima, Nannah and Mami J. of Tawovehun, and Mbalia of Heremakono all attended at least a few years of primary school. This theme of the vitality of education would also surface in Kaponpon, the last of the five communities in which I interviewed Peace Mothers concerning their experiences and philosophies toward peace and justice.

TALKING WITH THE PEACE MOTHERS OF KAPONPON, KOINADUGU DISTRICT

A Word on the Language of Peace in Limba

The people of Kaponpon, within the Wara Wara Bafodia Chiefdom, are native speakers of Limba, one of the principal languages of Koinadugu and Northern Sierra Leone overall. There are numerous ways to speak about peace in Limba. Like the Mende word *ndeleh*, there is a single word for peace in Limba, which is *matebe*. But just as the Fulbeh and Mandingo people speak of peace in terms of the calm or cool heart (*buti berende* in Fula and *jusu-suma* in Mandingo) the Limba people imagine peace as heartfelt forgiveness. Two similar idiomatic expressions illustrate the concept of peace in Limba culture—*peniyande ka nuthukuma* (forgiveness in the heart) and *nuthukuma ba peniyande* (a heart of forgiveness). Other Limba concepts linked to peacebuilding are *atenga katabante* (coming together or unity), *aniwali katabante* (collective work), and *akei ka katorkoi* (development).[75]

Cultural and Historical Notes on Kaponpon

A majority of Kaponpon's residents are ethnic Limba who make their living by farming, similar to the Mende of Palima and Tawovehun, the Fulbeh of Dogoloya, and the Mandingo of Heremakono. In addition to speaking Limba, most of the people we spoke with in Kaponpon are also fluent in Krio. In their religious practice, the Limba stand out from the other ethnic communities in certain regards. While it is common in communities throughout Sierra Leone for Muslims and Christians to intermarry, live, and work together, the

Limba endow their spiritual observance with an enhanced degree of syncretism. Their typical devotional practice blends aspects of the two monotheistic religions along with a more ancient reverence for the spirits of ancestors. Contemporary religious scholars identify in Limba spirituality the interwoven threads of these Muslim, Christian, and animist traditions.[76]

Assembling Our Research Team for Kaponpon, March 2016

Zainab Kamara, then the Peace Mothers coordinator for Koinadugu District, was raised in Kaponpon and knows the community well. She joined the team as Limba translator for our field visit to Kaponpon. From Heremakono along the main highway southwest of Kabala Town we took secondary roads, taking an hour to travel just ten miles over rough terrain.

When we arrived in Kaponpon, we were met by a friendly group of women who waited until we stepped down from the car and then pulled us into their dance of welcome, accompanied by women drummers. The sense of joyful celebration was palpable, and Lilian's and my willingness to participate and enjoy ourselves was appreciated. Artistry and teasing were in the air, amid respect and kindness. As a cross-cultural icebreaker, communal dancing has no rival.

Walking to a clearing in the middle of the settlement, we sat with the gathered townspeople. They offered prayers in Arabic and Limba from the Muslim and Christian traditions as they passed around cups of fresh kola nuts, encouraging each of us to take one in a sign of friendship. Included in the assembly were the town and section chiefs, both men; the Mammy Queen, who serves as the female ombudsperson for the women of her section; and the local Peace Mothers chairwoman for Kaponpon. Zainab Kamara provided Limba translation for the welcome ceremony, as she would for our focus group discussion immediately afterward.

Kaponpon Focus Group Discussions, 2016

The Kaponpon focus group followed the same general format utilized in all nine community dialogues across the women's collectives of Northern Uganda and Sierra Leone. Our research team invited a small group of Peace Mothers from the community to gather for a group conversation, deferring to the local Peace Mothers leadership to designate a representative group of women of different ages and roles. We welcomed six women of the community, of whom Fatumatah and Tenneh would go on to take part in the individual and follow-up interviews over the ensuing years. The discussion below focuses on their contributions. Fatumatah is the chairwoman of the Kapon-pon Peace Mothers. In 2016 she was the thirty-four-year-old mother of five children. Tenneh is the youngest Peace Mother I had the opportunity to in-terview. In 2016 she was eighteen years old and the new mother of a several-month-old baby boy named Yonson, who slept in a sling on her back throughout much of our group discussion.

As at the other interview sites, we started with the theme of *reconcilia-tion*. Not unlike several of the women of Dogoloya, Heremakono and both communities in Moyamba, the Peace Mothers of Kaponpon do not make a strict differentiation between reconciliation and accountability. Accountabil-ity ideally occurs within the reconciliation process, and both concepts serve the goal of community reunification. Thus, when the offender accepts respon-sibility for wrongdoing this facilitates unity, and reconciliation itself is often defined as reunification after a breach. Reconciliation is the outcome of a suc-cessful mediation process and does not normally require the participation of outside authorities. Like Peace Mother Boie Jalloh of Dogoloya, both Fa-tumatah and Tenneh stand out in their community as highly effective me-diators. As described by Fatumatah, 'Reconciliation is when conflict happens, and I can intervene. I don't have to wait until I'm asked. I can engage other stakeholders to help.' For her part, Tenneh focused on her interactions with her peers: 'As young people, we often had conflicts among ourselves. Now I can interview the quarrelling parties, and if I fail [to resolve their dispute], I can call in an elder to help. That is reconciliation.'

Next, we turned to *livelihood*, which the Peace Mothers of Kaponpon un-derstand on several different levels. Providing concrete examples of farming and other physical activities, they also envision livelihood as linked to other processes—such as reconciliation, progress toward gender equality, and the protection of women's inheritance rights. Fatumatah makes her living farm-ing rice and groundnuts and keeping goats, sheep, and poultry. She clarified that in addition to cultivating food crops, she raises her animals for sale, using the proceeds to finance the purchase of clothing and payment of her children's school fees. For Tenneh, 'livelihood is investing in education for the future.' She was the one Peace Mother who defined livelihood chiefly in terms of edu-cation rather than the production of food or the generation of income.

Finally, we turned to *accountability*. In contrast to the women of Moyamba, who often focused on financial transparency, and the Peace Mothers of Do-goloya, who spoke almost exclusively in terms of moral accountability, the Ka-ponpon focus group members talked about accountability in terms of both honesty in money management and loyalty to their community. For the Peace Mothers of Kaponpon, there is a strong connection between accountability and communal integrity. For Fatumatah, accountability is expressed through a willingness to contribute to community needs. She pointed to the fact that the closest health clinic is far from Kaponpon, and for this reason the Peace Mothers have collected funds for building a new health clinic. For Tenneh, accountability is a matter of personal integrity: "Trust is the first thing I refer to. Accountability is when you perform the responsibilities expected of you."

Individual and Follow-Up Interviews in Kaponpon, 2017 and Subsequent Years (2018–2023)

In July 2017, Lilian and I returned to Kaponpon with our Fambul Tok team. Zainab Kamara was ill the day we visited Kaponpon and hence not available to provide Limba interpretation as she had in the prior year.[77] Her husband Edward, a schoolteacher, stepped forward to translate in her place. On the morning of July 14, we arrived in Kaponpon in time for a community gathering. Despite the unpredictability of the rainy season, the welcome ceremony was unrushed and even more elaborate than the year before. The gathering of nearly fifty men and women included Fatumatah in her capacity as Peace Mothers chairwoman, the Mammy Queen, the head teacher of the local public school, the village chief, and the section chief.

First came the women's dance, which Lilian and I joined to the great bemusement of the children. We sat down for the Muslim invocation of *Al-Fatiha*, followed by a recitation of the Lord's Prayer in the Christian tradition.[78] Lilian expressed our appreciation of the community's willingness to welcome our research delegation once again. When she related that my father had passed away a few months before, the local imam led a special prayer in his honor. Even the children joined their elders, cupping their open palms to the sky as they bowed their heads and intoned the words. Afterward, the imam made brief remarks, honoring the suffering of the women of his community, encouraging the children to stay in school, and recognizing that education is the key to success.

Lilian spoke next, thanking our hosts and describing the project and my intention to publish a book about how women suffer and find a way forward in different countries in Africa. One community member spoke out spontaneously, suggesting that in addition to my publication, contributions to improved health care in the community would be particularly appreciated. 'Women in Kaponpon,' she noted wryly, 'deliver their babies in hammocks,'

Figure 22. Fatumatah, Peace Mother of Kaponpon, Koinadugu District, Sierra Leone. Photo by J. Moore, 2018.

and what they *really* need is a proper delivery room. The Mammy Queen interjected diplomatically, *"tenki-tenki"* (thank you in Krio), testifying that she and her fellow Peace Mothers have deep memories of the war, and so they value the writing of a book that will chronicle their suffering. I added that the manuscript was indeed meant to witness their hardships but also to acknowledge the depth of their contributions, conveying to readers what they as peacebuilders can teach people around the world about resilience and community transformation.

Finally, the village chief spoke with pride of his people's willingness to do anything it took to further develop their community. He wished the visitors a safe onward journey and prayed that I might keep the memory of Kaponpon close in my heart. Lilian finally suggested it was nearly time to start the individual interviews. But before that could happen, we were given more kola nuts, a live chicken, and a pot of rice for later consumption as well as roasted groundnuts and rice with fish and pepper sauce for a quick snack to fuel our one-on-one conversations.

For the two interviews with Fatumatah and Tenneh I used the standard Peacebuilders' Questionnaire.[79]

Linking Impressions and Insights from Kaponpon, 2017 and Subsequent Years (2018–2023)

Fatumatah and Tenneh were a special pair to interview in the sense that Fatumatah at thirty-six was an elder in the community, and Tenneh at nineteen was still a youth leader. In 2017 and since, Fatumatah has served as the Peace Mothers chairwoman of Kaponpon. She is a Muslim and Temne by birth, part of the largest ethnic community in Northern Sierra Leone. In addition to Temne, she speaks Limba, the native language of her husband, and Krio. Like many of the women I interviewed in Koinadugu District, Fatumatah was not able to attend school as a child. She explained that her parents had eight children, and only her three brothers were sent to school. Fatumatah stressed that times have changed, and families are now willing to send their daughters to school. She pointed to the experiences of the young women in her family. Her eldest, now twenty-five with three children herself, left school in Form 2 after nearly ten years of combined primary and secondary education. Her twenty-three-year-old daughter is presently in Form 3 and her youngest is about to complete Form 2.

In her interview, Tenneh described the day her young baby was born. She gave birth to Yonson in their local clinic in Bafodia, which she reached after a four-hour journey on foot.[80] As she labored, Tenneh was assisted by a trained nurse. By her recollection, Yonson's birth was 'not easy.' After delivering, she rested and recovered for two days before returning to Kaponpon with her son. Tenneh is of Limba ethnicity on both sides. In addition to Limba she speaks Krio and some English. While her Peace Mothers chairwoman Fatumatah is a Muslim, Tenneh is a Christian of the Wesleyan Methodist denomination. After completing her second year of junior secondary school, and in order to prepare for the birth of her son, she interrupted her education just as she was preparing to enter senior high school. In terms of access to medical care, Tenneh reported that recently she took Yonson to the clinic for his regular infant health checkup so that he could be weighed and treated for scabies with tablets and injections. She was continuing to treat his malaria with herbs and was happy that he was showing signs of improvement.

Both Fatumatah and Tenneh spoke about the importance of education, particularly in inspiring changed attitudes toward gender roles and a gradual acceptance of gender equality. Fatumatah explained that traditionally in her culture, 'when you're given to your husband [in marriage], you don't have rights. To me, that is not rightful.' She insisted, 'We have to send our children to school [and], in time, attitudes about women's rights will change. . . . It is important for children to know that both men and women have the same rights.'[81] For her part, when asked about education, Tenneh was adamant about the importance of 'investing in education for the future.' Having left school when she became a mother, Tenneh regards education as a means of livelihood, a form of wealth, and a measure of community vitality. We were happy to learn the following year that Tenneh had returned to her studies and was preparing for her entrance exams to senior secondary school.[82]

Additional keynotes in both Fatumatah's and Tenneh's interviews in 2017 were their perspectives on women's property and inheritance rights. Despite the Gender Laws and the formal protections for women in the 2007 Devolution of Estates Act, Fatumatah was quite clear on the existence of a double standard where women's inheritance rights are concerned. For a widow to inherit she must negotiate with the elders of the departed husband's family, and only in cases of special affection would she inherit even a portion. Fatumatah clarified that it helps the woman's case if she has given birth to a son by her deceased husband: 'If you are a woman, except you give birth to a baby boy, when your husband dies, you won't get a single cent. Even if you have a baby boy, the property will be kept for him.' As for Tenneh, she put even less credence in the formal inheritance rights of women: 'If you don't have a baby boy, you can't inherit' from your departed husband, she explained: 'It's the law.' Tenneh's views on women's property ownership reflected her personal priorities. She was not interested in owning property at the moment. 'I'd rather go to school,' she insisted, reinforcing her vision of education as a form of livelihood, a measure of wealth, and insurance for the future.

Linking Impressions from Kaponpon to Those of Peace Mothers Throughout Sierra Leone

Tenneh and Fatumatah are peacebuilders in their community, Tenneh just embarking on her leadership path, and Fatumatah in her capacity as chairwoman of the Kaponpon Peace Mothers. The elder had no formal education, while her younger colleague was required to suspend her schooling at the secondary level when she gave birth to her first child. One Muslim and one

Christian, both are engaged in agriculture, raising families, and resolving community conflicts as trained mediators. They share an understanding that peacebuilding grows out of common cause and shared labor. Fatumatah speaks of unity (togetherness or *atenga katabante*), and Tenneh stresses collective work (*aniwali katabante*) and development (*akei ka katorkoi*). For both, the fruit of unity and cooperation is peace (*matebe*), sustained by a heart of forgiveness (*nuthukuma ba peniyande*).

Fatumatah and Tenneh employ poetic conceptions of peacebuilding, yet they are not starry-eyed romantics. Like so many of their sister Peace Mothers, their idealism is grounded in realism and fired in the intense kiln of their daily lives. They understand that their strength as individuals and their solidarity as group members are essential to the transformation of their communities. They are often collaborative, and when necessary voice their opposition to the status quo. Their agency—both individual and collective—is expressed in myriad ways through physical labor, intellectual work, spiritual devotion, and jubilant celebration.

Comparative Insights Linking Women Peacebuilders in Sierra Leone and Northern Uganda

For this study on women's leadership in grassroots peacebuilding, thirty Sierra Leone Peace Mothers—from Palima, Tawovehun, Dogoloya, Heremakono, and Kaponpon—took part in focus group discussions in 2016. Of this larger set, ten women participated in one-on-one interviews the following year and in follow-up conversations in 2018. In turn, five of these continued to meet with our research team when we made follow-up visits in subsequent years, most recently in 2023.

Our interactions with individual Peace Mothers over a seven-year period reveal approaches to peacebuilding that resonate with some of the insights shared by women peacebuilders in Northern Uganda, particularly the role that reconciliation plays in collective survival and the importance of access to land, credit, health care, and education in women's efforts to empower themselves and their communities. Alongside the common themes are certain broad distinctions between the Peace Mothers of Sierra Leone and their counterparts in Northern Uganda. Most dramatically, the grassroots women's peace movement in Sierra Leone is characterized by much greater ethnic and religious pluralism than its sister movement in Northern Uganda. For its part, the grassroots women's peace movement in Northern Uganda is characterized by greater criticism and demands of its current government than is the case for the Peace Mothers. This difference partially reflects the fact that Sierra Leoneans have elected two new presidents since their Rebel War ended, whereas President Museveni of Uganda, in office during the LRA War, has remained in power ever since. Our comparative analysis of women peacebuilders in the two countries will be reinforced in the final concluding chapter of this volume.

What remains for this chapter on the Peace Mothers of Sierra Leone is to distill the experiences and insights of the women of Moyamba and Koinadugu Districts into a set of vital principles about the nature of justice and social transformation in the aftermath of communal violence. These themes have relevance to conflict transformation in other parts of the world.

Common Threads in the Fabric of Peacebuilding in Sierra Leone

Certainly, the Peace Mothers' views on the nature of reconciliation, accountability, and livelihood are not monolithic. Nevertheless, collectively these women present a coherent vision of women-centered grassroots social transformation in Sierra Leone. Through an open-textured synthesis of their individual reflections, we may distill six vital Peace Mother principles that enrich our broader understanding of peacebuilding in postconflict societies.

First, *reconciliation is the heart of peacebuilding.* Members of the five Peace Mothers groups take for granted the symbiosis between acknowledgment, forgiveness, and survival. For them, accountability promotes reconciliation, reconciliation furthers livelihood, and earning an honest living is itself a measure of accountability. While accountability, reconciliation, and livelihood are all crucial values to women active in community transformation throughout the Peace Mothers movement, it might be said that reconciliation is the first among equals. Reconciliation restores relationships. Without it, the collective survival of the community is under grave threat. This idea was stated with particular intensity by Peace Mothers in the Palima section of Moyamba District. As Hannah expressed it, 'The first and foremost thing is that the women of Palima . . . are working together. Even now, we are on it. We have no fear to enter any house in the village because we are all one.' Woven through all aspects of peacebuilding is the common thread of relationship; just as reconciliation occurs at the level of the community, accountability is owed to the collective, and livelihood is a collaborative struggle and a shared triumph.

Second, *livelihood for women requires access to income and credit.* Material well-being for many members of the Sierra Leone Peace Mothers flows from the labor they engage in to put food in their children's stomachs—namely, farming. At the same time, their livelihood is dependent upon their ability to earn a certain portion of cash income required to meet other familial needs, particularly the payment of school fees and the purchase of medications. In Heremakono and throughout Sierra Leone, Peace Mothers put great stock in their village savings associations (VSAs), which empower them to pool their resources, make loans, charge interest, reinvest profits, and give outright grants in the case of family emergencies. Linked to their community banks are the collaborative enterprises these funds can support—namely, community health clinics and schools, flour mills, and farming collectives.

Third, *accountability entails both moral and financial integrity.* For the Peace Mothers, it is well understood that an individual's expression of remorse for wrongdoing facilitates forgiveness by the injured party and the restoration of their relationship. Peace Mothers view an offender's acknowledgment of misconduct chiefly as a question of inner integrity, rather than an external sanction imposed through police power or judicial actors. Particularly as expressed by the Peace Mothers of Dogoloya, "accountability from within" is more essential and enduring than "accountability from without." Accountability is valued as a character trait that engenders trust, in turn facilitating community unity. Such accountability includes financial integrity, reflected in the respect that Peace Mothers have for the treasurer of their VSA.

Fourth, *gender equality promotes women's security and the family's welfare.* In communities across Moyamba and Koinadugu, women appreciate that the protection of their rights to own and inherit land—as women, as daughters, and as widows—is their due under the law. At the same time, the receipt of their just inheritance is critical to their ability to sustain themselves and to provide for their families. For all these reasons, they are deeply committed to advocacy and education leading to the proper implementation of Sierra Leone's Devolution of Estates Act.

Fifth, *dispute resolution facilitates partnership between women and men.* Peace Mothers throughout Sierra Leone have developed mediation and violence de-escalation techniques that are highly effective, such that the community is seldom reliant on the intervention of law enforcement or other external actors. Pride in their ability as Peace Mothers to combat domestic violence and to resolve their own disputes reflects a certain lack of confidence in the integrity of public institutions in rural Sierra Leone. At the same time, the Peace Mothers see their mediation skills as intrinsically valuable, and as a means of strengthening social solidarity between spouses, among neighbors, and across extended families.

Sixth and finally, *women's leadership empowers social transformation.* Members of all five Peace Mothers groups in Sierra Leone credit the role of Fambul Tok in helping instill a culture of reconciliation and collective development in their communities. They also acknowledge their own heroic efforts to ameliorate the Rebel War's destructive and still-pervasive impact on rural life in Sierra Leone. They are convinced that social cohesion and gender equality are vital antidotes to the violence and social rupture they have experienced. As Peace Mothers, they take great pride in their contributions as women in fueling a powerful resurgence in community spirit in the postwar period, activism that has continued through subsequent emergencies. Come what may—the devastation of Ebola, flooding, mudslides, economic stagnation, government disengagement, electoral irregularities, political unrest, family violence—the Peace Mothers "are on it." They understand that their leadership and collective activism are the lifeblood of social transformation in their communities.

CONCLUDING INSIGHTS FROM THE PEACE MOTHERS

The regenerative and redemptive power of solidarity in the face of suffering—the capacity of communities and individuals to emerge from violence with renewed vitality and deepened resilience—is eloquently expressed in dialogues with Peace Mothers in all five communities we visited in Sierra Leone. Whether expressed in Mende as *ndeleh*, in Fula as *buti berende* (calm heart), in Mandingo as *jusu-suma* (cool heart), or in Limba as *peniyande ka nuthukuma* (forgiveness in the heart), peacebuilding for the Peace Mothers is an organic and devotional process requiring both patience and courage. The work of peace is rooted in rites of reunification (*atenga katabante* or coming together in Limba), it matures through cooperative work projects (*fotande* in Fula and *jama-bara* in Mandingo), and it flowers in collective development (*ndeguloma* in Mende). But peacebuilding is not all hearts and flowers to grassroots women activists in Sierra Leone. It happens through hard work, against the odds, and despite governmental incapacity. The creativity and strength that enable women to survive by the sweat of their brows are the very qualities that enable them to collaborate in new endeavors and realms. Their expansive contributions include the promotion of women's property rights, the prevention of domestic violence, the expansion of economic enterprise and social services, and the development of women's leadership and participation in electoral politics.

The Peace Mothers as a collective celebrate their members' nurturing devotion to family and community. But that's not all. In a sweet and subtle form of irony, participation in their local Peace Mothers group is also an expression of women's defiance of oppressive traditions, their commitment to social change, and their dedication to the struggle for gender equality. As community peacebuilders, the Peace Mothers are powerful for others and for themselves.

Rural Women Peacebuilders: A Quiet Storm of Social Transformation

When we made it back home, back over those curved roads
that wind through the city of peace, we stopped at the
doorway of dusk as it opened to our homelands.
We gave thanks for the story, for all parts of the story
because it was by the light of those challenges we knew
ourselves—
We asked for forgiveness.
We laid down our burdens next to each other.

—Joy Harjo

I have more skills due to my suffering.
—Grace, Peacebuilder of Rwot
Lakica, Northern Uganda

I feel strongest as a woman when I
am working together with the group.
—Tenneh, Peace Mother of
Kaponpon, Sierra Leone

Figure 23. Peace Mothers of Dogoloya and the late Mr. Jalloh, Koinadugu District, Sierra Leone. Photo by J. Moore, 2017.

G race and Tenneh, Jane Orama and Boie Jalloh, and all their fellow women peacebuilders in Uganda and Sierra Leone, understand as few of us can the challenges of social transformation in societies emerging from armed conflict and burdened by entrenched poverty and enduring patriarchy. Their grounded perspectives on peacebuilding, justice, and human rights urge us to rethink the dominant global model for transitional justice, which stresses the establishment of formal judicial and national institutions in the postwar period, including war crimes tribunals for penal justice, truth commissions for restorative justice, and reparations programs for redistributive justice. Their rural women-centered vision of social change turns the global model inside out, demonstrating that top-down and near-term mechanisms are not the exclusive ways to engender accountability, reconciliation, and livelihood. In fact, the insights and experiences of rural women peacebuilders in Northern Uganda and Sierra Leone suggest that grassroots and long-term community practices serve these ends more concretely and sustainably, particularly if they are supported by progressive social welfare reforms at the national level.

If the norms of human rights law, the theories of feminism, and the practices of transitional justice are to be truly relevant, they should dovetail with the vision and priorities of the women who are doing the work of human dignity at the local level. Scholars, activists, and practitioners operating transnationally will better support and champion the work of women peacebuilders if we honor their priorities and become fluent in their vernaculars of reconciliation, accountability, and livelihood, even as we speak about and help create transformative justice for the benefit of everyone.

Peace Mothers of Sierra Leone—from the Mende communities of Palima and Tawovehun in the southern district of Moyamba to the Fulbeh, Mandingo, and Limba communities of Dogoloya, Heremakono, and Kaponpon in the northern hill district of Koinadugu—have much in common with the women of Rwot Lakica, Alany pa Mony Lit, Uketu wan Kwene, and Odoko Mit, who reside in sub-counties across Acholiland in Northern Uganda. A total of sixty women peacebuilders across these nine communities took part in the focus groups convened in 2016, thirty of whom were interviewed individually on several occasions over the ensuing seven years. These grassroots women peacebuilders span five ethnolinguistic groups, four faith traditions,[1] three climate zones, and two countries and civil war experiences. Nevertheless, all agree that their contributions—to trauma healing, collective agriculture, microfinance, conflict mediation, domestic violence prevention, and the defense of women's political and inheritance rights—are vital to healthy social life in their villages, parishes, and chiefdoms.

On the most basic level, to describe the daily activities of the Sierra Leone Peace Mothers and the women peacebuilders of Acholiland is to define peacebuilding and transformative justice in their communities. They model and promote reconciliation, generate and share livelihood, and seek and demand greater accountability from themselves and from others. Their solidarity energizes them for the work of surviving and thriving in the most difficult of circumstances. They are grateful and proud of what they have accomplished, and they aspire to much more. Chief among the endeavors that bring them joy and satisfaction are their community savings and loan associations; their record of successful mediation of disputes; and the mutual support, both moral and material, that they provide one another in times of difficulty or tragedy. Central to the unmet demands of women peacebuilders in both countries are greater burden sharing and partnership between men and women within families and communities and increased investments in education and health care from their national governments. In the case of Northern Uganda, members of women's community collectives are also waiting for basic acknowledgment and meaningful compensation by the government for its role in atrocities against civilians in the LRA War, over fifteen years after the signing of the Juba Peace Accords.

Grassroots women's conceptions of reconciliation, livelihood, and accountability in Sierra Leone and Northern Uganda supply missing cornerstones in the theoretical framework of feminism and transformative justice. Their experiences and insights hone our understandings of gender, class, and ethnicity as they humanize our notions of physical and systemic violence, justice, and healing. Entering into the life experiences of provincial women in these countries requires us to think about identity, power, and human agency in less abstract ways. First, we must acknowledge that women—so often depicted as victims of physical violence, enmeshed in structural violence and mired in poverty—are also the living, breathing survivors of the violence they continuously contend with. Even as they struggle, they often prevail, they always give thanks, and they relentlessly persevere in enlivening and enriching their families and communities in concrete acts of peacebuilding every day. They overcame the atrocities of war and they continue to sustain the fragile peace.

But women's resilience should not be stretched to the breaking point. Nor is it enough for women to be merely present in conversations about rebuilding war-torn societies. The work and contributions of non-elite women engaged in reconciliation, empowerment, and livelihood sustains resilience and subsistence in their communities. If their communities are to reach a point of social transformation, it will be their wisdom and values that drives such change, in collaboration with men. By the same token, if human rights advocates and academics have useful contributions to make, and if our theorizing about transformative justice has any relevance, our work must resonate with these women's work. *Their* work nourishing their families, strengthening their social networks, and speaking truth to power can nourish *our* justice work, and will help sustain the work that remains.

From Transition to Social Transformation

The three-pronged model of transformational justice presented in the Introduction to this book gets significant elaboration from the experiences of women peacebuilders in Northern Uganda and Sierra Leone. They acknowledge the importance of war crimes tribunals, truth commissions, and reparations programs, but they regard each of these aspects of the peacebuilding process as a point of departure, a placeholder, and sometimes a distraction from the more important organic work of social transformation. To each of these three strands of transitional justice as classically defined in the rhetoric of global scholars and diplomats, grassroots women peacebuilders demand a transformative component that will bear fruit over time. To their widening braid of transformative justice, they add a fourth strand, their dedication to gender equality, and finally a fifth, their vision of true partnership with men.

The Five Strands of Grassroots Women-Centric Transformative Justice in Uganda and Sierra Leone
ACCOUNTABILITY FOR STATE AND NONSTATE ACTORS ALIKE

Accountability is the first strand of women-centric peacebuilding. Prosecutions of notorious accused war criminals have occurred in both countries. In the Special Court for Sierra Leone there were nine convictions of leaders of all three of the armed factions plus Charles Taylor, the former president of Liberia. For Northern Uganda, there has been only one conviction of Dominic Ongwen; the LRA leader Joseph Kony remains on the lam; and the war crimes trial of the LRA commander Thomas Kwoyelo is still ongoing in the Ugandan High Court's International Crimes Division (ICD), some fifteen years after he was taken into custody.

What is problematic about the pursuit of postconflict penal justice in Northern Uganda from the perspective of grassroots women peacebuilders is that there have been no war crimes prosecutions of any government actors, including soldiers and officers who served in the Uganda Peoples' Defence Forces during the LRA War. Moreover, in Sierra Leone, in contrast to the primary position of criminal prosecutions in global models for transitional justice, the Special Court convictions scarcely came up in the interviews with Sierra Leone Peace Mothers. Not once—even in their eloquent definitions of accountability and their detailed descriptions of dispute resolution at the community level—did they themselves raise the issue of war crimes prosecutions.

The problem with the criminal justice model is not merely that it is retributive. More indicting is that too often penal justice is neither just nor even-handed. In Northern Uganda, the ICC trials trouble Acholi women peacebuilders, in large part because the focus has been so laser sharp on rebel offenders. As the late Daker Nighty of Uketu wan Kwene in Pader District insisted, the LRA commander "Dominic Ongwen can't take all accountability. The government must [as well]." She was referring to the government's responsibility to investigate the many disappearances of family members throughout Acholiland whose fates remain unknown since the cessation of the Rebel War, many of whom were victims of attacks by the Ugandan Army.

In both Northern Uganda and Sierra Leone, accountability is seldom seen in terms of individual criminal liability. It is more commonly seen in civil terms, particularly in recognition of the state's responsibility to *admit* and *remedy* human rights violations and war crimes. Thus, in Pader District of Northern Uganda, the late Daker Nighty's framing of the problem of "negative accountability" on the part of the state is a call for the provision of meaningful reparations to survivors of war atrocities. It is also a demand that the state answer for the fate of the disappeared to their surviving family members, who have been waiting for government acknowledgment of its role in conscriptions, displacement, and war deaths. Members of the Ugandan Women's Advocacy Network see considerable irony in the fact that they were required to seek amnesty from the very government that failed to prevent their capture and forced entry into the LRA in the first place. 'Since all of us were abducted,' one member argued, 'the government should acknowledge its part in our plight.' In short, accountability cannot be for insurgents only. War crimes prosecutions may even breed cynicism unless there is accountability on both the government and rebel sides, whether criminal or civil in nature.

Accountability from Within

For women peacebuilders, the first strand of restorative justice, *accountability, is a two-way street and an inside job.* Just as the government must account for its role in war injuries, community members must come clean to each other for the harms that have occurred between individuals and families. While Northern Ugandan women peacebuilders were particularly concerned with ending "negative accountability" on the part of their government, Sierra Leonean peacebuilders put their own distinctive spin on the term. They offer a vision of accountability as dictated by their own internal moral compasses rather than something imposed by an external authority. The Peace Mothers of Dogoloya in Koinadugu District emphasize that the best way to create accountability was to be honest about one's own actions, which crucially involves the individual's willingness to accept responsibility. As Ayeba expressed it: 'A wife should be able to apologize to her husband if she wrongs him . . . and men also should be able to apologize.' Despite all that has been taken from them, women peacebuilders in Sierra Leone and Uganda are modeling for their governments and societies what personal and collective integrity mean.

Reconciliation is the second strand of women-centric peacebuilding. Although proposals have been considered in the Justice Ministry and the Parliament, Uganda has not yet mandated a Truth and Reconciliation Commission to reestablish the historical record and provide an opportunity for public testimony by war survivors.[2] As for Sierra Leone, the national Truth and Reconciliation Commission's Final Report came out in 2004, some twenty years ago. Nevertheless, not one Peace Mother pointed to Sierra Leone's TRC when asked to define reconciliation. Moreover, few women peacebuilders in Gulu, Nwoya, Pader, or Kitgum spoke of proposals for a Ugandan Truth Commission. Rather, women peacebuilders from both countries focus on their own commitment to dispute resolution within their families and communities.

Reconciliation as Survival

Thus, our second strand of peacebuilding, *reconciliation, is also a local affair.* Women peacebuilders appreciate the importance of formal legal institutions and procedures to ensure a healthy historical reckoning at the national level. Nevertheless, they are most concerned with community reconciliation of conflicts past and present. As my translator and facilitator Lilian Morsay stressed, "Reconciliation is not an event. It is a process. It won't happen spontaneously. It goes on as long, as long, as long as you live." Moreover, without such reconciliation at the community level, collective subsistence may come to a standstill. As Nannah, Peace Mother of Tawovehun described it, '*Ngoyela* [reconciliation in Mende] is healing. If you refuse to heal or forgive, the wrong will continue. In community, wrongs will happen [but] life must continue.' Boie, Peace Mother of Dogoloya, talked about a conflict between clans on either side of a river who could not use the water for their daily needs until they took part in a ceremony of atonement. 'We should realize,' she insisted, 'that the water belongs to us all.'

REPARATIONS FUNDS AS A DOWN PAYMENT TOWARD ENHANCED LIVELIHOOD, THROUGH SYSTEMIC IMPROVEMENTS IN HEALTH CARE AND EDUCATION

Enhanced livelihood, both through reparations and social reforms, constitutes the third strand of women-centric peacebuilding. For Peace Mothers in Moyamba and Koinadugu, Sierra Leone, and for members of women's collectives in Gulu, Nwoya, Pader, and Kitgum in Northern Uganda, grassroots transformative justice requires improved material conditions of daily life for local people in their communities. They may not reference the International Covenant on Economic and Social Rights, but they know their government is falling short in its obligations to ensure a decent standard of living for all Ugandans.[3] For these women, social justice, if not *more* important than historical and courtroom justice, is the ultimate guarantor that reconciliation and accountability have been achieved in their societies. While following the ICC and ICD trials against Dominic Ongwen and Thomas Kwoyelo in The Hague and Gulu, Northern Uganda, and aware of the work of the Truth and Reconciliation Commission in Sierra Leone, women peacebuilders in both countries consider these mechanisms largely irrelevant until they are connected to social conditions at the local level, including the expansion of education, health care, and income generating opportunities.

But how to realize social justice? Certainly, compensation for war injuries is an essential component of accountability for rural women peacebuilders in both countries. In fact, *mato oput*, the traditional atonement ceremony in Acholi culture, involves the payment of livestock or some other material wealth by the clan of the wrongdoer to the clan of the victim, as described in minute detail by women residing in communities throughout Acholiland. In Sierra Leone, the government made significant, if modest, payments of US\$100 to nearly thirty thousand individuals with war-related injuries, including amputees and survivors of sexual violence, through the National Commission for Social Action described in Chapter 2. In Uganda, on the other hand, no payments on that scale have been made.

In this vein, several women peacebuilders from Nwoya and Pader noted their support for a petition that the Women's Advocacy Network submitted in 2014 to the Ugandan Parliament, seeking compensation for civilians who suffered at the hands of the UPDF (Ugandan Army) and the LRA during the civil war. The petition resulted in a unanimous parliamentary resolution calling on the government to increase social services for war survivors, which has not yet given birth to legislation in the Ugandan Parliament.[4] One Ugandan peacebuilder involved in the petition at the parish level spoke of the courage needed for citizens to call their government to account. She expressed great pride in her participation in women's collective action across Acholiland, which serves to effectuate essential improvements in human security within their region and in their nation overall.

Reparations in the Long Term

Structural reparations are as important as one-off payments. Those who participate in grassroots and national drives toward reparations do not merely demand monetary compensation for individual survivors. Women peacebuilders also seek systemic reforms to guarantee the ongoing provision of decent medical services and quality education, as required of Uganda as a signatory to the Banjul Charter.[5]

Alongside the important symbolic impact of one-off reparations payments, women peacebuilders in Northern Uganda and Sierra Leone have their eyes set on the government's commitment to ongoing expenditures for improved infrastructure for rural communities and the construction of new schools, clinics, and hospitals. Women peacebuilders understand the importance of roads and bridges, potable water, access to markets, and employment opportunities in sustaining a dignified standard of living in their communities. However, adequate medical care for all community members and quality primary and secondary education for the youth are their greatest preoccupations.

Women peacebuilders know all too well that public health and public education remain far from universal in their countries. As willing as they are to gather stones to build a new health clinic or primary school like the Peace Mothers of Dogoloya in Koinadugu District, they know that medicines must be paid for with cash and that even "free" public education requires the payment of school fees that are often prohibitively high. As one Sierra Leonean community member so wryly observed: How can we even talk about peacebuilding when "the women of Kaponpon deliver their babies in hammocks"? The advocacy of women peacebuilders and advocates is slowly paying off, particularly in the public health domain. Proposals for universal health care and a national health insurance program are still being debated in the Ugandan Parliament. Nevertheless, budgetary allocations to community health care in Uganda increased by nearly 30 percent from 2017 to 2018.[6] Moreover, state spending on health has continued to go up steadily if slowly in recent years, while not yet meeting the national goals of universal health coverage reflected in Uganda's National Health Financing Strategy.[7] As for Sierra Leone, in April 2018 the government enacted a policy to eliminate fees at public hospitals and health clinics throughout the country for pregnant and nursing mothers and children under the age of five.[8] In its 2022 Annual Report for Sierra Leone, the World Health Organization acknowledges important progress in Sierra Leone toward its goal of attaining universal health coverage by 2030.[9]

GENDER EQUALITY IN EDUCATION, HEALTH, INHERITANCE, AND THE HOME—WORKS IN PROGRESS

Gender equality is the fourth strand of transformative justice for women peacebuilders in Northern Uganda and Sierra Leone. Historical, courtroom, and social justice cannot exist without justice for women. Nor will one-off or structural reparations bear fruit without ensuring that women benefit equally with men. Certainly, women in both countries appreciate that their empowerment and equality are intrinsically linked to the well-being and integrity of their communities. Nevertheless, they also appreciate that "women power" is still an aspiration. While the difficulties of daily life are shared by all members of their communities, Northern Ugandan and Sierra Leonean women peacebuilders are constantly reminded of the ways in which their rights to education, health care, and property are more circumscribed than that of men. Girls do not have the same access to secondary education as boys, in either country; women die in childbirth at a staggering rate, particularly in Sierra Leone; and women do not yet enjoy de facto equality with men in property and inheritance rights. High rates of domestic violence against women continue. Nevertheless, familial violence is now widely understood to be both morally wrong and subject to criminal sanction, and this progress is a source of empowerment to women peacebuilders.

Enhancing Girls' and Women's Education As the Gateway to Social Well-Being

For our fourth strand of peacebuilding, *women's equal access to sustainable livelihood must start at the community level, and in the public schools.* This ideal faces the stark reality in both countries that it is still only a minority of young women who complete secondary school. Jane of Uketu wan Kwene in Pader, Northern Uganda is profiled in the Introduction to this book. She spoke of progress achieved thanks to public sensitization trainings on the importance of 'girl child education.' Nevertheless, she cautioned, 'if you have many children, boys tend to be prioritized. . . . When funds are short, women are seen as a source of money through work' and others leave school due to 'the problem of [early] pregnancy.' In Uganda, 20 percent of young women do not even begin their secondary studies, and for Sierra Leone women, about 50 percent lack access to secondary education.[10]

Tenneh, Peace Mother of Kaponpon in Sierra Leone's Koinadugu District, is the youngest peacebuilder it was my privilege to interview in either country. Her experience is illustrative of the difficulties that young women face and the lengths they are willing to go in furthering their studies. I interviewed her in 2016 with her newborn strapped in a bundle on her back. When we met the next time in 2017, baby Yonson was recovering from malaria in her arms. In 2018 Tenneh spoke to me with her toddler sitting attentively in her lap. During our most recent reunion on an October afternoon in 2023, we paused our conversation to greet the seven-year-old Yonson as he proudly reached home on foot after a day at primary school.

Tenneh left school for a time when she was pregnant with Yonson. She had a lot to say about education, and not just when asked directly. When we were discussing making a living, instead of talking about the wide diversity of crops women grow in her community, Tenneh defined livelihood as 'investing in education for the future.' When asked her views on women's property rights, she had this to say about purchasing land: 'I'd rather go to school.' True to her word, by the time we talked again in 2023, she had returned to her academic program and was awaiting her results in the exams that are the gateway to successful transition from senior secondary school to university studies.

Enhancing Access to Health Care and Alleviating the High Risk of Maternal Mortality

For women peacebuilders, the fourth strand of transformative justice, *gender equality, is not an abstract legal concept, particularly where health care is concerned.* Like accountability, reconciliation, and livelihood, gender equality must be realized in women's daily lives, and as girls grow and mature into adulthood. It entails quality education and much more. Gender equality means that women must be able to pursue their education past the primary level, yes. But women also require the resources to stay in school if they become pregnant, survive the births of their children, and enjoy health care for themselves and their children throughout their lives. However, for many women in both countries, childbirth remains a high-risk experience. Ugandan women are twenty-five times more likely to die when delivering their babies than women in the United States. In Sierra Leone, women are one hundred times more likely to die in childbirth than American women.[11]

Growing Advocacy Against Domestic Violence

For our fourth strand of women-centric peacebuilding, *gender equality requires safety in the home*. Rates of domestic violence are very high in both countries: nearly 50 percent for Ugandan women fifteen years of age or older and around 45 percent for Sierra Leonean women.[12] It is significant that not a single woman I interviewed in either country thought that it was right to beat a spouse or a child. Fatumatah, Peace Mothers chairwoman of Kaponpon in Sierra Leone's Koinadugu District, explained that in traditional Limba culture, 'when you're given to your husband [in marriage], you don't have rights. To me, that is not rightful.' She insisted, 'We have to send our children to school [and] in time, attitudes about women's rights will change. . . . It is important for children to know that both men and women have the same rights.'

With respect to domestic assault, numerous women peacebuilders were passionate about the right of women to be free from violence, particularly in the home. Christine, a peacebuilder from Kitgum District, Northern Uganda, insisted that 'the law is there against striking a woman. It wasn't always that way. Dialogue works better.' Pamela, also from Kitgum, was adamant that 'if a woman is assaulted, they arrest the man and take the woman to the hospital. . . . It is not proper for women and children to be beaten.' Bichentina, yet another woman peacebuilder from Kitgum, explained that women at risk can now go to a neighbor or the local authorities, indicating a community consensus regarding the criminality of domestic violence and the need for corrective measures.[13] On the other side of the continent, Sierra Leone Peace Mother Theresa spoke unequivocally about accountability for domestic violence. As section chairwoman for Palima, she is willing to bring her political power to bear: 'If a man beats a woman, I will take action.'

More Equal but Still Inequitable Property Rights

Also relevant to our fourth strand of women-centric peacebuilding, *gender equality begins on the land*. Alongside the other components of equality—women's access to secondary education, their enjoyment of reproductive health care, and their protection against domestic violence—the effective enjoyment by rural women of their property and inheritance rights is essential to their economic and political agency as well as their physical integrity. While women peacebuilders in both countries are involved in community sensitization about the lawful devolution of estates, there remains a significant lag between law and practice regarding women's property and inheritance rights. As discussed in Chapter 2, Sierra Leonean and Ugandan law clearly recognizes women's equal inheritance rights,[14] but there is a problem of uneven respect for these statutory rights on the ground. In both countries, women are mindful of the gap between de jure rights and de facto equality.

Hannah, Peace Mother of Palima in Moyamba District, Sierra Leone, spoke at some length about the challenges women face, particularly widows, whose property is often subject to land-grabbing by other relatives or community members. 'In our culture,' Hannah explained, 'if you don't have money to go to court, whether you are right or wrong, there is no justice. If there's not a strong man behind you, you are gone. They will grab everything. You are gone. They will pounce on you.' For her part, Fatumatah, Peace Mother of Kaponpon, clarified that it helps the woman's case if she has given birth to a son by her deceased husband: 'If you are a woman,' cautioned Fatumatah, 'except you give birth to a baby boy, when your husband dies, you won't get a single cent. Even if you have a baby boy, the property will be kept for him.' Mbalia, the late Peace Mothers chairwoman of Heremakono, was more sanguine about respect for women's inheritance rights: 'Before now, when the husband died, the relatives would take his property. Now, given the law and sensitization, property is left with the wife and kids.'

Across the continent in Uganda, Evelyn, the late chairwoman of Alany pa Mony Lit in Nwoya District, had strategic advice for women navigating uncertain legal waters: 'Women need to control their own finances. When women have a brain to think, and act, and use their own money, they can do so. If you wait for the man, he may block you.'

CHANGING GENDER ROLES AND SHARED RESPONSIBILITIES BETWEEN WOMEN AND MEN

Partnership between women and men is the fifth and anchoring strand of women-centric peacebuilding. Women peacebuilders in both countries are very proud of their expanding contributions toward sustaining their families and communities. When asked about her role as a woman in her community, Ayeba, Peace Mother of Dogoloya in Sierra Leone's Koinadugu District, expressed her view that women's overall status now is 'comparatively much better than during the war. Now, we women, we're doing more, like running the home. Before, men were shouldering everything, but now, we women are doing a bigger part.' Hannah, Peace Mother of Palima, was more concise: 'For women, if you don't work, you don't eat.' Finally, from Uganda, Bichentina of Odoko Mit focused on women's role in human rights advocacy: 'Because of the work we are doing as a group, women's rights and children's rights are being respected.'

Despite pride in their livelihood activities, several women peacebuilders on both sides of the continent spoke with ambivalence or frustration about their growing responsibilities, particularly in agricultural work and other forms of subsistence. Jane of Uketu wan Kwene in Uganda's Pader District put it this way: 'Women have become men in their homes. I see a negative strength. We women shouldn't have to take on such responsibility without support.' In neighboring Kitgum District, Concy of Odoko Mit raised the issue of men's consumption of alcohol: 'Almost all work in the home is being done by women. Most men drink.' The late Daker Nighty of Uketu wan Kwene put it less diplomatically: "Women suffer more because men behave as if they are insane."

Progress Toward Partnership Between Women and Men

There is no doubt that the fifth strand of women-centric peacebuilding, *partnership between women and men, is a very tall order.* At least in the short term, we can observe a pronounced tendency toward "zero-sum" thinking, whereby some men view the empowerment of women as leading to their own emasculation.[15] Nevertheless, there are also signs of growing collaboration between women and men in both countries. For the Peace Mothers, the idea of such partnership is explicit in the slogan "Woman power, man support." In fact, the late Mr. Jalloh of Dogoloya was dubbed a "change agent" because of his willingness to model for other men in his community a loosening of traditional Fulbeh gender restrictions. To start with, he encouraged other men to follow his lead in encouraging their spouses to speak publicly and to become active in their local Peace Mothers group. On multiple visits to Dogoloya, "Dr. J." came out to welcome our research team, expressing his profound appreciation for the Peace Mothers as a force for community development and the building of trust.

Individual women of Northern Uganda and Sierra Leone continue to express their hopes for strengthened common cause between women and men in the development of their villages and chiefdoms. Boie, Peace Mother of Dogoloya, spoke of a disaster she faced in her home: 'Thirty-five men and women came to help me,' without any payment of money, 'simply because I've been promoting peace in the community.' From Northern Uganda, Evelyn of Alany pa Mony Lit talked in more strategic terms about how women might more fully realize their equal inheritance rights: 'Women ... [must] start collaborating with their brothers from an early age [so that they are able] to become peers.' Lilian Morsay, my Fambul Tok translator and research partner, has participated over the past few years in community sensitization meetings regarding the rights of women under Sierra Leone's Devolution of Estates Act. She described men who accompanied their wives to these sessions and wept openly with relief, in the realization that when they died, their wives need not be left vulnerable, landless, or economically destitute.

Reflecting on the Quiet Storm of Women-Centered Social Transformation

The five strands of women-centric community-based peacebuilding are accountability, reconciliation, livelihood, women's equality, and women's partnership with men. Partnership remains a work in progress. Women peacebuilders in Northern Uganda and Sierra Leone clearly articulate that they need support from their spouses, their neighbors, and their governments in their efforts to uphold their communities. There are myriad examples of women's empowerment through collective action, but sometimes the collective takes more than it gives, requiring much from individual women without changing their reality in palpable ways. Women cannot stop violence and alleviate poverty alone.

It is crucial to acknowledge women's past wartime experiences of physical and psychic violence, but it is equally essential to address the abuses and deprivations they continue to face in the present day; to honor their visions of nonviolence, healing, and well-being; and to acknowledge their daily commitments to livelihood, dignity, and equality for themselves, their families, and their communities, now and in the future. While transformative justice requires accountability for perpetrators of crimes committed in wartime, women also demand access to health care, education, and legal protections in peacetime, and they seek partnership with men in all these endeavors. Justice is not transformative unless power dynamics in families and local communities change, such that women exercise greater personal, political, and economic agency in their daily lives, all the while sharing power with men.

In peacebuilding, the five strands circle back on one another. Partnership and equality between men and women require acknowledgment of wrongdoing, reconciliation of differences, and sustainable livelihood. For women peacebuilders practicing transformative justice in Northern Uganda and Sierra Leone, an important piece of unfinished business is the admission of responsibility for violence. Women demand acknowledgment of the abuse of power by all responsible actors, whether rebel fighters or soldiers, their spouses, members of their families, their neighbors, or the state itself. With regard to the integrity of state institutions, women continue to believe in their government's capacity and duty to represent and serve the people. They are profoundly concerned with the state's willingness to address the structural roots of conflict. They recognize that the poverty and violence that women disproportionately suffer are linked to legal and cultural systems regarding land tenure, inheritance, and domestic relations as well as the compromised integrity of state institutions dedicated to the provision of basic social services. They also know that it will require ongoing work by everyone—through public education, legislative reform, state expenditures, and community action by women and men—to realize the social transformation in the transformative justice that they seek.

While rural women's strategies for transformative justice serve as a model for political and socioeconomic reforms at the national and local levels, those systemic changes are long in coming and often face entrenched resistance, as the experiences of women and men in Uganda and Sierra Leone illustrate. Given the political machinations and economic impediments that frustrate positive change at the national level, rural communities have become essential generators of incremental and innovative social change. Women's activism at the grassroots level—within their families, villages, parishes, chiefdoms, sections, and districts—constitutes a quiet storm. Without the luxury to wait for national structural reform, women's groups in multiple locales continue to coordinate and germinate, maturing into ever more deeply engrained peace movements in both countries.

At the end of day, women peacebuilders return to the values that brought them together in the first place, when the Sierra Leone Peace Mothers and the Northern Ugandan women's collectives were founded over fifteen years ago. They came together to provide mutual support, compassion, and understanding to one another in the aftermath of brutal civil conflicts. Their unity became a foundation for restored relationships, collective decision-making, conflict resolution, women's empowerment, and cooperative development in their communities.

Figure 24. The late Mbalia Koroma, Jenny Moore, and Lilian Morsay, Heremakono, Koinadugu District, Sierra Leone. Photo by Mustafa Rogers, 2019.

There is still much work to be done. The obstacles to women-centered peacebuilding are daunting—from the enduring realities of patriarchy and poverty at the local level, to the crushing burdens of corruption, inflation, armed conflict, climate change, and disease at the national, regional, and global levels. Women peacebuilders envision systemic change, yet they don't waste time waiting for it. They make peace, piecemeal, in their daily lives, creating for themselves most of the justice and social transformation they may ever experience, on the ground and in their families, chiefdoms, and districts. As Sierra Leone Peace Mother Hannah explains, 'The first and foremost thing is that the women of Palima are working together. Even now, we are on it. We have no fear to enter any house in the village because we are all one.' And as Filda of Uganda's Alany pa Mony Lit reminds us, 'We bring forth the strength that we need.'

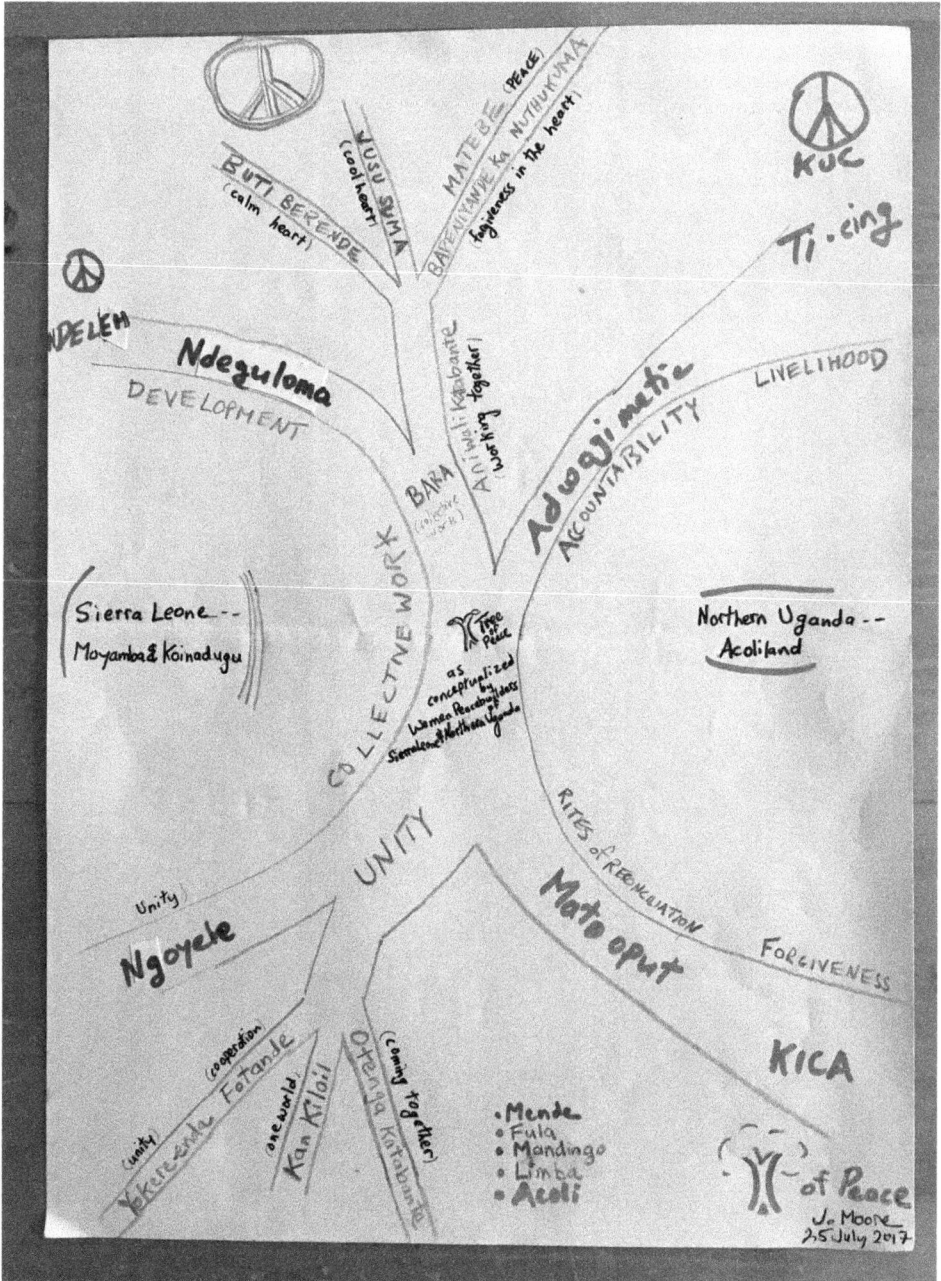

Figure 25. Tree of peace with peacebuilders' multilingual vocabulary of peace. Drawing by J. Moore, 2017.

APPENDIX 1

Women Peacebuilders' Questionnaire

Used for interviews with members of women's collectives in Northern Uganda and Sierra Leone conducted in 2016 and 2017.

1. What is your name? (*NB: my original notes included only the first name; I substituted the full name subsequently only if the interviewee indicated her willingness and preference to be cited by full name.*)
2. How many children do you have? What are their genders and ages? Where were they born (at home or elsewhere)? Did you have the help of a (traditional) birth attendant, nurse or other health worker?
3. What is your tribal community?
4. What is your first language? What other languages do you speak?
5. What is your religion if any?
6. What schooling have you completed if any?
7. Have you or your family been treated at a health clinic or hospital in the past year? When and where?
8. What are you most proud of/enthusiastic about in your work in your community?
9. What new activities would you like to accomplish in the next two years?
10. How do you resolve/are disputes resolved in your community?
11. I am interested in what you think of the word "reconciliation." To me, <u>reconciliation</u> means the healing of community divisions (caused by war or violence). <u>What is reconciliation to you?</u> [**POSSIBLE** follow-up questions: *If you believe more reconciliation is needed, what is the best way to seek reconciliation in your community? What if any reconciliation activities are taking place? Do they benefit women? Do women participate freely or are they pressured? What changes are needed?*]
12. I am interested in what you think of the word "livelihood." To me, <u>livelihood</u> is being able to provide for my family. <u>What is livelihood to you?</u> [**POSSIBLE** follow-up questions: *If you believe stronger support for livelihood is needed, what is the best way to enhance livelihood in your community? What forms of social support are most needed? What programs do women need especially? Do they need support for their families, themselves, or both? Should the government help provide for your community's livelihood needs or is it most important for community members to rely on themselves and their own organizations?*]
13. I am interested in what you think of the word "accountability." To me, <u>accountability</u> is taking responsibility for my own wrongful acts, or someone else taking responsibility for his or her own wrongful acts. <u>What is accountability to you?</u> [**POSSIBLE** follow-up questions: *If you believe more accountability is needed in your community, what is the best way to do this? Are women victims or perpetrators of offences or both? Are women able to testify freely about crimes? If they speak up, are they respected or criticized? What changes are needed?*]

14. In your community <u>is reconciliation, livelihood, or accountability the most important value</u>? Or are they all equal? Is one more important for women specifically? <u>Is something else more important</u> for women or your community that has not been discussed?

15. <u>What attitudes do women in your community have toward the central government</u>? Do most women trust the government to serve all Sierra Leonean people, regardless of gender, ethnicity, religion, economic status, or region?

16. <u>Do you feel stronger</u> in your community and in your family than before the war? On the contrary, are you more vulnerable or victimized? How so? What about for women in general?

17. What <u>protections against violence</u> in the home and the community can women call upon? Are these protections sufficient? How can protections be improved?

18. What <u>educational opportunities</u> are women and girls in your community able to pursue? Are these educational opportunities sufficient? How can opportunities be improved?

19. What <u>health care services</u> are women in your community able to gain access to? Are these health services sufficient? How can health services be improved?

20. What <u>employment and income-generated opportunities</u> are available for women in your community? Are employment opportunities sufficient? How can opportunities be improved?

21. <u>Can a woman buy land in her own name in your community</u>? If not, are the barriers to land ownership in the form of national law, local conditions, or both? What reforms are needed?

22. <u>Can a woman inherit property at the death of her parent or spouse</u>? If not, are the barriers to inheritance in national law, local conditions, or both? What reforms are needed?

23. <u>Can a woman run for public office and participate in elections</u>? If not, are the barriers to political participation in national law, local conditions, or both? What reforms are needed?

24. <u>Are women helping to make decisions about how to move your community forward</u>? Explain the ways women serve as leaders. How can you and other women become more active and effective in protecting each other and helping your community move forward?

Talking with Members of Gwoko Ter Kwaro in Kitgum District, Northern Uganda

The women and men of Gwoko ter Kwaro (Keeping the Culture) reside in the Pajong Parish of Mucwini Sub-County in Kitgum District, Northern Uganda. Seven people participated in our focus group discussion in July 2016, four women and three men. Subsequently, I conducted individual interviews with the four women. When I first met with members of Gwoko ter Kwaro in 2016, I had a general sense that as group members they benefited from trainings provided by HU-RIFO in mediation, human rights monitoring, and the prevention of gender-based violence. Yet in my interactions with the women of Gwoko over the next three years, I have come to appreciate the myriad aspects of their community healing work as well as the different ways they define reconciliation, accountability, livelihood, and other aspects of peacebuilding.

All members of Gwoko ter Kwaro are native Acholi speakers. The women had limited opportunities to pursue their education. Of the four I interviewed individually, two had no schooling and two had to interrupt their studies toward the end of primary school. They are farmers of maize, *simsim*, cassava, potatoes, groundnuts, sorghum, millet, and pigeon peas. They celebrate their work successfully mediating disputes and educating community members about women's rights and responsibilities. They appreciate the training and solidarity they have received from HURIFO. They take great pride in their VSLA, in which they regularly deposit small amounts of cash, thereby becoming eligible for small cash loans on a revolving basis. The women also contribute to collective farming activities, helping out as a group when an individual member is preparing a field for cultivation or bringing in a harvest. During the focus group discussion, the men also shared insights into their typical contributions to village life, including cultivating crops, weaving bamboo sleeping mats, and carving bamboo handles for hoes used in agricultural cultivation.

Focus Group Discussion with Gwoko ter Kwaro, 2016

Our focus group in 2016 started somewhat inauspiciously. Prior to our arrival, Winnie Arima had tried to contact Joseph, the Gwoko chairperson, but his cell phone was out of service, and thus we arrived unannounced. Joseph and his family members spontaneously gathered group members upon our arrival. Winnie and I joked that we likely gathered a neighbor or two who just happened to be passing by. Most participants arrived on foot. We sat together on a tarpaulin in a shady clearing next to Joseph's family compound, with later arrivals joining in. The initial mood of the Gwoko ter Kwaro focus group was quite subdued, possibly due to the lack of advance notice. It was hard to judge as a first-time visitor to Mucwini Sub-County, but I had the sense that individual participants may have been pressed into service out of a sense of obligation. Once the discussion was underway, awkwardness gave way to graciousness and greater sharing on all sides.

As with all the community groups in Northern Uganda and Sierra Leone, we started the Gwoko focus group with the theme of *reconciliation* (*mato oput*). Each participant was invited to share their understanding of the meaning of *mato oput* as we moved around the circle. Not unlike Rwot Lakica and the RLP affiliates, certain aspects of reconciliation were common touchstones for Gwoko ter Kwaro members. They spoke of *mato oput* in terms of a ritual sharing of food and drink and a means of restoring unity through the mediation of community leaders. They acknowledged that *mato oput* had not yet been used as a mechanism for restorative justice with state actors, while holding out hope that it could serve such a purpose in the future. Finally, Gwoko members identified an additional role for *mato oput*—namely, reconciliation within the home between husband and wife.

Of the four women of Gwoko ter Kwaro who took part in the focus group and individual interviews in 2016, Pamela was thirty-one and Ellen, Christine, and Jennifer were in their early to mid-forties. Pamela, mother of four, started the discussion by offering that 'reconciliation is rebuilding what has been spoiled.' She spoke of *mato oput* as a mechanism for alleviating strife in the community and also a way for her to come to terms with 'those who wounded me during the war.' Although 'this hasn't happened yet . . . I could reconcile' with such persons, she insisted. Ellen, mother of five, emphasized an important dimension of *mato oput*: according to traditional Acholi practice, the disputing families or clans could not break bread together until such a rite occurred. As she explained, 'We slaughter a goat and eat together, but it's more than a ceremony. [It leads to] unification, so that both parties start living together and forget the past.' The men who participated in the Gwoko ter Kwaro focus group struck resonant chords. The chairperson Joseph, fifty-five and father of seven, talked about 'drinking the bitter herb' (the literal meaning of *mato oput*) as a means of 'becoming one' at the community level. Alex, forty-three and father of nine, emphasized that *mato oput* is needed as a mechanism for ensuring that there is 'no recurrence' of strife.

The Gwoko focus group then proceeded to a discussion of *livelihood* (*tic-cing*). While members of Rwot Lakica touched on livelihood as a way to promote healing, and the members of Alany pa Mony Lit and Uketu wan Kwene emphasized collective aspects of *tic-cing*, Gwoko members highlighted the broad spectrum of livelihood activities in their community, requiring various levels of training. Examples included teaching and other government work; all kinds of cultivation, particularly for women; and crafting mats and wooden handles, typically for men. Pamela offered, 'I do it in the form of tailoring and farming—ground nuts, maize, and millet.' Jennifer noted that in their community 'most have not been to school, so we keep livestock and farm.' She went on to share details about Northern Ugandan cuisine, with some reverence regarding the paste (*alot*) made by grinding groundnuts together with *simsim* (sesame). She insisted that the best food is seasoned with *alot*. Harkening back to the passage from *Song of Lawino* at the beginning of Chapter 3, her words are a reminder that livelihood is often a blending of necessity and devotion, hardship and celebration. The three men added their own nuances. For Joseph, making baskets is an important occupation for men who are unable to secure government work. Alex engages in 'digging in the garden to provide for the kids, especially maize.' For Geoffrey, livelihood is 'making handles for hoes' as well as cultivating groundnuts, *simsim*, sweet potatoes, and beans.

Finally, Gwoko ter Kwaro members turned to *accountability*, introducing some interesting variations on themes explored by the other community groups. Rwot Lakica and Uketu wan Kwene members had spoken of the need for state accountability for wartime atrocities. Alany pa Mony Lit members had emphasized *adwogi metic* as the fruit or consequences of one's actions. Gwoko ter Kwaro members took a slightly different tack. They tended to define *adwogi metic* in the more literal sense of fair compensation for one's physical labor, rather than a moral accounting for one's behavior. On the moral side, they also acknowledged the ethical consequences of wrongdoing, but in such instances they tended to use another Acholi term, *kwayo kica*, which is the request for forgiveness.

Pamela started us off with the proposition that 'if I have done a wrongful act, I must admit to it, ask for *kwayo kica* and seek unity.' Ellen delved into the distinction between the two terms.

She stated that *adwogi metic* is the fruit of 'what I plant and produce' and *kwayo kica* is 'linked to acknowledging a wrongful act; I need to admit it and ask forgiveness.' For both *adwogi metic* and *kwayo kica* the payment of compensation is vital, whether as wages for labor or reparations for wrongdoing. The men contributed their own nuanced understandings, generally agreeing that *adwogi metic* requires appropriate recompense. In speaking of *kwayo kica*, Alex insisted that mediation is key in the granting of mercy (*timo kica*).[1] Geoffrey stressed that *kwayo kica* is most challenging for wartime abuses, which are harder to forgive than garden-variety offenses, so to speak, such as when a person's livestock trample their neighbor's crops.

Individual Interviews with Gwoko ter Kwaro, 2016

The focus group discussion ended with lunch, followed by individual interviews with each of the four women members, utilizing the Peacebuilders' Questionnaire, in Appendix 1. Pamela, Ellen, Christine, and Jennifer all gave permission for their names to be used in association with the quotes that are attributed to them below.

Life Circumstances and Experiences

Pamela, Ellen, Christine and Jennifer ranged in age from thirty-one to forty-four as of 2016. Of the four, two speak only Acholi, and two speak Acholi and also a bit of English. All four are Catholic. Two did not attend any school, and two concluded their studies in the seventh year of primary school. Unlike the majority of the women in the other community groups, all the Gwoko ter Kwaro interviewees gave birth to their children in a hospital or clinic. Only Jennifer mentioned that one of her children was born en route to the hospital. They named her Ayu, meaning "on the way." As of 2016, Pamela had four children; Ellen had six children and had lost five others; Christine had eight children; and Jennifer had six.[2]

When asked about the health of their family members, the women pointed to a variety of challenges, from current physical conditions to long-term war-related trauma. Christine has had a problem with a disc in her back since her youth. In July 2016, Jennifer was expecting her seventh child and Pamela's two-year-old son was receiving injections in the Mucwini health center for a persistent cough. Ellen spoke about her health in terms of war-related experiences. She lost her husband in 2002, one of fifty-six relatives and community members who were killed in an LRA massacre.[3] Thereafter, she and many of their neighbors fled to a camp for displaced persons. Her firstborn was abducted by the LRA and escaped after one year. He is now married and the father of three children.

Community Involvement

In speaking about those aspects of their community work they find most meaningful, the four women focused on their mediation, cooperative farming, and community banking activities. Pamela pointed to 'the work of mediation, which helps people live in *ribbe* [unity].' She described a quarrel between husband and wife that she helped resolve as a member of Gwoko ter Kwaro's mediation team. For her part, Ellen emphasized their farming cooperative, mentioning that just the day before Gwoko ter Kwaro members had helped her plow a field in preparation for planting *simsim*. Christine stated, 'I am most proud of my community sensitization and conflict resolution. I'm a good mediator.' Finally, Jennifer noted, 'I am proud of our VSLA because it helps us in many ways. I borrowed 20,000 [Ugandan shillings or around US$6] to pay a medical bill and I paid it back with interest.' Focusing on the methodology of conflict resolution that best serves their community, Jennifer gave a personal example: 'If I'm having a dispute with my husband, first we two sit down together. If we can't iron it out, then we get an elder to sit down with us . . . or I could rest at my parents' house for a while.'

Interrelationships Between Reconciliation, Livelihood, and Accountability

As in other communities, the interviewees from Gwoko ter Kwaro had their own ways of articulating the interconnections between reconciliation [*mato oput*], livelihood [*tic-cing*], and accountability [*adwogi metic* or *kwayo kica*]. While Ellen and Jennifer agreed that 'the three terms . . . are interrelated,' Christine took a different tack: '*Mato oput* is the priority—rebuilding what has been spoiled.'

Attitudes Toward Women's Empowerment

The women of Gwoko ter Kwaro shared insights and more than a few pithy comments regarding the national government of Uganda; the changing nature of women's roles before, during, and since the war; and whether there are sufficient remedies for women facing violence in the home and community. When asked if President Museveni cared about the women of Northern Uganda, their answers varied. One asserted that 'Museveni cares about the people' and another agreed, 'Museveni cares about our family.' Others took an opposing view: 'The government is not caring about women. People get nothing from the government.' One delved more deeply into their local history: 'The government is not caring equally for Ugandans. Sixteen from my family were killed by the LRA in 2002, including my parents, and the government has done nothing. In the camps, there was insufficient food. There were many deaths in 2002.'

Speaking of the changing status of women, all four Gwoko ter Kwaro interviewees spoke of improvements in their circumstances overall. Pamela and Christine believe that women are stronger than they were before and during the war. Ellen was willing to wade a bit further into gender politics: 'Women are doing a lot of good things. There is unity in the community. Women are hardworking peacemakers. Men of these days are not serious or responsible. Women have to step up.'[4]

All four Gwoko ter Kwaro interviewees wished to comment specifically about protections against gender violence. Pamela was adamant that 'If a woman is assaulted, they arrest the man and take the woman to the hospital. . . . It is not proper for women and children to be beaten.' Ellen explained that women at risk can now go to a neighbor or the local authorities. Christine insisted, 'The law is there against striking a woman. It wasn't always that way. Dialogue works better.' Jennifer hypothesized about a situation in which she has a dispute with her husband. She noted that an elder in the family or community could intervene and 'write a letter of protection for me to take to the police. Even a letter can be effective as a warning.'

Access to Education, Health Care, and Employment

In a similar vein as the women of Rwot Lakica, Alany pa Mony Lit, and Uketu wan Kwene, the four interviewees of Gwoko ter Kwaro emphasized extreme impediments to women's full enjoyment of their rights to education, health care, and employment. Pamela recognized women's formal right to equal educational opportunities but spoke of the difficulties families face in coming up with the funds to pay for school fees. The precise reason she left school after her P-7 year was insufficient family resources. Ellen acknowledged that those with funds can access health care but stressed that others go without, particularly given that their local health center is overwhelmed. Christine believes that employment opportunities are limited even for women with significant education. Jennifer insisted that 'even if you go to school, you must know someone' to get a job.

Property Ownership, Inheritance, and Women's Access to the Political Process

The women of Gwoko ter Kwaro expressed a great range of views regarding women's property and inheritance rights. There was general agreement that as a practical matter, married women were wise to consult with their husbands before purchasing land even if they had the necessary funds. There were some differences of opinion concerning a woman's right to inherit property upon the death of her husband or father. Both Pamela and Ellen stated that daughters and sons inherit equally from the father, although Pamela suggested that one son often takes the lead in the distribution of property. Christine saw it differently, insisting that while a woman could inherit from her late husband, daughters did not inherit—the father's property goes to the sons. For her part, Jennifer focused on the vulnerability of widows who, in her view, have no entitlement to inherit anything upon the death of the husband. Despite constitutional guarantees and newly revised statutory provisions that mandate gender equality in property ownership, Jennifer stated unequivocally that 'the law doesn't allow a married woman to purchase land without consulting her husband.' It is an understatement to acknowledge that women's property and inheritance rights are currently in flux in this part of Acholiland until the 2022 amendments to Uganda's Succession Law become ingrained culturally.

While Gwoko members lauded modest advancements in women's participation in electoral politics, they made an important distinction between women serving in women-designated seats in local councils—sometimes referred to as "affirmative action" seats[5]—and non-gender-specific positions. Most women lawmakers serve in local council, district council, and parliamentary positions that are set aside for women, and thus run against other female candidates exclusively. Nevertheless, several Gwoko members noted the growing trend of women contesting men for open electoral seats, including positions as members of Parliament (MPs).

Estimation of Women's Roles in the Community Overall

In addressing the last question regarding women's contributions to community development, the four individual interviewees of Gwoko ter Kwaro focused on their physical labor, particularly in the cultivation of crops. Pamela pointed to their collective farming activities as an essential way in which 'women are helping the community.' For her part, Christine cautioned that, while women do much of the work of development, they have yet to fully enjoy its fruits. She suggested that in order for the women of Pajong Parish to reach their fullest potential at the community level they will need to work more closely with elected leaders.

New Challenges and Opportunities for Gwoko ter Kwaro in 2023

In July 2023, upon returning to Pajong Parish for the last phase of interviews, Fred Ngomokwe, Winnie Abalo, and I drove along tarmac and unpaved roads, witnessing parched farmland on all sides, the maize and sorghum plants stunted by dry conditions. Kitgum was the district of Acholiland most impacted by drought conditions that year; Mucwini Sub-county where Gwoko ter Kwaro is based was particularly hard hit. In fact, in contrast to all the other groups, Gwoko ter Kwaro members said that of late they had been unable to generate significant funds through their microlending VSLA. Even the modest level of weekly contributions (typically 5,000 Ugandan shillings or slightly over US$1) was beyond the means of many women. Similarly, they were seldom hiring themselves out as work crews for agricultural tasks such as weeding because there hadn't been sufficient output in recent harvest seasons to merit the hiring of casual laborers.

Despite the downturn in their lending and livelihood activities, Gwoko's mediation and child protection activities continued during this period. Bichentina spoke of mediating a boundary dispute resulting in a compromise outcome that literally split the difference between the two claimed property lines. For her part, Jennifer declared 'I'm proud of my work on child protection and children's rights,' citing her advocacy for her own children in the school environment. Bichentina noted, 'I'm proud of myself as a mediator. I hold my head high and people listen to me.'⁶

Highlighting the Insights of Gwoko ter Kwaro Members

Five major themes were addressed during the focus group and individual interviews with members of Gwoko ter Kwaro: the value of partnership between men and women; *adwogi metic* (fair compensation for labor) and *kwayo kica* (requesting forgiveness) as alternative perspectives on accountability; a growing awareness of women's rights to be free from physical violence; the realization that to enjoy their social and economic rights women must become more politically active; and, finally, an emphasis on alternative dispute resolution of community conflicts.

The interviews with the members of Gwoko ter Kwaro were also notable for their insights into the essence of *mato oput* or reconciliation. For Gwoko members, rites of reconciliation and the concept of reconciliation itself are vital to the very survival of the community and its members. Christine and Ellen of Gwoko ter Kwaro gave the example of two clans whose territory bordered opposite sides of a river from which clanspeople drew water to drink, cook, and cultivate and which they crossed to get to their fields, to market, and to medical care. They stressed that in time of strife the river became an impermeable boundary. Only through *mato oput,* and the inspiration of their traditional leaders to reach out to one another across the divide, could they again 'freely cross the river.' At that point, agriculture, commerce, and daily nourishment could resume. Reconciliation is part spiritual and part material, and the two aspects are indivisible.

NOTES

Introduction

Epigraph: Joy Harjo, *Conflict Resolution for Holy Beings: Poems* (W. W. Norton, 2015), 16. Copyright © 2015 by Joy Harjo. Used by permission of W. W. Norton & Company, Inc.

1. Boie is her first name, but Jalloh is a pseudonym.

2. Jane is her first name, but Orama is a pseudonym.

3. See generally Chris Dolan, *Social Torture: The Case of Northern Uganda, 1986–2006* (Berghahn Books, 2011). Chris Dolan is the former director of the Refugee Law Project, an NGO affiliated with the University of Makerere School of Law in Kampala, Uganda.

4. See Jennifer Moore, Uganda Field Notebook, July 2023 (meeting with Uketu wan Kwene members, July 13), on file with author.

5. See generally United Nations, "Guidance Note of the Secretary General: United Nations Approach to Transitional Justice," April 2010, available at https://www.un.org/ruleoflaw/blog /document/guidance-note-of-the-secretary-general-united-nations-approach-to-transitional -justice/. See also International Center for Transitional Justice (ICTJ), "What Is Transitional Justice," available at http://www.ictj.org/about/transitional-justice; and Naomi Roht-Arriaza and Javier Mariezcurrena, eds., *Transitional Justice in the Twenty-First Century: Beyond Truth Versus Justice* (Cambridge University Press, 2006), 2.

6. Increasingly, the term "transformative justice" is used as an elaboration of or alternative to the term "transitional justice." See generally Paul Gready and Simon Robins, *From Transitional to Transformative Justice* (Cambridge University Press, 2019). The various meanings of these terms will be explored throughout the text below.

7. See generally Aisling Swaine, *Conflict-Related Violence Against Women: Transforming Transition* (Cambridge University Press, 2018).

8. United Nations Office on Drugs and Crime, *Global Study on Homicide*, Executive Summary, 14 (UNDOC, July 2019), available at https://www.unodc.org/documents/data-and-analysis /gsh/Booklet1.pdf.

9. See generally Jennifer Moore, *Humanitarian Law in Action Within Africa* (Oxford University Press, 2012).

10. The voices of Burundian women peacebuilders were meant to be included in this book. Given security conditions, the field research in Burundi was not feasible during the 2016–23 period. Burundi will be the subject of future research.

11. See Sally Engle Merry, *Human Rights and Gender Violence: Translating International Law into Local Justice* (University of Chicago Press, 2006), 204. Engle Merry explores the layered relationships between transnational human rights advocates, national and local NGOs, and non-elite women living in communities around the world. See also interview with Libby Hoffman, *African Peace Journal* (2016), available at http://www.africanpeacejournal.com/interview-with -libby-hoffman/. Hoffman, cofounder with John Caulker of the Sierra Leonean NGO Fambul Tok,

urges that human rights activists go into conflict-emergent communities to "discover the peace that is already there."

12. Northern Uganda's LRA War was concentrated in the traditional homeland of the Acholi and Langi language groups. Nevertheless, Acholi and Langi people were represented in all the major constituencies of that conflict—the LRA, the Uganda Peoples' Defence Forces, and certainly the affected civilian population, which both military forces claimed to defend and yet brutalized over a twenty-year period.

13. Joy Harjo, *Conflict Resolution for Holy Beings: Poems* (W. W. Norton, 2015), 77 (from the first stanza of the title poem in this work). Copyright © 2015 by Joy Harjo. Used by permission of W. W. Norton & Company, Inc.

14. See ICTJ, "What Is Transitional Justice."

15. The Fourth Geneva Convention of 1949 defines as grave breaches serious violations of humanitarian law, including attacks on civilian communities, which are also the basis for individual criminal liability in the Rome Statute of the International Criminal Court. See Geneva Convention No. IV, the Convention Relative to the Protection of Civilian Persons in Time of War, August 12, 1949, 675 U.N.T.S. 287, arts. 147 (defining grave breaches to include willful killing, taking of hostages, and wanton destruction) and 148 (states parties' liability/non-impunity for grave breaches). See also Rome Statute of the International Criminal Court, UN Doc. A/CONF.183/9 (1998), 2184 U.N.T.S. 3, entered into force July 1, 2002, arts. 7 (crimes against humanity) and 8 (war crimes).

16. In her monograph *Transitional Justice*, Ruti Teitel used the term to encompass the kinds of political and institutional changes implemented by societies in "periods of radical flux" between autocratic regimes and increasingly democratic systems. See Teitel, *Transitional Justice* (Oxford University Press, 2000), 223.

17. Naomi Roht-Arriaza defines transitional justice to include "that set of practices, mechanisms and concerns that arise following a period of conflict, civil strife or repression, and that are aimed directly at confronting and dealing with past violations of human rights and humanitarian law." See Roht-Arriaza, "The New Landscape of Transitional Justice," in *Transitional Justice in the Twenty-First Century*, ed. Roht-Arriaza and Javier Mariezcurrena (Cambridge University Press, 2006).

18. See J. Moore, *Humanitarian Law*, 333 (in some countries emerging from protracted armed conflict, transitional justice serves as a framework for "the simultaneous pursuit of criminal, social, and historical justice").

19. The 2004 Final Report of the Sierra Leone Truth and Reconciliation Commission made a variety of recommendations, some designated "mandatory," including the abolition of the death penalty, arbitrary detention, and corporal punishment of children; an end to customary practices by which rape victims were compelled to marry their rapists and pregnant girls were expelled from public school; the establishment of eighteen as the minimum age to marry; the repeal of legislation linking the prosecution of sex offenses to the "moral character" of the victim; and the repeal of both statutory and customary laws discriminating against women in inheritance and land acquisition. The Final Report also contained a number of recommendations that the government should "work toward" including directives concerning reparations—such as lifetime free health care, occupational therapy, and prosthetics for amputees, and free health care and fistula surgery for victims of sexual violence. See Sierra Leone Truth and Reconciliation Commission (TRC), Final Report of the Truth and Reconciliation Commission (TRC Final Report), 2004. The commission's recommendations are found in the text of vol. 2, chapter 3, and the Recommendations Tables at the end of that chapter, available at http://www.sierraleonetrc.org/index.php/view-report-text-vol-2/item/volume-two-chapter-three?category_id=20.

20. The Rainbo Initiative was the first provider of free medical and psychosocial services for survivors of gender-based violence in Sierra Leone. See Rainbo Initiative, "Mission and Vision

of Rainbo Initiative," available at https://rainboinitiative.org/our-programs/. The Rainbo Initiative is funded and supported by the international NGO International Rescue Committee and the Irish government under the auspices of Irish Aid (within Ireland's Department of Foreign Affairs and Trade). In addition to the inaugural Rainbo Centre in Freetown, founded in 2003, there are also Rainbo Centres in Kenema (founded in 2004), Kono (2005), Bo (2018), Makeni and Kambia (2018). See Jennifer Moore, Notes from interview with Rebecca Kallih, clinical director, Rainbo Initiative, Sierra Leone Field Notebook 2019 (May 23), 63–64, on file with author. See also Irish Aid, "Sierra Leone," available at https://www.dfa.gov.ie/irish-embassy/sierra-leone/our-role/irish-aid-in-sierra-leone/.

21. See Cristián Correa, Julie Guillerot, Lisa Magarrell, "Reparations and Victim Participation: A Look at the Truth Commission Experience," chapter 15 of *Reparations for Victims of Genocide, War Crimes and Crimes Against Humanity*, ed. Carla Ferstman, Mariana Goetz, and Alan Stephens (Martinus Nijhoff, 2009).

22. See South African Truth and Reconciliation Commission, "Legal Background [to the South African TRC]," available at http://www.justice.gov.za/trc/legal/index.htm.

23. International Center for Transitional Justice (ICTJ), "The Former Yugoslavia and Transitional Justice" (2015), available at https://www.ictj.org/our-work/regions-and-countries/former-yugoslavia.

24. ICTJ, "Cambodia and Transitional Justice" (2015), available at https://www.ictj.org/our-work/regions-and-countries/cambodia.

25. Roger Duthie, "Local Justice and Reintegration Processes as Complements to Transitional Justice and DDR [Disarmament, Demobilization, and Reintegration]" (ICTJ, 2010), available at https://www.ictj.org/publication/transitional-justice-and-ddr-case-rwanda-case-study.

26. Luis Vieira, "The CAVR [Commission for Reception, Truth, and Reconciliation] and the 2006 Displacement Crisis in Timor-Leste: Reflections on Truth-Telling, Dialogue, and Durable Solutions" (ICTJ–Brookings Project on Internal Displacement, 2012), available at https://www.ictj.org/resource-library/cavr-and-2006-displacement-crisis-timor-leste-reflections-truth-telling-dialogue.

27. Transitional and transformative justice mechanisms in Northern Uganda and Sierra Leone are discussed throughout the text, particularly in Chapters 2, 3, and 4.

28. See generally (re Chile) Correa et al., "Reparations"; see generally (re South Africa), Truth and Reconciliation Commission of South Africa, "Legal Background."

29. See generally (re International Criminal Tribunal for the Former Yugoslavia), UN ICTY, "About the ICTY," available at http://www.icty.org/en/about; see also UN ICTY, "Statute of the Tribunal"; see also link to UN Security Council Resolution 808 of February 22, 1993, available at http://www.icty.org/en/documents/statute-tribunal; see generally (re International Criminal Tribunal for Rwanda), UN ICTR, "The ICTR in Brief," available at http://www.unictr.org/en/tribunal; see also link to the UN Security Council 955 of November 8, 1994, available at http://www.unictr.org/en/documents.

30. Correa et al., "Reparations."

31. See Tonya Bolden, *Cause: Reconstruction America, 1863–1877* (Alfred A. Knopf, 2005), 23–26. See also Brenda Wineapple, *Ecstatic Nation: Confidence, Crisis, and Compromise, 1848–1877* (Harper Collins, 2013), 345.

32. K. Sue Jewell, *Survival of the Black Family: The Institutional Impact of U.S. Social Policy* (Praeger, 1988), 37 (discussion of the importance of Black social networks to supplement the limited support offered by the Freedman's Bureau to former slaves during Reconstruction). See also David Goldfield, *American Aflame: How the Civil War Created a Nation* (Bloomsbury Press, 2011), 407–8.

33. Mutual assistance organizations remain significant in postconflict societies today, particularly but not exclusively in implementing social-redistributive forms of justice. Contemporary

examples of civil society organizations engaged in communitarian postconflict social transformation include the Women's Advocacy Network based in Gulu District, Northern Uganda, and the Fambul Tok Peace Mothers of Sierra Leone.

34. See ICTJ, "What Is Transitional Justice."

35. In the earlier-cited edited volume *From Transitional to Transformative Justice* (ed. Gready and Robins), various contributors explore case studies of the transformative approach to postconflict justice in diverse countries including Australia, Brazil, Sri Lanka, and Uganda.

36. In Sierra Leone, the parties to the conflict included rebels of the Revolutionary United Front, soldier-rebels (*sobels*) of the Armed Forces Revolutionary Council, militia volunteers of the Civil Defense Forces as well as the ECOMOG peacekeepers. Arms, training, and funding to support the conflict were also provided by the former government of Liberia, transnational corporations, diamond mine impresarios, and cross-border gunrunners.

The role of transnational organized criminal syndicates in contemporary armed conflicts suggests that the model of civil wars as struggles between national army and popular insurgency is antiquated. The increasing complexity of modern civil conflicts in Africa reflects a global trend in which national and regional conflicts are increasingly enmeshed with counterinsurgency policy, immigration policy, and counternarcotics campaigns. For further discussion of "entrepreneurial insurgencies," see J. Moore, *Humanitarian Law*, 57–58. See also Joseph Sorrentino, "How the U.S. 'Solved' the Central American Migrant Crisis," *In These Times*, May 12, 2016, available at http://inthesetimes.com/article/17916/how-the-u.s.-solved-the-central-american-migrant-crisis.

In its assessment of the causes of the Rebel War, the Final Report of Sierra Leone's Truth and Reconciliation Commission famously condemned all Sierra Leonean elites—political, military, and mercantile—for their collective conspiracy of avarice, corruption, and "moral bankruptcy" in abandoning the youth of Sierra Leone and relegating the poor to lives of despair and misery. See J. Moore, *Humanitarian Law*, 262, citing TRC Final Report, vol. 2, chap. 1, paras. 21 and 22.

In Uganda, the LRA War had its own complex constellation of military and political actors, not limited to the rebels of the LRA and the soldiers of the UPDF. Like Sierra Leone's Truth and Reconciliation Commission, a variety of academic and community-based organizations in Uganda have sought to study the roots and conduct of recent wars in Uganda. In a collaborative effort called the National Reconciliation and Transitional Justice Audit, the Refugee Law Project of Makerere University School of Law compiled a "Compendium of Conflicts" which included an exhaustive analysis of the contributing forces and actors that fueled and guided the LRA War. See generally Refugee Law Project, *Compendium of Conflicts in Uganda: Findings of the National Reconciliation and Transitional Justice Audit* (2014), 149–53, available at https://www.refugeelawproject.org/index.php?option=com_content&view=article&id=90&catid=16&Itemid=101.

The various armed forces that became involved on one or both sides of the conflict in Northern Uganda encompassed the Sudanese People's Liberation Army, the government of Sudan, militant groups in the Democratic Republic of the Congo and the Central African Republic, and other foreign governments including the United States, which supported the Ugandan government's efforts to find and apprehend LRA leaders.

37. See generally Jennifer Moore, "From Nation State to Failed State: International Protection from Human Rights Abuses by Non-State Agents," *Columbia Human Rights Law Review* 31, no. 1 (Fall 1999): 81–121.

38. See Dolan, *Social Torture*, 5 (discussing "the importance of external involvement in the dynamics of supposedly internal situations").

39. See generally Erin Baines, *I am Evelyn Amony: Reclaiming My Life from the Lord's Resistance Army*; Sarah Nouwen, *Complementarity in the Line of Fire: The Catalysing Role of the International Criminal Court in Uganda and Sudan*; Dolan, *Social Torture*; Mark Drumbl, "Victims Who Victimize: Transcending International Criminal Law's Binaries," *London Review of International Law* (2016), available at https://is.muni.cz/el/1422/jaro2016/MVV196K/um/Victims

_as_Victimizers.pdf; Paul Bradfield, "Reshaping Amnesty in Uganda: The Case of Thomas Kwoyelo," *Journal of International Criminal Law* 15 (2017): 825–55, 829; see also J. Moore, *Humanitarian Law*, chapter 7; and Nicola Palmer, Phil Clark, and Danielle Granville, eds., *Critical Perspectives in Transitional Justice* (Cambridge: Intersentia, 2012).

40. See generally Hawa Kamara, "A Look at the Major Changes in the Three Gender Acts," Centre for Accountability and the Rule of Law, August 11, 2016, available at http://www.carl-sl .org/pres/a-look-at-the-major-changes-in-the-three-gender-acts/; Jimmy D. Kandeh, "Politicization of Ethnic Identities in Sierra Leone," *African Studies Review* 35, no. 1 (April 1992): 81–99; William Schabas, "The Conjoined Twins of Transitional Justice? The Sierra Leone Truth and Reconciliation Commission and the Special Court," *Journal of International Criminal Justice* 2, no. 4 (December 2004): 1082–99; Tom Perriello and Marieke Wierda, *The Special Court for Sierra Leone Under Scrutiny* (International Center for Transitional Justice, 2006); and Joseph Opala, "What the West Failed to See in Sierra Leone," *Washington Post*, May 14, 2000, B2; see also J. Moore, *Humanitarian Law*, chapter 8.

41. See Aisling Swaine, *Conflict-Related Violence Against Women*; Fionnuala Ní Aoláin, Dina Francesca Haynes, and Naomi Cahn, *On the Frontlines: Gender, War, and the Post-Conflict Process* (Oxford University Press, 2011).

42. See, e.g., J. Moore, *Humanitarian Law* generally and chapters 7 and 8 regarding Northern Uganda and Sierra Leone, respectively.

43. See Stephanie Figgins, "After Elections, Libya's Transitional Justice in the Balance," *Egypt Independent*, July 16, 2012, available at https://egyptindependent.com/after-libya-s-elections -transitional-justice-balance/. See generally Ian Martin, *All Necessary Measures? The United Nations and International Intervention in Libya* (C. Hurst, 2022), especially chapter 4, "The Day After: Post-Conflict Planning," 85–106.

44. See William Schabas, "Prosecutorial Discretion v. Judicial Activism at the International Criminal Court," *Journal of International Criminal Justice* 6 (September 2008): 731, 752, cited in J. Moore, *Humanitarian Law*, 135 and 149n90.

45. Rules of state responsibility for wrongful acts under international law were classically imposed by states against other states. See Mark Janis, *An Introduction to International Law*, 4th ed. (Little, Brown, 2003), 187–88 and 189, citing I. Brownlie, *Principles of Public International Law*, 4th ed. (Oxford University Press, 1990), 434. Modern human rights law provides increasing mechanisms for individuals to hold states responsible for their international obligations, particularly under regional human rights treaties. See, e.g., African Charter on Human and Peoples' Rights, adopted June 27, 1981, entered into force October 21, 1986, OAU Doc. CAB/LEG/67/3 Rev. 5 (1981), art. 55 (re individual petitions against states before the African Commission on Human and Peoples' Rights).

46. See generally Jennifer Moore, "Toward a More Responsive Sovereignty: Confronting Human Rights Violations Through National Reconstruction," in *Effective Strategies for Protecting Human Rights*, ed. David Barnhizer (Ashgate, 2001), 71–78.

47. See Merry, *Human Rights and Gender Violence*, 193–195 and 210–212. Sally Engle Merry has analyzed the importance of "translators" in collaborations between global human rights activists and local community activists: "Translators are people who can easily move between layers because they conceptualize the issue in more than one way. . . . Through their mediation, human rights become relevant to a local social movement even though the oppressed group itself did not talk about human rights" (210).

48. In Northern Uganda, the fighting and displacement occurred in the Northern Region, far from the centrally located capital city of Kampala, principally in the Acholi districts of Gulu, Kitgum, and Pader. (When the war began in 1986, Uganda had 33 districts, but due to subdivisions there were 135 as of July 1, 2020.) In Sierra Leone, the war impacted each and every one of its 14 provincial districts as well as the capital city of Freetown.

49. I use the term human rights agencies to refer to both nongovernmental organizations (NGOs) and community-based organizations (CBOs) engaged in community development initiatives broadly conceived.

50. In both countries, these local women's groups receive technical and moral support from NGOs and CBOs without relying on significant financial resources from such entities. The women's collectives are self-sustaining through microfinance activities while benefiting from NGO trainings in the areas of mediation, domestic violence prevention, and women's inheritance rights under national law.

51. The University of New Mexico has an Institutional Review Board that considers research projects with human subjects in order to maintain ethical standards including respect for vulnerable people and the values of confidentiality and consent. Based on the submission of my research protocol and proposal, the UNM Office of the IRB granted me permission to proceed with my research on November 9, 2015, with an exemption from continuing oversight. See Dr. J. Scott Tonigan, IRB chairperson, exemption letter to Jennifer Moore (reference #12115, November 9, 2015), on file with author. Out of 60 women, all 60 gave me consent to quote them at least by first name in this volume. While 58 of the 60 were willing for me to use their full names, I elected to use first names only for the women I paraphrase and quote in this book. The only exceptions are in the case of women who served as my translators or consultants, who have gone on to lead community-based organizations or died during the course of my research.

Because many of my interviewees, including Jane and Boie, are not fully literate in their maternal languages, I used an oral script for consent. See Uganda and Sierra Leone IRB consent forms, on file with author.

Chapter 1

Epigraph: Joy Harjo, *Conflict Resolution for Holy Beings: Poems* (W. W. Norton, 2015), 64. Copyright © 2015 by Joy Harjo. Used by permission of W. W. Norton & Company, Inc.

1. The interviews conducted for this book focus on women engaged in community activism. Nevertheless, in its exploration of grassroots transformative justice in Sierra Leone and Uganda, this work honors a vision of feminism that respects and intersects with movements for the liberation of queer, transgender, and nonbinary people throughout the world.

2. See Mona Eltahawy, "Enough with Crumbs. I Want the Cake," *New York Times International Edition*, May 30, 2019, 13. See also Eltahawy, *Headscarves and Hymens: Why the Middle East Needs a Sexual Revolution* (Farrar, Straus & Giroux, 2015).

3. Manchanda cautions that "the impulse to women's social transformation and autonomy is circumscribed by the nationalist project, which constructs women as purveyors of the community's accepted and acceptable cultural identity." Rita Manchanda, "Ambivalent Gains in South Asian Conflicts," in *The Aftermath: Women in Post-Conflict Transformation*, ed. Sheila Meintjes, Anu Pillay, and Meredith Turshen (Zed Books, 2001), 100.

4. Fionnuala Ní Aoláin conceives of "strategic essentialism" as a way to facilitate "women's presence" in conversations about transitional justice when so often "scholarly and policy rejoinders to the phenomena of political repression generally failed to take account of the experiences of women." Ní Aoláin, "Advancing a Feminist Analysis of Transitional Justice," in *Feminist Perspectives on Transitional Justice: From International and Criminal to Alternative Forms of Justice*, ed. Martha Fineman and Estelle Zinsstag (Intersentia, 2013), 46.

5. See UNSC Res. 1325 of October 31, 2000, S/RES/1325 (2000).

6. See Res. 2467 of April 23, 2019, S/Res/2467 (2019) (reiterating the Security Council's "intention to include provisions on the promotion of gender equality and the empowerment of women in conflict and post-conflict situations").

7. The focus of Res. 2467 is on "the prevention of and response to sexual violence" during and after armed conflict. The term "sexual violence" appears seventy-two times in the ten-page document.

8. Sheila Meintjes, Anu Pillay, and Meredith Turshen, There is No Aftermath for Women, in Meintjes, Pillay, and Turshen, *Aftermath*, 3–4.

9. Meintjes, Pillay, and Turshen, *Aftermath*, 4–5.

10. See Aisling Swaine, *Conflict-Related Violence Against Women: Transforming Transition* (Cambridge University Press, 2018), 15, 288 ("If violence against women is a feature of peace, it will inevitably be a feature of conflict").

11. According to data for 2020, only South Sudan and Chad have higher maternal mortality rates than Sierra Leone. See https://www.indexmundi.com/g/r.aspx?v=2223.

12. See Paul Gready, introduction to *From Transition to Transformative Justice*, ed. Paul Gready and Simon Robins (Cambridge University Press, 2019), 8.

13. See Ní Aoláin, "Advancing a Feminist Analysis," 59–60.

14. When introduced by the scholar Kimberlé Crenshaw in the 1980s, the notion of intersectionality highlighted the double oppression experienced by Black women facing discrimination on the basis of their gender and race. Crenshaw and others have elaborated the concept to apply in a variety of contexts and with respect to a range of identity markers. See generally Crenshaw, *On Intersectionality: Essential Writings* (2014; repr., New Press, 2017).

15. David C. Gray and Benjamin A. Levin, "Feminist Perspectives on Extraordinary Justice," in Fineman and Zinsstag, *Feminist Perspectives on Transitional Justice*, 69, 71.

16. Like intersectionality theory, "standpoint theory" appreciates that women's multiple perspectives are shaped by diverse social experiences. See, e.g., Dorothy Smith, *The Conceptual Practices of Power: A Feminist Sociology of Knowledge* (Northeastern University Press, 1990).

17. Eilish Rooney, "Intersectionality: A Feminist Theory for Transitional Justice," in Fineman and Zinsstag, *Feminist Perspectives on Transitional Justice*, 92.

18. See Rooney, "Intersectionality," 90.

19. See Chris Dolan, *Social Torture: The Case of Northern Uganda, 1986–2006* (Berghahn Books, 2011), 167 and 192–96.

20. In Northern Uganda traditional cattle husbandry was devastated during the LRA War, with cattle stocks looted and destroyed. As an attempt to restore traditional livelihood practices, NGOs and government agencies would from time to time donate cattle to women's microfinance groups, despite "the increasing economic desperation of men." Dolan, *Social Torture*, 177.

21. See, e.g., Jerker Edström, Chris Dolan, and Thea Shahrokh, with Onen David, "Therapeutic Activism: Men of Hope Refugee Association Uganda, Breaking the Silence over Male Rape in Conflict-Related Sexual Violence," Refugee Law Project, March 2016, available at https://www.refugeelawproject.org/files/others/Therapeutic_Activism_Brief.pdf.

22. Dolan, *Social Torture*, 262.

23. See generally Edström, Dolan, and Shahrokh, "Therapeutic Activism."

24. The difficulties in challenging the hegemony of the retributive justice model for post-conflict transition is explored by Mark Drumbl in his analysis of the trial of the Lord's Resistance Army commander Dominic Ongwen in the International Criminal Court. He writes, "Yet so long as the accoutrements of the criminal law—courtrooms, judgments, and jailhouses—expand as the iconic way in which to imagine post-conflict justice and solemnly authenticate the past, non-justiciability leads to invisibility." Drumbl, "Victims Who Victimize: Transcending International Criminal Law's Binaries," *London Review of International Law* (2016): 25, available at https://is.muni.cz/el/1422/jaro2016/MVV196K/um/Victims_as_Victimizers.pdf.

25. The Geneva Conventions of 1949, in common article 3, prohibit the cruel treatment of civilians in noninternational armed conflicts. The mistreatment of civilians, including "torture or inhuman treatment . . . or unlawful confinement" is defined as a "grave breach" of the Fourth

Geneva Convention in article 147, meaning that states must criminalize such acts under their domestic laws. See Geneva Convention Relative to the Protection of Civilian Persons in Time of War of August 12, 1949 (Fourth Geneva Convention), arts. 3 and 147, available at https://ihl-databases.icrc.org/en/ihl-treaties.

26. Moreover, the LRA leader Thomas Kwoyelo's trial in the International Crimes Division (ICD) of the Ugandan High Court is also ongoing, twelve years after he was taken into custody. Chapter 2 further discusses the International Criminal Court (ICC) trial of Ongwen, the ICD trial of Kwoyelo, and the nine war crimes convictions laid down by the Special Court for Sierra Leone in the context of Sierra Leone's Rebel War.

27. International law, including international human rights law, has three primary sources, as recognized by the Statute of the International Court of Justice: treaties, customary norms, and general principles. See Charter of the United Nations, signed June 26, 1945, entered into force October 24, 1945, 59 Stat. 1031, TS No. 993, 3 Bevans 1153 (1969), Statute of the International Court of Justice (ICJ Statute, art. 38[a]). See also Jennifer Moore, *Humanitarian Law in Action Within Africa* (Oxford University Press, 2012), 15–20 (exploring the sources of international law and the dynamic relationships between sources).

28. United Nations General Assembly, G.A. Res. 217A(III), U.N. Doc. A/810, 71 (1948).

29. All these treaties are cited in notes below.

30. See International Covenant on Civil and Political Rights (ICCPR), adopted December 19, 1966, entered into force March 23, 1976, 999 U.N.T.S. 171, art. 2, emphasis added.

31. See Convention on the Elimination of Discrimination Against Women (CEDAW), adopted December 18, 1979, entered into force September 3, 1981, UNGA Res. 34/180, 34 UN GAOR Supp. (no. 46), 193, UN Doc. A/34/46 (1980), art. 2; see also the Convention Against Torture and Other Cruel, Inhuman or Degrading Treatment or Punishment (CAT), adopted December 10, 1984, entered into force June 26, 1987, UNGA Res. 39/46, 39 UN GAOR Supp. (no. 51), 197, UN Doc. A/39/51 (1984), art. 2; and the International Convention on the Elimination of All Forms of Racial Discrimination (CERD), adopted March 7, 1966, entered into force January 4, 1969, 660 U.N.T.S. 195, art. 2.

32. African [Banjul] Charter on Human and Peoples' Rights, adopted June 27, 1981, entered into force October 21, 1986, OAU Doc. CAB/LEG/67/3 Rev. 5 (1981), art. 30 ("An African Commission on Human and Peoples' Rights . . . shall be established . . . to promote human and peoples' rights and ensure their protection in Africa").

33. CEDAW, art. 3.

34. See Hawa Kamara, "A Look at the Major Changes in the Three Gender Acts," Centre for Accountability and the Rule of Law, August 11, 2016, available at http://www.carl-sl.org/pres/a-look-at-the-major-changes-in-the-three-gender-acts/.

35. The Constitution of Uganda, 1995, arts. 21 and 33, available at https://www.parliament.go.ug/cmis/views/e138fbaf-95f5-4cbc-ac33-b4678be3577a%253B1.0.

36. See Banjul Charter, art. 28.

37. See, e.g., Universal Declaration of Human Rights (UDHR); ICCPR; and International Covenant on Economic, Social, and Cultural Rights (ICESCR), adopted December 19, 1966, entered into force January 3, 1976, 999 U.N.T.S. 3.

38. As the anthropologist Sally Engle Merry wrote in a kindred vein about indigenous women in Hong Kong: "These grassroots women came to think of themselves as having rights, but did not understand their problems in terms of human rights conventions. Nevertheless, they were able to create an effective working relationship with educated elites who did." See Merry, *Human Rights and Gender Violence: Translating International Law into Local Justice* (University of Chicago Press, 2006), 194.

39. Because Uganda and Sierra Leone have ratified many human rights instruments, some of their provisions are codified in national legislation, particularly regarding women's physical

integrity, or incorporated in their national constitutions, particularly relating to inheritance and property rights. Specific domestic laws of Uganda and Sierra Leone are further discussed in Chapters 2–4.

40. ICCPR, art. 4(1), emphasis added.

41. Banjul Charter, art. 2, emphasis added.

42. CEDAW.

43. Protocol to the African Charter on Human and Peoples' Rights on the Rights of Women in Africa (Banjul Women's Protocol), adopted July 11, 2003, entered into force November 25, 2005, available at http://www.achpr.org/instruments/women-protocol/.

44. CEDAW, art. 1.

45. Banjul Women's Protocol, art. 1.

46. CEDAW, art. 5; Banjul Women's Protocol, art. 2(2).

47. UDHR.

48. Despite the integrated approach of the Universal Declaration, the United Nations General Assembly put forth two international human rights treaties in 1966, suggesting a bifurcation of human rights into civil-political and economic-social-cultural branches. See ICCPR and ICESCR.

49. J. Moore, *Humanitarian Law in Action Within Africa*, 19 and n. 43.

50. The Banjul Charter stands out among regional human rights treaties in incorporating social and economic rights alongside civil and political rights. See Banjul Charter, arts. 6 (liberty), 7 (fair trial), 8 (freedom of religion), 15 (equal pay for equal work), 16 (health rights), and 17 (education rights).

51. See J. Moore, *Humanitarian Law in Action Within Africa*, 108–9. The 1995 Ugandan Constitution was amended in 2005 to provide for Kampala as the capital city and to constitute districts within the country. The 1991 Constitution of Sierra Leone was reaffirmed in 1996, during the war, and amended in 2008, to permit the Anti-Corruption Commission to prosecute corruption offenses.

52. ICESCR.

53. CEDAW.

54. CEDAW, arts. 7 (public life), 10 (field of education), 11 (field of employment), 12 (field of health care, including family planning), 13 (nondiscrimination to ensure right to "family benefits" and access to loans and other forms of credit).

55. CEDAW, art. 14, emphasis added. In particular, article 14 provides that states should "take all appropriate measures" to ensure that women and men equally benefit from rural development, particularly in ensuring women's rights to (a) participate in development planning; (b) have access to health care services; (c) benefit from social security programs; (d) take part in formal and informal education programs; (e) receive equal employment and self-employment opportunities, including participation in cooperatives; (f) participate in community activities; (g) have access to agricultural loans and other forms of credit; and (h) enjoy "adequate living conditions, particularly in relation to housing, sanitation, electricity and water supply, transport and communications."

56. The insights and experience of members of women's collectives in Northern Uganda are further presented and discussed in Chapter 3.

57. CEDAW, art. 3, emphasis added.

58. CEDAW, art. 16(e).

59. Banjul Women's Protocol, art. 14(b) (whether to have children) and (c) (any method of contraception), emphasis added.

60. Compare CEDAW, art. 16(b) (consent to marriage) with Banjul Women's Protocol, art. 6 (minimum age 18).

61. CEDAW, art. 15(2).

62. Banjul Women's Protocol, arts. 20 (widows), 21 (inheritance), 22 (elderly women). There are also provisions dedicated to "Special Protection of Women with Disabilities" (art. 23), and "Special Protection of Women in Distress" (art. 24), emphasis added.

63. Banjul Women's Protocol, art. 5, emphasis added.

64. See USAID, Desk Study (draft), available at https://www.usaid.gov/document/desk-study -female-genital-mutilationcutting-sierra-leone. Female genital cutting (FGC) is not explicitly criminalized under Sierra Leonean Law, although the Domestic Violence Act of 2007 protects women and girls from acts which may endanger their health or safety. See Equality Now, Fact Sheet on FGM in Sierra Leone, available at https://www.equalitynow.org/learn_more_fgm_in _sierra_leone/. FGM/FGC in Sierra Leone is further discussed in Chapter 4.

65. Banjul Women's Protocol, art. 10 (Right to Peace), emphasis added.

66. Banjul Women's Protocol, art. 11 (Protection of Women in Armed Conflicts), emphasis added.

67. Banjul Women's Protocol, art. 13 (Economic and Social Welfare Rights), emphasis added.

68. Banjul Women's Protocol, arts. 15 (food), 16 (shelter), 17 (culture), 18 (environment), and 19 (development).

69. See Banjul Charter, Part II (re African Commission). Art. 45(2) mandates the African Commission on Human and Peoples' Rights to "ensure the protection of human and peoples' rights." There is also a subsequent Protocol to the Banjul Charter constituting an African Court on Human and Peoples' Rights. See Protocol to the African Charter on Human and Peoples' Rights on the Establishment of an African Court on Human and Peoples' Rights (Banjul Protocol on the African Court), concluded June 9, 1998, entered into force January 25, 2004, OAU Doc. OAU/LEG/EXP/AFCHPR/PROT (III). However, only Uganda has ratified the African Court Protocol and even so has not made a declaration allowing individuals and agencies to bring claims against it before the new court.

70. Article 55 of the Banjul Charter allows individual and group petitions to be considered by the African Commission if a majority of the commission so decides.

71. Notably, Fambul Tok, the NGO that launched the Sierra Leone Peace Mothers, was founded by John Caulker, formerly of Forum of Conscience.

72. 223/98 Forum of Conscience / Sierra Leone (African Commission, November 6, 2000), paras. 18–20, available at http://caselaw.ihrda.org/doc/223.98/view/en/.

73. Forum of Conscience / Sierra Leone, para. 21.

74. See Death Penalty Information Center, press release of July 26, 2021, available at https:// deathpenaltyinfo.org/news/sierra-leone-becomes-23rd-african-country-to-abolish-the-death -penalty.

75. Notably, governmental authority in Sierra Leone was more recently challenged in 2023, the same year that the reelection of President Bio was marred by charges of voter fraud and at a time when ordinary Sierra Leoneans were experiencing punishing levels of inflation. On November 26, 2023, armed militants attacked the Pademba Road Prison in Freetown, releasing around two thousand prisoners, in what the government characterized as a thwarted coup attempt. Nighttime curfews were imposed nationwide. The level of fear among the civil population was high, due in part to uncertainty about the identity and motives of the perpetrators. See Mayeni Jones and Umaru Fofana, "Sierra Leone Lifts Curfew After Breakout from Freetown's Pademba Road Prison," BBC, November 27, 2023, available at https://www.bbc.com/news/world-africa-67536147. See also Shola Lawal, "Uneasy Calm in Sierra Leone as Freetown Uprising Reveals Underlying Tension," *Al Jazeera*, November 28, 2023, available at https://www.aljazeera.com/features/2023 /11/28/uneasy-calm-in-sierra-leone-as-freetown-uprising-reveals-underlying-tension.

76. See Justice and Reconciliation Project Press Release, "Parliament Adopts Resolution to Address the Needs of War-Affected," Kampala, April 10, 2014, available at http://www.justice

andreconciliation.org/media/newsroom/press-releases/2014/parliament-adopts-resolution-to
-address-the-needs-of-war-affected/.

77. See J. Moore, Uganda Field Notebook, July 2023 (meeting with WAN members, July 17), on file with author.

78. See Hawa Kamara, "Look at the Major Changes." It is the Devolution of Estates Act in particular that ratifies the equal inheritance rights of women.

79. As discussed in the text above, Uganda and Sierra Leone have ratified additional international human rights treaties that recognize the rights of women, men, and children to the full range of economic, social, civil, and political human rights, including freedom from torture and inhumane treatment and freedom from racial discrimination. Notable examples are the ICCPR, the Convention Against Torture and the Convention on the Elimination of Racial Discrimination. See ICCPR; CAT; and CERD.

80. When Lucy from Nwoya District of Northern Uganda refers to her constitutional rights to inherit property on an equal basis with male family members, she is supported by the weight of judicial precedent but stymied by legislative inaction.

Chapter 2

Epigraph: Joy Harjo, *Conflict Resolution for Holy Beings: Poems* (W. W. Norton, 2015), 7. Copyright © 2015 by Joy Harjo. Used by permission of W. W. Norton & Company, Inc.

1. See Andy Lancaster, "The Divisive Nature of Ethnicity in Ugandan Politics, Before and After Independence" (PhD diss., University of Leeds, May 2011), para. 7 and n. 30 ("The colonial authority's preferential treatment of Baganda was largely responsible for regional inequality within Uganda and a major cause of resentment toward Baganda by other ethnic groups"), available at http://www.e-ir.info/2012/05/25/the-divisive-nature-of-ethnicity-in-ugandan-politics -before-and-after-independence/.

2. Refugee Law Project, *Compendium of Conflicts in Uganda: Findings of the National Reconciliation and Transitional Justice Audit* (2014), 17 and n. 13, available at https://www .refugeelawproject.org/index.php?option=com_content&view=article&id=90&catid =20&Itemid=146.

3. According to a World Bank report released in May 2023, the national poverty rate for Uganda is 30 percent and for the Northern Region it is 40 percent. See Tonny Abet, "Eastern, Northern Regions Top in Poverty—WB report," *Daily Monitor* (Uganda), May 12, 2023, available at https://www.monitor.co.ug/uganda/news/national/eastern-northern-regions-top-in -poverty-wb-report-4231850. In fact, in 2023 the prime minister conceded that infrastructural investments in Northern Uganda in the postwar period had not succeeded in lowering the poverty rate in the region, likely due to corruption in disbursement of funds and a failure to focus expenditures on the areas most affected by the LRA War. In her presentation to Parliament, Prime Minister Robinah Nabbanja added that the government planned to utilize instead the Parish Development Model, in which state funds are directly invested in viable small-scale income-generating projects identified by clusters of households at the local level. See Elizabeth Kamurungi, "Govt Admits Poverty Fight Failure in Northern Uganda," *Daily Monitor* (Uganda), November 28, 2022, available at https://www.monitor.co.ug/uganda/news/national/govt-admits-poverty-fight -failure-in-northern-uganda-4035418.

4. See generally, J. Moore, *Humanitarian Law in Action Within Africa* (Oxford University Press 2012), Chapter 7 (on Uganda). See also Joseph Wasonga, "Exclusion of Women in Post-Conflict Peace Processes: Transitional Justice in Northern Uganda," in *Feminist Perspectives on Transitional Justice: From International and Criminal to Alternative Forms of Justice*, ed. Martha

Fineman and Estelle Zinsstag (Intersentia, 2013), 256. See Refugee Law Project, *Compendium of Conflicts in Uganda*, 17–18 and 85.

5. J. Moore, *Humanitarian Law in Action Within Africa*, 211–14.

6. Agence France-Presse, "Milton Obote, 80, Strongman in Uganda, Twice Overthrown," *New York Times*, October 11, 2005, available at https://www.nytimes.com/2005/10/11/world/milton -obote-80-strongman-in-uganda-twice-overthrown.html.

7. See National African Language Resource Center, University of Wisconsin–Madison, "Who Speaks Acholi," available at http://www.nalrc.indiana.edu/resources/brochures. Acholi-Langi cultural affinity derives in part from their common descent from the Nilotic Luo people who migrated from Southern Sudan into Uganda during the fifteenth and sixteenth centuries C.E. Ibid.

8. Refugee Law Project, *Compendium of Conflicts in Uganda*, 68 ("Obote, a northerner, abolished all Kingdoms, which were particularly strong in the south").

9. Agence France-Presse, "Milton Obote."

10. See J. Moore, *Humanitarian Law in Action Within Africa*, 211–12.

11. See Alois S. Mlambo, "Mugabe on Land, Indigenization, and Development" in Sabelo J. Ndlovu-Gatsheni (ed.), *Mugabeism?: History, Politics, and Power in Zimbabwe* (Springer, 2015) at 49 (tracing Zimbabwe President Robert Mugabe's model of black economic nationalism to Amin's expulsion policy in the 1970s).

12. See Joseph Wasonga, "Exclusion of Women in Post-Conflict Peace Processes," 256; J. Moore, *Humanitarian Law in Action Within Africa*, 212; see also Refugee Law Project, *Compendium of Conflicts in Uganda*, 80 ("Amin regarded the Acholi and Langi as supporters of Obote, and for that reason he turned against them and brutally murdered or exiled a large number of soldiers, . . . politicians and civilians").

13. Sheila Rule, "Man in the News: Yoweri Museveni, Winner in Uganda," *New York Times*, Jan. 31, 1986, available at https://www.nytimes.com/1986/01/31/world/man-in-the-news-yoweri -kaguta-museveni-winner-in-uganda.html.

14. Ibid.

15. Refugee Law Project, *Compendium of Conflicts in Uganda*, 85.

16. Sheila Rule, "Man in the News: Yoweri Museveni, Winner in Uganda."

17. Ibid.

18. See J. Moore, Uganda Field Notebook, July 2023 (meeting with Fred Ngomokwe, consultant, Refugee Law Project, Gulu, 14 July), on file with author.

19. See Refugee Law Project, *Compendium of Conflicts in Uganda*, 91.

20. Museveni served as head of state for a decade in an unelected capacity until his first election in 1996 under Uganda's 1995 Constitution. Museveni was subsequently reelected in 2001, 2006, 2011, and 2016, to his fifth five-year term, each time with very little or reluctant support from northerners. See J. Moore, *Humanitarian Law in Action Within Africa*, 213. See also Chris Dolan, *Social Torture: The Case of Northern Uganda, 1986–2006* (Berghahn Books, 2011), 46, 56.

21. See Refugee Law Project, *Compendium of Conflicts in Uganda*, 17.

22. Refugee Law Project, *Compendium of Conflicts in Uganda*, 17.

23. See J. Moore, *Humanitarian Law in Action Within Africa*, 213–14. See also Refugee Law Project, *Compendium of Conflicts in Uganda*, 145–47 (re Alice Auma Lakwena) and 149–150 (re Joseph Kony). Note that South Sudan separated and attained its independence from Sudan in 2011.

24. See Refugee Law Project, *Compendium of Conflicts in Uganda*, 151–52 ("feeling abandoned by the Acholi, Kony resorted to the use of violence against civilians and abduction as a recruitment strategy").

25. See Wasonga, "Exclusion of Women," 256–58.

26. See J. Moore, *Humanitarian Law in Action Within Africa*, 213. See also Refugee Law Project, *Compendium of Conflicts in Uganda*, 152 and n. 335, citing Chris Dolan, *Social Torture: The Case of Northern Uganda, 1986–2006*, 1st ed. (Berghahn Books, 2009).

27. The Acholi in Northern Uganda have experienced a history of discrimination, regional neglect, and underdevelopment dating back to the colonial period. See Lancaster, "Divisive Nature of Ethnicity."

28. See Wasonga, "Exclusion of Women," 259 ("Uprooting of the people was basically a government program").

29. P. Wegner, "Ambiguous Impacts: The Effects of the International Criminal Court Investigations in Northern Uganda" (Refugee Law Project Working Paper No. 22, October 2012), 16 (UPDF lootings and rapes in IDP camps as well as assaults, torture, and unlawful killings).

30. See Dolan, *Social Torture*, 187 ("Conditions in the protected villages created a metaphorical prison").

31. In Dolan's conception, the "social torture" of Northern Ugandans was characterized by the inhumane treatment of the Acholi community as well as the long-term toll that dislocation and encampment had on the physical and psychosocial health of individuals. See Dolan, *Social Torture*, 6–7 and 159–60. Dolan holds various actors responsible for such collective suffering, including military officials and humanitarian organizations (260–61).

32. See Amy Ross and Chandra Lekha Siram, "Catch-22 in Uganda: the LRA, the ICC and the Peace Process," JURIST Legal News and Research, University of Pittsburgh School of Law, July 17, 2006.

33. See Wasonga, "Exclusion of Women," 260 and n. 29.

34. See Paul Bradfield, "Reshaping Amnesty in Uganda," *Journal of International Criminal Law* 15 (2017), 825–55, 829.

35. See J. Moore, *Humanitarian Law in Action Within Africa*, 218–19. See also Bradfield, "Reshaping Amnesty in Uganda," 829–30.

36. See Bradfield, "Reshaping Amnesty in Uganda," 830–31 and 854.

37. Further details of the forced conscription, servitude, escape, and reintegration of members of the Women's Advocacy Network are the subject of a section of Chapter 3.

38. See, e.g., Agreement on Accountability and Reconciliation Between the Government of the Republic of Uganda and the Lord's Resistance Army/Movement, Juba, Sudan, June 29, 2004 (also known as "Juba Agenda #3"). The full text is available at https://peacemaker.un.org/uganda -accountability-reconciliation2007. For full citations of all six Juba Accords, see J. Moore, *Humanitarian Law in Action Within Africa*, 214 and nn. 32–37.

39. See "LRA and Uganda Sign Peace Pact," *Al Jazeera*, March 2, 2008, available at https:// www.aljazeera.com/news/2008/3/2/lra-and-uganda-sign-peace-pact.

40. See J. Moore, Uganda Field Notebook, July 2023 (meeting with Rwot Yusuf Adek, traditional Acholi chief, July 14), on file with author. (Rwot Adek's full name is used with his permission.)

41. See Jeffrey Gettleman and Eric Schmitt, "US Aided a Failed Plan to Rout Ugandan Rebels," *New York Times*, February 6, 2009, available at https://www.nytimes.com/2009/02/07/world /africa/07congo.html.

42. See "Lord's Resistance Army Kidnappings Hit Six-Year High," Reuters, July 20, 2016, available at http://af.reuters.com/article/drcNews/idAFL8N1A62ML.

43. "Lord's Resistance Army Steps Up Congo Attacks as U.S.-backed Force Pulls Out," Reuters, June 16, 2017, available at https://www.washingtonpost.com/world/africa/lords-resistance -army-steps-up-congo-attacks-as-us-backed-force-pulls-out/2017/06/16/f48c37fe-52bc-11e7 -91eb-9611861a988f_story.html?utm_term=.c76bc9df6762.

44. See United Nations Office for the Coordination of Humanitarian Affairs (OCHA), "Special Alert: Escalation of LRA Attacks Causes Displacement," May 20, 2020, available at https:// reliefweb.int/report/democratic-republic-congo-special-alert-escalation-lra-attacks-causes -displacement.

45. See J. Moore, *Humanitarian Law in Action Within Africa*, 198.

46. Vincent Otti, Kony's top deputy, was killed in 2007. BBC, "Uganda's LRA Confirm Otti's Death," January 23, 2008, available at http://news.bbc.co.uk/2/hi/africa/7204278.stm. See also Evelyn Amony, *I Am Evelyn Amony: Reclaiming My Life from the Lord's Resistance Army* (University of Wisconsin Press, 2015), 125–26 (Amony's report of receiving a telephone call in October 2007 informing her of Otti's execution by Kony, reportedly for insubordination).

47. See International Criminal Court, "Situation in Uganda," under "Situations and Cases," available at https://www.icc-cpi.int/uganda.

48. In 2015 ninety charges against Ongwen were confirmed by Pre-Trial Chamber II and initial hearings were scheduled for December 2016. "Gulu will not host Ong'wen trial just yet, ICC judges rule," August 2, 2016, available at http://www.jfjustice.net/en/icc-cases/gulu-will-not-host-onga-wen-trial-just-yet-icc-judges-rule.

49. See International Criminal Court, fact sheet on Ongwen Case ("Situation in Uganda"), available at https://www.icc-cpi.int/cases?field_defendant_t=693.

50. See Refugee Law Project, "Another Injustice—Victims' Consultations in the ICC Case Against LRA's Dominic Ongwen" (2016), available at https://www.youtube.com/watch?v=l3CthMxJ3jQ. See also interview with Daker Nighty discussed in Chapter 3.

51. See generally Refugee Law Project, "Ongwen's Justice Dilemma Part II, Ongwen's Confirmation of Charges Hearing: Implications and Way Forward?," 2016, available at http://refugeelawproject.org/resources/briefing-notes-and-special-reports/12-conflict-and-tj-special-reports/368-ongwen-s-justice-dilemma-part-ii-ongwen%E2%80%99s-confirmation-of-charges-hearing-implications-and-way-forward%E2%80%9D. "Legally, Ongwen's case will also set a precedent on a number of legal questions currently before the Court, including . . . how to determine intentional acts in situations of coercion . . . [and] *the fine line between victims turned perpetrators* as well as the plight of child soldiers in international criminal and humanitarian law" (13, emphasis added). See also Mark Drumbl, "Victims Who Victimize: Transcending International Criminal Law's Binaries," *London Review of International Law*, 2016, available at https://is.muni.cz/el/1422/jaro2016/MVV196K/um/Victims_as_Victimizers.pdf at 17 (Ongwen "endured what he subsequently inflicted"—in particular enslavement and child conscription).

52. See Author's Field Notebook, Uganda 2016 (notes from focus group interview with Uketu wan Kwene members), on file with author.

53. See J. Moore, *Humanitarian Law in Action Within Africa*, 136–37.

54. See Jimmy Wamimbi, "Thomas Kwoyelo Trial," Avocats sans Frontières (Lawyers Without Borders) policy briefing, April 25, 2023, available at https://asf.be/thomas-kwoyelo-trial-prosecution-moves-close-to-wind-up-presenting-its-witness/.

It is essential to acknowledge in this context that individuals suspected of involvement in terrorism have been held in US military detention in Guantanamo Bay for upward of twenty years, many without ever being charged with a crime. See BBC News, "Guantanamo Bay: US Releases Oldest Detainee Saifullah Paracha," available at https://www.bbc.com/news/world-us-canada-63438878 https://www.bbc.com/news/world-us-canada-63438878.

55. Kwoyelo was charged with violations of Uganda's Geneva Conventions Act of 1964, which domesticated provisions of the 1949 Geneva Conventions. See Paul Bradfield, "Reshaping Amnesty in Uganda," 837.

56. For some, Kwoyelo's prosecution flies in the face of Uganda's 2000 Amnesty Act, which has resulted in amnesty for 26,000 former combatants, including 13,000 LRA fighters. Bradfield notes that "local views in northern Uganda on the moral propriety of Kwoyelo's prosecution can vary significantly," contrasting those who emphasize his lack of "moral agency" due to his conscription as a child, with those direct victims who may have a "deep contempt" for Kwoyelo." Bradfield, "Reshaping Amnesty in Uganda," 838.

57. Justice Bart Magunda Katureebe, in his opinion for the Ugandan Supreme Court, elaborated that the Amnesty Act was designed to apply to acts of rebellion against the government of Uganda, not "terrible crimes … against innocent civilians who had nothing to do with government." See Derrick Kiyonga, "Why LRA Commander Kwoyelo Case Has Dragged on for 14 Years," *Monitor* (Uganda), June 11, 2023, available at https://www.monitor.co.ug/uganda/magazines/people -power/why-lra-commander-kwoyelo-case-has-dragged-on-for-14-years-4265436.

58. See Paul Bradfield, "Amnesty or No Amnesty? African Commission Weighs in on the Kwoyelo Case," *Beyond the Hague* (blog): Thoughts on International Justice from The Hague and Beyond, October 11, 2018, available at https://beyondthehague.com/2018/10/11/amnesty-or-no -amnesty-african-commission-weighs-in-on-the-kwoyelo-case/. The African Commission case concerning Kwoyelo is further discussed in Chapter 1.

59. See Communication 431/12 Thomas Kwoyelo v. Uganda (African Commission, decision adopted during the 23rd Extra-Ordinary Session, February 13–22, 2018), paras. 195, 245, 252, and 295(ii), available at http://www.achpr.org/files/sessions/23rd-eos/comunications/431 .12/communication_431_12.pdf. The African Commission decision in Kwoyelo is further discussed in Chapter 1..

60. See Jimmy Wamimbi, "Thomas Kwoyelo Trial."

61. See Wasonga, "Exclusion of Women," 259.

62. NB: Unlike for the majority of women quoted in this text, I use Ms. Amony's real name, with her permission, because she is a published author and a leader of an NGO. For others who are less known outside their communities, I use pseudonyms, regardless of their permission to use real names, out of an abundance of concern for their anonymity.

63. See Evelyn Amony, *I Am Evelyn Amony: Reclaiming My Life from the Lord's Resistance Army*, ed. Erin Baines (University of Wisconsin Press, 2015), 39.

64. United Nations statistics indicate that as of 2018, 49.9 percent of Ugandan women fifteen years old and older have experienced intimate partner violence, compared to 31.5 percent for least developed countries overall, and 45 percent for Sierra Leonean women. UNDP Human Development Statistical Update (2018), 91, 93, 94, Dashboard 3, available at http://www.hdr.undp.org /sites/default/files/2018_human_development_statistical_update.pdf.

65. See UNDP Human Development Report (HDR) 2021/2022, "Uncertain Times, Unsettled Lives: Shaping Our Future in a Transforming World," table 4 (Gender Development Index), available at https://hdr.undp.org/system/files/documents/global-report-document/hdr2021-22pdf _1.pdf. The corresponding data point for women in Sierra Leone is 61.4 years life expectancy.

66. See UNDP HDR 2021/22, table 4 (Gender Development Index). The corresponding statistics for Sierra Leone are 3.5 average years of schooling for women and 5.8 for men. In the United Kingdom, 13.4 years of schooling is the average for both women and men.

67. See UNDP HDR 2021/22, table 5 (Gender Inequality Index). The corresponding data point for Sierra Leone is a staggering 1,120 maternal deaths per 100,000 live births.

68. These two dates were chosen for beginning and concluding the Sixteen Days of Activism because both have great significance in the struggle for women's equality, integrity, and agency. November 25 is the International Day for the Elimination of Violence Against Women, the date on which the Mirabal sisters were assassinated in 1960 for standing up to the repressive dictatorship of Rafael Trujillo in the Dominican Republic. December 10 is Human Rights Day, the date on which the United Nations General Assembly adopted the Universal Declaration of Human Rights in 1948. See UN Women, "16 Days of Activism to End Violence Against Women and Girls," available at https://www.unwomen.org/en/what-we-do/ending-violence-against-women/unite/16-days-of -activism. As early as 2010, the U.S. ambassador to Uganda Jerry Lanier credited the Ugandan government with stating in its most recent National Development Plan that "domestic violence is recognized as a problem and actions are being taken to reduce it." See statement by the U.S.

ambassador to Uganda Jerry Lanier, published in the *Independent* (Uganda), November 30, 2010, available at https://www.independent.co.ug/16-days-activism-gender-based-violence/.

69. See Susan Ngongi-Namando, UN resident coordinator in Uganda, "Remarks at National Launch of 16 Days of Activism to End Violence Against Women and Girls," November 24, 2022, available at https://uganda.un.org/en/210673-remarks-national-launch-16-days-activism-end -violence-against-women-and-girls.

70. See Stephen Ssenkaaba, "Uganda: Violence Against Women Unabated Despite Law and Policies," *Africa @ The United Nations General Assembly* (blog), 2023, available at https:// www.un.org/africarenewal/news/uganda-violence-against-women-unabated-despite-laws-and -policies.

71. See Parliament of the Republic of Uganda, Uganda Succession Amendment Act (new Succession Act) of 2022, sec. 5 (amendment of prior sec. 9) and sec. 12 (amendment of prior sec. 23), available at www.gcic.go.ug/the-amended-succession-laws/.

72. See new Succession Act, sec. 13 (amendment of prior sec. 26).

73. See new Succession Act, sec. 14 (amendment of prior sec. 27).

74. See Parliament of the Republic of Uganda, "What New Amendments to the Succession Act Mean," February 9, 2022, available at https://www.parliament.go.ug/news/5646/what-new -amendments-succession-act-mean. See also LANDnet et al., Memorandum on [Uganda] Succession Amendment Bill, LANDnet, April 18, 2018, 1–4, available at http://www.landnet.ug /landwatch/wp-content/uploads/2018/06/SUCCESSION-BILL-Complete-to-SEND.pdf, citing *Law & Advocacy for Women in Uganda v. Attorney General of Uganda, Constitutional Petition No. 13 of 05* (Ugandan Constitutional Court, April 5, 2007).

75. See Parliament of the Republic of Uganda, Anti-Homosexuality Act, 2023, sec. 3 (Aggravated Homosexuality) and sec. 11 (Promotion of Homosexuality), available at https://www .parliament.go.ug/sites/default/files/The%20Anti-Homosexuality%20Act%2C%202023.pdf. See also Ashwani Budoo-Scholtz, deputy director Africa, Human Rights Watch, "Uganda's President Signs Repressive Anti-LGBTQ Law," May 30, 2023, available at https://www.hrw.org/news/2023 /05/30/ugandas-president-signs-repressive-anti-lgbt-law.

76. See Human Rights Awareness and Promotion Forum, "HRAPF Analysis of the Changes to the Anti-Homosexuality Bill," *HRAPF* (blog), May 3, 2023, available at https://hrapf.org/hrapfs -analysis-of-the-changes-to-the-anti-homosexuality-bill-2023/. See also Jackline Kemigisa, "Why I've Joined the Court Challenge Against Uganda's Anti-Gay Law," *Open Democracy* (blog), June 2, 2023, available at https://www.opendemocracy.net/en/5050/uganda-anti-homosexuality-act-2023 -petition-constitutional-court/.

77. The linkages between homophobia and stigma against survivors of sexual assault are evident at the community level. In 2023 interviews with members of Alany pa Mony Lit, one of the women's cooperatives in Northern Uganda, members referenced their inability to secure loans from financial institutions on account of bias due to their advanced age and status as sexual violence survivors. Fred Ngomokwe, one of my research partners and Acholi translators, explained after our interviews that the pejorative phrase in Acholi for rape survivors is similar to a slur used against gay men. This eliding of LGBTQ people with sexual assault victims creates a very real danger that survivors of war-related violence will be further marginalized in the climate of fear instilled by the Anti-Homosexuality Act alongside members of the gay community. See J. Moore, Uganda Field Notebook, July 2023 (meeting with Alany members, July 12), on file with author.

78. See J. Moore, *Humanitarian Law in Action Within Africa*, 215.

79. The Transitional Justice Working Group of Uganda's Justice, Law, and Order Section (JLOS) produced multiple drafts of a "National Transitional Justice Policy." See documents regarding JLOS National Transitional Justice Policy, available at http://www.jlos.go.ug/index.php /document-centre/transitional-justice/transitional-justice-policy. In 2023 the advocacy group Avocats sans Frontières welcomed "the government of Uganda's adoption of the National Tran-

sitional Justice Policy, a comprehensive and key framework designed to address past human rights violations with the aim of promoting justice, accountability, and reconciliation which are key pillars in achieving sustainable peace. However, there is a need to expedite the enactment of the legislative instruments to operationalize the policy and ensure that victims achieve justice." See Jimmy Wamimbi, "Thomas Kwoyelo Trial." See also Jeremy Sarkin, "Providing Reparations in Uganda: Substantive Recommendations for Implementing Reparations in the Aftermath of the Conflicts That Occurred over the Last Few Decades," *African Human Rights Law Journal* 14 (2014): 526–52, available at http://www.saflii.org/za/journals/AHRLJ/2014/27.html.

80. In tracing the taproots of the "Rebel War," an important historical source for students of Sierra Leonean history is the multivolume Final Report of the Sierra Leone Truth and Reconciliation Commission (TRC), published in 2004 after the cessation of civil war hostilities. As a component of the nation's postconflict national reconciliation process, the TRC Final Report is an expression of a collective commitment to expose the causes and conduct of the war in light of Sierra Leone's colonial and postindependence history and on that foundation to rebuild a culture of peace in Sierra Leone. See generally Sierra Leone Truth and Reconciliation Commission, Final Report of the Truth and Reconciliation Commission (TRC Final Report), 2004. The Executive Summary is found in vol. 2, chap. 1, available at http://www.sierraleonetrc.org/index.php/view-report-text-vol-2/item/volume-two-chapter-one?category_id=20. See also J. Moore, *Humanitarian Law in Action Within Africa*, 241–82.

81. One group of settlers was made up of families headed by freedmen and freedwomen who had supported the British in the American Revolution and came to the Freetown Colony after trying to survive in the farm country of Nova Scotia or on the streets of London. Other settlers were former slaves from Jamaica who had fought the British as guerrilla-style maroons and were offered passage to West Africa in exchange for ending their rebellion. A third group of early inhabitants were emancipated slaves who had been captured in raids throughout the African interior and liberated on shipboard before setting sail for the Americas. These so-called Liberated Africans were sent to the new coastal settlement after their slaving vessels were seized off the coast of West Africa by the British navy in its role enforcing the recent prohibition of the transatlantic slave trade. See J. Moore, *Humanitarian Law in Action Within Africa*, 244–45; see also Richard Dowden, *Africa: Altered States, Ordinary Miracles* (Public Affairs, 2009), 290–91.

82. In modern Sierra Leone, "Krio" is a linguistic, ethnocultural, and socioeconomic term. Krio is the national language of Sierra Leone, originally spoken by the Creole (Krio) settler community, and derived from English and many African languages. Krio is also a reference to the people who are descended from that multiethnic Creole community that developed the Freetown Colony after its founding in 1792. Finally, Krio as a sociological term denotes the greater relative economic and political privilege that the urban settler class generally had compared to the indigenous Africans of the inland communities of the Sierra Leone Protectorate. See generally Jimmy D. Kandeh, "Politicization of Ethnic Identities in Sierra Leone," *African Studies Review* 35, no. 1 (April 1992): 81–99.

83. Minority Rights Group International, *World Directory of Minorities and Indigenous Peoples—Sierra Leone, 2007*, available at http://www.refworld.org/docid/4954ce4823.html.

84. One notable exception was the considerable degree of social integration and intermarriage between the Krio and the Sherbro people of coastal Sierra Leone. Sherbro people had had contact with Europeans throughout the period of the transatlantic slave trade, and some urbanized Sherbro assimilated as Krio during the protectorate period. See Anaïs Ménard, *Integrating Strangers: Sherbro Identity and the Politics of Reciprocity Along the Sierra Leonean Coast* (Berghahn Books, 2023), 25 ("Sherbros are not 'fully' Krio, but are Krio nonetheless. Both identities can coexist to define an individual").

85. See Kandeh, "Politicization of Ethnic Identities in Sierra Leone," 83. The so-called natives of the protectorate were also economically exploited as migrant laborers in the Freetown Colony,

throughout Africa and as far as British Honduras (84–85). Compared to people living in the protectorate, "people in the Colony enjoyed vastly superior social, political and economic development and access to vital resources such as education." See TRC Final Report, vol. 2, chap. 1, para. 11.

86. See generally Kandeh, "Politicization of Ethnic Identities in Sierra Leone."

87. See CIA, *The World Factbook* (Sierra Leone, People and Society), last updated September 1, 2023, available at https://www.cia.gov/the-world-factbook/countries/sierra-leone/#people-and-society.

88. Milton Margai was knighted by Queen Elizabeth in 1950 for his service to Sierra Leone and the British Commonwealth. See Reuters, "Sir Milton Margai Dead at 68," *New York Times*, April 29, 1964, available at https://www.nytimes.com/1964/04/29/archives/sir-milton-margai-dead-at-68-prime-minister-of-sierra-leone.html.

89. See Kandeh, "Politicization of Ethnic Identities in Sierra Leone."

90. Despite the legacy of class and tribal inequalities, ethnic intermarriage and intermarriage between Muslims and Christians became and remain prevalent since independence throughout Sierra Leone. The Krio national language facilitates a national identity that transcends tribal or sectarian affiliation. See J. Moore, *Humanitarian Law in Action Within Africa*, 245.

91. See Joseph Opala, "What the West Failed to See in Sierra Leone," *Washington Post*, May 14, 2000, available at https://www.washingtonpost.com/archive/opinions/2000/05/14/what-the-west-failed-to-see-in-sierra-leone/097eb3e0-c671-4c8e-83a1-3d3dfd5efb45/.

92. See generally J. Moore, *Humanitarian Law in Action Within Africa*, 246–47.

93. See Kandeh, "Politicization of Ethnic Identities in Sierra Leone," 82.

94. See TRC Final Report, vol. 2, chap. 1, para. 69 (pdf file, 15).

95. See TRC Final Report, Executive Summary, vol. 2, chap. 1, para. 14 (found on p. 4 of the pdf file).

96. See J. Moore, *Humanitarian Law in Action within Africa*, 246. See also Dowden, *Africa*, 302.

97. See Tom Perriello and Marieke Wierda, *The Special Court for Sierra Leone Under Scrutiny* (International Center for Transitional Justice, 2006), 5.

98. See J. Moore, *Humanitarian Law in Action Within Africa*, 246.

99. See TRC Final Report Executive Summary, vol. 2, chap. 1, para. 24 (found on pp. 6–7 of the pdf file).

100. TRC Final Report Executive Summary, vol. 2, chap. 1, para. 25 (found on p. 7 of the pdf file).

101. See Jean-Christophe Rufin, "The Economics of War: A New Theory for Armed Conflicts," in *Forum: War, Money and Survival*, ed. International Committee of the Red Cross (2000), 22–26. Rufin discusses the increasing criminal-entrepreneurial nature of civil wars in the post–Cold War era. Armed movements, unable to rely on one international patron, increasingly rely on new income-generating activities, including "direct predation on civilians" (24). See also Opala, "What the West Failed to See" (Opala describes the "competitive banditry" of the factions in the Sierra Leonean civil war).

102. See Perriello and Wierda, *Special Court*, 6 (Perriello and Wierda stress the "massive human rights abuses against civilians" that resulted from the practice of armed "factions trading off control over villages").

103. TRC Final Report, vol. 2, chap. 1, paras. 29–36. As specifically noted by the authors of the TRC Final Report, "While most of the violations and abuses were attributed to the RUF, other significant perpetrators included the AFRC and the CDF" (para. 34).

104. The TRC Final Report focuses on the particular motivations of young male militants in the RUF, AFRC, and CDF: "Another common feature was the almost identical composition of the ground forces: impressionable, disgruntled young men eager for an opportunity to assert

themselves, either to ensure that no harm was done to their own people, to fight against perceived injustice, or for personal and group aggrandisement." TRC Final Report, vol. 2, chap. 1, para. 36.

105. See J. Moore, *Humanitarian Law in Action Within Africa*, 252–53.

106. This generalized fear of violence by armed militants endures to the present day. On November 26, 2023, armed militants attacked the Pademba Road Prison in Freetown, releasing around two thousand prisoners, in what the government characterized as a thwarted coup attempt. Nighttime curfews were imposed nationwide. The level of fear among the civilian population was high, due in part to uncertainty about the identity and motives of the perpetrators. See Mayeni Jones and Umaru Fofana, "Sierra Leone Lifts Curfew After Breakout from Freetown's Pademba Road Prison," BBC, November, 27, 2023, available at https://www.bbc.com/news/world-africa-67536147.

107. See TRC Final Report, vol. 2, chap. 1, para. 36.

108. See TRC Final Report, vol. 2, chap. 1, para. 35.

109. See insights on Sierra Leone's civil conflict shared by Lilian Morsay of Fambul Tok, quoted and discussed in Chapter 4.

110. The impact of the Rebel War reflected the integrated nature of Sierra Leonean society, the coexistence of the two religious traditions in most rural communities, and the prevalence of "Chris-Mus" marriages. See J. Moore, *Humanitarian Law in Action Within Africa*, 245.

111. Peace Agreement Between the Government of Sierra Leone and the Revolutionary United Front of Sierra Leone, Lomé, July 7, 1999 (Lomé Accords), available at http://www.sierra-leone.org/lomeaccord.html.

112. Lomé Accords, art. 9.

113. Lomé Accords, art 26.

114. See TRC Final Report, vol. 1, introduction, available at http://www.sierraleonetrc.org/index.php/view-report-text-vol-1/item/introduction?category_id=19.

115. See generally TRC Final Report, vol. 1, chap. 5, "Methodology and Processes," available at http://www.sierraleonetrc.org/index.php/view-report-text-vol-1/item/vol-one-chapter-five?category_id=19.

116. Since the end of the Rebel War, the former Koinadugu District was administratively split into the new Falaba and (smaller) Koinadugu Districts. Dogoloya today, while administratively part of Falaba District, retains its historical and cultural affiliation with Koinadugu.

117. See TRC Final Report, vol. 1, chap. 5, paras. 194–200.

118. See TRC Final Report, vol. 2, chap. 3, Recommendations, para. 54 (abolition of the death penalty), para. 93 (prohibition of corporal punishment), paras. 316–76 (protection of women's rights), and paras. 482–507 (implementation of reparations), available at https://www.sierraleonetrc.org/index.php/view-the-final-report/download-table-of-contents/volume-two/item/witness-to-the-truth-volume-two-chapter-3?category_id=12.

119. See Hawa Kamara, "A Look at the Major Changes in the Three Gender Acts," Centre for Accountability and the Rule of Law, August 11, 2016, available at http://www.carl-sl.org/pres/a-look-at-the-major-changes-in-the-three-gender-acts/.

120. See The Devolution of Estates Act, 2007, available at http://www.sierra-leone.org/Laws/2007-21p.pdf, section 8(a).

121. See Devolution of Estates Act, section 2.

122. See Devolution of Estates Act, section 22(3).

123. See The United States Institute for Peace, "Truth Commission: Sierra Leone," available at https://www.usip.org/publications/2002/11/truth-commission-sierra-leone.

In 2009 the International Center for Transitional Justice (ICTJ) published an evaluation of the reparations program, reporting that only around twenty thousand people in fact received cash payments. The authors of the ICTJ report concluded that to be meaningful, the NaCSA program needed to progress beyond one-off payments, to provide ongoing pension support and access to enhanced educational opportunities and health care for war survivors. See Mohamad Suma and Cristiàn Correa, "Report and Proposals for the Implementation of Reparations in Sierra Leone" (International Center for Transitional Justice, 2009), 7, 9–11, available at https://www.ictj.org/sites /default/files/ICTJ-SierraLeone-Reparations-Report-2009-English.pdf.

124. See Death Penalty Information Center, press release, July 26, 2021, available at https:// deathpenaltyinfo.org/news/sierra-leone-becomes-23rd-african-country-to-abolish-the-death -penalty.

125. See Death Penalty Information Center, press release, July 26, 2021. Three more African countries abolished the death penalty in 2022 (Central African Republic, Equatorial Guinea, and Zambia). Two additional African countries limit its implementation (Kenya abolished the mandatory death penalty for murder and Gabon removed the death penalty from its legislation, without explicitly abolishing it in all cases). See "Countries That Have Abolished the Death Penalty Since 1976," available at https://deathpenaltyinfo.org/policy-issues/international/countries-that -have-abolished-the-death-penalty-since-1976.

126. See Aaron Fichtelberg, *Hybrid Tribunals: A Comparative Examination* (Springer, 2015), 56 ("UN officials strongly opposed the immunities that the [Lomé] accord guaranteed") and n. 24 (the UN legal advisor Ralph Zacklin in particular viewed the amnesty as inapplicable to international crimes).

127. Agreement Between the United Nations and the Government of Sierra Leone on the Establishment of the Special Court for Sierra Leone, January 16, 2002, available at http://www.rscsl .org/documents.html (at link under "Special Court Agreement"), art. 1(1) (re type and timing of crimes within the jurisdiction of the Special Court).

128. See TRC Final Report.

129. See J. Moore, *Humanitarian Law in Action Within Africa*, 130.

130. Special Court for Sierra Leone, *The Prosecutor v. Charles Ghankay Taylor* (conviction in Trial Chamber, April 26, 2012; sentenced to fifty-year term of imprisonment, May 30, 2012; conviction upheld on appeal); available at http://www.rscsl.org/Taylor.html.

131. See Special Court for Sierra Leone, Status Sheet on the Case of Foday Sankoh, December 11, 2023, available at https://rscsl.org/the-scsl/cases/other-cases/foday-saybana-sankoh/.

132. See Statute of the Special Court for Sierra Leone (August 2000), art. 10 ("An amnesty granted to any person falling within the jurisdiction of the Special Court in respect of the crimes referred to in articles 2 to 4 of the present Statute shall not be a bar to prosecution"), art. 2 (re crimes against humanity), art. 3 (re violations of the 1949 Geneva Conventions), art. 4 (re other violations of international humanitarian law).

133. See Lomé Accords, art. 9(2). The Lomé amnesty provision applies to combatants' acts "committed in pursuit of their *objectives*" (emphasis added).

134. See Statute of the Special Court for Sierra Leone, art. 1 ("The Special Court shall . . . have the power to prosecute persons who bear the greatest responsibility for serious violations of international humanitarian law and Sierra Leonean law"). See also Figure 7.

135. See generally William Schabas, "The Conjoined Twins of Transitional Justice? The Sierra Leone Truth and Reconciliation Commission and the Special Court," *Journal of Criminal Justice* 2 (2004): 1082–99. Schabas concluded that the dynamic between the two institutions reflected "a genuinely complementary approach" and one "more synergistic than many might have thought." See Schabas, "The Relationship Between Truth Commissions and International Courts: The Case of Sierra Leone," *Human Rights Quarterly* 25 (2002): 1065–66.

136. See generally Rosalind Shaw, "Linking Justice with Reintegration? Ex-Combatants and the Sierra Leone Experiment," in *Localizing Transitional Justice: Interventions and Priorities After Mass Violence*, ed. Rosalind Shaw, Lars Waldorf, and Pierre Hazan (Stanford University Press, 2010), 111–132 and 122 (references to the TRC as "the child of the Special Court" and Special Court hiring practices regarding former TRC employees).

137. See Shaw, "Linking Justice with Reintegration?," 126.

138. As defined by UNDP, the Human Development Index (HDI) is "a composite index measuring average achievement in three basic dimensions of human development—a long and healthy life, knowledge and a decent standard of living." See UNDP HDR 2021/2022, Glossary of Definitions following table 4 (Gender Development Index).

139. See UNDP HDR 2021/2022, table 2 (Human Development Index Trends, 1990–2021), available at https://hdr.undp.org/system/files/documents/global-report-document/hdr2021-22pdf_1.pdf.

140. See generally European Union Election Observation Mission Sierra Leone 2023, Final Report on General Elections, June 2023, available at https://www.eeas.europa.eu/eom-sierra-leone-2023/sierra-leone-2023-final-report-general-elections-june-2023_en?s=410315.

Election improprieties in 2023 also contributed to concerns of increasing popular unrest, which seemingly bore fruit on November 26, 2023, when armed militants attacked the Pademba Road Prison in Freetown, releasing around two thousand prisoners. Responding to what the government characterized as a thwarted coup attempt, the civil population was put on high alert, due in part to uncertainty about the identity and motives of the perpetrators. See Mayeni Jones and Umaru Fofana, "Sierra Leone Lifts Curfew After Breakout from Freetown's Pademba Road Prison," BBC, November 27, 2023, available at https://www.bbc.com/news/world-africa-67536147.

141. See Shaw, "Linking Justice with Reintegration?," 11.

142. The Refugee Law Project of Uganda's Makerere University School of Law conducts pathbreaking social action research on behalf of male survivors of sexual violence. See Jerker Edström, Chris Dolan, and Thea Shahrokh, with Onen David, "Therapeutic Activism: Men of Hope Refugee Association Uganda Breaking the Silence over Male Rape in Conflict-Related Sexual Violence," Refugee Law Project, March 2016, available at https://www.refugeelawproject.org/files/others/Therapeutic_Activism_Brief.pdf.

143. See Sandesh Sivakumaran, "Sexual Violence Against Men in Armed Conflict," *European Journal of International Law* 18, no. 2 (2007): 259 ("male sexual violence [in conflict] has been recognized as regular and unexceptional, pervasive and widespread, although certainly not at the rate of sexual violence committed against women") and 258n37.

144. See Perriello and Wierda, *Special Court*, 8, citing Physicians for Human Rights, *War-Related Sexual Violence in Sierra Leone: A Population-Based Assessment*, 2002.

145. See Field Notebook Version of Chapter 7 of J. Moore's Women's Work Manuscript referencing May 15, 2018, interview with L. Morsay, saved electronically on May 18, 2018, on file with author.

146. See TRC Final Report, vol. 3B, chap. 3, paras. 263–68, available at http://www.sierraleonetrc.org/index.php/view-report-text-vol-3b/item/volume-three-b-chapter-three?category_id=9.

147. See Aisling Swaine, *Conflict-Related Violence Against Women: Transforming Transition* (Cambridge University Press, 2018), 57 (flagging racialized media depictions "pitching violence in the global south as peculiarly atrocious relative to the alleged civility of violence in the global north") and 86 (refusing to "posit any of the case studies, and especially Liberia, as 'different' or 'worse' from the other.")

148. Swaine explores the linkages between the baseline of violence against women in "time of peace" and the patterns of violence against women that occur during and after militarized armed conflict, "evidencing the varying and fluid dynamics between forms of extraordinary and ordinary violence." Swaine, *Conflict-Related Violence Against Women*, 25 and 185 ("gendered violence is ever-present").

149. See UNDP Human Development Statistical Update (2018), 91, 93, 94. For Uganda, the precise figure is 49.9 percent of women who have experienced such violence.

150. See UNDP HDR 2021/2022, table 4 (Gender Development Index), available at https://hdr.undp.org/system/files/documents/global-report-document/hdr2021-22pdf_1.pdf.

151. See UNDP HDR 2021/2022, table 4 (Gender Development Index). In the United Kingdom, the average duration of schooling for both women and men is 13.4 years.

152. See UNDP HDR 2021/22, table 5 (Gender Inequality Index).

153. See UNDP HDR 2021/22, table 5 (Gender Inequality Index).

154. Then-president Ernest Bai Koroma's apology continues:

> We will never as a nation move forward if we do not apologize to the women of this country for letting them down during the war; we will never as a nation know better days if we do not ask for the forgiveness of our mothers, sisters, partners, and female compatriots for what we let them go through during the war. It is almost a decade now since the war ended, but we must apologise for the wrongs of the war. As Head of State I apologise for the wrongs wrought on women, as Commander-in-Chief I ask for forgiveness for the armed forces, as Fountain of Honour and Justice I pledge this country's commitment to honour, protect, and defend the rights and aspirations of the women of this country. As a Sierra Leonean man, I urge all men of this nation to stand by women to defeat these long-standing injustices suffered by more than half our population.

See press release, "President Koroma Apologizes to Sierra Leonean Women," *Sierra Express Media*, March 27, 2010, complete text available at http://sierraexpressmedia.com/?p=6911.

155. See Palko Karasz and Dionne Searcey, "Sierra Leone Declares National Emergency over Rape of Young Girls," *New York Times*, February 8, 2019, available at https://www.nytimes.com /2019/02/08/world/africa/sierra-leone-girls-rape.html. When President Maada Bio announced the national emergency, he cited the data of the Rainbo Initiative, a Sierra Leonean NGO that operates a network of medical and psychosocial counseling centers for survivors of sexual assault. See J. Moore, Notes from interview with Rebecca Kallih, clinical director, Rainbo Initiative, Sierra Leone Field Notebook 2019 (May 23), 67, on file with author. The Rainbo Initiative reports that over the 2003–2019 period, their service providers have "helped more than 30,000 women and girls, 93% of whom are below the age of 17 and 24% below the age of 11." See Rainbo Initiative, available at http://rainboinitiative.sl/. The Rainbo Initiative operates five clinics throughout Sierra Leone—in Freetown, Kenema, Kono, Bo, and Makeni. See J. Moore, Kallih interview notes, Sierra Leone Field Notebook 2019 (May 23), 63–64, on file with author.

156. See UNICEF, Global Databases: Female Genital Mutilation/Cutting (FGM/C), updated as of October 2018, available at https://data.unicef.org/topic/child-protection/female-genital-mutilation/ (table I, Percentage of girls who have undergone FGM; and table III, Percentage of women and girls aged 15–49 years who have undergone FGM). See also Stephanie Nolen, "Growing Numbers of Girls Resist Genital Cutting in Sierra Leone," *New York Times*, June 15, 2022, available at https://www.nytimes.com/2022/06/14/health/female-genital-cutting-sierra-leone.html.

157. See Parliament of Sierra Leone, Gazette, Child Right Act of September 3, 2007, sec. 33, available at http://www.sierra-leone.org/Laws/2007-7p.pdf.

158. See Parliament of Sierra Leone, Gazette, Bill [proposed] Child Rights Act, November 24, 2022, sec. 12(2)(e), available at https://www.parliament.gov.sl/uploads/bill_files/The%20Child%20 Right%20Act,2022%20-%2024th%20November,%202022.pdf.

159. See TRC Final Report, vol. 3B, chap. 7, "Reconciliation," paras. 18 and 30. In chapter 7 of the Final Report, the TRC references the role of civil society organizations in the reconciliation process over one dozen times. See paras. 18, 30, 43, and 44, among others.

160. For information about the vision and work of Fambul Tok, see http://www.fambultok.org/.

161. The Kunduma Peace Farm is an example of a local agricultural cooperative that was established following a Fambul Tok–supported reconciliation process. See "Seeding Peace: Fambul Tok

Peace Farm, Kono District, Sierra Leone," video reported and produced by Jina Moore, available at https://www.youtube.com/watch?v=L7pdwxtYc9w.

162. Fionnuala Ní Aoláin, Dina Francesca Haynes, and Naomi Cahn explain that "public silences are a persistent feature of women's testimonial presentations in truth-telling contexts" and cite Venna Das's argument "that silence can be a powerful choice for women, an act of agency that is conscious and not passive and should not be understood to regulate the woman's choice of expression as a further act of victimization." Ní Aoláin, Haynes, and Cahn, *On the Frontlines: Gender, War, and the Post-Conflict Process* (Oxford University Press, 2011), 184.

163. See J. Moore, Sierra Leone Field Notebook 2017 (July 14), 16B (notes from conversation with Lilian Morsay, Fambul Tok Peace Mothers Coordinator), on file with author.

164. For information about the Fambul Tok Peace Mothers, see http://www.fambultokblog .org/program-updates-sierra-leone/announcing-new-short-film-on-peace-mothers and https:// vimeo.com/93511555 (since the founding of the Peace Mothers, women compose more than 50 percent of the participants in Fambul Tok activities nationwide).

165. Women's representation at the senior executive and legislative positions in recent years has ranged from 10 to 15 percent. In 2007, for example, there were two female cabinet ministers out of 24, and 16 female members of Parliament out of 124. See Claire Castillejo, "Women's Political Participation and Influence in Sierra Leone" (FRIDE Working Paper 83, June 2009), available at http://fride.org/descarga/wp83_women_political_eng_jun09.pdf (FRIDE is the acronym for the Madrid-based NGO Fundacíon Para Las Relaciones Internacionales y el Dialogo Exterior), 2. As of 2018, there were 18 female MPs. See Parliament of Sierra Leone Women's Caucus Information Note (2018), available at http://www.parliament.gov.sl/AboutUs/WomenCaucus.aspx.

166. Sierra Leonean "civil society has undoubtedly provided the greatest space for raising gender equality issues and has the most impact in changing gender roles." See Castillejo, "Women's Political Participation and Influence," 3.

167. Sylvester Samba, "Fambul Tok Takes Gov't to Task," Global Times: Sierra Leone's No. 1 News Portal, July 24, 2015, available at http://www.globaltimes-sl.com/fambul-tok-takes-govt-to -task/. See also Memunatu Bangura, "Fambul Tok Engages Neine Chiefdom," *Sierra Leone Concord Times* (November 26, 2015), available at http://slconcordtimes.com/fambul-tok-engages -neine-chiefdom/. See also J. Moore, Sierra Leone Field Notebook 2023, 7–8 (October 9 conversation with Lilian Morsay about the People's Planning Process). For more information on the People's Planning Process, see Chapter 4.

Chapter 3

The title of Chapter 3, "Peace in the Home, Peace in the Nation," is a slogan printed on a shirt I received as a gift in July 2016 from Winifred Arima Abalo, then field officer for the Ugandan NGO Human Rights Focus based in Kitgum, Northern Uganda. Ms. Abalo served as my Acholi interpreter and research facilitator during four years of successive research trips from 2016 to 2023. "*Kuc ikang, kuc ilobo*" in Acholi translates as "Peace in the home, peace in the nation."

Epigraphs: Okot p'Bitek, *"Song of Lawino," and "Song of Ocol"* (East African Publishing House, 1972), 82; two epic poems originally published separately in 1966). *Song of Lawino* is two hundred pages long.

Lucy is a member of the Alany pa Mony Lit women's community group in the village of Lukai, located in Nwoya District, west of Gulu in Northern Uganda. The insights she shared during interviews in 2016, 2017, 2018, and 2023 are discussed more fully in the text below.

1. The works of the renowned Ugandan poet Okot p'Bitek celebrate Acholi culture and history. Writing in the epic tradition, p'Bitek became famous for his characteristic "African long

poem" style, particularly displayed in *"Song of Lawino" and "Song of Ocol."* See also *Song of Fare-well* (Fountain Publishers, 1994), a volume of poetry by Jane Okot p'Bitek, written in tribute to her father Okot p'Bitek.

2. There are vignettes about Jane Orama and Boie Jalloh in the Introduction. The last names of Lucy, Jane, and Boie are pseudonyms.

3. Okot p'Bitek, *Song of Lawino*, 188, 198. Her husband gets his chance to respond in *Song of Ocol*.

4. Okot p'Bitek, *Song of Lawino*, 137–38.

5. Among the many ethnic groups of Uganda, an important but subtle distinction lies between Northern tribes and those associated with the Western and Southern Regions. Tribes traditionally from the West and South, like the Banyankole and Baganda, are Bantu speakers; whereas those in the North, including the Acholi and the Langi, speak Nilotic languages. Acholi and Langi people are very close linguistic cousins, speaking mutually comprehensible languages within the Luo branch of the greater Nilotic family. See Field Notebook 2018 Version of J. Moore's Women's Work Manuscript referencing July 10 conversation with the translator F. Ngomokwe, saved electronically on July 17, 2018, on file with author.

6. The causes and consequences of the LRA War are explored more fully in Chapter 2.

7. See J. Moore, Uganda Field Notebook, July 2023, notes from July 13 visit with Uketu wan Kwene, on file with author.

8. Social and economic vulnerability is particularly pronounced for women who married through a cultural ceremony without a marriage certificate, often the case for second wives in polygamous families.

9. As of 2023, Dr. Busingye Kabumba is HURIPEC's executive director. Dr. Zampewo is now serving as the deputy chief of Makerere University School of Law.

10. WAN, formerly a project of the Gulu-based Justice and Reconciliation Project, is now a freestanding NGO, directed by Evelyn Amony.

11. In 2016 I was also assisted in identifying partner organizations for my research by the Uganda Association of Women Lawyers (FIDA-U). FIDA-U, the Ugandan chapter of the Federación Internacional de Abogadas (FIDA), an international women lawyers NGO, was founded over a decade before the civil war began. Its vision is "a just and peaceful society where women's rights are realised and enjoyed in all spheres." See FIDA-Uganda, "Our Vision Statement," available at http://fidauganda.org/pages/about-us/. In recent years, FIDA-U has partnered with civil society organizations such as the Women's Advocacy Network (WAN), the Refugee Law Project (RLP), and Human Rights Focus (HURIFO) in their work with women survivors of the LRA War.

12. WAN is a network of women's groups; RLP supports women's groups and men's groups; and HURIFO partners with mixed groups.

13. External support for Alany and Uketu has somewhat abated in recent years, as the Refugee Law Project and other NGOs are impacted by changing priorities of funders in response to emergent political developments, such as the Anti-Homosexuality Act enacted by the Ugandan Parliament in 2023. For a variety of reasons, women's collectives in the Acholi Sub-region of Northern Uganda are largely sustained by their own microfinance and cooperative agricultural initiatives. See J. Moore, Uganda Field Notebook, July 2023, on file with author.

14. "Alany" and "Uketu" are shorthand names for the two collectives, used for purposes of brevity. The members of these community groups prefer to use the full titles, as a reflection of their life experiences and the reason for their coming together. As discussed below, Alany pa Mony Lit in Acholi means "Mistreatment of women is painful" and acknowledges the women's status as survivors of sexual assault by the military. Uketu wan Kwene is Acholi for "Where have you put them?"—a reference to its members' missing relatives who disappeared during the LRA War and whose fates remain unknown.

15. An ideal situation arises when an NGO works with a community group that was self-organized prior to any interactions with the agency. Such a group has its own vision, track record, and activities. While the affiliated NGO may provide training and moral support, it can do so without providing life support. Where the material support is minimal, it is more feasible for the community group to maintain its own integrity and initiative, even when the NGO founded the community group in the first instance, as with some of the women's groups affiliated with WAN. As Victoria Nyanjura of WAN put it, "When you own your own vision you work toward realizing it." See Field Notebook 2018 Version of J. Moore's Women's Work Manuscript referencing July 8 conversation with V. Nyanjura, saved electronically on May 17, 2018, on file with author. The balance is a tricky one to maintain.

16. See J. Moore, Uganda Field Notebook, July 2023, interviews with Alany members, July 12, on file with author.

17. As my RLP interpreter Fred Ngomokwe put it, "The women's groups formed primarily to provide peer support due to the similarity of their experiences." See Field Notebook 2018 Version of J. Moore's Women's Work Manuscript referencing July 9 conversation with F. Ngomokwe, saved electronically on July 17, 2018, on file with author.

18. As of 2023, plans for the TRC are still held up in the Ugandan cabinet within the Justice Law and Order Sector and have not yet reached the Ugandan Parliament. See Field Notebook 2018 Version of J. Moore's Women's Work Manuscript referencing July 8 conversation with V. Nyanjura, saved electronically on July 17, 2018, on file with author. See also discussion in Chapter 2 of Uganda's postconflict justice policies.

19. In 2023 the Ugandan Parliament took up a new draft of a Reparations Bill, giving individuals affiliated with the Women's Advocacy Network renewed hope for government support for survivors of the LRA War, including help in tracing their lost relatives. WAN's director Evelyn Amony was instrumental in pushing legislators to add specific language about missing persons to the bill. Despite renewed momentum, WAN members have modest expectations, given past government inaction in the reparative realm. See J. Moore, Uganda Field Notebook, July 2023, interviews with Women's Advocacy Network members, July 14, on file with author.

20. Odoko Mit is one of the community groups in Kitgum District that has benefited from trainings facilitated by Human Rights Focus. Another one is Gwoko ter Kwaro (Keeping the Culture). Interviews with members of Odoko Mit are analyzed in depth in this chapter. Interviews with Gwoko members are found in Appendix 2 of this volume.

21. Grace of Rwot Lakica translated resilience as *oteka*. Fully bilingual in Acholi and English, she provided her own insights into certain Acholi concepts, as further explored in the text below.

22. See Field Notebook 2018 Version of J. Moore's Women's Work Manuscript referencing July 10 and July 12 conversations with F. Ngomokwe and W. Abalo, saved electronically on July 17, 2018, on file with author.

23. Acholi concepts of resilience, such as Grace's notion of *oteka*, are resonant with terms used by Sierra Leonean Peace Mothers to describe their strength. For example, the Fula word *mijade* (deep thought), suggests an attitude of mindfulness, focused reflection, and discernment. Boie Jalloh, Peace Mother of Dogoloya in Koinadugu District, says *mijade* helps her face a conflict with uncertain resolution. Boie's perspectives on peacebuilding are explored in Chapter 4.

24. The Peacebuilder's Questionnaire is in Appendix 1 of this volume. It is also utilized in my interviews with the Peace Mothers of Sierra Leone.

25. We seized on the metaphor of a tree for the process of building peace because of the abundant references to the cultivation of trees in our interviews and because so often our focus group discussions took place under one. My interviewees' poetic contributions are referenced selectively in this chapter. A photograph of my pencil-drawn rendering of the composite tree of peace, inspired by women peacebuilders of Northern Uganda and Sierra Leone, is found in the text just after the Conclusion of this volume.

26. The Tree of Peace is the author's impressionistic compilation of the various components of peace as understood by women across Northern Uganda and Sierra Leone. It is reproduced as Figure 25. The drawing incorporates words and phrases from the five different mother tongues spoken by these women peacebuilders, whose insights are shared throughout the text.

27. The follow-up interviews in 2017 and 2018 allowed individual women to elaborate on their views on peace, subsistence, and women's empowerment in their communities. The analysis presented below centers on the focus group and first round of individual interviews conducted in 2016, making use of notes to present the clarifications participants provided in 2017 and 2018.

28. The Women's Advocacy Network was initially a project of the Gulu-based Justice and Reconciliation Project (JRP) and is now a free-standing NGO. For historical background on the JRP, see http://justiceandreconciliation.com/about/history/. For information on the establishment of the Women's Advocacy Network, see http://justiceandreconciliation.com/initiatives/womens-advocacy-network/.

29. Gulu Town is the district capital and largest city in Gulu District as well as the largest city in the Acholi Sub-region of Northern Uganda. Gulu and Kitgum were the districts most impacted by the LRA War.

30. See Field Notebook 2018 Version of J. Moore's Women's Work Manuscript referencing July 8 conversation with V. Nyanjura, saved electronically on July 17, 2018, on file with author.

31. Sister Nyirumbe's work with former abductees of the LRA is the subject of a book by Reggie Whitten. See generally R. Whitten, *Sewing Hope: Joseph Kony Tore These Girls' Lives Apart—Can She Stitch Them Back Together* (Dust Jacket Press, 2013). In addition to welcoming former abductees of the LRA, St. Monica's educates girls from local families in the Gulu area as well as the children of women incarcerated in the nearby Gulu Women's Prison. Author's Field Notebook, Uganda 2016, 32A (July 14), on file with author.

32. Aboke is a town in the Kole District of the Lango Sub-region, south of Acholiland.

33. See Field Notebook 2018 Version of J. Moore's Women's Work Manuscript referencing July 8 conversation with V. Nyanjura, saved electronically on July 17, 2018, on file with author.

34. Another notable exception, her friend Grace, abducted with her in 1996, was awarded a degree in business and development studies from Gulu University.

35. As clarified in the Introduction, throughout this book I use my interviewees' names only with the permission of the individual interviewee. While many were willing to be quoted by full name, I elected to use first names only, with few exceptions, as specifically explained in the text.

In this chapter, I use single quotes for statements by individuals that were translated from Acholi by my interpreters. I use double quotes when the individual spoke directly to me in English. In the case of the members of Rwot Lakica, Grace spoke with me in English; Agnes, Santa, and Stella spoke with me in Acholi; and Victoria translated from Acholi into English.

36. See references to 2016 interviews with Grace and fellow Women's Advocacy Network members in Gulu Town, Author's Field Notebook, Uganda 2016, 21B (July 12), on file with author.

37. Of the focus group participants in Gulu Town, all six are members of the Women's Advocacy Network. In terms of specific women's groups, four (Grace, Evelyn, Santa, and Agnes) are members of Rwot Lakica (God Is Merciful); Alice is a member of Kica Pa Rwot (God's Mercy); and Stella is a member of Can Rwede Pe (No One Wants Poverty). All three groups are affiliated with the Women's Advocacy Network. With the exception of Grace Acan, who has published under her own name, I use first names (or first names and last name pseudonyms) as a rule for the women of WAN. This practice generally applies to all the women peacebuilders I have interviewed across Northern Uganda and Sierra Leone. The exceptions are for women whose names

are available in print (like Grace Acan and Evelyn Amony of WAN), for members who have gone on to found an NGO or CBO of their own (like Victoria Nyanjura, one of my translators), or for those who have passed on (like Daker Nighty of Uketu wan Kwene).

38. When we met subsequently in June 2017 for follow-up interviews, Stella stressed that 'reconciliation is the root of peacemaking.' Author's Field Notebook, Uganda 2016, 3A (June 10), on file with author.

39. *Tic-cing* in Acholi means "the work of one's hands."

40. *Adwogi metic* and *kwayo kica* emphasize different components of accountability. *Adwogi metic* means, quite literally, as much as one is owed, or what one has earned and thus what one deserves. Members of the Alany pa Mony Lit women's group, affiliated with RLP and based in Nwoya District, stressed that *adwogi metic* signifies "a result accruing from something" or "a result from a specific issue at hand." See Field Notebook 2018 Version of J. Moore's Women's Work Manuscript referencing July 10 community visit with the women of Alany pa Mony Lit in Nwoya District, including the insights of F. Ngomokwe, saved electronically on July 17, 2018, on file with author. *Adwogi metic* bears an important connection to livelihood (*tic-cing*), through the notion of compensation, but here the emphasis is on payment for wrongdoing. In short, your "just deserts" are the fruit of your labor and your actions, good or bad. *Kwayo kica*, on the other hand, means the acknowledgment of responsibility and the request for forgiveness, which then may lead to the granting of forgiveness (*timo kica*), a necessary component of reconciliation. See Field Notebook 2018 Version of J. Moore's Women's Work Manuscript referencing July 8 conversation with V. Nyanjura, saved electronically on July 17, 2018, on file with author.

41. The Peacebuilders' Questionnaire is in Appendix 1 of this volume.

42. As of 2023, Grace was working with the Women's Advocacy Network.

43. When I returned to Gulu in July 2023 for the final phase of my research in Northern Uganda, I had the opportunity to meet with Grace and ask her how she and her WAN compatriots were faring. Grace by this time was on contract with the Refugee Law Project and still collaborating with members of the Women's Advocacy Network. I also learned that Agnes had gotten married; Santa had launched a small produce-selling enterprise; and Victoria Nyanjura, our interpreter from 2016 to 2018, was active in the eastern part of Acholiland directing her new community-based organization, Women United for Women. See J. Moore, Uganda Field Notebook, July 2023, meeting with Grace Acan, July 11, on file with author.

44. As elsewhere, double quotes for Grace are used because she spoke during her interview in fluent English.

45. The Women's Advocacy Network submitted a petition to the Uganda Women Parliamentary Association in 2014 calling for reparations to survivors of wartime atrocities during the LRA War, which resulted in a unanimous parliamentary resolution in April of that year, calling on the government of Uganda to set up a gender-sensitive reparations fund, to provide health services for war-affected women and children, and to resettle and reintegrate abducted women and children born in captivity. See Justice and Reconciliation Project press release, "Parliament Adopts Resolution to Address the Needs of War-Affected" (Kampala, April 10, 2014), available at http://www.justiceandreconciliation.org/media/newsroom/press-releases/2014/parliament -adopts-resolution-to-address-the-needs-of-war-affected/. See also Author's Field Notebook II, Uganda 2016, 26A and 28A (July 14), referencing author's briefing with Isaac Okwir, acting coordinator, Justice and Reconciliation Project (JRP), on file with author. In 2016 JRP was the parent organization of the Women's Advocacy Network. While of symbolic importance, the 2014 parliamentary resolution did not immediately bear fruit in the form of legislation appropriating monies for reparations. After preliminary text for a reparations bill was debated in Parliament, efforts stalled. As recently as 2023, there was renewed momentum for reparations legislation in Parliament.

46. See Xan Rice, "Uganda Bomb Blasts Kill at Least 74," *Guardian*, July 12, 2010, available at https://www.theguardian.com/world/2010/jul/12/uganda-kampala-bombs-explosions-attacks. See also Lino Owor Ogora, "Why Victims 'Feel Abandoned' by the Ugandan Government," International Justice Monitor blog, May 30, 2017, available at https://www.ijmonitor.org/2017/05/why-victims-feel-abandoned-by-the-ugandan-government/.

47. See J. Moore, Uganda Field Notebook, July 2023, meeting with WAN members, July 17, on file with author.

48. During the LRA War, Nwoya was originally a sub-county of Gulu District, which became its own district after the LRA War. The same is true of Pader, originally a sub-county of Kitgum District, and subsequently its own district in the postwar period.

49. As of 2023, a legal challenge to the constitutionality of the Anti-Homosexuality Act is being brought by individual staff members and affiliates of the Makerere University School of Law. The lead petitioner in the legal suit is Dr. Sylvia Tamale, former dean of the law school and a retired lecturer in gender and sexuality studies. The second petitioner is Dr. Busingye Kabumba, director of the Human Rights and Peace Centre (HURIPEC), also a unit of the Makerere University law school. The Refugee Law Project has fallen under the administrative rubric of the law school since HURIPEC, under the leadership of Dr. Joe Oloka-Onyango, launched RLP as a research and advocacy organization over twenty years ago.

50. The RLP field office in Gulu Town oversees activities in the districts of Gulu, Nwoya, and Pader. The RLP field office in Kitgum Town established and runs the Kitgum National Memory and Peace Documentation Center.

51. *Alany pa mony lit* is translated as "Mistreatment of women is painful." *Uketu wan kwene* means "Where will you put us?"

52. See Field Notebook 2018 Version of J. Moore's Women's Work Manuscript referencing July 9 conversation with F. Ngomokwe, saved electronically on July 17, 2018, on file with author.

53. *Alany* is the Acholi word for "mistreatment," "torture," "abuse," or "humiliation." As Fred Ngomokwe explains, it encompasses harassment of any kind—from bothersome to criminal behavior. As a reference to rape, the use of *alany* is euphemistic. "Acholi love speaking in parables," Fred notes. Author's Field Notebook, Uganda 2018, 11A (July 10), on file with author.

54. The linkages between homophobia and stigma against survivors of sexual assault are further discussed in Chapter 2.

55. See generally Chris Dolan, *Social Torture: The Case of Northern Uganda, 1986–2006* (Berghahn Books, 2011). Dolan talks about disruptions in the provision of rural health care and public education in Northern Uganda dating back to the LRA War. Dolan, *Social Torture*, 131–44. He also highlights the cumulative experience of trauma and "psychological debilitation" in the war-affected population overall (164–67). Finally, Dolan addresses the impact of war and economic misery on gender roles and expectations, leading to feelings of inadequacy on the part of women and men, the "increasing economic desperation of men," and men's movement into "what had previously been women's areas of work" (177).

56. Pamela Angwech, of the Gulu Women's Economic Development and Globalization Project (GWED-G), emphasizes the importance of partnership between men and women in the community and in the home. Shared decision-making between parents in the family setting models the notion of a "democratic household" for other men and women in the community. See notes from author's briefing with Pamela Angwech, executive director of GWED-G, Author's Field Notebook, Uganda 2016, 22A and 23B (July 13), on file with author. Further references to Ms. Angwech are available at https://www.facebook.com/GULUGWEDG/posts/executive-director-pamela-angwech-shares-the-gwed-g-story-with-chicagos-wbez-rad/391839627521383/.

57. As with all the community groups I met with in Northern Uganda and Sierra Leone, I asked each woman if it was her wish to participate in the interviews and if she was willing for me

to use her name and to paraphrase and/or quote her remarks, translated into English. For Alany pa Mony Lit, all the women I interviewed gave their consent for me to quote them by name. They confirmed their consent during follow-up interviews in 2017 and again in 2018.

58. Esther was a member of Alany pa Mony Lit during the full research period, 2016–23.

59. Noting again that Okello is a pseudonym.

60. Evelyn, Alany pa Mony Lit's chairwoman, died of complications from leukemia in July 2023. After her belated diagnosis in hospital in Gulu in early July, she was able to return to Lukai, where she passed away surrounded by family, neighbors, friends, and fellow Alany members, who mourn her passing and dedicate themselves to continuing her legacy of leadership and service. See J. Moore, Uganda Field Notebook, July 2023, notes regarding Alany pa Mony Lit, on file with author.

61. As noted earlier in this chapter, while the Ugandan government has yet to constitute a reparations fund for LRA war survivors, there was renewed momentum in Parliament in 2023 to resurrect efforts toward passage of the long-discussed but yet-to-be-enacted Reparations Bill.

62. The Peacebuilders' Questionnaire is in Appendix 1 of this volume. It was used with all nine community groups whose members I interviewed throughout Northern Uganda and Sierra Leone from 2016 to 2023.

63. The majority of Alany members (like the other community groups interviewed across Northern Uganda and Sierra Leone) gave me permission to use their full names. Nevertheless, I elected to use first names only in case of any future security risks. The last names of Jane Orama of Uketu wan Kwene and Lucy Okello of Alany pa Mony Lit are pseudonyms.

64. Two RLP summer legal interns in their final year of law studies at Makerere University conducted an additional interview, after observing the focus groups and sitting in on several of the individual interviews. George Ocen, a native Langi speaker, provided Acholi-English translation for the interview with Esther. Dorah Kukunda took notes and transcribed Esther's insights. Dorah has since completed her LLB and has enrolled in a postgraduate program at Makerere University. See Field Notebook 2018 Version of J. Moore's Women's Work Manuscript referencing July 10 conversation with F. Ngomokwe, saved electronically on July 17, 2018, on file with author.

65. The similarities and resonances between the responses of the members of Alany pa Mony Lit are striking, particularly given that I conducted the individual interviews separately in July 2016.

66. Lucy's reference to the Ugandan Constitution is an example of community women's awareness of human rights as incorporated in national law. This is an illustration of the concept of "complementarity" between international and domestic law, explored in the human rights law section of Chapter 1.

67. As of 2018, Aida explained, school fees had increased to 120,000 Ugandan shillings per term for her fifteen-year-old son to attend the school for the hearing impaired in Gulu municipality.

68. Pader District is located east of Gulu District and south of Kitgum District, in the Acholi Sub-region of Northern Uganda. See the map of Uganda, with detail regarding Acholi Sub-region, printed opposite the first page of this chapter.

69. See Field Notebook 2018 Version of J. Moore's Women's Work Manuscript referencing July 14 follow-up interview with Daker Nighty, saved electronically on July 17, 2018, on file with author.

70. In Acholi, *rwot* is chief and *daker* is queen.

71. I met Nighty in 2016, 2017, and 2018, each time I traveled to Pader District. Daker Nighty died of an illness on August 12, 2018, a month after our last visit. The Uketu wan Kwene women's group, and the people of Paibwore Chiefdom generally, continue to honor her legacy and her contributions to women's empowerment and the development of her community.

72. See Field Notebook 2018 Version of J. Moore's Women's Work Manuscript referencing July 14 follow-up interview with Daker Nighty, saved electronically on July 17, 2018, on file with author.

73. Daker Nighty is referring to the former LRA commander convicted of war crimes and crimes against humanity in the International Criminal Court, discussed in Chapter 2.

74. During our interviews with the members of Uketu in 2016, our two RLP interns Dorah Kukunda and George Ocen interviewed an additional group member, Doreen. Based on that experience, Dorah published a blog on women's inheritance and property rights in Northern Uganda. See Dorah Kukunda, "Clipped Wings," Refugee Law Project blog, October 31, 2016, available at https://www.refugeelawproject.org/index.php?option=com_content&view=article&id =185:clipped-wings&catid=27&Itemid=101.

75. Daker Nighty's understanding of the long-term commitment required to engage in a meaningful process of reconciliation echoes the words of Lilian Morsay, field coordinator for the Sierra Leone Fambul Tok Peace Mothers. Lilian understands reconciliation as a nonspontaneous process that "goes on as long, as long, as long as you live." See Chapter 4 text related to Lilian Morsay.

76. Nighty went even further during our follow-up interview in July 2018, suggesting that women are better suited to leadership than men: 'Women are not violent, they do not encourage violence,' and they are less likely to organize demonstrations that become chaotic. See Field Notebook 2018 Version of J. Moore's Women's Work Manuscript referencing July 14 conversation with Daker Nighty, saved electronically on July 17, 2018, on file with author.

77. See J. Moore, Uganda Field Notebook, July 2023, meeting with Uketu members and notes from conversation with Christine, July 13, on file with author.

78. See J. Moore, Uganda Field Notebook, July 2023, meeting with Uketu members and notes from conversation with Mary, July 13, on file with author.

79. See J. Moore, Uganda Field Notebook, July 2023, meeting with Uketu members and notes from conversation with Evelyn, July 13, on file with author.

80. Note that findings from interviews with a second women's collective of Kitgum, called Gwoko ter Kwaro (Keeping the Culture), are analyzed in Appendix 2 of this volume.

81. See Field Notebook 2018 Version of J. Moore's Women's Work Manuscript referencing July 12 conversation with W. Abalo, saved electronically on July 17, 2018, on file with author.

82. See Author's Field Notebook, Uganda 2018, 12B (July 13, with notes from follow-up interview with Bichentina), on file with author.

83. Odoko Mit members have collaborated with Winifred Arima Abalo, formerly the HURIFO field officer based in Kitgum Town. The group looks to HURIFO and other NGOs for solidarity rather than financial support.

84. The afternoon ended with a spontaneous women's dance, which Winnie and I were invited to join. This resulted in more hilarity, apparently because we were wearing slacks not skirts. At first, I donated my shawl to Winnie, who wrapped it around her waist and followed the procession. This was followed by an awkward moment when I was pulled into the swaying throng until Winnie relinquished the shawl and wrapped it around my waist. Several dancers smiled approvingly, one observing to the others, 'She's a woman now.' Community order was restored. See author's notes from visit with Odoko Mit members, Author's Field Notebook, Uganda 2016, 36B (July 19), on file with author.

85. See discussion in prior section quoting the late Daker Nighty of Uketu wan Kwene women's group in Pader District.

86. By 2023 the duration of the journey from Kitgum to Lagoro was shorter than in the past due to recent infrastructure improvements including more tarmac on the main Gulu-Kitgum Road.

87. A special benefit of spending time with women peacebuilders in Northern Uganda and Sierra Leone over a three-year period is that I have had the opportunity to watch a number of

babies grow into toddlers. When I returned to Laber Parish in June 2017, Pasca's healthy ten-month-old nursed and slept through most of our interview in her mother's arms.

88. Five thousand shillings is approximately US$1.50.

89. Our interpreter Winnie Abalo explained to me that among the Acholi when there is a suicide by hanging, the tree must be cut down to the roots to prevent recurrence and a sheep or goat is then sacrificed. See Field Notebook 2018 Version of J. Moore's Women's Work Manuscript referencing July 2016 follow-up conversation with W. Abalo, saved electronically on July 17, 2018, on file with author.

90. Concy's awareness of her skill in mediation is comparable with Sierra Leonean peace-builders, particularly Boie Jalloh, Peace Mother of Dogoloya in Koinadugu District. As Concy remarks that the families 'continue well' after her intervention, Boie also notes that after repeated mediation of a challenging marital dispute, the couple 'are now good together.' Boie's mediation work is profiled in the introduction and her perspectives on peacebuilding are explored more fully along with those of her fellow Peace Mothers in Chapter 4.

91. These set-asides are sometimes referred to as "affirmative action" positions, as referenced elsewhere in the text, specifically in Chapter 4 regarding the Sierra Leone Peace Mothers.

Chapter 4

Epigraph: Abioseh Nicol, "The Meaning of Africa," published in *Poems from Black Africa*, ed. Langston Hughes (Indiana University Press, 1963), 41. This excerpt from Mr. Nicol's poem is gratefully reprinted with permission of the late author's daughter, Mrs. Anna Addo Yobo. Abioseh Nicol is the pen name of Davidson Nicol, a Sierra Leonean poet, physician, and diplomat of Krio ethnicity who lived from 1923 to 1994. He served as Sierra Leone's ambassador to the United Nations and taught at Cambridge University in the UK and Fourah Bay College in Freetown. See Eric Pace, "Davidson Nicol Is Dead at 70; Was Doctor and U.N. Official," *New York Times*, September 28, 1994, available at https://www.nytimes.com/1994/09/28/obituaries/davidson-nicol-is-dead-at-70-was-doctor-and-un-official.html.

1. Bah is a pseudonym. The insights Lamrana shared during interviews conducted over the course of the 2016–2023 research period are discussed more fully in this chapter.

2. By 2014, seven years after its founding in 2007, Fambul Tok projects had been established in 2,500 villages across Sierra Leone. See Libby Hoffman, "Peace from the Inside Out," *Porch-light* (blog), December 21, 2022, available at https://www.porchlightbooks.com/blog/changethis/2022/answers-are-there. See also Libby Hoffman, *The Answers Are There: Building Peace from the Inside Out* (Blue Chair Press, 2022).

Fambul Tok has gone through two distinct stages: Phase I, beginning in 2007, focusing on postwar community reconciliation and economic revitalization; and Phase II, beginning in 2015, devoted to implementing the Wan Fambul (One Family) Framework, also known as People's Planning Process, a program of long-term social development in Sierra Leone.

The idea for the People's Planning Process came out of local responses to the Ebola crisis in 2014 and 2015. In the climate of chaos and fear surrounding the deadly epidemic, Fambul Tok and Peace Mothers groups throughout the country mobilized to support families coping with illness and death. Relationships and coordination between Peace Mothers became vital in restoring trust between neighbors and public health officials and in conducting public education campaigns on handwashing, isolation of ill persons, and safe burial of bodies. These efforts were as important as the construction of state-of-the-art clinics in containing the epidemic. The grassroots response to the Ebola crisis demonstrated the nimbleness of Fambul Tok community networks in crisis response as well as the potential of these networks to help shape national development policies that resonate with local needs and priorities.

The People's Planning Process (PPP) is a partnership between the government and Fambul Tok, which is focused on catalyzing development projects that are conceived and carried out at the village level, with minimal to no financial support from outside. The program, still at the pilot stage in 2023, has been rolled out in five districts. Villages are chosen through a consensus selection process first between paramount chiefs within a particular district, to identify a chiefdom; within that chiefdom there is a selection process between the section chiefs, to identify a section; and finally there is a selection process between village chiefs to identify a particular village. If consensus is not reached at any level, lots are drawn.

At the village level, the village appoints a Village Development Commission (VDC), consisting of five men and five women. At that point the VDC works alongside the village's Peace Mothers group to choose a development project that is meaningful to all members of the village—such as building a village meeting place, a platform to dry harvested grain, or a health clinic. All village members, even children, are expected to contribute in any way they can, gathering local materials like tree branches, manufacturing mud bricks, or carrying individual stones to lay a foundation. In some cases, the VDC and the Peace Mothers choose side-by-side projects that progress in tandem. The goal is to mobilize the collective to create sustainable projects that are independent of outside funding. Fambul Tok provides training in communication, dispute resolution, and project management but does not provide financial support. See J. Moore, Sierra Leone Field Notebook 2023, 7–8 (October 9 conversation about the PPP with Lilian Morsay), on file with author. See notes from May 1 and October 5, 2018, conversations with Libby Hoffman, Catalyst for Peace director and Fambul Tok cofounder, on file with author.

3. See http://www.fambultokblog.org/tag/peace-mothers and related links. See also Peace Mothers film (December 2013), available at https://vimeo.com/93511555.

4. Information provided by Lilian Morsay in her presentation on the Sierra Leone Peace Mothers during the conference "Celebrating and Nurturing Women's Leadership in Peacebuilding," Malindi, Kenya, January 18, 2018. See author's conference notes, p. 21, on file with author. Updated information provided by Lilian Morsay in interview with author, May 16, 2019. See J. Moore, Sierra Leone Field Notebook 2019, 15 (May 16), on file with author.

5. The 2007 Devolution of Estates Act, referenced in Chapter 2, seeks to ensure women's inheritance rights. As discussed below, the Fambul Tok Peace Mothers have organized community trainings to help ensure the full understanding and implementation of the act.

6. The Krio literal translation is "women in power, with men's support." Translation provided by Komba Moiwa, Fambul Tok Inter-District field coordinator and research facilitator, July 2018.

7. See also discussion of "strategic essentialism" in Chapter 1.

8. See Peace Mothers film, on-camera interview with Lilian Morsay (December 2013), available at https://vimeo.com/93511555.

9. After communicating electronically, Lilian Morsay and I spoke by telephone in early 2016 and spun out a basic plan for my research. My response to her "I'll take you wherever you want to go" was "Lilian, just tell me where and we'll go there." This approach remains the core of our collaborative methodology, sustained by respect, occasional irreverence, and abiding friendship.

10. Throughout our field trips and since, she has responded to questions about the history and contemporary dynamics of Sierra Leone, readily sharing her experience and insights on politics, the war and postconflict transition, and changing gender roles. See, e.g., Field Notebook 2018 Version of J. Moore's Women's Work Manuscript referencing May 15 interview with L. Morsay, saved electronically on May 18, 2018, on file with author.

11. See Field Notebook 2018 Version of J. Moore's Women's Work Manuscript referencing May 15 interview with L. Morsay, saved electronically on May 18, 2018, on file with author.

12. I did not visit Sierra Leone in 2020 or 2021 due to travel restrictions during the COVID-19 public health emergency.

13. The Peacebuilder's Questionnaire is in Appendix 1 of this volume.

14. See J. Moore, Sierra Leone Field Notebook 2022, 76 (July 28), on file with author; see also J. Moore, Sierra Leone Field Notebook 2023 (Boie questionnaire), on file with author.

15. See Cost of Living in Sierra Leone, available at https://livingcost.org/cost/sierra-leone.

16. See generally Carol P. Hoffer, "Madam Yoko: Ruler of the Kpa Mende Confederacy," in *Women, Culture and Society*, ed. Michelle Zimbalist Rosaldo and Louise Lamphere (Stanford University Press, 1974), 173–87. Hoffer explains, "In the Mende ethnic area of Sierra Leone, women produce a scarce resource: offspring for their husbands' patrilineages. . . . Women paramount chiefs within this context are seen as mothers writ large, calling into question any theoretical dichotomy in women's influence between the domestic and the juro-political domains" (173). See also J. Moore, Field Notebook 2018, 1B, referencing May 10 conversation with Joseph Benjie, Fambul Tok field officer for Moyamba District, and Komba Moiwa, Fambul Tok Inter-District field coordinator, regarding the continuing historical legacy of Madam Yoko, on file with author.

17. Traditional Mende women's societies are also referred to as Sande societies. Sande is in fact the traditional Mende term. Nevertheless, the more common usage in Sierra Leone today is Bondo, or Bundu, the corresponding term in Temne, the other major language of Sierra Leone. See Hoffer, "Madam Yoko," 173n2.

18. See Hoffer, "Madam Yoko," 173n1 (indicating that in 1914 women chiefs amounted to 15 percent of the total, and in 1970, 9 percent). See also Lynda R. Day, "The Evolution of Female Chiefship During the Late Nineteenth-Century Wars of the Mende," *International Journal of African Historical Studies* 27, no. 3 (1994):48 (indicating that from the 1890s to the 1990s, women served as 10 percent of the Mende paramount chiefs in Sierra Leone).

19. Female genital cutting is performed as a coming-of-age ceremony in numerous cultures throughout the world. It is not limited to Africa, nor is it exclusive to one religious tradition. The type of cutting ranges widely in different cultural contexts from pricking the clitoris; to removing part or all of the clitoris (clitoridectomy); to excising all or part of the labia majora and minora, sometimes restitching the remaining vaginal tissue to leave a small opening for urination and menstruation (the latter procedure is known as infibulation). The FGC that girls and young women are most commonly subjected to in Sierra Leone is a type of clitoridectomy. See Pam Belluck and Maddie McGarvey, "Lifelong Scars from Genital Cutting," *New York Times International Edition*, May 30, 2019, 4.

20. See J. Moore, Field Journal 2016, 6B–7B, referencing discussion with Fambul Tok staff members of Mende ethnicity about the practice of FGC in Sierra Leone.

21. The Bondo tradition remains controversial given its historical promotion and performance of female genital cutting as a component of young women's coming-of-age ceremonies. Bondo traditions more generally play an important role in sustaining and nurturing women's cultural life and political solidarity. The women's societies, at least since the time of Madam Yoko, have sponsored the selection and training of *soweis*, the women elders who serve as traditional birth attendants. Some *soweis* are also trained to perform the female genital cutting procedure. See Lisa O'Carroll, "Sierra Leone's Secret Societies Spread Silent Fear and Sleepless Nights," *Guardian*, August 24, 2015, available at https://www.theguardian.com/global-development/2015/aug/24/sierra-leone-female-genital-mutilation-soweis-secret-societies-fear.

22. The practice of FGC was largely suspended during the Ebola emergency in 2014–15, given the huge concern about the spread of infection and the threat to young women's survival. See O'Carroll, "Sierra Leone's Secret Societies." The procedure has since been restored at least in parts of Sierra Leone. Popular opposition to FGC continues to grow in Sierra Leone among women and men, both on public health grounds as a threat to the reproductive and mental health of women, and in terms of civil liberties as a violation of women's integrity and equality in the public and private domains. See J. Moore, Field Journal 2016, 6B–7B, referencing discussion with Fambul Tok staff members about FGC in Sierra Leone. See also Claire Castillejo, "Women's

Political Participation in Sierra Leone" (FRIDE Working Paper 83, June 2009), available at http://fride.org/descarga/wp83_women_political_eng_jun09.pdf.

23. According to UNICEF, as of October 2018, 8 percent of Sierra Leonean girls 14 years of age and younger had been subjected to FGC, based on data reported by their mothers. Also, as of October 2018, UNICEF reports that 85 percent of Sierra Leonean women between 15 and 49 years of age had undergone the practice. See UNICEF, Global Databases: Female genital mutilation/cutting (FGM/C), updated as of October 2018, available at https://data.unicef.org/topic/child-protection/female-genital-mutilation/ (Table I, Percentage of girls who have undergone FGM; and Table III, Percentage of women and girls aged 15–49 years who have undergone FGM).

24. In contrast to data from 2018 of an overall 93 percent prevalence of FGC among Sierra Leonean women and girls, at that time only 68 percent of Sierra Leonean women between 15 and 49 years of age believed that the practice should continue (80 percent of rural woman support the practice, and only 56 percent of urban women). See UNICEF, Global Databases: Female genital mutilation/cutting (Table II, Percentage of women and girls aged 15–49 years who have heard about FGM and think the practice should continue).

25. See Stephanie Nolen, "Growing Numbers of Girls Resist Genital Cutting in Sierra Leone," *New York Times*, June 15, 2022, available at https://www.nytimes.com/2022/06/14/health/female-genital-cutting-sierra-leone.html. Notably, Sierra Leone's Child Right Act prohibits harmful practices that endanger children, without mentioning female genital cutting. Some activists are calling for the act to be amended to specifically list FGC as a harmful and prohibited practice. See Nolan, "Growing Numbers."

26. See J. Moore, Field Journal 2016, 6B–7B, referencing discussion with Fambul Tok staff members about changing attitudes toward FGC in Sierra Leone.

27. In subsequent visits to Palima and Tawovehun I benefited from the Mende interpretation skills of Theresa Kamara (2017), Bashiru Yankuba (2018), and Joseph Benjie (2017 and 2018).

28. Most Sierra Leoneans say that the Muslim-Christian demographic breakdown is approximately 60:40 in Moyamba, as in most parts of Sierra Leone as a whole, with the exception of certain majority Fulbeh and Mandingo areas of Northern Province, which are high-majority Muslim. See J. Moore, Field Notebook 2018, 2A, referencing May 11 conversation with Joseph Benjie, Fambul Tok field officer for Moyamba District, and Komba Moiwa, Fambul Tok interdistrict field coordinator, on file with author.

29. Ademah's use of the plural form "religions" is a reference to Islam and Christianity.

30. While meeting with Fambul Tok colleagues in Kampala to plan our visits, I raised the possibility of traveling by bus and motorcycle to the communities in order to save money and to avoid tying up a Fambul Tok vehicle for the second year in a row. Thankfully, wiser heads deemed that plan unworkable given the uncertainties of travel by public means during the rainy season. The Fambul Tok director John Caulker graciously made a four-wheel drive Fambul Tok vehicle available and asked Mustapha Rogers to serve as our driver for the second year in a row.

31. Our conversation was interrupted periodically by some teasing of the stranger from a distant land who had so innocently suggested the possibility of saving funds by taking mopeds to the villages. Each time we came upon another drenched or mud-spattered bicyclist intrepidly navigating potholes of rainwater, there was a renewed chorus of ironic asides: "What fun!" and "Yes, next time, Jenny, we will definitely come by bike."

32. The Peacebuilder's Questionnaire is in Appendix 1 of this volume.

33. Theresa talked about 'taking action' in cases of domestic violence during her individual interview in 2017. However, she affirmed this statement in even stronger terms on May 11, 2018, by mentioning her prerogative to demand that the chief intervene. She clarified that the chief typically upholds her finding of wrongdoing and her authority to fine the perpetrators. See Field Notebook 2018 Version of J. Moore's Women's Work Manuscript referencing May 11 conversation with Theresa, saved electronically on May 18, 2018, on file with author.

34. Palima postscript: follow-up visit in 2018. In May 2018, when I returned to the community for follow-up interviews, the assembled Peace Mothers treated me like an old friend. They expressed their affection in various ways, from gentle teasing to outright provocation. Although the dancing time in 2018 was pared down to five or ten minutes, expectations of my by-now familiarity with the local steps were formidable and I could not disappoint. Peace Mothers Theresa and Hannah insisted that I participate in their version of the Lindy Hop, which entails shimmying into a near crouch while rotating ones fists in a pantomime of grinding grain until muscle exhaustion prompts jumping up in an exuberant stomp of both feet accompanied by an exultant pop of the forearms in a double wave. This move needed to be executed repeatedly. Actually, I don't know if this is an actual dance step, or simply something they developed for me on the fly. In any case, by the end of that morning in May 2018 I was bestowed my "native name"—Ngotoboliboli—which apparently means "good dancer" in Mende. Although when I waved goodbye to the local kids as I walked by the shaded verandas of their homes, given the peals of laughter that resounded each time one of them called out my new name, I wondered if it actually meant something quite different. It was doubtless some kind of tribute in any case.

35. Mami J. is referred to by the initial of her last name to provide the same degree of anonymity accorded all the Peace Mothers who took part in the field research for this book.

36. Women throughout Sierra Leone are impacted by high levels of infant and childhood mortality. Their reference to the children who "remain" is both an identification of the number of those who survived childhood diseases and also their honoring of the children they had lost.

37. After the prayer in his memory, I was able to convey how happy my father would have been that I was present in this place and learning from the Peace Mothers about their vital community work.

38. See Field Notebook 2018 Version of J. Moore's Women's Work Manuscript referencing May 11 conversation with Mami J., saved electronically on May 18, 2018, on file with author.

39. Nannah talked about the relationship between reconciliation and peace during her individual interview in July 2017 and delved further into these Mende terms during our follow-up conversation in May 2018. See Field Notebook 2018 Version of J. Moore's Women's Work Manuscript referencing May 11 conversation with Nannah, saved electronically on May 18, 2018, on file with author.

40. Since 2016, when my qualitative interviews first began, Koinadugu District has been split into two districts, Koinadugu and Falaba. Somewhat confusingly, people still often refer to both districts as Koinadugu since the partition was for administrative purposes and is still relatively recent. I sometimes refer to both districts as Koinadugu since the term has cultural resonance in Sierra Leone as the large and multiethnic region of the Northern Province that shares a border with Guinea.

41. The process of alluvial (riverbed) mining was described by Komba Moiwa on one of our field visits to Koinadugu in May 2018. See Field Notebook 2018 Version of J. Moore's Women's Work Manuscript referencing May 12–15 conversations with K. Moiwa, saved electronically on May 18, 2018, on file with author.

42. Loma Mansa, in Koinadugu District, Northern Province, is at an elevation of 6,391 feet. See *Encyclopaedia Britannica*, s.v. "Mount Loma Mansa," available at https://www.britannica.com/place/Mount-Loma-Mansa.

43. J. Moore, Field Journal 2016 at 15B (drawn from insights of Fambul Tok staff).

44. In 2023, for the first time, our research team included a volunteer research assistant from the United States, Ms. Taylor Noya. Taylor is a 2021 graduate of the University of New Mexico School of Law and a pro bono lawyer who has worked with immigrants and people facing homelessness. As a law student at UNM, she studied international law and human rights and refugee law. In those classes, she learned about the Peace Mothers and maintained a desire to accompany her former professor on one of her research trips. In October 2023, she joined the team.

During our visits to Kaponpon, Dogoloya, and Heremakono, she observed the follow-up interviews. Utilizing her proficiency in Arabic and other languages, she learned to greet community members in all three native languages, to the great appreciation of the Peace Mothers and our interpreters and colleagues.

45. The term *mijade* was utilized by Boie of Dogoloya, whose individual interview is discussed in the text below. Further insight into the concept of *mijade* or contemplation was provided by Issa Kamara, May 14–15, 2018. See Field Notebook 2018 Version of J. Moore's Women's Work Manuscript referencing May 14–15 conversations with I. Kamara, saved electronically on May 18, 2018, on file with author.

46. Dogoloya was the only place in Sierra Leone where I had the opportunity to drink fresh as opposed to powdered milk, given the lack of refrigeration in rural communities throughout the country. In Dogoloya and other Fulbeh communities, milk is consumed fresh or slightly fermented. Driving along graded roads in 2016, our research team stopped at a Fulbeh settlement, marked by split-rail fencing. A Pulloh (i.e., an individual member of the Fulbeh community) businesswoman sold us a plastic sack of milk, still warm from the cow and just starting to curdle into a tangy yogurt.

47. Conversation with Fambul Tok staff in Koinadugu. See J. Moore, Field Journal 2016, 21A.

48. *The Encyclopedia of World Cultures* (Gale, 1996), s.v. "Fulani," available at http://www.encyclopedia.com/social-sciences-and-law/anthropology-and-archaeology/people/fulani.

49. *Encyclopedia of World Cultures*, s.v. "Fulani."

50. As noted in Chapters 1 and 2, despite the relative peacefulness that accompanied the re-election of President Bio in June 2023, the results were marred by charges of voter fraud at a time when ordinary Sierra Leoneans were also experiencing punishing levels of inflation. The ensuing months led to political unrest at the national level. On November 26, 2023, armed militants attacked the Pademba Road Prison in Freetown, releasing around two thousand prisoners in what the government characterized as a thwarted coup attempt. Nighttime curfews were imposed nationwide. The level of fear among the civil population was high, due in part to uncertainty about the identity and motives of the perpetrators. See Mayeni Jones and Umaru Fofana, "Sierra Leone Lifts Curfew After Breakout from Freetown's Pademba Road Prison," BBC, November 27, 2023, available at https://www.bbc.com/news/world-africa-67536147.

51. In Sierra Leone around 14,000 people were infected with the Ebola virus, of whom nearly 4,000 died in 2014 and 2015. See Kevin Sieff, "Sierra Leone Is Free of Ebola, 18 Months and 4,000 Deaths After Outbreak," *Washington Post*, November 7, 2015, available at https://www.washingtonpost.com/world/sierra-leone-is-free-of-ebola-18-months-and-11000-deaths-after-outbreak/2015/11/07/b483b56e-8488-11e5-8bd2-680fff868306_story.html?utm_term=.f5bf6796bc7d. Around 60 percent of those who died of Ebola were women. See Lauren Wolfe, "Why Are So Many Women Dying from Ebola?," *Foreign Policy*, August 20, 2014, available at http://www.foreignpolicy.com/articles/2014/08/20/why_are_so_many_women_dying_from_ebola. The need for strengthened public health and educational infrastructures at the community level has never been more urgent for women and their families.

52. Traveling with our team—myself as team leader, Lilian Morsay as research facilitator, and Mustapha Rogers our driver—was Issa Kamara, a Fambul Tok staff member based in Kabala who is fluent in Fula.

53. Issa Kamara, Fambul Tok field officer for Koinadugu District, explained that Mr. Jalloh was an important "change agent" or progressive trendsetter for his community of Dogoloya because of his willingness, since Fambul Tok's arrival nearly a decade ago, to model a new style of community partnership between wife and husband. "Dr. J" self-consciously embraced the notion that women should express their opinions in the home as well as in public spaces. He is credited with facilitating subtle but important changes in attitudes in his community toward greater women's empowerment. See Field Notebook 2018 Version of J. Moore's Women's Work

Manuscript referencing May 14 conversation with I. Kamara, saved electronically on May 28, 2018, on file with author. Mr. Jalloh died of an illness in the fall of 2018. His passing was widely mourned in his community.

54. Lamrana, Peace Mother of Dogoloya, spoke these words during the focus group interview in her home village that took place in March 2016. Her words are the source of the first epigraph found at the beginning of this chapter. She confirmed this statement during our follow-up interview in May 2018. See Field Notebook 2018 Version of J. Moore's Women's Work Manuscript referencing May 14 conversation with Lamrana, saved electronically on May 18, 2018, on file with author.

55. Ayeba confirmed this statement during our follow-up interview in May 2018. See Field Notebook 2018 Version of J. Moore's Women's Work Manuscript referencing May 11 conversation with Ayeba, saved electronically on May 18, 2018, on file with author.

56. Boie affirmed this statement during our May 2018 follow-up conversation. See Field Notebook 2018 Version of J. Moore's Women's Work Manuscript referencing May 11, conversation with Boie, saved electronically on May 18, 2018, on file with author.

57. The Peacebuilders' Questionnaire is in Appendix 1 of this volume.

58. Many of the women interviewed in Northern Uganda and Sierra Leone analogized the various components of the peacebuilding process to the roots, trunk, branches, and fruit of a tree. A photograph of my pencil-drawn rendering of the composite Tree of Peace, inspired by the women peacebuilders of Northern Uganda and Sierra Leone, is reproduced as Figure 25 just after the Conclusion of this volume.

59. Mende, Fula, Mandingo, and Limba terms relating to peacebuilding are compelling in meaning and poetic in form, in particular the parallel metaphors of the calm heart in Fula (*buti berende*) and the cool heart in Mandingo (*jusu-suma*). At the same time, I could get a bit confused tossing around words and phrases in so many different languages. I am grateful that during my follow-up visits to Dogoloya, Heremakono, and Kaponpon in May 2018, Issa Kamara, Komba Moiwa, and Zainab Kamara, along with Peace Mothers like Boie Jalloh and Mbalia, helped ensure that I had the proper pronunciation, spelling, and understanding of the relevant terms in each language. See Field Notebook 2018 Version of J. Moore's Women's Work Manuscript referencing May 15 and May 21 conversations with Mbalia, Issa Kamara, and Komba Moiwa, saved electronically on May 18, 2018, on file with author.

60. Fula and Mandingo are distinct languages, although both fall within the expansive Niger-Congo lineage, the largest linguistic family in Africa, spanning the mother tongues of nearly 85 percent of the continent's population. See John T. Bendor-Samuel, "Niger-Congo Languages," *Encyclopaedia Britannica*, available at https://www.britannica.com/topic/Niger-Congo-languages.

61. While in American English "Fulani" is commonly used to refer to the Fulbeh people and their language, it is not the proper usage within the cultural context of Sierra Leone. As Issa Kamara clarified to me during my May 2018 visit to Dogoloya, "Fula" is the way we should refer to the language of the "Fulbeh" people. The precise singular form of Fulbeh is "Pulloh"—used when referring to one Fula speaker or one member of the Fulbeh ethnic community. See Field Notebook 2018 Version of J. Moore's Women's Work Manuscript referencing May 15 conversation with I. Kamara, saved electronically on May 18, 2018, on file with author.

62. See John L. Hirsch, *Sierra Leone: Diamonds and the Struggle for Democracy* (Lynne Rienner, 2001), 22.

63. Komba Moiwa confirmed this demographic and ethnographic information during our consultation in May 2018. See Field Notebook 2018 Version of J. Moore's Women's Work Manuscript referencing May 21 conversation with K. Moiwa, saved electronically on May 18, 2018, on file with author.

64. Issa Kamara is a native Fula speaker, but he also speaks Mandingo and is a practicing Muslim. Emanuel Mansaray is a native Mandingo speaker who was raised as a Muslim and later

became an ordained Christian minister. The dynamic linguistic and cultural identities of Issa and Emanuel are emblematic of Sierra Leone's pluralistic national culture.

65. As stated earlier, my first visit to Heremakono in March 2016 coincided with the funeral of a community member. At that time, while I learned the Mandingo expression *woma-toro*, I did not have the occasion to delve into its deeper meaning. As with the other communities in Sierra Leone and Uganda, I returned to Heremakono in July 2017 and May 2018. During my follow-up interview with the Peace Mother chairwoman Mbalia in 2018, I asked her to elaborate further on the significance of the term. My question led to a very interesting and philosophical discussion in which Mbalia, Issa Kamara serving as Mandingo interpreter, and my facilitator Komba Moiwa who happens to speak some Mandingo as well, each weighed in on the meaning of the phrase. They contrasted *woma-toro* ("We are part of your loss") with *won-toro*, which is also a way of expressing sympathy but where there is more of a separation between the bereaved person and the sympathizer. Mbalia stressed that to say *won-toro* is to suggest that you are sorry for the person's loss, but 'you are not part of it.' By expressing *woma-toro*, you are saying essentially that we are in this together. See Field Notebook 2018 Version of J. Moore's Women's Work Manuscript referencing May 15 conversation with Mbalia, I. Kamara, and K. Moiwa, saved electronically on May 18, 2018, on file with author.

66. Mbalia died of an illness in 2019. As a recognized leader of her community with a loving extended family, she is sorely missed.

67. I visited with Mbalia, the chairwoman of the Peace Mothers of Heremakono, on four occasions throughout the course of the 2016–2019 field research. Since her untimely passing in late 2019, she is mourned by her community and the loss of her leadership leaves a void. In addition to the context she provided during our 2016 Heremakono focus group and 2017 interview regarding their VSA (village savings association), Mbalia shared additional details and insights during our follow-up conversations in May 2018 and May 2019. First, she verified that each of the twenty members of the Heremakono Peace Mothers group indeed contribute 2,000 leones every Sunday. They also contribute 500 leones on a weekly basis for 'problems such as bereavement or sickness or accident or other urgent need.' In case of such exigent circumstances, the individual woman is given the funds necessary to solve her problem. Such monies come out of the separate social support portion of the VSA, and they are outright grants. Mbalia stressed that if a member needs school fees for a child, wants to invest in a small business endeavor, or has some other nonurgent need, she should take out a loan. Typical loans are 100,000 leones (approximately US$5) but can range to as much as one million leones (US$50). All loans are assessed at 10 percent when the loan is due, unless fully paid off. Mbalia illustrated a typical scenario in which a loan of 100,000 leones would be made by the VSA with a term of one month. In such circumstances, either the loan would be paid in full at the end of the month or the borrower would pay 10,000 leones in interest at that time. Mbalia specified that while the 10 percent interest rate is standard for Heremakono VSA loans, the period of the loan is negotiable, with the possibility of longer terms for larger amounts. See Field Notebook 2018 Version of J. Moore's Women's Work Manuscript referencing May 15 follow-up interview with Mbalia, saved electronically on May 18, 2018, on file with author.

68. Mbalia verified the accuracy of this quote during our follow-up conversation in May 2018. See Field Notebook 2018 Version of J. Moore's Women's Work Manuscript referencing May 15 follow-up interview with Mbalia, saved electronically on May 18, 2018, on file with author.

69. The Peacebuilder's Questionnaire is in Appendix 1 of this volume.

70. The assistant section chief for Heremakono and the section chairwoman of Heremakono are quite distinct positions. The position of Heremakono assistant section chief was created by the then–section chief especially for Mbalia, in a self-conscious attempt on his part to bring activist women into more formal leadership roles in their section. Contrastingly, the chairwoman of the section is a more common position given to a woman who serves as ombudsperson for women's concerns, ideally with the ear of the section chief, and reflecting the reality that men

have traditionally dominated official governance positions. It is feasible that as more women get access to formal political positions, the role of chairwoman of the section will become obsolete.

71. Sierra Leone's current reformist approach to local governance promotes initiatives to decentralize political power. Various governance structures are being created at the local level throughout the country, some of which are not yet fully operational. The Inclusive District Peace and Development Committees (IDPDCs), like the People's Planning Process (PPP) of which they are a part, seek to bring more local stakeholders into the planning of socioeconomic development projects at the local level. Mbalia and Issa Kamara, Fambul Tok field officer for Koinadugu District, provided more details regarding the PPP during our follow-up conversation in May 2018. The IDPDC for Koinadugu District includes representatives of the district office, the district council, the council of paramount chiefs, international governmental organizations working in Koinadugu, and a variety of civil society leaders like Mbalia herself. See Field Notebook 2018 Version of J. Moore's Women's Work Manuscript referencing May 15 follow-up interview with Mbalia, saved electronically on May 18, 2018, on file with author.

72. Sierra Leone and Northern Uganda are experiencing similar challenges and opportunities for women in the political sphere. Chapter 3 includes a kindred discussion of the contemporary dynamics of women's political empowerment in Northern Uganda. Pamela Angwech, of the Gulu Women's Economic Development and Globalization Project (GWED-G), emphasizes the importance of partnership between men and women in the community and in the home. Shared decision-making between parents in the family setting models the notion of a "democratic household" for other men and women in the community. See notes from author's briefing with Pamela Angwech, executive director of GWED-G, Author's Field Notebook, Uganda 2016, 22A and 23B (July 13), on file with author.

73. Although as of 2018 Mbalia was no longer serving in her assistant section chief role, she had retained her roles as Peace Mothers chairwoman for Heremakono, section chairwoman for Heremakono, and vice-chairperson of the IDPDC for Koinadugu District. See Field Notebook 2018 Version of J. Moore's Women's Work Manuscript referencing May 15 follow-up interview with Mbalia, saved electronically on May 18, 2018, on file with author.

74. A reference to the Devolution of Estates Act, discussed above and referenced in Chapters 1 and 2.

75. In Limba the literal translation of *aniwali katabante* is "working together." Other Limba terms relevant to peacebuilding and reconciliation are love, *mathimiyande*; encouragement from a friend, *gbonkitande mtonda*; and confiding in a friend, *thuruye mtonda*.

76. See Agatha Clark, *Religion and Beliefs of Sierra Leone*, chapter 4, "Interfaith Fusion," available at http://classroom.synonym.com/religion-beliefs-sierra-leone-5307.html. Last accessed December 30, 2023.

77. In 2016 Zainab was serving as the Fambul Tok Peace Mothers coordinator for Koinadugu. In 2017, she was elected ward councilor for Ward 145. She clarified in May 2018 that Ward 145 encompasses three sections, one of which is Kaponpon. As ward councilor she serves on the Koinadugu District Council, which meets monthly in Kaponpon. See Field Notebook 2018 Version of J. Moore's Women's Work Manuscript referencing May 14 conversation with Z. Kamara, saved electronically on 18 May 2018, on file with author.

78. Lilian Morsay clarified the name of the traditional Muslim invocation and that of the Christian prayer during our consultation in May 2018. See Field Notebook 2018 Version of J. Moore's Women's Work Manuscript referencing May 15 follow-up consultation with L. Morsay, saved electronically on May18, 2018, on file with author.

79. The Peacebuilder's Questionnaire is in Appendix 1 of this volume.

80. Zainab Kamara, who translated for my interview with Tenneh in 2018, provided further details about the nature of the clinic where Yonson was born. She explained that the Bafodia clinic is referred to as a PHU—or peripheral health unit. PHUs are typically staffed by community

health officers and traditional birth attendants. Trained nurses are assigned to PHUs on a rotational basis. They serve full time when posted to that particular PHU. See Field Notebook 2018
Version of J. Moore's Women's Work Manuscript referencing May 14 conversation with Z. Kamara, saved electronically on May 18, 2018, on file with author.

81. Fatumatah confirmed the accuracy of these quotes during our follow-up conversation in
May 2018. See Field Notebook 2018 Version of J. Moore's Women's Work Manuscript referencing
May 14 follow-up consultation with Fatumatah, saved electronically on May 18, 2018, on file with
author.

82. Our interpreter Zainab Kamara filled me in on an essential detail after our follow-up
interview with Tenneh in May 2018. Zainab was proud of Tenneh's discipline and clarity of purpose, insisting that the younger woman's resumption of her secondary school studies as of 2018
was a prodigious accomplishment for a twenty-year-old mother. She had joined her classmates
in Form 3 and was preparing to sit in the summer for her Basic Education Certificate Examination, the gateway between junior secondary and senior secondary school. Tenneh thus continues to actively pursue her vision of education as both a means of livelihood and an investment
for her future and that of her community. When I returned to Kaponpon in 2023—along with
Lilian Morsay, Komba Moiwa, and Issa Kamara—Tenneh had recently completed her secondary
schooling and was awaiting the results of her university admissions examination.

Conclusion

Epigraph: This epigraph is the final stanza of Joy Harjo's poem "Conflict Resolution for Holy
Beings" from her volume of poetry by the same name. Joy Harjo, *Conflict Resolution for Holy Be-
ings: Poems* (W. W. Norton, 2015), 84. Copyright © 2015 by Joy Harjo. Used by permission of
W. W. Norton & Company, Inc.

1. The range of faith practices conducted by Ugandan and Sierra Leonean peacebuilders encompass the prevalent Catholic devotional practice of the Acholi women of Northern Uganda;
the side-by-side Protestant and Muslim ritual lives of the Mende women of Sierra Leone's Moyamba District; the Muslim faith of the Fulbeh women of Dogoloya and the Mandingo women of
Heremakono in Sierra Leone's Northern Province; and the syncretic Christ-Mus traditions of
the Limba women of Kaponpon in Sierra Leone's Koinadugu District.

2. See documents relating to Uganda's proposed National Transitional Justice Policy, available at http://www.jlos.go.ug/index.php/document-centre/transitional-justice/transitional-justice
-policy.

3. International Covenant on Economic, Social, and Cultural Rights (ICESCR), adopted December 19, 1966, entered into force January 3, 1976, 999 U.N.T.S. 3, art. 11 ("the right of everyone
to an adequate standard of living").

4. In March 2014, the Women's Advocacy Network submitted a petition to the Uganda
Women Parliamentary Association calling for reparations to survivors of wartime atrocities during the LRA War. See Justice and Reconciliation Project press release, "Parliament Adopts Resolution to Address the Needs of War-Affected" (Kampala, April 10, 2014), available at http://www
.justiceandreconciliation.org/media/newsroom/press-releases/2014/parliament-adopts-resolution
-to-address-the-needs-of-war-affected/, referencing the Ugandan Parliament's 2014 resolution on
reparations for Northern Uganda, not yet implemented by the government of Uganda. There has
been renewed momentum for a reparations bill in the Ugandan Parliament as of 2023.

5. See African Charter on Human Peoples' Rights, art. 1 (state obligation to give effect to enumerated rights), art. 16 (health care provision), art. 17 (education), and art. 30 (establishment of
the African Commission on Human and Peoples' Rights to ensure protection of human rights
in Africa), as cited and discussed in Chapter 1, in the section The Essence of Human Rights Law.

6. Dicta Asiimwe, "Uganda Embarks on Journey Toward Universal Health Coverage," *East African*, June 25, 2018, available at https://allafrica.com/stories/201806260367.html.

7. UNICEF, "Sustaining Public Investments in Health Sector," Uganda Budget Brief, Fiscal Year 2023/24, 3 and 10, available at https://www.unicef.org/esa/media/13261/file/UNICEF-Uganda -Health-Budget-Brief-2023-2024.pdf.

8. See UNICEF, Country Office Annual Report 2018, Sierra Leone, 16, available at https:// www.unicef.org/about/annualreport/files/Sierra_Leone_2018_COAR.pdf.

9. WHO, Sierra Leone Annual Report 2022, 4 and 12, available at https://www.afro.who .int/sites/default/files/2023-07/WHO%20Sierra%20Leone%20Annual%20Report%20for%20 2022.pdf.

10. See human development data for Sierra Leone and Uganda compiled by the United Nations Development Program in 2018, discussed in Chapter 2 and available at http://www.hdr.undp .org/sites/default/files/2018_human_development_statistical_update.pdf (Tables 5 and 9).

11. See human development data for Sierra Leone and Uganda compiled by the United Nations Development Programme in 2018, discussed in Chapter 2 and available at http://www.hdr .undp.org/sites/default/files/2018_human_development_statistical_update.pdf (Tables 5 and 9).

12. For the period 2005–2018, data from the UN Development Program indicates that 49.9% of Ugandan women 15 years old and above and 45.3 percent for Sierra Leonean women have experienced intimate partner violence at least once. This is compared to 31.5 percent for least developed countries overall. The United States has no data recorded by UNDP for this period. The corresponding rate for the United Kingdom is 29 percent. UNDP Human Development Statistical Update (2018), 91, 93, 94, Dashboard 3, available at http://www.hdr.undp.org/sites/default/files /2018_human_development_statistical_update.pdf.

13. See Author's Field Notebook, Uganda 2018, 12 B (July 13, with notes from follow-up interview with Bichentina), on file with author. See also Author's Field Notebook, Uganda 2023, 2 (July 18, with notes from interview with Bichentina), on file with author.

14. See Hawa Kamara, "A Look at the Major Changes in the Three Gender Acts," Centre for Accountability and the Rule of Law, August 11, 2016, available at http://www.carl-sl.org/pres/a -look-at-the-major-changes-in-the-three-gender-acts/. It is the Devolution of Estates Act in particular that ratifies the equal inheritance rights of women.

15. This book has explored the complex dynamics between women and men during and after war, particularly in the context of women's empowerment. Chris Dolan has written about the destructive impact of the LRA war and the enforced encampment of Acholi civilians by the Ugandan military, including the debilitating and humiliating impact of this experience on women and men. See Chris Dolan, *Social Torture: The Case of Northern Uganda, 1986–2006* (Berghahn Books, 2011), 177. Dolan addresses the impact of war and economic misery on gender roles and expectations, leading to feelings of inadequacy on the part of women and men, including the "increasing economic desperation of men" and their movement into "what had previously been women's areas of work, such as traditional healing." He also describes the destructive impact of long-term encampment on men's traditional roles as husbands, economic providers, and physical protectors of their families. See generally Dolan, *Social Torture*, chapter 7, 191–218.

Appendix 2

Chiefly in the interest of greater brevity, this analysis of the interviews with members of Gwoko ter Kwaro was not incorporated into the main body of the text of Chapter 3 on women peacebuilders of Northern Uganda. This choice was also made in order to achieve a tighter comparative analysis among the four Acholi community groups addressed in Chapter 3—namely, Rwot Lakica, Alany pa Mony Lit, Uketu wan Kwene, and Odoko Mit.

1. *Kwayo kica* is the asking for forgiveness and *timo kica* is the granting of forgiveness.

2. Jennifer was pregnant in July 2016 with her seventh child. She gave birth to her daughter later that year, and brought her six-month-old baby girl to our follow-up interview in June 2017. When we met once more in July 2018, her toddler sat in her lap during our conversation. See Field Notebook 2018 Version of J. Moore's Women's Work Manuscript referencing June 2017 and July 2018 conversations with Jennifer and saved electronically on July 17, 2018.

3. Ellen confirmed in 2018 that after the death of her husband she was remarried for a time to the brother of her husband through "inheritance," a traditional practice that is sometimes followed whereby a widow cohabitates with one of her husband's brothers, in order to ensure her material support. Evidently, this practice is somewhat ad hoc, as in Ellen's case, where she is no longer married to her brother-in-law. 'He is still around, but we are not living together.' See Field Notebook 2018 Version of J. Moore's Women's Work Manuscript referencing July 12 follow-up interview with Ellen and saved electronically on July 17, 2018. On file with author.

4. At our follow-up interview in June 2017, Ellen added an important qualification of her statement in 2016 about men's lack of initiative. Despite their faults, 'we still respect the men.' See Field Notebook 2018 Version of J. Moore's Women's Work Manuscript referencing June 13, 2017, follow-up interview with Ellen and saved electronically on July 17, 2018. On file with author.

5. Pamela Angwech, of the Gulu Women's Economic Development and Globalization Project (GWED-G), speaks of the progress women have made in contesting successfully against men for legislative positions. She noted in 2016 that around a dozen women were currently serving as Members of the Ugandan Parliament "outside affirmative action political spaces." See notes from author's briefing with Pamela Angwech, executive director of GWED-G, Author's Field Notebook, Uganda 2016, 22A and 23A (July 13), on file with author.

6. See J. Moore, Uganda Field Notebook, July 2023 (meeting with Gwoko ter Kwaro members, July 19), on file with author.

INDEX

ACKNOWLEDGMENTS

My first thanks go to the women of Northern Uganda and Sierra Leone who shared with me their time and thoughtful reflections on peace and justice over six summers from 2016 to 2023. I met with sixty women in ten communities, and while I only name half of them here by first name, my heartfelt gratitude goes to all the members of the local peacebuilding collectives to which they belong and to their families who support them and whom they support in turn. Special appreciation to Grace, Agnes, Evelyn, Santa, and Stella of Gulu; to Christine, Ellen, Jennifer, Pamela, Bichentina, Concy, and Pasca of Kitgum; to Ayeba, Boie, Lamrana, Fatumatah, and Tenneh and the late Mbalia of Koinadugu; to Hannah, Theresa, Nannah, and Mami J. of Moyamba; to Agnes, Aida, Esther, Filda, Lucy and the late Evelyn of Nwoya; and to Jane, Mary, and the late Daker Nighty of Pader.

Second, I thank my four research guides—Lilian Morsay of Fambul Tok, Sierra Leone; Victoria Nyanjura, a founder of the Women's Advocacy Network, Uganda; Fred Ngomokwe of the Refugee Law Project, Gulu, Uganda; and Winnie Arima Abalo of Human Rights Focus, Kitgum, Uganda. You helped me to realize the kind of deep and respectful personal narrative research that I imagined. Your expertise and commitment to grassroots peace and justice work in your countries and home districts are reflected in this book. I am also grateful for the skills of my interpreters and research facilitators—Komba Moiwa, Theresa Kamara, Joseph Benjie, Bashiru Yankuba, Issa Kamara, Emmanuel Mansaray, Zainab Kamara, and Edward Kamara. My research also benefitted from the support, advice, and referrals of Joe Oloka-Onyango and Zahara Nampewo of Makerere University's Human Rights and Peace Center, Kampala, Uganda; Chris Dolan, former director of the Refugee Law Project, Makerere University; Ibrahim George of the International Committee of the Red Cross; John Caulker of Fambul Tok, Freetown, Sierra Leone; and Libby Hoffman of Catalyst for Peace, Portland, Maine. And for transporting our research teams into the communities, I thank our drivers Mustapha Rogers, Alhaji Sankoh, Tamba Nyama, and Emanuel Ochan, who also imparted their own insights on war and peace.

For critical and constructive reading of my chapters, I thank Dr. Paul Bradfield, PhD, Irish Centre for Human Rights, University of Galway; Mary Louise Pratt, emeritus professor of language and comparative literature at New York University; Nathalie Martin, Professor of Law at the University of New Mexico School of Law, and Felipe Gonzales, UNM emeritus professor of Sociology. For their painstaking copy editing of early drafts of the manuscript my heartfelt thanks go to my former law students Taylor Noya, Kateri Eisenberg, and Daniel Silverstein.

To my friends at the University of Pennsylvania, I also extend my appreciation. My heartfelt thanks to Bert Lockwood, who encouraged me ten years ago to submit a proposal to Penn Press; my gratitude to Peter Agree, Penn Press' former editor-in-chief, who helped shepherd me through the first stages of the review process; and my appreciation to Walter Biggins, editor-in-chief, along with his editing and production teams, including Mel Smith and Noreen O'Connor-Abel. It has been a pleasure to work with you all.

Last, but not least, thanks to my family, friends, and UNM colleagues. My deepest gratitude goes to my dear daughter Kyra, who inventoried my chapters with care; alongside her beloved sister, my late daughter Tessa, who contributed her art and artistry throughout. While Tessa passed away before the book was finished, she gave her permission for her artwork to be on the cover of *Women's Work*. For all that she taught me about women's work and mothers' work, I am forever blessed. Thanks also to friends Janet Buck and Maggie Montgomery for their poetic insights; to Valerie Sobel and Cindy Nee for their photographic expertise; to Emilie McVay-Ash, Cheryl Burbank, Stephanie Grant, Marlene Valdez and the late Margaret Harrington for helping me plan my trips to Africa; and to my colleague Nathalie Martin and my Deans Alfred Mathewson, Sergio Pareja, and Camille Carey for always giving me the support to incorporate my field work and scholarship into my calling as a law professor. Special appreciation to Taylor Noya, who accompanied me on my last round of interviews in Sierra Leone in 2023. The portraits she drew and shared with the Peace Mothers and our Fambul Tok colleagues further strengthened our bonds of friendship and collaboration. Finally, deep thanks to Joy Harjo for her generosity in allowing me to incorporate her evocative and life-affirming poetry about conflict resolution into this book.

www.ingramcontent.com/pod-product-compliance
Lightning Source LLC
Chambersburg PA
CBHW031405270326
41929CB00010BA/1332